Informatik – Fachberichte

Band 4: Computer Architecture. Workshop of the Gesellschaft für Informatik 1975. Edited by W. Händler. VIII, 382 pages. 1976.

Band 5: GI – 6. Jahrestagung. Proceedings 1976. Herausgegeben von E. J. Neuhold. X, 474 Seiten. 1976.

Band 6: B. Schmidt, GPSS-FORTRAN, Version II. Einführung in die Simulation diskreter Systeme mit Hilfe eines FORTRAN-Programmpaketes, 2. Auflage. XIII, 535 Seiten. 1978.

Band 7: GMR–GI–GfK. Fachtagung Prozessrechner 1977. Herausgegeben von G. Schmidt. XIII, 524 Seiten. 1977.

Band 8: Digitale Bildverarbeitung/Digital Image Processing. GI/NTG Fachtagung, München, März 1977. Herausgegeben von H.-H. Nagel. XI, 328 Seiten. 1977.

Band 9: Modelle für Rechensysteme. Workshop 1977. Herausgegeben von P. P. Spies. VI, 297 Seiten. 1977.

Band 10: GI – 7. Jahrestagung. Proceedings 1977. Herausgegeben von H. J. Schneider. IX, 214 Seiten. 1977.

Band 11: Methoden der Informatik für Rechnerunterstütztes Entwerfen und Konstruieren, GI-Fachtagung, München, 1977. Herausgegeben von R. Gnatz und K. Samelson. VIII, 327 Seiten. 1977.

Band 12: Programmiersprachen. 5. Fachtagung der GI, Braunschweig, 1978. Herausgegeben von Klaus Alber. VI, 179 Seiten. 1977.

Band 13: W. Steinmüller, L. Ermer, W. Schimmel: Datenschutz bei riskanten Systemen. X, 244 Seiten. 1978.

Band 14: Datenbanken in Rechnernetzen mit Kleinrechnern. Fachtagung der GI, Karlsruhe, 1978. Herausgegeben von W. Stucky und E. Holler. X, 198 Seiten. 1978.

Band 15: Organisation von Rechenzentren. Workshop der Gesellschaft für Informatik, Göttingen, 1977. Herausgegeben von D. Wall. X, 310 Seiten. 1978.

Band 16: GI – 8. Jahrestagung, Proceedings 1978. Herausgegeben von S. Schindler und W. K. Giloi. VI, 394 Seiten. 1978.

Band 17: Bildverarbeitung und Mustererkennung. DAGM Symposium, Oberpfaffenhofen, 1978. Herausgegeben von E. Triendl. XIII, 385 Seiten. 1978.

Band 18: Virtuelle Maschinen. Nachbildung und Vervielfachung maschinenorientierter Schnittstellen. GI-Arbeitsseminar. München 1979. Herausgegeben von H. J. Siegert. X, 231 Seiten. 1979.

Band 19: GI – 9. Jahrestagung. Herausgegeben von K. H. Böhling und P. P. Spies. XIII, 690 Seiten. 1979.

Band 20: Angewandte Szenenanalyse. DAGM Symposium, Karlsruhe 1979. Herausgegeben von J. Foith. XIII, 362 Seiten. 1979.

Band 21: Formale Modelle für Informationssysteme. Fachtagung der GI, Tutzing 1979. Herausgegeben von H. C. Mayr und B. E. Meyer. VI, 265 Seiten. 1979.

Band 22: Kommunikation in verteilten Systemen. Workshop der Gesellschaft für Informatik e.V.. Herausgegeben von S. Schindler und J. Schröder. VIII, 338 Seiten. 1979.

Band 23: K.-H. Hauer, Portable Methodenmonitoren. XI, 209 Seiten. 1980.

Band 24: N. Ryska, S. Herda: Technischer Datenschutz. Kryptographische Verfahren in der Datenverarbeitung. V, 401 Seiten. 1980.

Band 25: Programmiersprachen und Programmierentwicklung. 6. Fachtagung, Darmstadt, 1980. Herausgegeben von H.-J. Hoffmann. IV, 236 Seiten. 1980.

Band 26: F. Gaffal, Datenverarbeitung im Hochschulbereich der USA. Stand und Entwicklungstendenzen. IX, 199 Seiten. 1980.

Band 27: GI-NTG Fachtagung, Struktur und Betrieb von Rechensystemen. Kiel, März 1980. Herausgegeben von G. Zimmermann. IX, 286 Seiten. 1980.

Band 28: Online-Systeme im Finanz- und Rechnungswesen. Anwendergespräch, Berlin, April 1980. Herausgegeben von P. Stahlknecht. X, 547 Seiten, 1980.

Band 29: Erzeugung und Analyse von Bildern und Strukturen. DGaO – DAGM Tagung, Essen, Mai 1980. Herausgegeben von S. J. Pöppl und H. Platzer. VII, 215 Seiten. 1980.

Band 30: Textverarbeitung und Informatik. Fachtagung der GI, Bayreuth, Mai 1980. Herausgegeben von P. R. Wossidlo. VIII, 362 Seiten. 1980.

Band 31: Firmware Engineering. Seminar veranstaltet von der gemeinsamen Fachgruppe „Mikroprogrammierung" des GI Fachausschusses 3/4 und des NTG-Fachausschusses 6 vom 12. – 14. März 1980 in Berlin. Herausgegeben von W. K. Giloi. VII, 295 Seiten. 1980.

Band 32: M. Kühn, CAD Arbeitssituation. VII, 215 Seiten. 1980.

Band 33: GI – 10. Jahrestagung. Herausgegeben von R. Wilhelm. XV, 563 Seiten. 1980.

Band 34: CAD-Fachgespräch. GI - 10. Jahrestagung. Herausgegeben von R. Wilhelm. VI, 184 Seiten. 1980.

Band 35: B. Buchberger, F. Lichtenberger: Mathematik für Mathematiker I. Die Methode der Mathematik. XI, 315 Seiten. 1980.

Band 36: The Use of Formal Specification of Software. Berlin, Juni 1979. Edited by H. K. Berg and W. K. Giloi. V, 388 pages. 1980.

Band 37: Entwicklungstendenzen wissenschaftlicher Rechenzentren. Kolloquium Göttingen, Juni 1980. Herausgegeben von D. Wall. VII, 163 Seiten. 1980.

Band 38: Datenverarbeitung im Marketing. Herausgegeben von R. Thome. VIII, 377 pages. 1981.

Band 40: Kommunikation in verteilten Systemen. Herausgegeben von S. Schindler und J.C.W. Schröder. IX, 459 Seiten. 1981.

Band 41: Messung, Modellierung und Bewertung von Rechensystemen. GI-NTG Fachtagung. Jülich, Februar 1981. Herausgegeben von B. Mertens. VIII, 368 Seiten. 1981.

Band 42: W. Kilian, Personalinformationssysteme in deutschen Großunternehmen. XV, 352 Seiten. 1981.

Band 43: G. Goos, Werkzeuge der Programmiertechnik. VI, 262 Seiten. 1981.

Band 44: Organisation informationstechnik-gestützter öffentlicher Verwaltungen. Fachtagung, Speyer, Oktober 1980. Herausgegeben von Heinrich Reinermann, Herbert Fiedler, Klaus Grimmer und Klaus Lenk. VIII, 651 Seiten. 1981.

Band 45: R. Marty, PISA – A Programming System for Interactive Production of Application Software. VII. 297 Seiten. 1981.

Band 46: F. Wolf, Organisation und Betrieb von Rechenzentren. VII, 244 Seiten. 1981.

Band 47: GWAI-81 German Workshop on Artificial Intelligence. Bad Honnef, January 1981. Herausgegeben von J. H. Siekmann. XII, 317 Seiten. 1981.

Informatik-Fachberichte

Herausgegeben von W. Brauer
im Auftrag der Gesellschaft für Informatik (GI)

47

GWAI-81

German Workshop on Artificial Intelligence
Bad Honnef, January 26-31, 1981

Edited by Jörg H. Siekmann

Springer-Verlag Berlin Heidelberg GmbH 1981

Herausgeber

J. Siekmann
Universität Karlsruhe, Institut für Informatik I
Postfach 6380, 7500 Karlsruhe 1

GWAI-81

Der Fachausschuß 6, Kognitive Systeme, Unterausschuß
"Künstliche Intelligenz" bildete das Programmkomitee:

W. Bibel   (Universität München, Mathematisches Institut)
P. Deussen   (Universität Karlsruhe, Institut für Informatik I)
J. Foith   (Fraunhofer Gesellschaft, IITB, Karlsruhe)
P. Raulefs   (Universität Bonn, Institut für Informatik III)
W. Wahlster   (Universität Hamburg, Germanisches Seminar)

Vorsitzender des Programmausschusses: J. Siekmann

Die Fachtagung wurde von der Firma Nixdorf und der Firma
ATM Computer GmbH finanziell unterstützt.

Die Reisekosten der Referenten wurden zum Teil durch einen Zuschuß
des Bundesministeriums für Forschung und Technologie finanziert.

CR Subject Classifications (1981): 3.61, 3.62, 3.64, 3.65, 3.69

ISBN 978-3-540-10859-7   ISBN 978-3-662-02328-0 (eBook)
DOI 10.1007/978-3-662-02328-0

2145/3140 − 5 4 3 2 1 0

Einleitung

Die erste Fachtagung *Künstliche Intelligenz* der Gesellschaft für
Informatik (wenngleich bereits der fünfte Workshop zu diesem Thema in
Deutschland) wurde vom 26.1. bis 30.1.1981 im Physikzentrum in Bad Honnef
abgehalten. Damit wird nach fast fünfundzwanzigjähriger Verspätung [1]
auch bei uns langsam ein Gebiet salonfähig, das zum Schaden der deutschen Informatik bisher vernachlässigt wurde und das in den USA (und
anderen Ländern) bereits seit langem unter dem Namen "Artificial
Intelligence" zu den Kernfächern der Informatik gehört [2].

Die Tagung wurde geprägt durch den Wechsel von eingeladenen Hauptvor-
trägen von jeweils einstündiger Dauer mit anschließender halbstündiger
Diskussion und den speziellen Fachvorträgen von jeweils halbstündiger
Redezeit.

Die Hauptvorträge (HV) geben auch in etwa die Forschungsschwerpunkte
wieder, durch die die *Künstliche Intelligenz* in Deutschland vertreten
ist:

W. Radig (Hamburg) gibt in seinem HV "Modelle und Strukturen in der
Bildverarbeitung" einen Überblick über die Forschung auf dem Gebiet
Computersehen. Der Beitrag konzentriert sich dabei besonders auf die
Aspekte, die über das traditionelle "pattern recognition" hinausgehen
und steht damit in engem Zusammenhang mit dem zweiten HV: J. Foith
(Karlsruhe) "Roboterforschung: Von Spielzeugwelten zur industriellen
Anwendung". Dieser Beitrag dürfte besonders für Leser aus der Industrie
von Interesse sein. Beide Gebiete demonstrieren besonders anschaulich,
mit welchem Tempo der Verlust *wissenschaftlicher* Konkurrenzfähigkeit
zum Verlust *industrieller* Wettbewerbsfähigkeit führen kann: die Grundlagenforschung wurde vor ca. 10 Jahren in den USA begonnen [3] und von
der deutschen Informatik weitgehend ignoriert. Heute sind in Japan über
15.000 Industrieroboter im Einsatz [4] und es ist bekannt, daß die
mangelnde Konkurrenzfähigkeit deutscher Produkte auch auf den höheren
Automatisierungsgrad beispielsweise der japanischen Industrie [5] zu-
rückzuführen ist. Allerdings ist einschränkend zu bemerken, daß die
japanischen Industrieroboter, die derzeit eingesetzt werden, weitgehend starr programmiert sind und wenig eigene 'Künstliche Intelligenz'
besitzen. Die Bedeutung der Roboterforschung ist jedoch in der Bundesrepublik nicht in der wünschenswerten Weise erkannt worden und es gibt
bis heute keine Grundlagenforschung oder universitätre Ausbildung auf
diesem Gebiet.

Zwei weitere wichtige Forschungsschwerpunkte werden in den nächsten beiden Beiträgen vorgestellt: W. Wahlster (Hamburg): "Natürlichsprachliche KI-Systeme: Entwicklungsstand und Forschungsperspektiven" und P. Raulefs (Bonn) "Expertensysteme: Entwicklungsstand und Forschungsperspektiven". Diese beiden Gebiete sind in ganz besonderer Weise geeignet, falsche Vorstellungen über die Grenzen eines Computers zu korrigieren und zu demonstrieren, wie weit es bereits gelungen ist, Fähigkeiten auf dem Computer zu realisieren, die bisher nur menschlicher Intelligenz vorbehalten waren.

Auf dem Gebiet der Verarbeitung natürlicher Sprache hat sich im Laufe der letzten zehn Jahre der Forschungsschwerpunkt von den Problemen des reinen Sprachverstehens [6] auf die zusätzlichen Probleme, die in einem Dialog auftreten, verlagert. Diese zusätzliche Problemstellung ist durch die abwechselnde Initiative der Dialogpartner, die Fähigkeit,ein Ausufern des Dialogs zu verhindern und die Rückführung des Gespräches auf spezielle Punkte sowie die unterschiedliche Motivation der Dialogpartner gekennzeichnet. Ein sehr gutes Beispiel für das derzeitig Machbare liefert der folgende Dialog zwischen einem Benutzer (Ben.) und dem Hamburger Redepartnermodell (HAM-RPM) [7]. Das Computerprogramm, also HAM-RPM, simuliert das sprachliche Verhalten eines Hotelmanagers, dessen Interessenlage durch eine möglichst positive Darstellung seines Hotels und durch den Versuch, ein Zimmer zu vermieten, gekennzeichnet ist:

DIALOG		ERLÄUTERUNGEN
Ben.	040 293758	Simulation des Anrufs
HAM-RPM	Hotel Alsterblick, Guten Abend!	
Ben.	Guten Abend, hier spricht Briegel DFG Bonn	echte Namenerkennung
HAM-RPM	Was kann ich für Sie tun, Herr Briegel?	
Ben.	Ich möchte ein Doppelzimmer für 3 Nächte mit Bad	Wortstellung
HAM-RPM	Gewiß, ich mal sehen ... Ein Doppelzimmer mit Bad bis zum 15.11. hätten Sie gern?	Umrechnung Vorannahme: ab heute
Ben.	Ja bitte	
HAM-RPM	Ja, da ist noch was frei. Haben Sie noch irgend einen besonderen Wunsch?	Abgabe der Initiative
Ben.	Gibt es ein Radio oder einen Fernseher im Zimmer?	Kombinierte Frage

HAM-RPM	Ja, es steht kein Fernsehgerät zur Verfügung, aber das Zimmer hat ein Radio	Kombinierte Antwort
Ben.	Ein Telefon?	Syntaktisch unvollständige Frage
HAM-RPM	Ja.	
Ben.	Ist ein Schreibtisch vielleicht vorhanden?	Zweifel über Zutreffen
HAM-RPM	Ja, ein Schreibtisch ist tatsächlich vorhanden.	Bestätigung
Ben.	Wieviele einzelne Betten sind im Zimmer?	frz. Betten?
HAM-RPM	Zwei.	Syntaktisch unvollständige Antwort.
Ben.	Hoffentlich ist eins von den Betten einigermassen hart.	Vorannahme
HAM-RPM	Ja, eins von den Betten ist vermutlich hart.	vage Antwort
Ben.	Wie meinen Sie das?	Metasprachl. Dialog
HAM-RPM	Seine Matraze ist neu. Darf ich das Zimmer für Sie buchen, Herr Briegel?	Schlußfolgerung auf Wissen Übernahme der Initiative
Ben.	Ja gerne	
HAM-RPM	Ich habe also ein Doppelzimmer für Herrn Briegel vom 12.11. bis zum 15.11. gebucht. Vielen Dank und auf Wiedersehen	Zusammenfassung

Das Computerprogramm 'versteht' die gesprochene Sprache in dem Sinn, daß es eine *interne Repräsentation* der ausgesprochenen Sachverhalte aufbaut und mit Hilfe einer Wissensbasis über diese Sachverhalte sinnvolle Antworten generieren kann.

Die enormen technologischen Konsequenzen, die aus Forschungsbeiträgen dieser Art erwachsen, werden besonders deutlich, wenn ein Dialogsystem mit einem Expertensystem gekoppelt wird, wie es in dem Beitrag von P. Raulefs dargestellt wird.

Beide Gebiete werden in den USA wegen der zu erwartenden technologischen Konsequenzen mit einem Aufwand erforscht, der bei uns nicht realisierbar wäre.

In dem Beitrag von H. Boley (Hamburg): "KI-Sprachen und KI-Maschinen, eine Übersicht" werden die speziellen Hardware- und Softwareentwicklungen für die KI-Forschung vorgestellt. Dieser Vortrag ist wegen der bevorstehenden Anschaffung von LISP-Maschinen für einige deutsche Universitäten von besonders aktuellem Interesse: mit einer solchen Anschaffung würden wir gleichzeitig mit den amerikanischen Forschungsgruppen eine ihnen vergleichbare Ausrüstung erhalten. Gruppen, denen heute eine solche Maschine zur Verfügung steht, dürften in kurzer Zeit einen Forschungsvorsprung haben, der kaum noch aufzuholen ist.

Der nächste Tag war ausschließlich theoretischen Fragestellungen und dem automatischen Beweisen vorbehalten und begann mit dem HV von W. Bibel (München): "Matings in Matrices: Eine Einführung in neuere Beweisverfahren", in dem die zur Zeit am aussichtsreichsten erscheinenden Verfahren vorgestellt werden. Der HV von R. Loos (Karlsruhe), "Termreduktionssysteme und algebraische Algorithmen" gibt eine Übersicht über das Gebiet der 'Rewrite-Systeme', das inzwischen auch für die Kerninformatik (abstrakte Datentypen, Programmverifikation, funktionales Programmieren usw.) von fundamentaler Bedeutung zu werden verspricht. Der Vortrag ist von besonderem Interesse durch die Verbindung der theoretischen Verfahren der Termreduktionssysteme mit den klassischen Fragestellungen der Computeralgebra.

Der HV des letzten Tages: W. Polak (Stanford): "Programmverifikation in Stanford - gestern, heute und morgen" stellt das derzeit erfolgreichste PV-System vor und gibt interessante Ausblicke einerseits auf die in den nächsten Jahren zu erwartende industrielle Anwendung und andererseits auf die zu erwartenden Forschungsschwerpunkte. Das Hauptziel ist dabei die Integration der Programmverifikation in den Softwareerstellungszyklus, ein Problem, auf das inzwischen eine Reihe von Wissenschaftlern hingewiesen haben, für das bisher jedoch keine an einem größeren Projekt demonstrierte Lösung gefunden wurde.

Die Evaluierung einer einwöchigen Tagung und der vorgetragenen Ergebnisse ist immer subjektiv: meine persönliche Einschätzung - nicht nur auf Grund dieser Tagung - ist die, daß die deutsche Forschung auf diesem Gebiet noch immer sehr stark von den USA abhängig ist. Das gilt für die sonstigen (Standard-)Gebiete der Informatik ganz genauso und war nach so lange verzögertem Start und so kurzer Entwicklungszeit auch nicht anders zu erwarten. Andererseits haben zumindest die Gebiete "Verarbeitung Natürlicher Sprache" (Hamburg); "Szenenanalyse" (Hamburg), "Programmiersprachenentwicklung" (Bonn) und "Automatisches Beweisen" (München, Karlsruhe) einen gewissen internationalen Standard erreicht und Ergebnisse vorzuweisen, die auch außerhalb Deutschlands zunehmend Beachtung finden.

Die Teilnehmerzahl, die mit ca. 100 Teilnehmern fast doppelt so hoch war, wie erwartet, mag ebenfalls ein Hinweis auf das erwachende Interesse sein, das diesem Gebiet neuerdings auch von der Industrie entgegengebracht wird.

[1] Die "Dartmouth Conference" (1956) gilt als die Geburtsstunde der Artificial Intelligence, wenn auch die eigentlichen Anfänge auf v. Neumann (USA) und A. Turing (England) zurückgehen. P. McCorduck, "Machines Who Think", Freeman and Co., 1979, gibt eine mehr journalistisch orientierte historische Übersicht.

[2] Siehe z.B. die Curriculum Empfehlungen der ACM '78 in CACM 1979, vol 22, no 3 und CACM 1981, vol 24, no 3. Die großen Universitäten (MIT, Stanford, CMU etc.) haben ohnehin seit über 10 Jahren spezielle Schwerpunktprogramme für die AI.

[3] Siehe den SRI-International Roboter 'Shakey' oder den Edinburgh-Roboter 'FREDDY' als Vorläufer in den unten angegebenen Lehrbüchern.

[4] E. Feigenbaum, Hauptvortrag der 10. GI-Jahrestagung, 1980.

[5] Siehe z.B. Abegglen, A. Etorie "Japans Technologie Heute", Spektrum der Wissenschaft, April 1981 (Scientific American).

[6] Siehe die beiden unten angegebenen Fachbücher für Natural Language Processing.

[7] W. v. Hahn, Computer als Dialogpartner, HAM-RPM, Universität Hamburg, Germanisches Seminar.

Die folgende Liste gibt eine kleine Auswahl aus der Standardliteratur zur Künstlichen Intelligenz:

Empfehlenswerte einführende Lehrbücher:

B. Raphael "The Thinking Computer: Mind inside Matter", 1976, San Francisco, W.H. Freeman
N. Nilsson "Problem Solving Methods in Artificial Intelligence", 1971 New York, McGraw Hill
N. Nilsson "Principles of Artificial Intelligence", Tioga Publ. Comp., Palo Alto, 1980

Fachbücher zur Verarbeitung Natürlicher Sprache:

T. Winograd "Understanding Natural Language" Edinburgh University Press, 1970
E. Charniak, Y.A. Wilks (eds) "Computational Semantics" North Holland, 1976

Fachbücher zum Automatischen Beweisen:

D. Loveland "Automated Theorem Proving", North Holland, 1978
C. Chang, R. Lee "Symbolic Logic and Mechanical Theorem Proving, Academic Press, 1973

Fachbücher zum Computersehen:

P.H. Winston (ed) "The Psychology of Computer Vision"
McGraw Hill, 1975
A.R. Hanson, E.M. Riseman (eds) "Computer Vision Systems"
Academic Press, 1978

Künstliche Intelligenz und Psychologie:

K.M. Colby "Artificial Paranoia", Pergamon General Psychology
Series, 1975

Philosophische Aspekte der Künstlichen Intelligenz:

M. Boden "Artificial Intelligence and Natural Man",
Harvester Press, 1977
A. Sloman "The Computer Revolution in Philosophy",
Harvester Press, 1978

Kritische KI-Literatur:

J. Weizenbaum "Computer Power and Human Reason",
W.H. Freeman, 1976
H.L. Dreyfus "What Computers Can't Do" Harper and Row, 1972

Fachliteratur:

Journal of Artificial Intelligence, North Holland

Cognitive Science, North Holland

Machine Intelligence (vol 1 bis 9), Edinburgh University Press

Proceedings of the International Joint Conference on Artificial
Intelligence (seit 1969 zweijährig)

Proceedings der AISB-Conference on Artificial Intelligence
(seit 1974 zweijährig)

Proceedings of Theoretical Issues in Natural Language Processing
(seit 1975 zweijährig)

Proceedings of Workshop on Automated Deduction
(seit 1974 zweijährig)

Im übrigen gibt der Fachausschuss 6 der Gesellschaft für Informatik
eine Informationsbroschüre heraus, die viermal jährlich erscheint und
über die Forschungsaktivitäten, insbesondere in Deutschland informiert.

Der "Rundbrief der Fachgruppe KI" kann bei den derzeitigen Editoren

H. Boley, P. Schefe, W. Wahlster
Universität Hamburg
Institut für Informatik
Schlüterstr. 70
2000 Hamburg

bestellt werden.

INHALTSVERZEICHNIS

Einleitung

COMPUTERSEHEN UND ROBOTERFORSCHUNG

NATÜRLICHSPRACHLICHE KI-SYSTEME

EXPERTENSYSTEME/VERARBEITUNG NATÜRLICHER SPRACHE

Ferner wurden in der Reihe "open shop" die folgenden, nicht referier-
ten Vorträge gehalten, die über gerade angelaufene Forschungsprojekte
oder "last minute results" berichteten:

Th. Christaller, Augmented Transition Networks zur formalen
   Beschreibung von Dialogsituationen

W. Dzida, S. Herda, C. Hoffmann, W. Valder, Ein Modell vom
   Benutzer als Grundlage für den Entwurf eines kongitiven
   Systems

K.D. Hess, Petri-Netze als Simulationsmittel natürlichsprachlicher Handlungsabläufe

L. Sokolowski, Die MIT LISP-Maschine

MODELS AND STRUCTURES IN IMAGE PROCESSING

B. RADIG
Fachbereich Informatik
Universität Hamburg

1.0   INTRODUCTION

"AI is the 'study of how to use knowledge to achieve intelligent
action, which often implies selection from a large space of
alternatives'. Vision and speech are two problems which require
the application of diverse sources of knowledge, including both
symbolic knowledge and knowledge of the signal space, to the
interpretation of a noisy signal (image or speech waveform). AI
systems which solve vision and speech problems differ from purely
symbolic problem solving systems since they must explicitly deal
with errors, noise, and uncertainty in the input data."
[REDDY ROSENFELD 79]

2.0   THE VISION PROBLEM

The analysis of digitized images and sequences thereof puts an
AI-system in a special environment due to the large amount of
fuzzy input data which is usually involved.

"The vision problem begins with a large gray-level intensity
array, and culminates in a description, that depends on that
array, and on the purpose for which it is being viewed.   The
question is, what has to go on in between." [MARR 75]

This description, usually called the interpretation of an image,
can be regarded as the result of a heuristic search; the
organization of the search and the heuristics involved partially

answer Marr's question.

A heuristic search - according to the definition by NEWELL and ERNST 65 - involves a set $\{X\}$ of objects and a list $\{Q\}$ of operators. If we partition the set of objects $\{X\}$ into a subset of initial objects $\{X_I\}$, e.g. the components of the intensity array, and a set of final objects $\{X_F\}$ which comprise the description to be generated, then the question 'what has to go on in between' can be reformulated as the search for a sequence $S: Q_1, \ldots, Q_n$ of operations which transform $\{X_I\}$ into $\{X_F\}$. Note the similarity to a state-space representation [NILSSON 71], [KANAL 79].

Such a cognitive system has to be supplied with a knowledge base which contains three types of information:
- A definition of the objects $\{X_I\}$ the system has to start with, and the objects $\{X\}$ which might be generated applying the operators.
- A definition of the operators $\{Q\}$ and their applicability to the various objects X.
- Information to reduce the search space for the transformation sequence S, since an enumerative generation of S is usually far beyond the limits of computational feasibility.

A modern cognitive system contains most of the above information in an explicitly accessible database (compare [KELLY 70] and [BAIRD KELLY 74] for an improvement of system design and performance using explicit models, here formalized as production rules). Such a database is usually called 'long term memory' or 'world model'. The first name emphasizes that its content is not altered by a current interpretation process, whereas it might be changed by an adaptive 'learning' mechanism, as in WINSTON's 75 classical approach. The second naming stresses the fact that an important component of the database are 'stored models' [SHAPIRO HARALICK 80] as a structural description of prototypical, generic objects and their interdependency. Again, the prefix 'world' expresses that the content is not a snapshot of a distinct situation, rather it describes the general knowledge of the system about its environment [ZUCKER ET AL. 75].

The database which receives the results, intermediate or final, of an analysis process is sometimes termed 'short term memory' [LEVINE 78]. It is populated by instances of stored models which culminate in the desired system internal model of the scene. Systems which analyse and relate images from a sequence of visual observations may be attributed a 'medium term memory'. It contains the structures which are selected to be compared from frame to frame, together with the established links which denote the correspondence of (time varying) structures from different frames. From them a description of the whole image sequence can be obtained. An example is the volumetric description of a moving car, reconstructed from coordinate sequences of corresponding object points [DRESCHLER NAGEL 81].

The point of view of image interpretation as a sequence of instantiations of eventually more and more complex models leads to another aspect of the heuristic search, namely the matching of structural descriptions. The stored model as a structural description of a prototype object is compared with candidate objects which have been hypothesized on the image content. PREPARATA and RAY 72 expressed this point of view as follows, where stimulus may be identified with the intensity array, and map with the model base:

"Understanding and recognition can be characterized as the linking of components of the stimulus to concepts in the map . . . By interpretation we mean
(1) the formulation of hypotheses upon the stimulus-map linkage suggested by the evidence provided by the preprocessed stimulus, followed by
(2) experiments aimed at testing the hypotheses, until a decision is made as the selection of the hypothesis scoring the highest confidence."

Several questions arise in this context:
- how to reduce the cardinality of candidates (e.g. by hierarchical organization of prototypes [BARROW ET AL. 72] and knowledge [NIEMANN 80]);
- how to cope with imperfect matches (e.g. by 'ε-homomorphism' [SHAPIRO HARALICK 80]), and how to carry the confidence value as a measure of the mismatch between a prototype and its instance over to higher-level instances which use this incomplete instance as a constituent [BERTELSMEIER RADIG 77b];
- what are the primitive structures on the lowest level which are usually computed by a segmentation process which interfaces the intensity array with the symbolic description (e.g. 'vertex-string-surface' graphs which are re-encoded as 'half-chunk' graphs [JACOBUS ET AL. 80]).

To solve these problems, techniques drawn from the repertoire of artificial intelligence enter the game.

3.0 FROM INTENSITY ARRAYS TO THEIR INTERPRETATION

It is usually prohibitive to start with the heuristic search from the pixel level. One of the rare exceptions is MARTELLI's 76 approach, employing the classical A^* algorithm [HART ET AL. 68], which inputs gray-value pixels and ends up with edges; but this approach is not practical, in general.

Some typical steps can be identified in the course from a - let's say 10Mbit multispectral - image to the one bit answer to a user's yes/no question.

```
                    physics                     10Mbit

recording                   │   digitized image       │
                            │   transformed,          │
preprocessing               │   smoothed,             │
                            │   enhanced image        │
segmentation                │   regions, edges        │
                            │                         │   abstraction
symbolic description        │   relational structure  │
                            │                         │
hypothize-test              │   model instances       │
                            │                         │
interpretation              ▼   result                ▼

           scene description                    1bit
```

3.1 Image Sequences

A sensor converts radiation intensity into an electrical signal. The radiation may range from ultrasonic waves, infrared, visible, and Roentgen light to elementary particle radiation. The signal is quantized with 1 to 12bit resolution and stored in a digital memory.

If an image is taken for industrial purposes to be processed in real-time the data volume is kept low, typically 128*128*1 ≈ 0.02Mbit. Systems which process standard TV-images have to handle about 512*580*8 ≈ 2.4Mbit. High resolution satellite scanners deliver up to 200Mbit per image. Pixels which form such black-and-white images have three components, p=(x,y,gray), the two coordinates and the gray-value. The field of research and application is growing where further components have to be added in order to observe phenomena of interest; see [NAGEL 81], [RADIG NAGEL 80] for an overview.

Spectral components are added for
- color images, p=(x,y,red,green,blue), data volume ≈ 1 to 10Mbit;
- multispectral satellite images, p=(x,y,IR,...,UV), up to 1Gbit;
- digital image processing for high quality color printing devices, p=(x,y,color1,...,color10), up to 2Gbit.

An increasingly important application, where the third spatial component is added, p=(x,y,z,gray), is computer tomography. Here, a set of slices of about 10Mbit resolution each, comprise a 3-D image ([Herman 80], see [SHANI 80] for a typical application).

In order to record dynamic processes an additional component, time, is needed. Industrial applications of visual inspection of (rotating) surfaces sometimes use linear detector arrays with resolution up to 4096 pixels and 10000 lines per surface [BERTELSMEIER HILLE 79], [HARA ET AL. 80]. Here, a pixel has the components p=(x,gray,t).

A sequence of TV-images generates about 50Mbit/sec, p=(x,y,gray,t) [JAIN NAGEL 79], [RADIG 81]. For color-TV sequences, data rates are up to three times as large, p=(x,y,red,green,blue,t).

X-ray image sequences have become important for studying the dynamics of human organs and blood circulations [ONOE ET AL. 80], [BÖHM ET AL. 80], [BRENNECKE ET Al. 80]. Tremendous demands for processing and storage capabilities arise in dynamical 3-D computer tomography, p=(x,y,z,gray,t), [WOOD 76], [HEINTZEN BÜRSCH 78].

3.2 Preprocessing

The preprocessing prepares the data for the segmentation (see the textbook by ROSENFELD and KAK 76), and incorporates such processes as coordinate transforms, e.g. from a red-green-blue color space to an intensity-hue-saturation image.

Noise may be reduced by application of a smoothing procedure. This is essentially a low pass filtering technique, since the spectral distribution of the most disturbing noise peaks at the high frequency tail. But care has to be taken not to blur sharp edges [NAGAO MATSUYAMA 79], and not to destroy the details of the boundary of a region, but rather restore them [TRIENDL 78]. Most of these filter operations are non-linear (median or general rank filters [HEYGSTER 80]) and experimentally designed due to the difficult theoretical prediction of their results.

To prepare an image for edge detection digital approximations of gradient and Laplace operators [ROSENFELD KAK 76] may be applied. Least-squares approximation of the gradient [HOLDERMANN KAZMIERCZAK 72] come in use again [RADIG 78], [HARALICK 80].

3.3 Segmentation

Usually, symbolic description of an image (sequence) is based on a partition of the pixel matrix into equivalence classes. Two classical techniques are well investigated (see [DAVIS 75], [ZUCKER 76], [RISEMAN ARBIB 77], [HILLE 81], [FU MUI 81] for a survey).

One approach searches for discontinuities of the image function, locates edge elements there, and assigns pixels within a closed boundary formed by linked edge elements to a region. The other approach defines some uniformity attributes and collects adjacent pixels into a region as long as the uniformity attribute (e.g. color [OHTA ET AL. 80]) is not violated. It is also possible to split regions until their properties are uniform enough. In a natural way, borders of regions may be identified as edges. In a considerably different approach, EHRICH and FOITH 78 start from a tree-like description of intensity profiles along scan lines.

In the past, research was mainly directed to develop segmentation techniques which offer acceptable performance within the limits of memory and run-time constraints. These approaches are ad hoc in nature and their design implicitly reflects the designer's knowledge and expectations about the scene domain. This kind of segmentation program is still important for applications which employ small computers or dedicated hardware processors.

Several arguments support the use of explicit knowledge in image segmentation. There is no optimal method for all images. The selection of an appropriate method is far easier if the a priori knowledge is clearly stated in the segmentation algorithm. Explicit representation of such knowledge may enable a user to adapt a segmentation algorithm to the specific scene domain he has in mind. The most supporting argument is the insight that

"It very well may be true that no region formation algorithm can ever work properly without semantic feedback."
[HANSON RISEMAN 75].

There is no quantitative measure of the quality of a segmentation result unless a segmentation algorithm is part of a cognitive system, where some kind of interpretation is based on these results. If the segmentation becomes unreliable in the opinion of higher level procedures, a cognitive system could optimize the performance of its lower level frontend. This is only possible if information gathered so far in the system is able to alter those knowledge chunks in the long term memory which control the segmentation.

However, semantic feedback implies that models of edges and regions as well as merging or splitting parameters have to be inferred from interpretation hypotheses which rely on previous segmentation results. Here, we are in a situation that search has to compensate for a lack of knowledge. KANADE 80 adresses this problem in developing his paradigm of image understanding.

It is not surprising that industrial applications - where a lot of a priori knowledge is available - may be able to successfully incorporate semantic segmentation into vision systems [TROPF 80].

3.4 Symbolic Description

The segmentation results are converted into a symbolic description dedicated to the interpretation process. The description might be strings of terminal symbols in the case of a subsequent syntactical analysis (for a short survey see [FU 78]). More common is the representation as graphs or relational structures, e.g. the vertex-string-surface graphs of JACOBUS ET AL. 80, or the region-segment-vertex graphs of HANSON and RISEMAN 78. Examples of typical structures can be found in [BERTELSMEIER RADIG 77a], [KRAASCH ZACH 79], [RADIG ET AL. 80]: regions (R), boundaries (B), straight lines (L), and endpoints (E). Properties are ROW(E), COL(E) = image coordinates, LENGTH(B), AREA(R), GRAYMEAN(R), SLOPE(L), etc. Relations are WITHIN(R,R) = one region is completely enclosed by another, NEIGHBOR(R,R) = both regions have a common boundary, BORDER(B,R), HEADPOINT(E,B), TAILPOINT(E,B), APPROXIMATES(L,B) = the boundary is approximated by the indicated straigth line, etc.

Since the symbolic description, sometimes called 'sketch' or 'sketch map' in this context, interfaces the segmentation and the interpretation process, it should be carefully designed in order to preserve segmentation information and to allow efficient hypothesis-test cycles. SHNEIER 79 developed a compact relational structure representation, CHENG and HUANG 80 discuss some alternatives.

3.5 Interpretation

Several techniques are in use in order to relate the sketch map to the information stored in the long term memory or world model. Among them are syntactical approaches, e.g. [YOU FU 79], and [MOHR HATON 76], [MOHR MASINI 80] who parse even imperfect patterns.

In relaxation labeling, developed by Rosenfeld and his coworkers [ROSENFELD ET AL. 76], a set of labels (meanings) is distributed over each item, e.g. pixels or nodes of a graph. Each label carries an initial confidence value, obtained from a priori knowledge. A set of rules determines which pair of labels at adjacent items support each other and which does not. An iterative and parallel application of these rules alters the confidence values in such a way that the system is expected to approach a state where each item is uniquely labeled.

Related to (but independent from) discrete relaxation labeling is the method of constraint propagation [WALTZ 75], [TENENBAUM BARROW 76]. Here, constraints on the relationship between objects, if carefully imposed, disambiguate the meaning of the objects in an iterative cycle.

If both the sketch map and the stored models are represented as graph structures, the hypothesis-test paradigm is equivalent to the search for graph homomorphisms [PREPARATA RAY 72], [NEVATIA PRICE 78], [HARALICK 78], [BROOKS ET AL. 79], [RADIG ET AL. 80], [JACOBUS ET AL. 80]. Since the sketch map usually contains more elements than a stored model, a subgraph of the sketch has to be identified with the instance of an object. CHENG and HUANG 80 start this search from prominent nodes which exhibit some extraordinary feature. BERTELSMEIER and RADIG 77a,b use cliques in a 'compatibility graph' to solve this problem, according to an idea of BARROW and BURSTALL 76. The long term memory contains a hierarchy of models; the nodes of the compatibility graph are hypothetical assignments of instances of submodels to constituents of the model in question. Arcs in the graph express the fact that two hypothetical assignments do not violate the relational constraints prescribed in the model for these two parts. Maximal cliques in this graph correspond to instances of the model.

Of course, interpretation does not end with instantiating models or accumulating other descriptors in the short term memory. The conversion of interpretation results - from the control of the manipulator of an industrial robot to a natural language dialogue with a human user - should be part of a cognitive system, but is a more or less separate field of research.

4.0 TRENDS

Interaction between AI and vision research becomes more and more productive. This is evident in the research which is done in order to represent the various types of knowledge which guide the analysis of images [NAGEL 79].

Progress made so far is an essential basis for the development of versatile cognitive systems. In order to improve the performance of such systems one current trend in research is to extend the application of AI methods towards the low level processors of a vision system. Since semantic segmentation burdens such a system by enlarging its search space, efficient heuristics and backtracking mechanisms have to be employed. Conventional AI languages which provide appropriate control structures are not designed for processing large amounts of data. The ADA programming language might be a future tool to combine efficiency with powerful control and representation structures, and a tool to distribute the load over a network of cooperating computers. As another alternative, dedicated hardware such as the LISP machine, may add the efficiency to AI languages which is needed in order to process images and image sequences.

Image segmentation can be supported by a better non-purposive preprocessing of the images. Horn's work [HORN 77] who determined lightness and reflectance from gray-value images is such an example, another is the recovery of 'intrinsic images' [BARROW TENENBAUM 78] which describe range, orientation, reflectance, and incident illumination; see [BRADY 81] for a discussion of related topics. Even these low level processes are strongly related to AI methods employing the ideas of consistency by constraint satisfaction.

With the increased interest in the evaluation of image sequences [NAGEL 81] a special aspect of knowledge representation becomes important, too. If sketch maps are represented as relational structures two maps from different images can be mapped one to the other, in order to detect differences between them [JACOBUS ET AL. 80]. Since models are represented as relational structures, a scetch map can easily be converted into a model for the interpretation of the next image. RADIG ET AL. 80 used this technique to solve the correspondence problem for the 3-D reconstruction of simple moving objects from a sequence of images. Here, techniques of hierarchical composition of models and scene descriptors offer the chance to meet the computational challenge.

5.0   REFERENCES

BAIRD KELLY 74
   M. L. Baird, M. D. Kelly: "Recognizing Objects by Rules of
   Inference on Sequentially Thresholded Gray-Level Pictures",
   Comp. Graphics Image Proc. 3 (1974) 1-22.
BARROW ET AL. 72
   H. G. Barrow, A. P. Ambler, R. M. Burstall: "Some Techniques
   for Recognizing Structures in Pictures", in Frontiers of
   Pattern Recognition, S. Watanabe (ed.), Academic Press, New
   York 1972.
BARROW BURSTALL 76
   H. G. Barrow, R. M. Burstall: "Subgraph Isomorphism,
   Matching Relational Structures and Maximal Cliques",
   Information Proc. Letters 4 (1976) 83-84.
BARROW TENENBAUM 78
   H G. Barrow, J. M. Tenenbaum: "Recovering Intrinsic Scene
   Characteristics from Images", in Computer Vision Systems, A.
   R. Hanson, E. M. Riseman (eds.), Academic Press, New York
   1978.
BERTELSMEIER HILLE 79
   R. Bertelsmeier, G. Hille: "Anwendungen von
   Bildanalysetechniken zur automatischen Sichtkontrolle von
   Bauteilen im Automobilbau", in Angewandte Szenenanalyse, J.
   P. Foith (ed.), Informatik Fachberichte 20, Springer
   Berlin-Heidelberg-New York 1979.
BERTELSMEIER RADIG 77a
   R. Bertelsmeier, B. Radig: "Kontextunterstützte Analyse von
   Szenen mit bewegten Objecten", GI/NTG Fachtagung Digitale
   Bildverarbeitung, H.-H. Nagel (ed.), München Mar. 28-30,
   1977, Informatik Fachberichte 8, 101-128, Springer
   Berlin-Heidelberg-New York 1977.
BERTELSMEIER RADIG 77b
   R. Bertelsmeier, B. Radig: "Context Guided Analysis of
   Scenes With Moving Objects", Report IFI-HH-B-41/77,
   Fachbereich Informatik, Univ. Hamburg, Feb. 1977.
BÖHM ET AL. 80
   M. Böhm, U. Obermöller, K. H. Höhne: "Determination of Heart
   Dynamics from X-Ray and Ultrasound Image Sequences",
   ICPR-80, Miami Beach, Dec. 1-4, 1980, 403-408.

BRADY 81
M. Brady: "Artificial Intelligence Approaches to Image
Understanding", Nato Adv. Study Inst. on Pattern Recognition
Theory and Applications, Oxford, March 29 - April 11, 1981.
BRENNECKE ET AL. 80
R. Brennecke, H. J. Hahne, P. H. Heintzen: "A
Multiprocessor-System for the Acquisition and Analysis of
Video Image Sequences", in Erzeugung und Analyse von Bildern
und Strukturen, S. J. Pöppl, H. Platzer (eds.), Informatik
Fachberichte 29, Springer Berlin-Heidelberg-New York 1980.
BROOKS ET AL. 79
R. A. Brooks, R. Greiner, T. O. Binford: "The ACRONYM
Model-Based Vision System", IJCAI-79, Tokyo, Aug. 20-23,
1979, 105-113.
CHENG HUANG 80
J.-K. Cheng, T. S. Huang: "Algorithms for Matching
Relational Structures and their Applications to Image
Processing", Report TR-EE 80-53, School of Electr. Engg.,
Purdue Univ., Dec. 1980.
DAVIS 75
L. S. Davis: "A Survey of Edge Detection Techniques", Comp.
Graphics Image Proc. 4 (1975) 248-270.
DRESCHLER NAGEL 81
L. Dreschler, H.-H. Nagel: "On the Frame-to-Frame
Correspondence between Greyvalue Characteristics in the
Images of Moving Objects", this volume.
EHRICH FOITH 78
R. W. Ehrich, J. P. Foith: "Topology and Semantics of
Intensity Arrays", in Computer Vision Systems, A. R. Hanson,
E. M. Riseman (eds.), Academic Press, New York 1978.
FU 78
K. S. Fu: "Recent Advantages in Syntactic Pattern
Recognition", IJCPR-78, Kyoto, Nov. 7-10, 1978, 95-105.
FU MUI 81
K. S. Fu, J. K. Mui: "A Survey on Image Segmentation",
Pattern Recognition 13 (1981) 3-16.
HANSON RISEMAN 75
A. R. Hanson, E. M. Riseman: "The Design of a Semantically
Directed Vision Processor", COINS Technical Report 75C-1,
Univ. of Massachusets, 1975.

HANSON RISEMAN 78

    A. R. Hanson, E. M. Riseman: "Segmentation of Natural
Scenes", in Computer Vision Systems, A. R. Hanson, E. M.
Riseman (eds.), Academic Press, New York 1978.

HARA ET AL. 80

    Y. Hara, K. Okamoto, T. Hamada, N. Akiyama: "Automatic
Visual Inspection of LSI Photomasks", ICPR-80, Miami Beach,
Dec. 1-4, 1980, 273-279.

HARALICK 78

    R. M. Haralick: "Scene Analysis, Arrangements, and
Homomorphisms", in Computer Vision Systems, A. R. Hanson, E.
M. Riseman (eds.), Academic Press, New York 1978.

HARALICK 80

    R. M. Haralick: "Edge and Region Analysis for Digital Image
Data", Comp. Graphics Image Proc. 12 (1980) 60-79.

HART ET AL. 68

    P. E. Hart, N. J. Nilsson, B. Raphael: "A Formal Basis for
the Heuristic Determination of Minimum Cost Paths", IEEE
Trans. Sys. Sci. Cyber. SSC-4 (1968) 100-107, and
corrections in SIGART Newsletter No. 37, Dec. 1972, 28-29;
see also D. Gelperin: "On the Optimality of A^*", Artificial
Intelligence 8 (1977) 69-76.

HEINTZEN BÜRSCH 78

    P. H. Heintzen, J. H. Bürsch (eds.):
"Roentgen-Video-Techniques for Dynamic Studies of Structure
and Function of the Heart and Circulation", Georg Thieme
Verlag, Stuttgart 1978.

HERMAN 80

    G. T. Herman: "Image Reconstruction from Projections",
Academic Press, New York 1980.

HEYGSTER 80

    G. Heygster: "Two-Dimensional Rank Filters - Deterministic
and Spectral Properties", ICPR-80, Miami Beach, Dec. 1-4,
1980, 1165-1167.

HILLE 81

    G. Hille: "Methoden und Modelle in der Bildsegmentation -
Eine Übersicht", Fachbereich Informatik, Univ. Hamburg, in
preparation.

HOLDERMANN KAZMIERCZAK 72

    F. Holdermann, H. Kazmierczak: "Preprocessing of Gray Scale
Pictures", Comp. Graphics Image Proc. 1 (1972) 66-80.

HORN 77
    B. K. P. Horn: "Understanding Image Intensities", Artificial
    Intelligence 8 (1977) 201-231.
JACOBUS ET AL. 80
    C. J. Jacobus, R. T. Chien, J. M. Selander: "Motion
    Detection and Analysis of Matching Graphs of
    Intermediate-Level Primitives", IEEE Trans. Pattern Anal.
    Mach. Intell. PAMI-2 (1980) 495-510.
JAIN NAGEL 79
    R. Jain, H.-H. Nagel: "On the Analysis of Accumulative
    Difference Pictures from Image Sequences of Real World
    Scenes", IEEE Trans. Pattern Anal. Mach. Intell. PAMI-1
    (1979) 206-214.
KANADE 80
    T. Kanade: "Region Segmentation: Signal vs Semantics", Comp.
    Graphics Image Proc. 13 (1980) 279-297.
KANAL 79
    L. N. Kanal: "Problem-Solving Models and Search Strategies
    for Pattern Recognition", IEEE Trans. Pattern Analysis
    Machine Intell. PAMI-1 (1979) 193-201.
KELLY 70
    M. D. Kelly: "Visual Identification of Peoples by Computer",
    Memo AI-130, Comp. Sc. Dept. Stanford Univ. 1970.
KRAASCH ZACH 79
    R. Kraasch, W. Zach: "Dreidimensionale Beschreibung
    einfacher bewegter Gegenstände", Diploma thesis, Fachbereich
    Informatik, Univ. Hamburg, July 1979.
LEVINE 78
    M. D. Levine: "A Knowledge-Based Computer Vision System", in
    Computer Vision Systems, A. R. Hanson, E. M. Riseman (eds.),
    Academic Press, New York 1978.
MARR 75
    D. Marr: "Early Processing of Visual Information", Memo
    AI-340, MIT Cambridge /MA, Dec. 1975, and Phil. Trans. Royal
    Society, Series B, 275 (1976) 483-524.
MARTELLI 76
    A. Martelli: "An Application of Heuristic Search Methods to
    Edge and Contour Detection", C.ACM 19 (1976) 73-83.
MOHR HATON 76
    R. Mohr, J.-P. Haton: "A Parsing Algorithm for Imperfect
    Patterns and its Application to Speech and Image
    Recognition", talk given at IJCPR-76, published as Report
    76-R-018, Univ. de Nancy I, 1976.

MOHR MASINI 80

R. Mohr, G. Masini: "Knowledge Directed Recognition: A Syntactical Approach", ICPR-80, Miami Beach, Dec. 1-4, 1980, 337-339.

NAGAO MATSUYAMA 79

M. Nagao, T. Matsuyama: "Edge Preserving Smoothing", Comp. Graphics Image Proc. 9 (1979) 394-407.

NAGEL 79

H.-H. Nagel: "Über die Repräsentation von Wissen zur Auswertung von Bildern", in Angewandte Szenenanalyse, J. P. Foith (ed.), Informatik Fachberichte 20, Springer Berlin-Heidelberg-New York 1979.

NAGEL 81

H.-H. Nagel: "Image Sequence Analysis: What Can we Learn from Applications?", to appear in Image Sequence Analysis, T. S. Huang (ed.) Springer Berlin-Heidelberg-New York 1981; and Report IFI-HH-M-79/80, Fachbereich Informatik, Univ. Hamburg, 1980.

NEVATIA PRICE 78

R. Nevatia, K. Price: "Locating Structures in Areal Images", ICPR-80, Miami Beach, Dec. 1-4, 1980, 686-690.

NEWELL ERNST 65

A. Newell, G. Ernst: "The Search for Generality", Proc. IFIP Congress 65, W. A. Kalenich (ed.), Spartan Books, Washington D.C., and Macmillan, London, 1965.

NIEMANN 80

H. Niemann: "Hierarchical Graphs in Pattern Analysis", ICPR-80, Miami Beach, Dec. 1-4, 1980, 213-216; see also "Zur Repräsentation von Kontrollstrukturen und Wissen in der Musteranalyse", in Erzeugung und Analyse von Bildern und Strukturen, S. J. Pöppl, H. Platzer (eds.), Informatik Fachberichte 29, Springer Berlin-Heidelberg-New York 1980.

NILSSON 71

N. J. Nilsson: "Problem-Solving Methods in Artificial Intelligence", McGraw Hill, New York 1971.

OHTA ET AL. 80

Y. I. Ohta, T. Kanade, T. Sakai: "Color Information for Region Segmentation", Comp. Graphics Image Proc. 13 (1980) 222-241.

ONOE ET AL. 80

M. Onoe, K. Preston, A. Rosenfeld (eds.): "Real-Time Medical Image Processing", Plenum Press, New York 1980.

PREPARATA RAY 72
    F. P. Preparata, S. R. Ray: "An Approach to Artificial
    Nonsymbolic Cognition", Information Sciences 4 (1972) 65-86.
RADIG 78
    B. Radig: "Parameterized Region Extraction for the
    Description of Moving Objects", Proc. AISB/GI Conf. on
    Artificial Intelligence, Hamburg, July 18-20, 1978.
RADIG NAGEL 80
    B. Radig, H.-H. Nagel: "Evaluation of Image Sequences: A
    Look Beyond Applications", Nato Adv. Study Inst. on Digital
    Image Proc. and Anal., Bonas, France, June 23 - July 4,
    1980, published by INRIA, to be published by Reidel.
RADIG ET AL. 80
    B. Radig, R. Kraasch, W. Zach: "Matching Symbolic
    Descriptions for 3-D Reconstruction of Simple Moving
    Objects", ICPR-80, Miami Beach, Dec. 1-4, 1980, 1081-1084.
RADIG 81
    B. Radig: "Image Region Extraction of Moving Objects", to
    appear in Image Sequence Analysis, T. S. Huang (ed.),
    Springer Berlin-Heidelberg-New York 1981.
REDDY ROSENFELD 79
    R. Reddy, A. Rosenfeld: Final Report on Workshop on Control
    Structures and Knowledge Representation for Image and Speech
    Understanding, April 3-4, 1979, Center for Adult Education,
    Univ. of Maryland, College Park.
RISEMAN ARBIB 77
    E. M. Riseman, M. A. Arbib: "Segmentation of Static Scenes",
    Comp. Graphics Image Proc. 6 (1977) 221-276.
ROSENFELD ET AL. 76
    A. Rosenfeld, R. A. Hummel, S. W. Zucker: "Scene Labeling by
    Relaxation Operation", IEEE Trans. System, Man, Cybernetics
    SMC-6 (1976) 420-433
ROSENFELD KAK 76
    A. Rosenfeld, A. C. Kak: "Digital Picture Processing",
    Academic Press, New York 1976.
SHANI 80
    U. Shani: "A 3-D Model-Driven System for the Recognition of
    Abdominal Anatomy from CT Scans", ICPR-80, Miami Beach, Dec.
    1-4, 1980, 585-590.
SHAPIRO HARALICK 80
    L. G. Shapiro, R. M. Haralick: "Algorithms for Inexact
    Matching", ICPR-80, Miami Beach, Dec. 1-4, 1980, 202-207.

SHNEIER 79
    M. O. Shneier: "A Compact Relational Structure
    Representation", IJCAI-79, Tokyo, Aug. 20-23, 1979, 818-826.
TENENBAUM BARROW 76
    J. M. Tenenbaum, H. G. Barrow: "IGS: A Paradigm for
    Integrating Image Segmentation and Interpretation", in
    Pattern Recognition and Artificial Intelligence, C. H. Chen
    (ed.), Academic Press, New York 1976, and "Experiments in
    Interpretation Guided Segmentation", Artificial Intelligence
    8 (1977) 241-274.
TRIENDL 78
    E. E. Triendl: "How to Get the Edge into the Map", IJCPR-78,
    Kyoto, Nov. 7-10, 1978, 946-950.
TROPF 80
    H. Tropf: "Analysis-By-Synthesis Search for Semantic
    Segmentation - Applied to Workpiece Recognition", ICPR-80,
    Miami Beach, Dec. 1-4, 1980, 1165-1167.
WALTZ 75
    D. Waltz: "Generating Semantic Descriptions from Drawings of
    Scenes with Shadows", in The Psychology of Computer Vision,
    P. H. Winston (ed.), McGraw Hill, New York 1975.
WINSTON 75
    P. H. Winston: "Learning Structural Descriptions from
    Examples", in The Psychology of Computer Vision, P. H.
    Winston (ed.), McGraw Hill, New York 1975.
WOOD 76
    E. H. Wood: "New Horizons for Study of the Cardiopulmonary
    and Circulatory Systems", Chest 69 (1976) 394-408.
YOU FU 79
    K. C. You, K. S. Fu: "A Syntactic Approach to Shape
    Recognition Using Attributed Grammars", IEEE Trans. System,
    Man, Cybernetics SMC-9 (1979) 334-344.
ZUCKER ET AL. 75
    S. W. Zucker, A. Rosenfeld, L.-S. Davis: "General Purpose
    Models: Expectations About the Unexpected", IJCAI-75,
    Tbilisi, Sept. 3-8, 1975, 716-721.
ZUCKER 76
    S. W. Zucker: "Region Growing: Childhood and Adolescence",
    Comp. Graphics Image Proc. 5 (1976) 382-393.

On the Frame-to-Frame Correspondence
between Greyvalue Characteristics in the Images
of Moving Objects

L. Dreschler and H.-H. Nagel
Fachbereich Informatik
Universitaet Hamburg
Schlueterstrasse 70
D-2000 Hamburg 13

Abstract

A system approach is outlined for the derivation of 3D polyhedral descriptions of moving objects by evaluation of monocular TV-frame sequences from real-world scenes. An implementation of this approach facilitated the study of the correspondence problem between descriptors extracted from images of moving cars in consecutive TV-frames. Our experience forced us to modify the relaxation approach of Barnard and Thompson 79+80 [1] in order to obtain acceptable results. These modifications are described and discussed.

1. Introduction

Visual observation of changes in the environment can be combined with general knowledge about moving bodies and about the image formation process in order to derive a description of a specific scene, its objects and their motion. A system which exploits general knowledge in order to extract scene-specific knowledge from visual sensors with time-varying input may be said to "learn from observations". It is obvious that the notion of "learning" has more aspects than those covered by a capability as indicated. Nevertheless, it appears useful to study approaches which attempt to implement such capabilities.

One such approach has been outlined by NAGEL 77 [12], based on considerations related to the evaluation of digitized TV-frame sequences - see NAGEL 78 [13]. Based on experiences accumulated in the meantime, a somewhat restricted and modified version of this approach has been implemented. It can be broken down into the following steps.

(1) A scene with moving rigid objects - e. g. , a street scene with a moving car - is sensed by a black/white TV-camera. The video signal is stored in real-time on an AMPEX MD400 analog video magnetic disc, one track per TV-frame, 25 frames per second.

(2) Consecutive frames are digitized without real-time constraints by locking the reading head to a single track until the 574 TV-lines used for that frame have been digitized (512 pixels with 8 bit greyvalues per TV-line). These raw data are condensed into a 192 line x 256 column image.

(3) The actual frame is compared with a reference frame - usually taken to be the first frame of a sequence. Significant differences between actual and reference frame are clustered to determine a rectangular window around the image of a moving object - see JAIN and NAGEL 79 [8]. An example is shown in figure 1.

a) First frame   b) Last frame

Fig. 1: A series of 22 frames showing a moving car.

(4) Within such a 'moving object window', descriptors are located which are hypothesized to represent the image of an identifiable point on the surface of the moving object - see DRESCHLER 81 [3], DRESCHLER and NAGEL 81 [4].

(5) An approach to the 'correspondence problem' (DUDA and HART 73 [5]) between descriptors extracted from consecutive frames attempts to pair those descriptors which correspond to the same point on the surface of the moving object. This step will be discussed in more detail in the subsequent sections.

(6) Repeating these steps for a sequence of consecutive frames should result in a set of 'descriptor chains'. Each chain comprises the 2D image coordinates of those descriptors which have been linked

from frame to frame through pairwise correspondences according to step (5). Global criteria - which consider an entire image sequence and not only pairs of consecutive frames - could be used to reject unacceptable chains, for example too short ones.

(7) The relative three-dimensional configuration of object points - each of which corresponds to a chain accepted in the preceding step (6) - will be computed by minimizing a suitably chosen error function (BONDE and NAGEL 79 [2], NAGEL 80 [14]). This error function reflects the assumption that the object points form a rigid 3D configuration. All 2D image coordinate variations measured throughout the perspective image sequence must be attributed to the displacement between this 3D point configuration and the sensor. This approach yields the 3D point configuration from series of 2D measurements up to a common scale factor. In addition, the space trajectory for a reference point of this 3D configuration will be obtained with respect to the camera coordinate system as a function of time - i.e. frame number -, but again only up to the same common scale factor. Related approaches for perspective projection have been investigated by ROACH and AGGARWAL 80 [21], by NAGEL 81 [15], and by NAGEL and NEUMANN 81 [16].

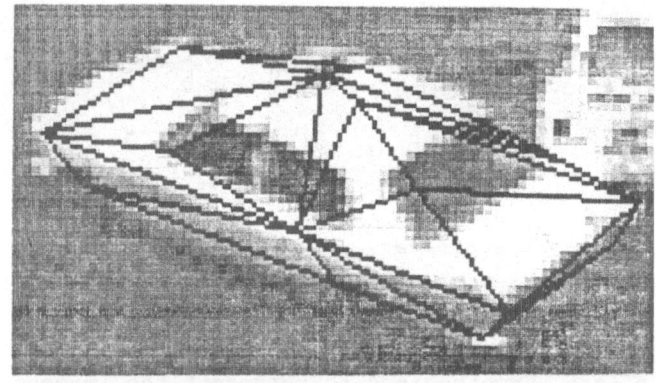

Fig. 2a:
Visible edges of
the convex hull
projected back into
the car image from
fig. 1a.

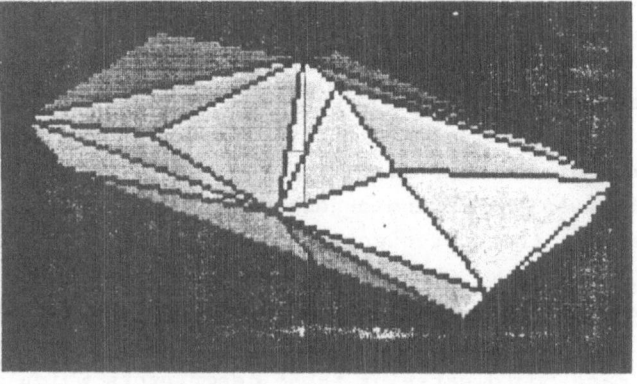

Fig. 2b:
The visible surfaces
of the convex hull
shaded according
to Lambert's
reflectivity law.
A hypothetical
light source is
assumed to illumi-
nate the convex
hull from the
viewing direction.

(8) A polyhedral approximation to the desired description of the moving object can be derived by computing the three-dimensional convex hull for the 3D point configuration obtained according to step (7). Computer graphic techniques may be employed to visualize this approximate object representation, for example in the position and attitude corresponding to the moving object selected from figure 1 - see figures 2a+b.

(9) Further work will be required to refine this convex hull into a better approximation of the object description - see, e. g. , the explorations by O'ROURKE 80 [17].

This concise presentation outlines our approach in order to provide a framework for a more detailed discussion of a particular question.

2. On the Correspondence Problem

The correspondence problem can be formulated as the search for a suitably defined match between 2D descriptor configurations from two different image frames. Such a problem occurs not only during the evaluation of temporal image sequences, but also in the disparity determination required for binocular stereovision.

In their efforts towards developing a computational theory of human vision, Marr and coworkers studied the correspondence problem (MARR and POGGIO 79 [11], GRIMSON and MARR 79 [6], see also MARR and HILDRETH 80 [10]). Their approach, however, did not appear to be immediately applicable to the comparatively low resolution digitized TV-frame sequences available to us. ULLMAN 79 [23] introduced a simple heuristic cost function to compare various possible matches between configurations of isolated dots in binary images. A solution to the correspondence problem should be obtained by minimizing the cost associated with a match.

The structure of this cost function yields a minimum of zero cost if no descriptor will be matched at all. In order to avoid this situation, ULLMAN 79 requests that all descriptors from one frame must be matched to at least one descriptor in the next frame and vice versa. In our situation, however, we do not feel that a match must be enforced for each descriptor. Apart from the cases where a descriptor disappears or appears from one frame to the next due to object rotation or (dis-)occlusion, the algorithm for locating descriptors is not foolproof either. Forced matching of a descriptor for which no acceptable partner exists in the other frame may introduce errors. If the density of descriptors is high, the forced match may be found in the vicinity of the desired one and the resulting error may not be too disturbing. ULLMAN 79 studied his minimal mapping approach for simulated data. No experience is known to us how his approach might react to real-world data corrupted by noise or shortcomings of the descriptor locating process .

RANADE and ROSENFELD 80 [20] studied a relaxation algorithm to determine a translation which provided the best global match between two 2D point configurations - even if these had been distorted slightly from one frame to the next, for example by a small rotation. A general discussion of relaxation mechanisms can be found in ROSENFELD et al. 76 [22], with additional basic considerations presented, e.g., by HUMMEL and ZUCKER 80 [7].

BARNARD and THOMPSON 79+80 [1] employed a relaxation algorithm to determine a confidence value for selected pairings between descriptors extracted from two digitized images. They evaluated the supporting evidence provided by similar pairings in a local environment around the descriptor match investigated - as opposed to the global environment of the entire 2D point configuration used by RANADE and ROSENFELD 80.

Let $p(i,k,L)$ represent the confidence at the k-th iteration that a 2D vector $L = (Lx,Ly)$ - restricted to a square environment R of sidelength $2*r+1$ around descriptor position $Pi=(Pix,Piy)$ - provides the proper displacement to match the descriptor i with the appropriate descriptor from the next frame. Given a local environment R" around the descriptor position Pi, the value $q(i,k,L)$ denotes the sum over $p(j,k,L")$ with descriptor j from R" - provided its displacement L" is compatible with L. Two displacements are considered compatibel if $|Lx-Lx"|<t$ and $|Ly-Ly"|<t$, using an empirical threshold t. Based on these definitions, BARNARD and THOMPSON 79+80 determine unnormalized weight values $w(i,k+1,L)$ for the next iteration k+1 according to

$$w(i,k+1,L) = p(i,k,L)*[a+b*q(i,k,L)] \quad \text{for all L from R} \qquad (1a)$$

$$w(i,k+1,L@) = p(i,k,L@) \quad \text{for the 'undefined displacement' L@.} \qquad (1b)$$

New confidence values $p(i,k+1,L)$ are determined by normalizing the sum over $w(i,k+1,L)$ for all admitted L, including L@, to the value 1.

The initial values are determined from

$$w(i,1,L) = 1 / (1 + c*s(L)) \qquad (2)$$

with a constant factor c and s(L) denoting the sum of squared differences between corresponding greyvalues from 5*5 pixel environments around the descriptor positions Pi = (Pix, Piy) and the candidate match Pi+L = (Pix+Lx, Piy+Ly). These w(i,l,L) attempt to estimate the greyvalue similarity of 5*5 pixel environments around the descriptor positions for candidate matches between two different frames. The initial weight w(i,l,L@) for the 'undefined displacement' - i.e. no match appears possible - is taken to be

$$w(i,l,L@) = 1 - MAX(w(i,l,L)) \qquad\qquad (3)$$

where L varies over all displacements possible within R for which a candidate match is available in the next frame.

After a certain number k of iterations, candidate matches are selected if their p(i,k,L) exceeds an empirical acceptance threshold. If there is only one displacement L for which p(i,k,L) is selected then the match between the descriptors at position Pi in the current frame and Pi+L in the next frame will be finally accepted. In all other cases the descriptor at position Pi will not be matched.

3. Modifications to the BARNARD-THOMPSON Approach

Our experience has forced us to modify several aspects of this approach in order to obtain acceptable results for our data.

First, it is noted that the determination of confidences by BARNARD and THOMPSON is asymmetric. It evaluates the 'split competition' (see ULLMAN 79) between one descriptor i from the current frame and possible matching descriptors at various displacements L in the next frame. It neglects, however, the 'merge competition' where various descriptors from the current frame have to be considered as matches for the same descriptor in the next frame. The confidence values of BARNARD and THOMPSON 79+80 have only been normalized with respect to the source descriptor i. It is not possible, therefore, to compare confidence values from different source descriptors i and j tentatively paired with the same target descriptor in the next frame. This weakness could be remedied by applying the relaxation algorithm in both directions and using the mean of the two resulting confidence values for updating the weight factor w(i,k+1,L) from which the new confidence values are determined by normalization for each descriptor in each frame.

It is noted, moreover, that the weights w(i,k+1,L) can only increase during the updating process. The only possibility to decrease a confidence value is given during the normalization - if competing weights w(i,k+1,L") for L" different from L have been increased more strongly. If, however, the candidate match from Pi to Pi+L is the only pairing considered, the confidence p(i,k,L) cannot decrease because contradictory evidence from the environment cannot enter in the formalism outlined above.

In order to obtain a more balanced update, supporting evidence as well as contradictory evidence is taken into account. Let u(i,k,L) = q(i,k,L) denote the sum over all p(j,k,L") for neighboring descriptors j from R" with displacement vectors L" compatible with L. In analogy, v(i,k,L) denotes the sum over all p(j,k,L') for descriptors j from R" with displacement vectors L' incompatible with L. These sums are weighted by a factor which compensates the different apriori probabilities to find compatible displacements (factor = wc) and incompatible ones (factor = wi). Within R there are $(2*r+1)^2$ possible displacements, out of which at most $(2*t+1)^2$ are compatible with L for a given compatibility threshold t. We set

$$1/wc = (2*t+1)^2 / (2*r+1)^2 \quad \text{and} \quad 1 / wi = 1 - 1 / wc \quad (5)$$

Using these definitions, we replace the updating formula of BARNARD and THOMPSON 79+80 by

$$w(i,k+1,L) = p(i,k,L) * (1 + (u*wc - v*wi) / (u*wc + v*wi)) \quad (6)$$

The weight w(i,k+1,L) will increase only if the evidence from the environment R" which supports a displacement L - i.e. u(i,k,L)*wc - is greater than the evidence v(i,k,L)*wi which contradicts it.

In case of isolated descriptor pairs - i.e. no other descriptor in the environment R" around Pi or around the single match candidate positioned at Pi+L in the next frame - the confidence values will not change during the iterations. In such a case, a candidate match will be accepted if the initial estimate for the confidence p(i,1,L) exceeds the mean initial confidence value derived from all descriptors in the 'moving object window'.

A third modification exploits the fact that our descriptors comprise considerably more information about the greyvalue distribution at selected descriptor locations than those obtained with the Moravec operator employed by BARNARD and THOMPSON 79+80. Our descriptors have been selected by evaluating the main curvatures of the greyvalue surface as a function of the raster coordinates (DRESCHLER 81, DRESCHLER and NAGEL 81). Only descriptors characterized by the same

25

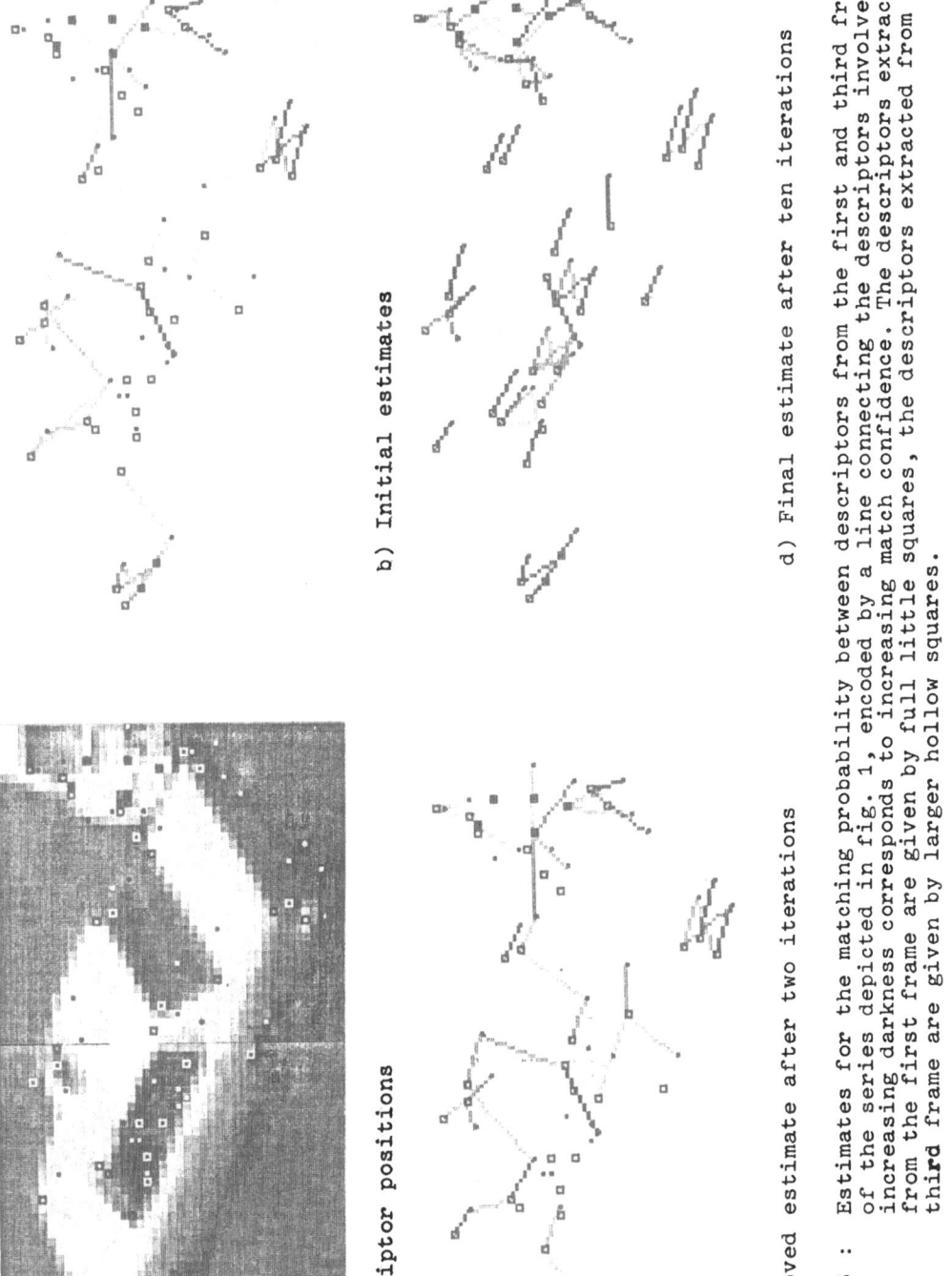

a) Descriptor positions

b) Initial estimates

c) Improved estimate after two iterations

d) Final estimate after ten iterations

Figure 3 : Estimates for the matching probability between descriptors from the first and third frame of the series depicted in fig. 1, encoded by a line connecting the descriptors involved - increasing darkness corresponds to increasing match confidence. The descriptors extracted from the first frame are given by full little squares, the descriptors extracted from the third frame are given by larger hollow squares.

combination of signs for the main curvatures involved will be admitted
as candidate pairings. This is essentially equivalent to a test which
avoids pairing a dark corner in bright background with a bright corner
in dark background or vice versa. The application of such a test
corresponds to an evaluation of the 'node compatibility' in the
terminology of MACKWORTH 77 [9].

The constant c used for estimating the initial weight $w(i,1,L)$ - see
equation (2) - has been set to the inverse of the area for which the
squared greyvalue difference $s(L)$ has to be evaluated. Moreover, the
initial weight $w(i,1,L)$ is multiplied by a confidence value derived
for each descriptor during step (4) outlined in the first section.
The number of iterations has been fixed to 10. The maximum acceptable
displacement has been set to $r = 10$ with a compatibility threshold of
$t = 3$. The environment R" has been chosen to be a square with a
sidelength of $2*r"+1 = 41$. Representative results for such data are
shown in figure 3. Figure 4 depicts the chain of descriptor locations
for which pairwise correspondence from frame to frame has been
established using the modified relaxation approach described in this
section. Such descriptor chains provided the input for the
determination of the 3D point configuration according to step (7) in
the first section (figure 2).

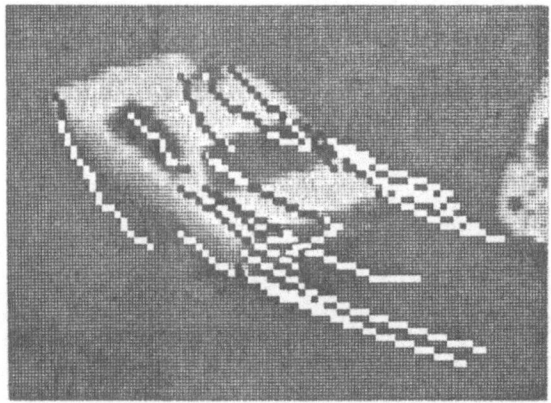

Fig. 4: Chains of matched descriptors connecting the descriptor
        locations of every other frame between frame 1 and
        frame 14 of the series from fig. 1.

4. Discussion

Various reasons caused us to investigate refinements of the relaxation approach to the correspondence problem as it has been reported by BARNARD and THOMPSON 79+80 [1]. First of all, the correspondence problem has been studied within a system for the evaluation of entire image sequences, not only of image pairs. This facilitated an investigation of many frame pairings with essentially smooth transitions from frame to frame. Extensive graphical debugging aids enabd us to scrutinize a large variety of phenomena encountered while working with images of real-world scenes. Moreover, our system approach provided a framework to study the effects of various modules - as outlined in the introductory section - on the 3D result.

After having improved the process for the extraction of descriptors (DRESCHLER 81, DRESCHLER and NAGEL 81), attention naturally focussed on the correspondence problem. Our intention has been to replace numerical parameters such as the constants a and b in equation (1a) or c in equation (2) by computations which are based on an improved understanding of the actual problem structure. Although the modifications described in the preceding section yield already acceptable results, the compatibility between neighboring tentative matches and its influence on the result has to be investigated further. Moreover, the fixed number of iterations should be replaced by an adaptively determined stop - see, e.g., PELEG 80 [18].

Alternatives to the relaxation approach should be explored, for example the 'minimal mapping' of ULLMAN 79 [23] - provided some descriptors can be excluded from the interframe match rather than subjected to a forced match. Current investigations attempt to evaluate other evidence in order to decide which descriptors might not have an appropriate match in the preceding or the subsequent frame - for example due to occlusion of the moving object by other scene components.

As another possibility, we studied a nearest-neighbor match. In order to avoid erroneous matches, the separation between two descriptor positions in one frame must be at least twice as large as the largest acceptable interframe displacement of a descriptor caused by object motion. By comparing successive half-frames - which are recorded only 20 msec apart - the expected displacements are usually small enough for the kind of street scenes studied by us. If, however, the first half-frames from two successive TV-frames - i.e. 40 msec apart - have to be compared, descriptors may already be too close to each other so that mismatches by a nearest-neighbor approach cannot be avoided reliably - see, e.g., some of the descriptors related to the door window in figure 3a.

Other approaches such as the graph match procedures investigated by RADIG et al. 80 [19] for analogous purposes could be studied in our framework as alternative solutions to the correspondence problem.

So far we have discussed only the matching between descriptors from two consecutive frames. We have only limited experience with nontrivial consistency tests for extended chains of matched descriptor pairs. Further research is required in this direction. Our contribution should be understood as an attempt to formulate more precise questions based on the reported experience with imagery from real-world scenes rather than any final solution to the correspondence problem.

5. Acknowledgement

We thank Mrs. R. Jancke for her help during the preparation of this text. We gratefully acknowledge a grant of the Deutsche Forschungsgemeinschaft which partially supported these investigations.

6. References

[1] Barnard, S.T. and Thompson, W.B., Disparity Analysis of Images
    IEEE Trans. Pattern Analysis and Machine Intelligence
    PAMI-2 (1980) 333-340, see also
    Technical Report 79-1 (January 1979), Computer Science Department
    University of Minnesota, Minneapolis/MN
[2] Bonde, T. and Nagel, H.-H., Deriving a 3-D Description of
    a Moving Rigid Object from Monocular TV-frame Sequences
    WCATVI-79, pp. 44-45
[3] Dreschler, L., Ermittlung markanter Punkte auf den Bildern bewegter
    Objekte und Berechnung einer 3D-Beschreibung auf dieser Grundlage
    Fachbereich Informatik der Universitaet Hamburg
    Hamburg/Germany (in preparation)
[4] Dreschler, L. and Nagel, H.-H.
    Volumetric Model and 3D-Trajectory of a Moving Car
    Derived from Monocular TV-Frame Sequences of a Street Scene
    submitted for publication
[5] Duda, R.O. and Hart, P.E., Pattern Classification and Scene
    Analysis, John Wiley & Sons, New York, 1973

[6] Grimson, W.E.L. and Marr, D.
A Computer Implementation of a Theory of Human Stereo Vision
Proc. Image Understanding Workshop, pp. 41-47
L.S. Baumann (ed.), Palo Alto/CA, April 24-25, 1979
Science Applications, Inc., Arlington/VA 22209

[7] Hummel, R.A. and Zucker, S.D.
On the Foundations of Relaxation Labeling Processes
ICPR-80, pp. 50-53

[8] Jain, R. and Nagel, H.-H.
On the Analysis of Accumulative Difference Pictures
from Image Sequences of Real World Scenes
IEEE Trans. Pattern Analysis and Machine Intelligence
PAMI-1 (1979) 206-214

[9] Mackworth, A.K., Consistency in Networks of Relations
Artificial Intelligence 8 (1977) 99-118

[10] Marr, D. and Hildreth, E., Theory of Edge Detection
Proc. R. Soc. Lond. B 207 (1980) 187-217

[11] Marr, D. and Poggio, T., A Computational Theory of Human
Stereo Vision, Proc. Royal Society London B 204 (1979) 301-308

[12] Nagel, H.-H., Analysing Sequences of TV-Frames:
System Design Considerations, IJCAI-77, p.626

[13] Nagel, H.-H., Formation of an Object Concept by Analysis of
Systematic Time Variations in the Optically Perceptible Environment
Computer Graphics and Image Processing 7 (1978) 149-194

[14] Nagel, H.-H., From Digital Picture Processing to Image Analysis
Proc. International Conference on Image Analysis
and Processing, Pavia/ Italy, October 22-24, 1980 (in press)

[15] Nagel, H.-H., On the Derivation of 3D Rigid Point Configurations
from Image Sequences
IEEE Conference on Pattern Recognition and Image Processing
August 3-5, 1981, Dallas/TX (to appear)

[16] Nagel, H.-H. and Neumann, B.
On 3D Reconstruction from two Perspective Views
(submitted for publication)

[17] O'Rourke, J., Polyhedral Object Models from 3D-Points
IfI-HH-M-77/80, Fachbereich Informatik, Universitaet Hamburg 1980

[18] Peleg, S., Monitoring Relaxation Algorithms Using Labeling
Evaluations, ICPR-80, pp. 54-57

[19] Radig, B., Kraasch, R., and Zach, W.,
Matching Symbolic Descriptions for 3-D Reconstruction
ICPR-80, pp. 1081-1084

[20] Ranade, S. and Rosenfeld, A., Point Pattern Matching by Relaxation
Pattern Recognition 12 (1980) 269-275

[21] Roach, J.W. and Aggarwal, J.K.
Determining the Movement of Objects from a Sequence of Images
IEEE Trans. Pattern Analysis and Machine Intelligence
PAMI-2 (1980) 554-562

[22] Rosenfeld, A., Hummel, R.A. and Zucker, S.W.
Scene Labelling by Relaxation Operations
IEEE Trans. Systems, Man, and Cybernetics, SMC-6 (1976) 420-433

[23] Ullman, S., The Interpretation of Visual Motion
The MIT Press, Cambridge/Mass., 1979

ROBOTICS RESEARCH : FROM TOY WORLDS TO INDUSTRIAL APPLICATIONS

Jörgen P. Foith

Fraunhofer-Institut f. Informations-
und Datenverarbeitung (IITB)

Karlsruhe, West-Germany

Summary

The idea of constructing artificial devices that act like humans or animals has
intrigued mankind for a long time. Early designs were supposed to be decorative,
astonishing, and amusing. Today, there is a strong interest in applying robots
to practical tasks, particularly in manufacturing.

Modern robotics has its roots in teleoperators, NC machine tools, and Artificial
Intelligence. Main developments that have led to present day industrial robots
are briefly discussed. Today, industrial robots of the first and second generation
are applied in a variety of tasks, yet their number is far from a long predicted
'robot revolution'. It is strongly felt that this is due to the lack of sensors
and the lack of high level task representations.

In order to provide these robots with some kind of 'practical intelligence', work
is going on in a number of Artificial Intelligence research laboratories around
the world, in particular in USA and Japan. The paper summarizes the efforts that
are being made in manipulator design, development of sensory equipment, and design
and implementation of robot control languages. It is noted that, despite all the
progress that has been achieved, much remains to be done.

1.   ROBOTS AS TOYS

The idea of constructing artificial devices that act and behave like humans or animals
has intrigued mankind for a long time. In earlier centuries such devices were called
'automata' and were mechanical devices that imitated a human or an animal, generally
without performing useful work /ENCYCLOPAEDIA BRITANNICA '79/. The notion of "robots"
originated in 1920 through the play "R.U.R." ("Rossum's Universal Robots") by the
Czechoslovak dramatist K. Čapek. "Robot" is a derivation of the Czech word "robota"
meaning "forced labor". Today, robots are indeed supposed to perform useful work and
are to relieve the blue collar worker from dangerous, uncomfortable, and tedious tasks.

Typically, automata looked like a copy of the organism whose behaviour was to be
simulated. Indeed, the idea of effigies that are brought to life by means of a charm
is found in myth and folklore in many cultures. An example is the "Golem" that in
many tales was to be a perfect servant to his creator and master, according to Jewish
folklore. The construction of automata may go back as far as to the 3rd century BC :
there exist accounts of a mechanical orchestra for the emperor during the Han dynasty.
Later records from China report about flying fish, an otter which caught fish, and
figures engaged in numerous activities.

In Europe, automata were usually designed to be decorative, astonishing, and amusing.
One of the earliest accounts refers to a wooden model of a pigeon constructed by the
Greek Archytas (400 - 35o BC). The Greek Hero of Alexandria (1st century) is said to
have built birds that chirped, drank, and flew. One of the most sophisticated "animal
automata", by French J. de Vaucanson (18th century), was a mechanical duck that flapped
its wings, drank water and pecked corn, and even "digested" to the degree of dis-
solving the corn. The most complicated automata were "androids", i.e. automata that
resembled humans and that could be made to walk about, play music, or write and draw.
Medieval examples are a "talking head" by R. Bacon (13th century), and an "iron man"
by Albertus Magnus (13th century). Androids were especially popular in the Renaissance;
one well preserved example is a mandolin-playing lady that is attributed to Italian
G. Torriano (16th century). The highest degree of sophistication seems to have been
reached in the 18th century by artists such as J. de Vaucanson (French) or father and
son P. & H.-L. Jaquet-Droz (Swiss). De Vaucanson created among others a flute player
capable of playing a dozen songs; the Jaquet-Droz constructed figures that could write
and draw, or others that did play musical instruments. Alas, one of the most astonishing
and most powerful automata - the chess player by Baron W. von Kempelen (18th century) -
turned out to be a fake because it was controlled by a human chess player !

It is outside the scope of this paper to discuss the underlying ideas that drove ancient
engineers to construct such automata. One feature that all these devices share, is the
fact that they are all driven by fixed "programs" where programs are sequences of

mechanical operations that are performed in a deterministic way. As such, these machines do not differ from modern NC-machines that are driven by fixed programs -- although these are no longer stored in mechanical devices but rather in solid-state memories. Despite the progress that has been made in the electronic field, today's first generation industrial robots are basically not that much different from early mechanical automata. Yet, with the advent of computers that could react to sensory signals, it was soon felt that it was possible to construct a new generation of robots that could adapt to changing environments.

In a way, the engineers that constructed these early automata were merely trying to simulate natural behaviour by using a "black box" approach; despite its sophistication we certainly havn't learned anything about "duckhood" from the mechanical duck by de Vaucanson, except that behaviour can be simulated on the basis of deterministic rules. The understanding of "reasoning", "intelligent behaviour", and "logic" has been the center of interest for more than two millenia; yet, most approaches were simply concerned with actions of the mind. In robotics, we have to be concerned with the logic of actions as well as the apparently trivial task of "doing things". Among other definitions of "Artificial Intelligence" (AI) has been defined as : "the experimental and theoretical study of perceptual and intellectual processes using computers. Its ultimate goal is to <u>understand</u> these processes well enough to make a computer perceive, understand, and act in ways now only possible for humans" /STANFORD UNIV '73/. Only recently have researchers begun to understand that these goals are not confined to "problem solving", "reasoning" or "game playing". Rather, there is a wide area where sensory and intellectual tasks are required when a robot "simply" has to pick up an object in a scene. Because we humans are so good at doing things, and are also unable to introspect about our actions, we just don't evaluate how much effort is needed to develop adequate computer programs /HORN '8o/. Just how much effort is needed, is one of the questions that this artiele tries to assess.

2.   ROBOTS APPLIED TO PRACTICAL TASKS

In the course of production engineering development one has become increasingly interested in the design of automata or robots that could perform practical work instead of amusing on-lookers. Automation of manufacturing was first attained for mass production. Here, conveyor systems link together consecutive workplaces in an efficient, although fixed way. Few human interactions are necessary, and workpieces are handled and processed automatically. It is obvious that much highly specialized machinery is needed, and this can only be justified by the large volume produced. Although it is difficult to get numbers - let alone exact ones - it is estimated that the major percentage of products is still being manufactured by small and medium size machine shops in small batches. The increase of productivity that could be obtained through intensified automation in these shops may be seen from an example from the U.S.A. . While only three percent of machine tools are numerically controlled, they account for about 33 percent of all production /SUGARMAN '80/.

Instead of putting highly specialized machinery to work one needs highly flexible production systems for small-lot and medium-lot manufacturing. Two types of actions are of importance during production: the manipulation of workpieces and the manipulation of tools. When handling workpieces the following manipulative operations are performed /BEJCZY '72/ : grasping, holding, moving, orienting, guiding, forcing, and sensing. These operations are used to load/unload machines, to assemble complex parts, or to transport/acquire/deposit workpieces. Manipulative operations for tool handling fall into similar categories. Here, they are used to grind, deburr, paint, weld, drill, etc. In order to cope with this variety of manipulative operations the concept of 'Industrial Robots' was conceived. An industrial robot is defined to be a manipulator system that can easily be programmed to perform a required task. It was one of the misconceptions of early developments that such a robot could indeed be applied to the broad range of tasks that occur in industry. Today, we have learned that the state-of-the-art is far from such a universal industrial robot. Rather, one has to define workstation functions to which certain individual robots are adapted.

2.1. THE DEVELOPMENT OF INDUSTRIAL ROBOTICS

While industrial robots may be the descendents of early automata in general, there are three developments that have led to the present day industrial robot: 1) tele-operators, 2) NC machine tools, and 3) computers. Let us briefly survey the sequence of projects from early developments until today.

Tele-operators were developed to perform manual tasks in a master-slave mode where the human master works at a safe distance from a dangerous environment. In 1947 the first servoed electric-powered tele-operator was developed. Due to the lack of force-feedback, the master didn't know what exactly was going on. This situation was remedied when in 1948 force-feedback was introduced /PAUL '79/. This brings forth an important issue : in order to operate properly one must have information about the position of the manipulator as well as the forces that are exerted on it. In other words, what is needed is an internal model of the manipulator that is always updated in the course of action. Indeed, present day industrial robots are equipped with proprioceptors such as angle encoders that report to the control computer the position of the axes of the manipulator. The values of these proprioceptors constitute the simplest possible model. We will discuss this point again in a later section.

Numerically controlled (NC) machines are often considered to be predecessors of robots:
from our point of view, most present day industrial robots are just another type of
NC machine, or rather CNC machine, since their programs are stored and run in a computer.
The beginning of NC machines dates back to the punched paper tape controlled Jacquard
loom; yet their importance has increased considerably with the advent of computers.
The combination of features of tele-operators and NC machines by G. Devol in the early
sixties has led to the first industrial robot, the 'Unimate'.

While the Unimate performs under the control of a fixed program, a second line of
development was introduced by M.I.T. in 1961. A tele-operator arm with touch sensors
was connected to a computer in order to guide the robot by touch-feedback /PAUL '79/.
As of the early sixties the development of sensors for industrial robots has found an
ever increasing interest. Yet, with very few exceptions, commercially available
industrial robots still lack sensory equipment.

In contrast to the commercial situation, many research groups have investigated the
use of sensor systems for robots. Among all senses that were studied, vision has
certainly found the greatest interest and there have been quite a number of 'hand-eye'
projects throughout the seventies.

The classical work of /ROBERTS '63/ demonstrated that it is possible to recognize
objects visually from a given scene and to determine their location and orientation.
Yet, despite almost two decades of research in scene analysis, the state-of-the-art
is still far from the analysis of complex scenes such as parts in a bin. The use of
optical feedback was first reported in 1967 by /WICHMAN '67/ who used a TV camera to
guide a robot in picking objects. By 197o the Stanford hand-eye system solved the
'instant insanity' puzzle where four multi-colored cubes on a table are stacked up such
that each side of the resulting tower shows no color twice /FELDMAN et al. '71/.
Another hand-eye system,called 'Freddy', at the Department of Artificial Intelligence
at Edinburgh, was capable of sorting wooden parts from a heap and assembling them into
toy objects such as a car or a boat /AMBLER et al. '75/. Freddy could handle mixed heaps
containing parts for two assemblies but it took an hour or two to do so ! A similar
system was 'SIRCH' of the Nottingham University; as opposed to Freddy it worked only
flat parts and binary images /HEGINBOTHAM et al. '73/. While Freddy assembled parts in
a fixed sequence and picked those parts from fixed positions (where it had put them in
the sorting phase), SIRCH determined itself where best to grasp the parts.

Many of these hand-eye projects were mostly concerned with recognizing objects and
guiding the robot to grasp them correctly. Only little interest was paid to issues of
programming the necessary movements or generating plans for actions. This line of
research was investigated at Stanford Research Institute (SRI) where a moving robot,

called 'Shakey', served as a testbed. Shakey was a computer-controlled vehicle equipped
with TV camera, range finder, and mechanical bumpers that communicated with its central
computer through radio channels /HART et al. '72/. Shakey could rove around, explore
its environment, and solve such tasks as pushing a large box from one room to another.
The development of Shakey brought a new line into robotics since Shakey was able to act
autonomously : it could solve problems with the aid of several levels of programs
that performed problem analysis, strategic planning, tactical execution, and low level
actions. The use of a world model and theorem proving methods permitted Shakey to find
a sequence of intermediate-level actions consisting of a variable sequence of low-level
actions leading to the solution of the problem. Successful intermediate-level actions
added to Shakey's experience and were included as new library routines. In Shakey we
find for the first time the notion of a world model that can be used to determine
a sequence of actions.

The generation of sequences of actions can basically be accomplished in two different
ways. Either one explicitly programs every step, or the robot has available a world
model and mechanisms of reasoning within this model in order to derive the required
sequences. The first approach is referred to as 'explicit programming', the second as
'world modeling' /PARK '77/. In the first case everything is left to the human operator,
in the second everything to the robot. An approach that falls between these two basic
concepts was chosen at the Stanford University Artificial Intelligence Laboratory (SAIL).
A language, called WAVE, allowed to specify a task symbolically in cartesian coordinates
together with necessary force compliances and gripper commmands /PAUL '77 A/. Run on
a robot system with two arms, power tools, TV sensor, position and torque sensors,
WAVE programs successfully controlled in 1972 the assembly of a water pump /PAUL '79/.
WAVE combines features of explicit programming with features of world modeling:
although the sequence of actions is programmed explicitly, WAVE maintains a model of
the arm for planning trajectories. WAVE was the first system to integrate force, touch,
vision, and position information and to relate these to one another in a world model.
In continuation of the work that was begun with WAVE, a more powerful world modeling
robot-control language, 'AL' (for 'Assembly Language'), was being developed as of 1974
at SAIL /FINKEL et al. '74/. The issue of robot programming languages has been taken
up by various other groups who have developed languages of their own. All these
approaches will be discussed in a later section.

Two mainstreams of research and development have thus evolved over the past two
decades - the investigation of sensory equipment and the design and implementation of
robot control languages. These two issues are closely related: control structures must
take into account sensory informations since these will ususally determine what actions
are taken. The control language must therefore attach sensory information to specific
segments in a program and it must react to that information. If different kinds of

sensory information are available at the same time, then it is necessary to translate these informations into a representation that relates these informations to each other. This requires the use of a model. This is really the central question that we have to cope with in robotics - how do we best represent the knowledge that we have about objects, their appearances, and their manipulation ? From the examples that were given the unexperienced reader may have the impression that many problems have already been solved. A word of caution is here in order; in most instances only very rudimentary problems have been solved and we are far from general solutions.

2.2.   ROBOTICS TODAY AND TOMORROW

The picture that we have painted for the seventies remains much the same for the beginning of this decade. A number of industrial robots have been put to practical work all over the world in a variety of tasks. Today, industrial robots perform loading/unloading, palletizing/depalletizing, spray painting, spot welding, press welding, arc welding, deburring, and grinding. Indeed, this list could be continued with many more examples. Yet, the length of such a list may be deceiving. If we look at the number of robots that are actually applied, we find that there are relatively few of them, considering that industrial robots have been available for quite some time. To give a few numbers (these are estimations from a 1980 survey by the Robot Institute of America /SUGARMAN '80/). Japan takes the lead with 14,000 robots (not counting the numerous pick-&-place devices that are often included in these figures!). In the U.S.A. there are about 3,000 units; in West-Germany about 850 units (although this number may well have doubled over the last year); Sweden 57o units; Britain and Norway about 200 units, each. The exact numbers are here of no importance since this is indeed a rather small labor force ! It may be noted, that with very few exceptions all these robots are of the first and second generation, $\underline{i}.\underline{e}$., without sensory equipment.

Robotics revolutions have been predicted for the last 20 years. In a 1978 Delphi forecast /COLDING et al. '79/ it was estimated that in the early eighties robots would arrive in masses and that they would have human capabilities on the assembly line by 1990. For 1995 the study predicted a take-over of 50% of all direct labor in automotive final assembly. Of the predictions for 1980 very few have become true, and it seems today that this forecast has been rather over-optimistic. Today we find articles raising questions such as "what is delaying the manipulator revolution?" or "why didn't robotics catch on?". There are numerous reasons. In many cases there are other means of automation. The complexity of "apparently simple" handling and manipulation tasks was completely underestimated. The cost factor was underestimated since in almost all robotics applications it is necessary to redesign the complete workstation. The low abilities of present day robots in no way compete with the highly developed skills that humans have acquired during evolution.

One severe difficulty in applying robots stems from the fact that the order of parts is seldom kept from one workstation to another one. Since humans easily pick scattered parts from a bin, preservation of orientation was not deemed important in a factory. But "to emulate man's hand-eye coordinations in orienting parts, is beyond today's robot" /ENGELBERGER '77/. The same holds for assembly tasks. No industrial robot today can pick up, for example, a part, inspect it for imperfections, fit it into place and screw it tight - a task that a blue collar worker performs easily. Although such a task could be solved by some research robot systems - at least for selected examples - it would take several days to program such a system; yet production changeovers must be done within the hour. Let me summarize the situation by quoting /PAUL '79/: "Currently available industrial robots will not have a major impact on manufacturing. .... Their use frequently requires the redesign of products and/or manufacturing systems. ... Their economic justification ... is based on many intangible assumptions and is frequently marginal in more sophisticated applications." On the other hand, to quote PAUL once more: "A low-cost, mass-produced, sensor-controlled robot could have a revolutionary effect on manufacturing."

A present day robot has only one arm, two claws without joints, moves along a fixed path, and has no idea about the objects it handles nor the task it performs. Whenever trouble arises, its only choice is to stop all action and call for human help. This is quite in contrast to the blue collar worker who has a mental model of his task and ways to reason about it. This allows him to solve it in various ways and he knows what to do when something goes wrong. He is not disturbed if a part is oriented the wrong way; he simply flips it over into the right orientation. A robot,in order to do this, has to have a three-dimensional model of the part as well as the fitting and has to compute how to rotate the part in 3-D for the assembly.

In summary, there is a lot to be done about industrial robots before these will make a breakthrough in manufacturing. They must be made much more flexible and intelligent to apply them in an efficient way. In particular we see the following avenues in tomorrow's robotics:
- more complex and more flexible machinery is needed such as two arms and   better hands;
- there is much to be done in the development of sensory equipment (and here I do not agree with other authors that, for instance, 'rudimentary vision' will do);
- the representation of sensory information and manipulative operations is still in its infancy;
- given such representations, mechanisms to reason upon that knowledge are required;
- once appropriate sensory equipment and good modeling techniques are available, then it will be a logical next step to implement robot self-surveillance and error-recovery mechanisms.

All this calls for a lot of research on models at various levels that include the robot, the workstation, the parts, and the task. What is badly needed are integrated solutions that cover all aspects mentioned here. Obviously this is an interdisciplinary task that must be tackled from many view points such as Artificial Intelligence, production engineering, control theory, mechanical engineering, computer science, and electronics.

3. "INTELLIGENT" ROBOTS

When we talk about "intelligence" today we usually refer to it as the reasoning power required to solve highly complicated problems. We often forget that there is a "practical intelligence" which allows us "to do things" and to get by in every day life. It is this practical intelligence that is sought here when we talk about "intelligent" robots. In the following we will discuss research and development projects that work on various aspects of such "intelligent" robots.

3.1. THE WORKSTATION, MANIPULATORS, AND GRIPPERS

At the outset of practical robot projects, naive minds may have thought that a robot - once being able to,say, handle parts for machine loading - would simply be mounted at the workstation and replace the human worker directly. Experience over the years has taught us otherwise. Today we know that a complete redesign of the workstation is often necessary. Let us therefore briefly examine a workstation that is to be robotized.

Typically, parts must be transported to that station, be stored there in sufficient numbers, picked from the storage and fed into the machine, grasped from the machine and be stored again before being transported away. In most instances the task of the robot is the handling of parts, not the machining of them (although there are some examples where the robot does the machining, too). If a robot without sensors is used, the parts must be strictly ordered and oriented, e.g. on a pallet or in a magazine. In order to guarantee exact position one must use special pallets that provide shape-fit of the parts - obviously this requires a new pallet every time a new workpiece must be handled. If the sensor is sensor-equipped, more general pallets can be used, and order and orientation of parts need not be as strictly kept. Still, given the state-of-the-art, parts should be well isolated from each other. If scattered parts are stored at the workplace then special feeding systems must be used before the robot can handle the parts (there are a few exceptions where the robot serves as the feeding system as well). After the parts have been machined, the robot places them in a deposit for further transport.

It is obvious that the layout of the workstation must well be engineered to ensure optimal operation. Much of the layout will depend on the robot that is used. Some robots move along an axis while others swivel around (for a survey on available industrial robots see /ABRAHAM et a. '77/). In each case the robot, the machine, and storage and deposit must be positioned differently. Thus the robot geometry determines the relative positions of all components of a workstation as well as the length of paths that the robot has to cover. Clearly, short paths and small size workstations are desirable. Quite often the oversize of a robot workstation can be one of the major obstacles to putting it into the factory.

Another practical problem is the robot gripper. Many present day grippers operate pneumatically; neither gripper width nor the gripping forces can be controlled. A number of research groups investigate the development of flexible grippers, but we are far from being able to emulate the human hand. For approaches towards flexible grippers see the Proceedings of the 1th - 10th International Symposium on Industrial Robots.

As with so many other things, grasping is not as trivial as it may seem. In general, a grasping point (i.e. a location for the center of the hand) must be reached, the hand must be aligned with the object surfaces and positioned at the proper angle. In grasping an object one must consider the geometry of the object as well as that of the hand - orientation of surfaces, dimensions of the object, number of fingers and their relative positions to each other, and minimal and maximal width of grasp; all these parameters determine possible grasping points. Among these, one must be selected that permits the robot to deposit the workpiece in the required orientation. Otherwise it must be put down in an intermediate position and be re-oriented. Today, the selection of grasping points is performed by the human operator during the instruction phase. For each stable position that the workpiece can assume one such grasping point is stored relative to a "zero" orientation of the workpiece in that position.

If automatic planning of grasping points is to be performed, one needs three-dimensional models of the objects as well as a set of rules that determine what a good grasping point could be. At the moment very little work is being done in this area - with the exception of ACRONYM /BROOKS et al. '79/, a vision system that is based on geometric models. When reasoning about grasping one must consider the shape of the object and the shape of the hand, the position of the object on its support, and the goal position to which the object is to be brought. Grasping rules may deal with parallel surfaces or edges, holes, centers of gravity, centers of rotation, symmetry axes, "clear-path" to the grasping point, accessibility of surfaces (hidden by support or goal-position), and so on. There may be a large number of constraints that must be taken into account, especially when dealing with complex shapes.

3.2.   SENSORS AND SMART INTERFACES

As was explained in Chapter 2 sensors are one of the keys to more intelligent robots. Without being aware of it, we humans make use of a lot of sensory information in doing things. Apparently much of this information is also kept in our memory. There are numerous sensors available today and many of these are useful for robots. In the following we will exclude standard sensors used as proprioceptors in industrial robots. These measure displacement, velocity, and acceleration and have been available for quite some time. Among the remaining sensors the following seem to be of importance in robotics tasks :

- proximity and touch sensors ("whisker" sensors)
- area tactile sensors
- force and torque sensors ("wrist" sensors)
- 3-D sensors ("range finders")
- visual sensors.

The notion of 'sensor' is often used in an ambigious way. The original meaning of the word refers only to the transducer that transforms a physical phenomenon into some kind of signal. Today, 'sensor' usually stands for 'transducer with signal and information processing system' whose output can be the result of a complex analysis. It is in the latter sense that we use the notion of 'sensor' in this article.

PROXIMITY AND TOUCH SENSORS

Proximity and touch sensors provide direct local information, help to avoid collisions, and detect the presence of objects or obstacles in the robot workspace. There is a wide range of commercially available systems based upon inductivity, capacity, pneumatic pressures, optical reflectances, or mechanical forces. One example of a mechanical/ electrical touch sensor can be found in /WANG & WILL '78/ where a thin wire serves as "whisker" that can detect objects without pushing them around. Such "cat's whiskers" are useful in many assembly tasks.

AREA TACTILE SENSORS

While proximity and touch sensors usually only provide binary information ('object present/absent'), area contact sensors can provide more complex information. Placed into the fingers of a robot hand one can deduce from their signals how well a part was grasped, whether it slips from the hand and what its shape is. Area tactile sensors are matrices of touch sensors and are useful in handling and assembly tasks.

FORCE AND TORQUE SENSORS

Force and torque sensors play an important role in handling and assembly; they are
installed in the wrist (sometimes in the fingertips) and often guide the final steps
in fitting operations. A typical example /SCHMIEDER et al. '79/ determines force and
torque in three dimensions. This sensor is based on deformations of four rods that are
parallel to the axis of symmetry and four spokes that are perpendicular to that axis.
Eight bridges of strain-gauges measure pairwise the deformations that are due to forces
and torques acting upon the hand. The tactile sensor computes the components of force
and torque in cartesian coordinates. Since most robots have coordinate systems that are
quite different from a cartesian one, it is necessary to transform these coordinates
into robot joint coordinates. We will discuss the topic of coordinate spaces below.

3-D SENSING

In robotics applications the most important information that one seeks about a scene
is three-dimensional in nature. The most direct way to obtain this information is by
3-D-sensing ("range finding"). This can be achieved in various ways using either light
(laser, infrared,LED) or ultrasonic waves for time-of-flight or phase shift measurements,
stereo or triangulation methods /WANG & WILL '78/. One particular instance of
triangulation is the use of 'structured light' where a plane of light is intersected
with the three-dimensional scene /AGIN '72/, /SHIRAI & SUWA '71/. From the resulting
light profile one can determine the 3-D coordinates of the objects in the scene
(today this method is referred to as 'light sectioning'). While some 3-D sensing
techniques are one-dimensional in nature, others use two-dimensional transducers such
as TV or solid state cameras; among these are the light sectioning techniques. Basically,
images that stem from light sectioning are easily transformed into images that one
obtains from other visual systems, i.e., they can be processed in much the same way as
images from TV or solid state cameras. A good example of a practical light sectioning
system is CONSIGHT /WARD et al. '79/. This system uses two strips of light and a
linear diode array. Since workpieces are presented on a moving conveyor belt, CONSIGHT
acquires silhouettes of passing objects. These are recognized with the aid of shape
features such as area, first and second moments, or hole shape features. In this
respect CONSIGHT performs as many other vision systems do that analyze TV or solid
state camera images.

VISUAL SENSORS

It is widely agreed upon that visual sensors are most badly needed as sensors for
industrial robots /EVANS et al. '78/. The most important applications for these sensors
are visual inspection, part handling, process control, and workstation surveillance.
Some of these applications are not directly related to robotics but rather to more
general issues of automation of manufacturing. Early approaches for industrial visual

sensors started in the seventies; the first approaches were typically simulations that did not perform in real-time - an important requirement for practical applications. Today there are numerous attempts to build visual sensors that are usable for the industry. For an extensive survey see /FOITH et al. '81/.

There are three principal types of systems: 1) software based systems store the (binarized) image immediately and analyze it completely by software; 2) hardware based systems process the image directly during the image scan. Most often only simple operations are performed such as discrete template matching (based on a few points). 3) Mixed systems use both on-line hardware and software. Here, hardware is applied whenever many data must be processed quickly; software is used when data must be analyzed in a flexible way.

Examples for highly developed practical sensor systems are the 'SRI vision module' /GLEASON & AGIN '79/ and the 'IITB Sensorsystem for Automation and Measurement' ('S.A.M.') /FOITH et al. '81/. The SRI vision module is a software based system whose hardware basically consists of a binarization unit, a run length encoder with image memory, and a DEC LSI-11. Its software provides efficient programs for the computation of numerous features such as area, perimeter, centroid coordinates, etc. Much of the recognition is based on models that are stored during the instruction phase. Typical performance times vary from 25 ms to 2.5 sec.

S.A.M. is a mixed system with several layers of hardware and software. The core of the hardware system is the feature extraction layer that computes on-line from a binary TV image the following features: component labels, area, perimeter, centroid coordinates, and number of holes. These features are further processed with a Z-80 microcomputer. Recognition is also based on models as in the SRI system. Typical performance times vary from 25 ms to 500 ms.

Both systems are commercially available (the SRI vision module is sold as 'VS-100' by Machine Intelligence Corporation/Calif.; S.A.M. is sold by Bosch/W-Germany). Probably half a dozen more vision systems are on the market (or will be soon) and many more are likely to follow. It is generally predicted that these systems will find wide-spread use.

Two remarks are in order. First, all models used in such simple vision systems are 'discrete aspect' models, i.e. they describe what an object looks like in a discrete position. These models provide no further knowledge about the objects and if an object changes its position in yaw, pitch or roll, then a new model becomes necessary. Second, all vision systems compute their results in cartesian coordinates. This makes it necessary to transform them into robot joint coordinates.

In a handling task, say the grasping of workpieces from a conveyor belt, the output of the vision system specifies the X-Y-(Z)-coordinates of the grasping point, the orientation of the workpiece in the belt plane, the positional class of the recognized workpiece, and a counter value which refers to the belt position at the moment of image acquisition. Coordinate and orientation data are all expressed in the sensor's own coordinate system which is cartesian. This system must be related to the robot system that is determined in joint coordinates. This transformation is usually done in two steps; a cartesian system is defined for the robot itself. First, sensor data are transformed into the robot cartesian system, and then a second transformation converts these data into the robot joint coordinates. These calculations are computed with the aid of homogenous transformations /PAUL '77 B/. These have been solved for a number of manipulators (such transformations are straightforward if the manipulator has a polar or cylindrical geometry; unfortunately some manipulators have a very complicated geometry which makes the establishment of these transformations rather difficult). As can be seen, the interfacing of sensory systems with a robot is not just a matter of transmitting data from one device to the other. What is needed here is a smart interface that will transform the data from one system into the other - and it must be able to do this both ways. For practical reasons, the task of such a smart interface is divided between the sensor and the manipulator: the sensor transforms data into (and from) the robot cartesian system; the robot interface performs the transformation into (and from) the joint coordinate system. The inverse transformations are necessary for the calibration phase between the sensor and the robot. Here, the manipulator is used to determine the relative position of the sensor system within the robot cartesian system by pointing to specific points in the visual field and transmitting the cartesian robot coordinates to the sensor. With these data the sensor-robot cartesian transformation can be determined automatically.

3.3.   PROGRAM GENERATION AND CONTROL

The programming of a present day industrial robot is a tedious operation because it is done by guiding the manipulator step by step through all points in space that are necessary to accomplish the task. On command, the sequence of points is stored as a sequence of joint coordinates together with necessary functions ('open/close hand',...) to be performed as each position is reached. Task performance is then obtained by playback of these joint positions. Joint coordinate teaching is feasible when all positions in a task are fixed. Once complex sensory information is available, more refined methods of programming must be sought. One way to do this is to increment the number of functions that are attached to the stored sequence of joint coordinates. These functions could include instructions to read sensors, to modify actions or to change the execution sequence. However, programming at this level can rapidly become an impossible task for the human operator, especially when dealing with complex

operations. In order to avoid cumbersome 'programming by guiding' techniques, a lot
of effort is being put into the development of high level robot control languages.
Obviously, programming by guiding will be rather easy for simple tasks; yet it is
generally believed that for complex tasks it will be worth while to use high level
languages. The ultimate goal would be the description of, say, an assembly task in a
few sentences in natural language: "Put that pump together! First, get the body, then
insert .... Finally, screw the cover tight!" Of course, we are far from such a level
of programming and will have to settle for more intermediate task descriptions.

There are several lines along which robot control languages can be discussed :
  - the level of programming
  - the use of models vs explicit programming
  - compilation vs interpretation of programs.
Basically, there are three levels of programming /FALEK et al. '80/ :
  - task level
  - object level
  - manipulation (execution) level.
The lowest level is that of manipulation where the program specifies the movements of
the manipulator step by step. At the object level programs describe actions on objects
- a representation which leads to more compact programs and thus to higher levels of
description. The highest level is obtained at the task level where complex descriptions
can be used. Work has been done at all three levels. Interestingly, early work
concentrated on the task level and dealt with plan generation. The investigations
performed with Shakey are a good example /FIKES et al. '72/. Yet, these approaches
did not have much impact on the development of control languages for industrial robots.
Here, work centered around the manipulator level (examples are: WAVE /PAUL '77 A/,
SIGLA /SALMON '78/, EMILY /WILL '78/ or VAL /SHIMANO '79/) or the object level
(examples are : AL /FINKEL et al. '74/, LAMA /LOZANO-PEREZ '76/, AUTOPASS
/LIEBERMAN & WESLEY '77/, or RAPT /POPPLESTONE et al. '78/).

The second line of distinction is the use of models, i.e. the question whether the
control system has some internal model about the world in which the robot operates
or not. In the second case all actions must be explicitly programmed. If models are
available then it is possible to incorporate automatic plan generation, program
verification as well as error diagnosis and recovery. Clearly, the modeling approach
has a number of appealing features although their pay-off may not come immediately.
Most control languages for industrial robots are explicit programming types. Among
those that use models are AL, LAMA, AUTOPASS, and RAPT. Although a step in the right
direction, the implementation of these languages is still a long way from applications
in industrial situations.

The final line of discussion is concerned with program behaviour at run time. Some of the languages require a compiler to translate the programs into basic actions before the programs are run. If compiled programs were written at the manipulation level (as for example in WAVE) then the program could not react to sensory input at run time. If such programs are written at the object level and are then compiled into manipulation statements that are interpreted one at a time (as in AUTOPASS/MAPLE) then the program can indeed react to sensory information. Therefore, most control languages are interpretative languages.

In concluding this section let me state that it is certainly desirable to program at the highest level possible; to use models about the objects, the robot, the workstation and the task; and to use interpretative languages as to be able to react to sensory input during run time. In particular, the use of models facilitates the automatic generation of plans, for instance to avoid collisions (for examples of planning of collision free paths see /UDUPA '77/ or /LOZANO-PEREZ & WESLEY '79/).

4.   CONCLUSION

Let me summarize the situation as I see it: obviously we cannot expect to see a universal robot in the near future that can handle all practical tasks efficiently and in an economical way. Rather, we will have to define specific tasks at workstations and build robots that are adapted to these tasks. In order to be able to apply industrial robots to practical tasks it will be necessary to improve the articulation of robots, to develop more powerful systems for tactile and visual sensing, to design more flexible transfer machinery, and to develop hierarchical computer programs that control the robot, the workstation as well as the entire assembly or machining operation.

The long predicted 'robot revolution' seems to get started after all. The Japanese government plans to install an unmanned, fully automatic factory for metal-work by 1984. The plant is supposed to produce machinery components ranging from hydraulic pumps to heavy duty transmissions. The US National Bureau of Standards plans to have a robot metal-working shop operative by 1988. These and other projects will demonstrate the use of "intelligent" robots. In the meantime actual robot sales, though still modest, seem to be growing rapidly. Swedish car manufacturer Volvo, for instance, has ordered 100 Cincinnati-Milacron robots, Japan's Toyota ordered 72o Kawasaki robots, American General Motors plans to employ 47o robots by 1983. Many more examples could be given. Optimistic estimations predict an annual growth of 30% of the robot market. As was discussed in this paper, only "intelligent" robots will have a real impact on manufacturing. Thus, in order to make all these predictions come true, a lot of research and development has still to be done.

5. LITERATURE

ABRAHAM, R.G.
STEWART, R.J.S.
SHUM, L.Y.

"State-Of-The-Art in Adaptable-Programmable Assembly Systems".
International Fluidics Services Ltd. (Publ.),
Kempston, Bedford, UK, 1977

AGIN, G.J.

"Representation and Description of Curved Objects".
Stanford Univ. Art. Intelligence Lab. (SAIL), Memo AIM-173,
CS-305, Stanford, Calif., October 1972

AMBLER, A.P.
BARROW, H.G.
BROWN, C.M.
BURSTALL, R.M.
POPPLESTONE, R.J.

"A Versatile System for Computer-Controlled Assembly".
Artificial Intelligence 6 (1975), pp. 129 - 156

BEJCZY, A.K.

"Machine Intelligence for Autonomous Manipulation".
in: Heer, E. (Ed.): 'Remotely Manned Systems',
Proc. 1st National Conference at CalTech, Pasadena, Calif.,
September 1972, pp. 377 - 396

BROOKS, R.
GREINER, R.
BINFORD, T.O.

"ACRONYM : A Model-Based Vision System".
Proc. 6th Int. Joint Conf. on Artificial Intelligence (IJCAI),
Tokyo, Japan, August 1979

COLDING, B.
COLWELL, L.V.
SMITH, D.N.

"Delphi Forecasts of Manufacturing Technology".
International Fluidics Services (Publ.),
Kempston, Bedford, UK, 1979

ENCYCLOPAEDIA
BRITANNICA

15th edition, Chicago, Ill., 1979
Articles on:
"Automata", 2; pp. 494 - 496
"Golem", IV; pg 614
"Robot Devices", 15; pp. 910 - 913

ENGELBERGER, J.F.

"A Robotics Prognostication".
Proc. of the 1977 Joint Automatic Control Conf.,
San Fransisco, Calif., June 1977, pp. 197 - 204

EVANS, J.M.
ALBUS, J.S.
BARBERA, A.J.

"National Bureau of Standards (NBS)/Robot Institute of America
(RIA) Robotics Research Workshop".
Proceedings, Dearborne, Mich., 1978

FALEK, D.
PARENT, M.

"An Evolutive Language for An Industrial Robot".
The Industrial Robot (1980) 9, pp. 168 - 171

FELDMAN, J.A.
et al.

"The Use of Vision and Manipulation to Solve The Instant Insanity Puzzle".

Proc. 2nd IJCAI,
London, September 1971, pp. 350 - 358

FIKES, R.
et al.

"Learning and Executing Generalized Robot Plans".

Artificial Intelligence 3 (1972) 4

FINKEL, R.
TAYLOR, R.H.
BOLLES, R.C.
PAUL, R.
FELDMAN, J.A.

"AL, A Programming System for Automation".

SAIL, Memo AIM-243, Stanford, Calif., November 1974

FOITH, J.P.
EISENBARTH, C.
ENDERLE, E.
GEISSELMANN, H.
RINGSHAUSER, H.
ZIMMERMANN, G.

"Real-Time Processing of Binary Images for Industrial Applications".

in: Bolc,L. & Z.Kulpa (Eds.): 'Digital Image Processing Systems',
Lectures in Computer Science, Springer-Verlag, Berlin, 1981

GLEASON, G.J.
AGIN, G.J.

"A Modular Vision System for Sensor-Controlled Manipulation and Inspection".

Proc. 9th Int. Symp. on Industrial Robots,
Washington, D.C., March 1979, pp. 57 - 70

HART, P.
et al.

"Artificial Intelligence - Research and Applications".

Annual Tech. Report to ARPA, SRI, Menlo Park, Calif.,
Decmber 1972

HEGINBOTHAM, W.B.
et al.

"The Nottingham 'SIRCH' Assembly Robot".

Proc. 1st Conf. on Industrial Robots,
Nottingham, UK, 1973, pp. 129 - 142

HORN, B.K.

"What Is Delaying The Manipulator Revolution ?".

M.I.T. AI Lab, Memo,
Cambridge, Ma., 1980

LIEBERMAN,L.I.
WESLEY, M.A.

"AUTOPASS: An Automatic Programming System for Computer Controlled Mechanical Assembly".

IBM Journal of Res. & Development 21 (1977) 6, pp. 321 - 333

LOZANO-PEREZ, T.

"The Design of A Mechanical Assembly System".

M.I.T. AI Lab, Memo AI-TR 397,
Cambridge, Ma., December 1976

LOZANO-PEREZ, T.
WESLEY, M.A.
"An Algorithm for Planning Collision-Free Paths Among Polyhedral Obstacles".

Comm. of the ACM 22 (1979) 10, pp. 560 - 570

PARK, W.T.
"Minicomputer Software Organization for Control of Industrial Robots".

Proc. of the 1977 Joint Automatic Control Conf.,
San Fransisco, Calif. June, 1977, pp. 164 - 171

PAUL, R.
(A)
"WAVE : A Model-Based Language for Manipulator Control".

The Industrial Robot 4 (1977) 1, pp. 10 - 17

PAUL, R.
(B)
"The Mathematics of Computer Controlled Manipulators".

Proc. 1977 Joint Automatic Control Conf.,
San Fransisco, Calif., June 1977, pp. 124 - 131

PAUL, R.
"Robots, Models, and Automation".

IEEE Computer (1979) 7, pp. 19 - 26

POPPLESTONE, R.J.
AMBLER, A.P.
BELLOS, I.
"RAPT : A Language for Describing Assemblies".

The Industrial Robot 5 (1978) 3, pp. 131 - 137

ROBERTS, L.G.
"Machine Perception of Three-Dimensional Solids".

in: J.Tipett, D.Berkowitz, L.Clapp, C.Koester, & A.Vanderbrugh
(Eds.): 'Optical and Electro-Optical Information Processing',
M.I.T. Press, Cambridge, Ma., 1965, pp. 159 - 197

SALMON, M.
"SIGLA: The Olivetti SIGMA Robot Programming Language".

8th Int. Symp. on Industrial Robots,
Stuttgart, W-Germany, May/June 1978

SCHMIEDER, L.
VILGERTSHOFER, A.
METTIN, F.
"Kraft-Drehmoment-Fuehler".

German Patent Pending, G 01 L 1/22, June 1979

SHIMANO, B.
"VAL :A Versatile Robot Programming and Control System".

Proc. of IEEE Comp. Soc. 3rd Int. Computer Software & Applications
Conf.COMPSAC, Chicago, Ill., November 1979, pp. 878 - 883

SHIRAI, Y.
SUWA, M.
"Recognition of Polyhedrons With A Range Finder".

Proc. 1st IJCAI,
London, 1971

STANFORD UNIV.
"Final Report: The First Ten Years of Artificial Intelligence
Research at Stanford".

Stanford Univ., Stanford, Calif., 1973

SUGARMAN, R.   "The Blue-Collar Robot".
                       IEEE Spectrum (1980) 9, pp. 53 - 57

UDUPA, S.M.   "Collision Detection And Avoidance in Computer Controlled
                       Manipulators".
                       Proc. of the 6th IJCAI,
                       Tokyo, Japan, August 1977, pp. 737 - 748

WANG, S.M.   "Sensors for Computer Controlled Mechanical Assembly".
WILL, P.M.
                       The Industrial Robot (1978) 3, pp. 9 - 18

WARD, M.R.   "CONSIGHT : A Practical Vision-Based Robot Guidance System".
ROSSOL, L.
HOLLAND, S.W.   Proc. 9th Int. Symp. on Industrial Robots,
DEWAR, R.   Washington, D.C., March 1979, pp. 195 - 211

WICHMAN, W.M.   "Use of Optical Feedback in The Computer Control of An Arm".
                       CS Dept., Stanford Univ., AI Project Memo 56,
                       Palo Alto, Calif., August 1967

WILL, P.M.   "Computer Controlled Mechanical Assembly".
                       The Industrial Robot (1978) 3

NATÜRLICHSPRACHLICHE KI-SYSTEME:
ENTWICKLUNGSSTAND UND FORSCHUNGSPERSPEKTIVE

W. Wahlster

Universität Hamburg

ABSTRACT.   After 20 years of research the first natural language AI systems are
beginning to enter the commercial market. Although computational models for many
of the linguistic, communicative and cognitive abilities underlying intelligent
language behavior are still open issues for basic research, an engineering discipline
for natural language interfaces is emerging. The paper surveys the state-of-the-art
in natural language AI systems with special emphasis on the situation in Germany and
discusses future directions for basic and applied research. Hot topics in current
natural language processing research are identified and illustrated with examples.

Zielsetzung der Übersicht

Der vorliegende Aufsatz versucht, einen Überblick zum Entwicklungsstand im Bereich der
natürlichsprachlichen KI-Systeme und zu aktuellen Fragestellungen der sprachorientierten KI-Forschung zu geben. Die Komplexität und die Breite des hier zu behandelnden Fach-
gebietes machen es unmöglich, einen solchen Überblick mit einer allgemeinverständlichen
Einführung in die Modelle und Methoden der Sprachverarbeitung zu kombinieren. Im Gegensatz zu den neueren Überblicksartikein von Grosz [18], Hendrix [26] und Fauser/Rathke
[16] liegt der Schwerpunkt der folgenden Übersicht auf natürlichsprachlichen Systemen
der Künstlichen Intelligenz, in denen Deutsch als Interaktionssprache benutzt wird. Die
vorliegende Arbeit unterscheidet sich in ihrer Zielsetzung außerdem von den Übersichts-
aufsätzen von Lenders [31] und Eisenberg [13], indem sie nicht zur KI-Forschung gehörende Aufgabenstellungen der maschinellen Sprachverarbeitung völlig ausklammert. Da hauptsächlich deutschsprachige KI-Systeme als Beispiele verwendet werden und sich die linguistischen Probleme bei der Sprachverarbeitung für eine Fremdsprache oft völlig anders
stellen, schien es wenig sinnvoll, den Beitrag auf Englisch zu verfassen. Die Zielgruppe,
an die sich dieser Überblick wendet, besteht einerseits aus Wissenschaftlern, die auf
einem anderen Teilgebiet der KI arbeiten, andererseits aber auch aus interessierten Informatikern und Linguisten, die sich über den Entwicklungsstand in der Bundesrepublik
und die internationalen Forschungsperspektiven der sprachorientierten KI informieren
möchten.

Fachgebiete, Forschungsschwerpunkte und Arbeitsrichtungen

Der Entwurf, die Implementation und die praktische Erprobung natürlichsprachlicher
Systeme sowie die Erforschung der damit verbundenen theoretischen Grundlagen bilden
seit dem Erfolg von Winograds SHRDLU-System [54] anfangs der 70iger Jahre ein etablier-
tes und weiterhin expandierendes Teilgebiet der Künstlichen Intelligenz (KI) Forschur
dessen Nutzen für hochentwickelte Industriegesellschaften unbestreitbar ist (vgl. [28],
[47]).

Dabei spricht man in der sprachorientierten KI-Forschung von *natürlichsprachlichen Systemen* (NSS, vgl. [49]), wenn

- eine Teilmenge der in das System eingegebenen oder vom System ausgegebenen Nachrichten natürlichsprachlich codiert ist und
- zur Verarbeitung der Nachrichten syntaktische und semantisch-pragmatische Verfahren
  zur Analyse und Generierung natürlicher Sprache eingesetzt werden.

Die erste Bedingung sichert, daß auch solche Systeme als NSS bezeichnet werden können,
die neben einer natürlichsprachlichen Ein- oder Ausgabe auch anders codierte Nachrichten
mit ihrer Umgebung austauschen. Beispielsweise wird in einem laufenden KI-Projekt der
Firma BBN [5] ein NSS entwickelt, das auf Eingaben des Benutzers wie (1), in der eine
natürlichsprachliche Äußerung mit einer Zeigehandlung verknüpft ist, mit einer entspre-

(1) BEN: *Entferne diesen* < der Benutzer zeigt z.B. mit einem Lichtgriffel auf
           ein graphisches Objekt, das er auf dem Sichtgerät sieht > *Zustand und
           zeige mir den Rest genauer.*

chenden Veränderung der gezeigten Graphik und einer zusätzlichen natürlichsprachlichen
Ausgabe (z.B. der Rückfrage '*Ist das genau genug?*') reagieren kann.

In der sprachorientierten KI-Forschung wird langfristig durchaus angestrebt, die viel-
fältigen Möglichkeiten der Integration von Mimik, Gestik und anderen nicht-verbalen
Handlungen in einen natürlichsprachlichen Dialog, wie sie der alltäglichen menschlichen
Kommunikation zugrundeliegen, auch für die Mensch/Maschine-Kommunikation verfügbar zu
machen.

Die zweite Bedingung verhindert, daß Systeme, die lediglich einfachste Zeichenketten-
operationen über natürlichsprachlich codierten Texten durchführen (z.B. Texteditoren,
sprachstatistische Systeme) als NSS aufgefaßt werden können.

Für die sprachorientierte KI-Forschung sind als Ausgangspunkt neben der *Informatik*
besonders Ergebnisse und Methoden der Fachwissenschaften *Linguistik* und *Psychologie*
relevant, genauso wie für das Theorembeweisen die Mathematik oder für Teile der Bildverarbeitung die Physik notwendige Grundlagen liefern.

Neben der KI gibt es mindestens noch die folgenden drei, ebenfalls interdisziplinären Forschungsgebiete, die wichtige Beiträge zur Entwicklung natürlichsprachlicher Systeme leisten:

- die Linguistische Datenverarbeitung (LDV)
- die Informationswissenschaft (IuD)
- die Kognitionswissenschaft

Zur Zeit gelten als Hauptarbeitsgebiete der sprachorientierten KI-Forschung die ersten drei der im folgenden genannten Forschungsschwerpunkte:

- Frage-Antwort-Systeme und Dialogsysteme
- Textverstehende Systeme
- Verstehen gesprochener Sprache
- Natürlichsprachliche Wissensaufnahme
- Natürlichsprachliche Programmierung
- 'Abstract'-Generierung
- Sprachliche Bildbeschreibung
- Automatische Übersetzung

Das bisher erfolgreichste Arbeitsgebiet ist die Konstruktion von Frage-Antwort- und Dialogsystemen, die oft als sog. natürlichsprachliche Schnittstellen einen besonders komfortablen Zugang zu den in der folgenden Liste zusammengestellten Systemklassen ermöglichen:

- Datenbanksysteme und Methodenbanksysteme
- Wissensbasierte Experten- und Beratungssysteme
- Tutorielle KI-Systeme
- Theorembeweiser
- Szenenanalysesysteme
- Graphik-Systeme

In der anwendungsorientierten KI-Forschung haben sich zwei Arbeitsrichtungen[1] herausgebildet, die sich hauptsächlich durch ihre Beurteilung der natürlichen Sprache als Kommunikationsform für den Mensch/Maschine-Dialog unterscheiden. Der Ausgangspunkt der ersten Arbeitsrichtung ist folgende These:

Die an die natürliche Sprache gebundenen Kommunikationsformen zwischen Menschen sind optimal für die Mensch/Maschine-Kommunikation geeignet. Daher muß das Ziel beim Entwurf natürlichsprachlicher KI-Systeme die möglichst vollständige Rekonstruktion aller syntaktischen, semantischen und pragmatischen Merkmale natürlichen Sprachverhaltens und der damit verbundenen kognitiven Leistungen sein.

[1] Während der Arbeitstagung 'Models of Dialogue: Theory and Application', die am 15./16. Januar 1981 in Linköping stattfand, wurden diese beiden Arbeitsrichtungen anschließend an das Einführungsreferat von S. Hägglund und U. Hein diskutiert. Es wurde gefordert, daß zur Zeit beide Arbeitsrichtungen weiterverfolgt werden.

Diese Arbeitsrichtung wurde bisher am meisten verfolgt. Die zweite Arbeitsrichtung geht von folgenden Prämissen aus:

Die an die natürliche Sprache gebundenen Kommunikationsformen zwischen Menschen sollten für die Mensch/Maschine-Kommunikation noch durch neue technische Möglichkeiten wie Mehrkanalkommunikation, überlappende Ein/Ausgabeoperationen und Graphik ergänzt werden. Daher wird nicht die perfekte Nachbildung menschlicher Kommunikationsformen angestrebt, sondern der Entwurf möglichst effizienter, neuer Kommunikationsmöglichkeiten zwischen Mensch und Maschine, die neben den für natürliches Sprachverhalten typischen Eigenschaften auch auf technischen Neuentwicklungen (z.B. interaktive Umgebung der LISP-Maschinen, Alto, Jericho, Dorado usw.) basieren.

Ein Beispiel für ein Projekt, in dem die zweite Arbeitsrichtung verfolgt wird, enthält der Bericht von Hayes/Reddy [23].

Wissensbereiche und Anwendungssituationen für natürlichsprachliche Systeme

Natürlichsprachliche Systeme zeichnen sich durch *zielgesteuertes Verhalten* aus, wobei das Hauptziel meist aus einer *Hilfestellung* für den Systembenutzer besteht, z.B. bei der

- Auskunftserteilung (z.B. PLIDIS [30], USL [34], BACON [20], HAM-RPM [21])
- Beratung (z.B. GUS [4], POL [48])
- Kooperation bei der Lösung einer Aufgabe (z.B. BBN-Graphik-System [5])
- Ausbildung (z.B. SCHOLAR [11])

In letzter Zeit wurden auch experimentelle NSS entwickelt, deren Verhalten zusätzlich durch solche vorgegebenen Ziele gesteuert wird, die keine reine Hilfsfunktion des Systems bewirken; solche Ziele sind z.B.

- Informationsgewinnung durch das System (z.B. ULLY [23], TEIRESIAS [12], KLAUS [19])
- Verkauf (z.B. Hotelreservierungssituation in HAM-RPM [27])

Selbstverständlich werden anfangs jegliche 'Systemziele' entweder bereits beim Entwurf eines KI-Systems fest vorgegeben oder beim Systemstart explizit als Parameter übergeben (z.B. in POLITICS [8], das verschiedene 'politische Zielvorstellungen verfolgen' kann). Abstrakt betrachtet kann allerdings auch das Verhalten eines menschlichen Gesprächspartners in einigen Situationen dadurch charakterisiert werden, daß dieser versucht, eine z.B. durch seine berufliche Rolle (für einen Angestellten im Reisebüro: Urlaubsberatung mit Verkaufsabsicht) von außen vorgegebene Intention im Rahmen seiner eigenen kommunikativen und kognitiven Fähigkeiten (z.B. Planung von Subzielen, Gesprächsstrategien, tendentiöse Beschreibung von Sachverhalten) zu verwirklichen.

Obwohl zunächst lediglich aus wissenschaftlichem Erkenntnisinteresse heraus entwickelt, zeichnen sich künftige Anwendungssituationen für die letztgenannte Klasse von KI-Systemen ab, in denen die typisch menschlich-persönlichen Züge des Gesprächspartners eine

untergeordnete Rolle spielen (z.B. Expertengespräche, vgl. [22]). Durch die kommerzielle
Entwicklung von sog. Heim- und Hobbycomputern ist schon jetzt abzusehen, daß darüber
hinaus natürlichsprachliche Systeme auch für reine *Unterhaltungszwecke* (z.B. sprach-
basierte Spiele) konstruiert werden, eine m.E. gesellschaftspolitisch sehr fragwürdige
Perspektive.

NSS werden heute grundsätzlich als *wissensbasierte Systeme* konzipiert, d.h. sie beruhen
nicht etwa auf einem einzigen allgemeinen Algorithmus zur Sprachanalyse und -generierung
sondern auf mehreren interagierenden Komponenten, die jeweils auf spezielle in der
Wissensbasis enthaltene *Wissensquellen* zugreifen (vgl. [46]). Im allgemeinen bestehen
NSS mindestens aus zwei Wissensbereichen: den diskursbereichsunabhängigen Wissensquellen,
die das für intelligentes Sprachverhalten notwendige *allgemeine Hintergrundwissen* enthalten, und den diskursbereichsabhängigen Wissensquellen, die zumeist *situations- und
anwendungsspezifisches Faktenwissen und Inferenzregeln* zur Verfügung stellen. Typische
Beispiele für diskursbereichsunabhängige Wissensquellen sind:

- Lexikon
- grammatische Regeln
- begriffliches Wissen
- allgemeine Inferenzregeln
- Dialogstrategien

In neueren Dialogsystemen kommen als dritter Bereich noch *dialogbezogene Wissensquellen*
hinzu, in denen sich während des Dialogs ergebende Information temporär gespeichert
wird. Typische Beispiele für dialogbezogene Wissensquellen sind:

- Fokus
- Inferenzgedächtnis
- Partnermodell
- syntaktische und semantische Dialoggedächtnisse

Während noch anfangs der 70iger Jahre das diskursbereichsabhängige Wissen der meist
rein experimentellen NSS verglichen mit dem Hintergrundwissen des Systems recht kleine
Datenbestände bildete, zeichnen sich die heutigen NSS meist durch Wissensbasen realisti-
scher Größe aus. Obwohl für die von neueren NSS abgedeckten Gegenstandsbereiche Bezeichnungen wie 'Mikrowelt, Miniwelt, Spielzeugwelt', die von unseriösen Kritikern der sprachorientierten KI-Forschung fälschlicherweise auch heute noch benutzt werden, irreführend
sind, unterscheiden sich NSS von traditionellen Informationssystemen dadurch, daß sie
über einen Bestand an allgemeinem Hintergrundwissen verfügen und für komplexe, heteroge-
ne Wissensbereiche, aber weniger für homogene Massendaten entwickelt wurden.
Die semantische Reichhaltigkeit der gewählten Bereiche anwendungsspezifischen Wissens
wird durch die folgende, alphabetisch geordnete Zusammenstellung von ausgewählten NSS
und ihren Diskursbereichen verdeutlicht (die Auswahl erfolgte nicht unter qualitativen
Gesichtspunkten sondern in Hinblick auf die Dokumentation eines breiten Anwendungs-

spektrums und unter besonderer Berücksichtigung deutschsprachiger Systementwürfe, die
durch einen Stern gekennzeichnet sind[1]):

* ATN-BIC: Wegebeschreibungen [33]
* BACON: medizinische Daten des BGA, Kongreßreisen [20]
   BLAH: US-Einkommenssteuergesetze [52]
   CO-OP: Militärausrüstung [29]
* Erlanger System für gesprochene Sprache: Fahrplanauskünfte über IC-Bahnverkehr [25]
* FAS-80: Dokumentation einer Programmbibliothek [55]
   GUS: Reiseplanung [4]
* HAM-RPM: Straßenverkehrsszene, Hotelreservierung [27]
* KIPUS: Arbeitsmarktberichte [14]
   LADDER: Ausrüstungs- und Personalbestand der Marine [43]
   LUNAR: Gesteinsproben der Apollo-11-Expedition [56]
* NATAN: Meldungen über militärische Kampfhandlungen [32]
   PHLIQUA1: Computerinstallationen [7]
   PLANES: Betriebsstatistik der Luftwaffe [51]
* PLIDIS: Abwässerüberwachung [30]
   POL: Schiffsbeladung [48]
* USL: Personaldaten, Schulnoten [34]

Wie die angeführte Zusammenstellung zeigt, zeichnen sich zwei Anwendungsschwerpunkte
ab:

• Buchungs- und Reservierungssituationen
• Verwaltungs- und Planungsbereich

Beispiele für den Entwicklungsstand in der Bundesrepublik

Um einen Eindruck vom Entwicklungsstand deutschsprachiger Systeme zu vermitteln, werden
im folgenden Dialogbeispiele für vier größere, in der Bundesrepublik entwickelte NSS
angeführt, allerdings ohne dabei auf Einzelheiten der zugrundeliegenden Verarbeitungs-
prozesse und Wissensquellen einzugehen.

Das vom Wissenschaftlichen Zentrum Heidelberg der IBM Deutschland entwickelte System
USL (User Specialty Languages, [34]) übersetzt natürlichsprachliche Anfragen in eine
auf der Relationenalgebra basierende formale Sprache Information System Base Language
(ISBL) und wertet die ISBL-Ausdrücke über einer relationalen Datenbank aus (vgl. Fig.
1). Bei USL handelt es sich um ein anwendungsorientiertes NSS mit breitem sprachlichem
Wissen, dessen kommunikative und kognitive Fähigkeiten bezogen auf die in der KI gel-
tenden Standards gering sind.

1) Eine Zusammenstellung von 54 NSS bis 1977 findet man in [50].

BEN: *Welcher Mitarbeiter des Managers Schmidt wohnt in Heidelberg?*

ISBL-Ausdruck:

((WOHN; C2 = 'HEIDELBERG')*(MITARBEITER * (MANAGER; C1 = 'SCHMIDT'); C2 = C3);
C1 = C3)%C1

SYS: *Braun.*

BEN: *Wer verdient mehr als sein Manager?*

ISBL-Ausdruck:

((VERDIEN * (VERDIEN * MANAGER; C1 = C3); C2 > C4); C1 = C6)%C1

SYS: *Niemand.*

Fig. 1: Beispielsequenz mit dem System USL

Das am Institut für deutsche Sprache in Mannheim entwickelte System PLIDIS (Problem-
lösendes Informationssystem mit Deutsch als Interaktionssprache, [30]) verfügt mit der
sog. Konstruktsprache (KS) über eine wesentlich mächtigere Repräsentationssprache als
USL (vgl. Fig. 2).

BEN: *Von welchen Laboren wurden die letzten 5 Proben des Betriebs Gärtner&*
Klinger untersucht?

Ergebnis der KS-Überführung (PASS2):

```
(LAMBDA X7
 (EXIST X6.STOFFKOLL
  (EXIST X8.INT
   (EXIST X9.ABSTROBJ
 (UND
  (LETZTNVOR
    5
    <LAMBDA X5.STOFFKOLL
     (EXIST X2.ORT
              (EXIST X3.BETRIEB
                   (EXIST X4.INT
                        (UND (BETRIEB GAERTNER&KLINGER X2.ORT)
                             (PROBE X3.BETRIEB X4.INT X5.STOFFKOLL>
         HEUTE X6.STOFFKOLL)
  (LABORBERICHT X7 X6.STOFFKOLL  X8.INT
                 X9.ABSTROBJ))))))
```

SYS: *CHEMISCHES-UNTERSUCHUNGS-LABORATORIUM*
CHEMISCHE-LANDESUNTERSUCHUNGSANSTALT

Fig. 2: Beispiel für die Performanz von PLIDIS

Wie PLIDIS so weist auch das an der TU Berlin entwickelte System BACON (Berlin Automatic
Construction of Semantic Networks, [20]) neben den sprachlichen auch inferentielle Fähigkeiten, aber nur geringfügige kommunikative Fähigkeiten auf (vgl. Fig. 3).

BEN: *Welche Nebenwirkungen traten in den den Dokumenten, in denen Human-Albumin angeschuldigt wurde, auf?*

SYS: *Schuettelfrost, Asthma, Atemnot und Dyspnoe.*

BEN: *In welchen Dokumenten, in denen Schuettelfrost auftrat, wurde Bisolvon verabreicht?*

SYS: *5/303.*

BEN: *In 5/303 wurde Bisolvon nicht verabreicht.*

SYS: *?Dem widerspricht der Datenbankeintrag:*

In 5/303 wurde SP Bisolvon verabreicht.

Soll ich aendern?

BEN: *Nein.*

SYS: *Habe nichts veraendert.*

Fig. 3: Beispieldialog mit BACON

Das an der Universität Hamburg implementierte System HAM-RPM (Hamburger Redepartner-modell, [21],[27]) stellt den Versuch dar, möglichst viele sprachliche, kommunikative und kognitive Leistungen, die intelligentem Dialogverhalten zugrundeliegen, in einem KI-System zu integrieren. Während es sich bei den Systemen USL, PLIDIS und BACON um eher anwendungsorientierte Projekte handelt, die von der Industrie bzw. dem BMFT ge-fördert wurden, ist das System HAM-RPM ein Ergebnis der von der DFG geförderten Grund-lagenforschung im Bereich KI. Eines der wesentlichen Unterscheidungsmerkmale von HAM-RPM, das sich bereits aus einem Vergleich der angeführten Beispieldialoge ergibt, be-steht darin, daß HAM-RPM über eine leistungsfähige Sprachgenerierungskomponente ver-fügt, in die neben syntaktisch-semantischem Wissen auch partnertaktische Überlegungen (z.B. in Fig. 4: der Versuch einer vom Benutzer offensichtlich erwünschten positiven Beantwortung) eingehen.

BEN: *Befindet sich in der Naehe jedes Bettes ein Nachttisch?*

SURF-Struktur:

```
(AF-D: IS
       (T-S: (Q-QT: E-) (LAMBDA: X97 (AF-A: ISA X97 NACHTTISCH)))
       (LAMBDA: X95
               (AF-A: RAEUMLICH IN/ DER/ NAEHE X95
                      (T-S: (Q-W: JED) (LAMBDA: X93 (AF-A: ISA X93 BETT]
```

Elliptifizierte SURF-Struktur der Antwort:

```
(LAMBDA: X106 (AF-A: RAEUMLICH IN/ DER/ NAEHE X106
              (T-S: (Q-W: (QW-H: FAST JED))(LAMBDA: X107 (AF-A: ISA X107 BETT]
```

SYS: *Ja, in der Naehe von fast jedem.*

Fig. 4: Performanzbeispiel aus HAM-RPM

Die in Fig. 5 dargestellte 'Systemlandschaft' wurde mit dem Ziel entworfen, einen möglichst vollständigen Überblick zu den in der BRD und DDR entwickelten NSS sowie den einschlägigen Forschungszentren zu ermöglichen. Zur Bezeichnung der Städte in der Bundesrepublik werden dabei die jeweiligen Autokennzeichen benutzt. Als Kriterium für die Größe des Schriftzuges für die Systembezeichnung wird das Produkt aus der Projektgröße und dem Umfang, in dem Techniken der sprachorientierten KI zum Einsatz kommen, verwendet. Die an den einzelnen Orten entwickelten Systeme sind in chronologischer Reihenfolge geordnet. Der größere Teil der Projekte ist bereits abgeschlossen. Eingeklammerte Angaben verweisen auf Studien, die bestehende NSS in Hinblick auf spezielle Eigenschaften auswerten. Literaturhinweise für einige der angeführten Systeme, die der vorliegende Überblick aus Platzgründen nicht enthalten kann, findet man in [15], [31], [37].

• HH: HASY, SNP, HASE, HANSA, HAM-RPM, SWYSS, GESA

• BI: EQBAS, HBASE, KOPRO, ATN-BIC

• B: BACON

• OSTBERLIN: SYSAN

• BO: AUTOMATISCHE ÜBERSETZUNG

• E: DENTAL

• DRESDEN: FAS-75/80

• BN: ISLIB, (FRAGANT-STUDIE) (LEXIKON-STUDIE)

• ER: HEX, SPEECH-PROJEKT

• MA: ISLIB, PLIDIS

• HD: LIANA, SALAT, PLAIN, USL

• SB: SUSY

• KA: KAIFAS

• R: (EVALUIERUNGSSTUDIE)

• S: PROTEX, KIPUS, (FAS-STUDIE)

• M: CONDOR, NATAN

• KN: SALAT

Fig. 5: Geographie natürlichsprachlicher Systeme in BRD und DDR

Aktuelle Forschungsthemen der sprachorientierten KI-Forschung

Der folgende Abschnitt enthält eine Zusammenstellung und Einordnung aktueller Forschungsthemen der sprachorientierten KI, wie sie sich aufgrund einer Auswertung z.B. neuerer
Tagungsbände einschlägiger internationaler Konferenzen (vgl. [35], [36], [37], [38], [39],
[40]) und meiner Gespräche[1] mit führenden Forschungsgruppen ergibt. Die Forschungsthemen
betreffen sprachliche, kommunikative und kognitive Fähigkeiten von NSS. Obwohl diese
Klassifikation der Fähigkeiten im folgenden als Gliederungshilfe benutzt wird, muß be-
tont werden, daß in der KI-Forschung zwischen den einzelnen Fähigkeiten und damit auch
zwischen den Verfahren zu ihrer formalen Rekonstruktion zahlreiche Interdependenzen ge-
sehen werden. Denn es ist ja gerade die holistische Betrachtungsweise aller am Sprachverstehen und der Sprachproduktion beteiligten informationsverarbeitenden Prozesse,
die KI-Ansätze von dem oft stark isolierenden Vorgehen in der reinen Linguistik und
Psychologie unterscheiden.

Wir unterscheiden im folgenden drei Forschungsstadien: zur Zeit weltweit besonders in-
tensiv bearbeitete Forschungsthemen ('intensive Forschung'), Problemstellungen, die als
wichtig erkannt wurden, zu denen aber erst wenige Lösungsansätze vorliegen ('beginnende
Forschung') und ältere, noch nicht befriedigend gelöste Fragestellungen, die weiterhin
verfolgt werden ('fortgesetzte Forschung').

- Sprachliche Fähigkeiten:

  - Intensive Forschung:

    - Flexibles und robustes Parsing, z.B. bei abgebrochenen, umformulierten und
      ungrammatischen Eingaben
    - Parser für gesprochene Sprache und deterministische Parser
    - Ellipsenauflösung und Elliptifizierung

  - Beginnende Forschung:

    - Erzeugung ausweichender Antworten
    - Verstehen deiktischer Ausdrücke
    - Analyse kontrafaktischer Konditionale
    - Semantisch-pragmatische Auswertung von Modalpartikeln
    - Erzeugung von Reduktionspartikeln

  - Fortgesetzte Forschung

    - Referenzsemantische Analyse und Generierung definiter Kennzeichnungen
    - Verstehen natürlicher Quantoren
    - Analyse und Generierung von Anaphern und Kataphern
    - Analyse und Generierung vager Ausdrücke
    - Behandlung von Präsuppositionsverletzungen in der Benutzereingabe

[1] Ich danke der DFG für die Unterstützung einer Vortragsreise durch die USA.

- Kommunikative Fähigkeiten:

  - Intensive Forschung:

    - Erkennung und Erzeugung direkter und indirekter Sprechakte
    - Wechsel der Sprecherinitiative
    - Verfolgen von Dialogstrategien' und Dialogtaktiken
    - Argumentative Fähigkeiten
    - Fähigkeit zur Überbeantwortung von Fragen

  - Beginnende Forschung:
    - Strategien zur Verstehenssicherung und -überprüfung
    - Berücksichtigung phatischer Ausdrücke
    - Themensicherung durch explizite Fokussierung

  - Fortgesetzte Forschung:

    - Erkennung und Erzeugung von Dialog- und Textkohärenz oder -diskohärenz
    - Klärungsdialoge
    - Beherrschen ritualisierter Dialogabschnitte
    - Erkennen von Dialog- und Textabschnitten und -typen
    - Variabler Detaillierungsgrad der Systemantworten

- Kognitive Fähigkeiten:

  - Intensive Forschung:

    - natürlichsprachlicher Wissenserwerb
    - Planerkennung, Planerzeugung, Planabstimmung
    - Planung in Situationen mit multiplen Zielen, rekurrenten Zielen oder multiplen Akteuren
    - Aufbau und Verwaltung eines Partnermodells
    - Verstehen von Metaphern
    - Nicht-monotone Inferenzen

  - Beginnende Forschung:

    - Koordination visueller Eingaben mit sprachlichem Verhalten
    - Verstehen indirekter Rede
    - Erzeugung tendentiöser, gefärbter Antworten
    - Einbringen von Subjektivität durch Glaubens- und Überzeugungssysteme

  - Fortgesetzte Forschung:

    - Verbale Beschreibung zeitlicher Abläufe
    - Approximative Inferenzen
    - Aufbau von Dialog- und Textgedächtnissen
    - Objektbeschreibung als kognitiver Entscheidungsprozeß

- Aufbau eines Inferenzgedächtnisses
- Verstehen der logischen Beziehungen zwischen konjunktionslos aneinanderge-
  reihten Satzfolgen

Obwohl es wegen der Vielzahl der genannten Forschungsthemen im Rahmen der vorliegenden
Überblicksarbeit unmöglich ist, auf alle derzeit verfolgten Fragestellungen der sprachorientierten KI-Forschung einzugehen, sollen im folgenden wenigstens drei der genannten
Problemkreise anhand ausgewählter Beispiele erläutert werden, wobei versucht wird, einen
allgemeinen Entwicklungstrend herauszuarbeiten.

Die Systemreaktion in Fig. 6 ist ein typisches Beispiel für *kooperatives Dialogverhalten*:
Es wird nicht nur die eigentlich erfragte Abfahrtzeit sondern zusätzlich auch noch das
Abfahrtsgleis genannt, womit eine sog. *Überbeantwortung* vorliegt. Das gezeigte System-

BEN: *Wann fährt der nächste Zug nach Frankfurt ab?*

SYS: *16.34, Gleis 13.*

Fig. 6: Beispiel für eine Überbeantwortung aufgrund einer Planerkennung

verhalten mag gerade wegen seiner hohen Plausibilität und Natürlichkeit für einen KI-
Laien trivial erscheinen. Doch wie die Arbeiten von Cohen, Perrault und Allen [10], [1]
überzeugend nachweisen, erfordert die formale Rekonstruktion dieses Verhaltens in einem
NSS aufwendige Planerkennungs- und Planerzeugungsprozesse. Um zu der in Fig. 6 angegebenen Überbeantwortung zu gelangen, muß das System ein allgemeines Verfahren mit fol-
gender Grobstruktur anwenden:

(1) Beobachte das Benutzerverhalten
(2) Erkenne den Plan des Benutzers
(3) Suche nach evtl. Hindernissen für den inferierten Plan, indem du die
    geplanten Schritte in einer gedachten Welt des Benutzers ausführst
(4) Mache dir die evtl. entdeckten Hindernisse zum eigenen Ziel
(5) Erzeuge einen Plan zum Erreichen dieses Ziels
(6) Führe den Plan aus und gehe nach (1)

Bei Anwendung des skizzierten Verfahrens auf die Benutzerfrage in Fig. 6 inferiert
das System zunächst als Plan des Benutzers, daß dieser mit dem Zug nach Frankfurt
fahren will. Das System stellt dann fest, daß die fehlende Information über das Abfahrtsgleis ein Hindernis für den Plan des Benutzers darstellen könnte, und beseitigt
dieses durch die Zusatzinformation. Das Beispiel verdeutlicht die oben bereits beton-
te Abhängigkeit kommunikativer Leistungen wie der Überbeantwortung von kognitiven Fähigkeiten der Planerkennung und -erzeugung.

Die zweite Frage-Antwort-Sequenz (vgl. Fig. 7) ist einem Hotelreservierungsdialog mit HAM-RPM entnommen und zeigt die Kombination sprachlicher Fähigkeiten zur semantisch-pragmatischen Verarbeitung von Partikeln wie 'sogar' und 'natürlich' (vgl. [27]) mit der kognitiven Fähigkeit, ein internes Modell des Dialogpartners aufzubauen, dem Dialog-verlauf anzupassen und für die eigenen Dialogziele einzusetzen.

> BEN: *Hat das Zimmer vielleicht sogar ein Fernsehgerät?*
>
> SYS: *Ja, natürlich.*

Fig. 7: Beispiel für die Verarbeitung von Partikeln auf dem Hintergrund eines Partnermodells

'Sogar' signalisiert dem System u.a., daß der Benutzer das Vorhandensein eines Zimmer-fernsehers für eine Normabweichung bzgl. der von ihm erwarteten Hotelkategorie hält. Aufgrund von allgemeinem Wissen über prototypische Benutzerpräferenzen wird das System im Partnermodell speichern, daß der Gast einen Zimmerfernseher wünscht. Daß dieser Schluß keineswegs trivial ist und Wissen über Präferenzen erfordert, wird evident, wenn man in der Benutzerfrage 'ein Fernsehgerät' gegen 'ein Regenloch in der Decke' austauscht. Angenommen, das angebotene Zimmer gehört zu einem Hotel der gehobenen Kategorie, dann wird das System nach Analyse der Benutzerfrage und weiterer Inferenzen schließlich im Partnermodell speichern, daß der Kunde ein Hotel geringerer Kategorie erwartet. Die elliptische Systemantwort 'Ja, natürlich' in Fig. 7 enthält wesentlich mehr Information als die einfache Bestätigung, da durch sie versucht wird, beim Benutzer eine Korrektur der vorher durch 'vielleicht sogar' signalisierten Erwartungshaltung herbeizuführen.

Das abschließende Beispiel in Fig. 8 enthält Dialogabschnitte, die kommunikative Fähig-keiten eines NSS beim Wechsel der Sprecherinitiative und der Anwendung von Dialogstra-tegien aufzeigen. Im ersten Dialogabschnitt liegt die Initiative beim Hotelier, der

> BEN: *040 58 29 13*
>
> SYS: *Hotel Alsterblick, guten Abend*
>
> Eröffnungsskript   : Initiative liegt beim System
>
> SYS: *Ja, da ist noch was frei. Haben sie noch einen besonderen Wunsch?*
>
> BEN: *Gibt es im Zimmer ein ...*
>
> Freier Dialog über
> Eigenschaften des   : Initiative liegt beim Benutzer
> angebotenen Zimmers SYS: *Ist selbstverständlich vorhanden.*
>
> SYS: *Darf ich das Zimmer für sie buchen ...*
>
> Buchungsskript   : Initiative liegt beim System
>
> BEN: *Auf Wiederhören.*

Fig. 8: Wechsel der Sprecherinitiative aufgrund einer Dialogstrategie

versucht, die für ein Zimmerangebot notwendige Information (z.B. Art des Zimmers, Zeit-
raum) vom Gast zu erhalten. Im angegebenen Beispiel gibt der Hotelier dann durch die
Frage 'Haben Sie noch einen besonderen Wunsch?' die Initiative ab. Nach einem Dialogabschnitt, in dem der Gast initiativ wird, übernimmt aufgrund einer Dialogstrategie des
Hoteliers dieser wieder die Initiative, indem er fragt 'Darf ich das Zimmer für Sie
buchen?'. Im einfachsten Fall, der in der aktuellen Version von HAM-RPM implementiert
ist, bezieht sich die Strategie auf die Dialoglänge (der Hotelier drängt auf eine
Buchung); in einem verfeinerten Modell sollte die Bitte um Bestätigung der Buchung erfolgen, wenn laut Partnermodell der Kunde durch eine Systemantwort einen besonders guten
Eindruck vom angebotenen Zimmer gewonnen hat.

Die drei angegebenen Beispiele weisen auf einen deutlichen Trend in der sprachorientierten KI-Forschung hin: Die Analysekomponente zukünftiger NSS hat weniger das Ziel, eine
rein wörtliche Interpretation der Benutzereingabe zu finden, sondern vielmehr, die mit
der eingegebenen Äußerung verbundene Sprecherintention zu erkennen. Wie Fig. 9 zeigt,
fließen in diesen Forschungstrend zwei vorher getrennte Wissenschaftsgebiete ein: die
Sprechakttheorie der Linguistik und die in der KI entwickelten Planungssysteme.

Linguistische Pragmatik   KI-Planungsliteratur
Sprechakttheorie   (z.B. NOAH [20], BELIEVER
(z.B. Austin [3], Searle [44])   [45] und PANDORA [53])

Sprachorientierte KI-Forschung:
- Planerkennung bei der Sprechaktanalyse
- Sprechaktplanung
- Planabstimmung der Dialogpartner
(vgl. z.B. [10] [1] [2])

Fig. 9: Ein Entwicklungstrend der sprachorientierten KI-Forschung

Zusammenfassung und Ausblick: 8 Thesen zur sprachorientierten KI

In den ersten vier der folgenden Thesen wird der Entwicklungsstand und die Forschungsperspektive für natürlichsprachliche KI-Systeme zusammengefaßt. Da die weiteren vier
Thesen zur Ausbildungssituation und Förderungspolitik für das behandelte Fachgebiet
in der sich an den Vortrag anschließenden Diskussion sehr positiv aufgenommen wurden,

wurden sie auch in die schriftliche Version des Vortrags übernommen, obwohl sie nur in-
direkt mit der Forschungsperspektive und dem Entwicklungsstand in der Bundesrepublik
zusammenhängen.

THESE 1:

Nach 20 Jahren Grundlagenforschung gibt es jetzt in den USA die ersten kommerziell ein-
setzbaren natürlichsprachlichen Systeme (z.B. ROBOT, LIFER). Wichtige Grundkonzepte
des Entwurfs, der Konstruktion und Implementation natürlichsprachlicher Systeme, die
robust und produktreif sind, wurden gefunden (natural language interface engineering).
In der Bundesrepublik fehlt allerdings bisher ein in der Anwendung erfolgreiches
deutschsprachiges System.

THESE 2:

Während die sprachorientierte KI-Forschung in den 70iger Jahren durch einen deutlichen
Übergang von syntaktischen zu semantischen Fragestellungen gekennzeichnet war, scheint
für den Anfang der 80iger Jahre typisch zu sein, Sprachverhalten im größeren Zusammenhang von allgemeinem zielgerichtetem Verhalten (Handeln, Planen, Problemlösen) zu sehen.

THESE 3:

Obwohl für die Hauptkomponenten eines natürlichsprachlichen Systems heute eine Auswahl
von bewährten Modellen und Techniken zur Verfügung stehen, sind noch viele Einzelpro-
bleme, auch in klassischen Gebieten wie der lexikalischen Analyse und des Parsing
(z.B. Wortbildung, Ellipsen) ungeklärt und erfordern Grundlagenforschung in enger Zu-
sammenarbeit mit Linguisten.

THESE 4:

Bisher wurde anspruchsvolle sprachorientierte KI-Forschung, die hohe Anforderungen an
Rechenzeit und Speicherplatz stellt, durch die zu geringe Verfügbarkeit entsprechender
Betriebsmittel behindert. Durch Einführung von Spezialhardware wie den LISP-Maschinen
zeichnet sich jetzt eine Lösung des Hardware-Problems ab, die wegen der relativ geringen
Kosten langfristig auch Anwendungen von natürlichsprachlichen Systemen in kleineren und
mittleren Betrieben, Organisationen und Verwaltungen ermöglichen wird.

THESE 5:

Es herrscht noch immer ein großer Mangel an Informatikern mit guten Kenntnissen in sprachorientierter KI und Linguistik. Der Vermittlung der in der sprachorientierten KI-Forschung entwickelten Methoden sollte ein fester Platz im Lehrplan der Informatik und Informationswissenschaft zugewiesen werden. Entsprechende Ausbildungskapazitäten und eine kontinuierliche Forschungsentwicklung können nur durch die Einrichtung entsprechender Hochschullehrerstellen und einen zügigen Ausbau der Studiengänge Informatik mit Anwendung Linguistik und Informationswissenschaft erreicht werden.

THESE 6:

Bisher fehlt ein Standardwerk im Bereich der natürlichsprachlichen KI-Systeme, das alleine zur Ausbildung verwendet werden kann. Die bisher erschienen KI-Lehrbücher decken die sprachorientierte KI-Forschung nur schlecht ab. Die Grundausbildung wird immer noch durch mangelnde deutschsprachige Literatur über NSS erschwert.

THESE 7:

Seit langem geförderte Großprojekte zur Sprachverarbeitung, die oft linguistische und informatische ad-hoc-Verfahren einsetzen, sollten zu Gunsten mehrerer mittlerer KI-Projekte zügig abgeschlossen werden. Aufgrund der schnellen Weiterentwicklung von KI-Techniken sind NSS mit einer Entwicklungszeit von mehr als 5 Jahren schon veraltet, bevor es zu ihrem praktischen Einsatz kommt.

THESE 8:

Es sollte in den Projektzielen von sprachorientierten KI-Vorhaben eine klarere Trennung zwischen Grundlagenforschung und Anwendungsforschung vorgenommen werden, so daß mangelnder Anwendungserfolg nicht durch zusätzliche Grundlagenforschung oder umgekehrt mangelnde wissenschaftliche Ergebnisse nicht durch Anwendungsdruck entschuldigt werden können.

Literatur

[1] Allen, J., Perrault, C.: Participating in dialogues: understanding via plan deduction. In: Proc. of the second national conference of the Canadian Society for Computational Studies of Intelligence, Toronto 1978

[2] Appelt, D.E.: Problem solving applied to language generation. In: Proc. of the 18th annual meeting of the Association for Computational Linguistics, Philadelphia 1980

[3] Austin, J.L.: How to do things with words. Cambridge, Ma. 1962

[4] Bobrow, D.G., Kaplan, R.M., Kay, M., Norman, D.A., Thompson, H., Winograd, T. :
GUS - a frame-driven dialog system. In: AI, 8, 2, 155-173, 1977

[5] Brachman, R.J., Bobrow, R.J., Cohen, P.R., Klovstad, J.W., Webber, B.L., Woods, W.
A.: Research in natural language understanding. Annual Report, BBN Report
No. 4274, Cambridge, Ma. 1979

[6] Brecht, W.: Natürlichsprachliche Ansätze zu Datenbanksystemen. In: Krallmann, D.
(ed.): Kolloquium zur Lage der Linguistischen Datenverarbeitung. Essen 1978

[7] Bronnenberg, W.J.H.J., Bunt, H.C., Landsbergen, S.P.J., Scha, R.J.H., Schoenmakers,
W.J,. van Utteren, E.P.C.: The question answering system PHLIQUA1. In:
Bolc, L. (ed.): Natural language question answering systems. München, London:
Hanser/Macmillan 1980

[8] Carbonell, J.G.: POLITICS: An experiment in subjective understanding and integrated
reasoning. In: Schank, R.C., Riesbeck, C.K. (eds.): Inside computer understanding: five programs and miniatures. N.J.: Erlbaum 1980

[9] Christaller, Th., Metzing, D. (eds.) Augmented Transition Network Grammatiken.
Teil 1 und Teil 2, Berlin: Einhorn 1979 und 1980

[10] Cohen, P.R.: On knowing what to say: planning speech acts. Univ. of Toronto,
Dept. of Computer Science, Technical Report No. 118, 1978

[11] Collins, A., Warnock, E.H., Aiello, N.E., Miller, M.C.: Reasoning from incomplete
knowledge. In: Bobrow, D.G., Collins, A.(eds.): Representation and understanding: Studies in cognitive science. N.Y.: Academic 1975

[12] Davis, R.: Applications of meta level knowledge to the construction, maintenance
and use of large knowledge bases. In: Davis, R., Lenat, D.(eds.) Knowledge-
based Systems in Artificial Intelligence. N.Y.: McGraw Hill 1980

[13] Eisenberg, P.: Computerlinguistik. In: Althaus, H.P., Henne, H., Wiegand, H.E.(eds.):
Lexikon der Germanistischen Linguistik. Tübingen: Niemeyer 1980

[14] Fauser, A.: Inferenz und Kohärenz in KIPUS. In: Rollinger, C.-R., Schneider, H-J.
(eds.) Inferenzen in natürlichsprachlichen Systemen der Künstlichen Intelligenz. Berlin: Einhorn 1980

[15] Fauser, A., Roesner, D.: Computational Linguistics in West Germany - a selected
bibliography. Univ. Stuttgart, Inst. für Informatik, 1979

[16] Fauser, A., Rathke, C.: Studie zum Stand der Forschung über Frage-Antwort-Systeme.
(im Auftrag der GID), Vorversion, Univ. Stuttgart, Inst. für Informatik,
Februar 1981

[17] Görz, G.: The HEX-System: Experiences with an expectation-based parser. In: Bolc, L.
(ed.): Natural language based computer systems. München, London: Hanser,
Macmillan 1980

[18] Grosz, B.J.: Utterance and objective: issues in natural language communication.
In: Proc. of 6IJCAI, S. 1067-1076, 1979

[19] Haas, N., Hendrix, G.G.: An approach to acquiring and applying knowledge. In: Proc.
of the first national conference on artificial intelligence, Stanford Univ.,
S. 235 - 239, 1980

[20] Habel, C.U., Rollinger, C.-R., Schmidt, A., Schneider, H.-J.: A logic-oriented
approach to automatic text understanding. In: Bolc, L. (ed.): Natural
language based computer systems. München, London: Hanser/ Macmillan 1980

[21] v. Hahn, W., Hoeppner, W., Jameson, A.: The anatomy of the natural language dialogue system HAM-RPM. In: Bolc, L. (ed.) Natural language based computer
systems. München, London: Hanser/Macmillan 1980

[22] v. Hahn, W.Computer als Dialogpartner - Simulation von Sprachverstehen. Schriftl.
Version eines öffentl. Vortrags der DFG im Wissenschaftzentrum Bonn- Bad
Godesberg, erhältlich als HAM-RPM Bericht, Univ. Hamburg, Germanisches Se-
minar, 1981

[23] Hayes, P., Reddy, R.: An anatomy of graceful interaction in spoken and written
man-machine communication. Carnegie-Mellon Univ., Dept. of Computer Science,
Report CS-79-144, 1979

[24] Hayes, P.J., Rosner, M.A.: ULLY: A program for handling conversations. In: Proc.
of the AISB summer conference, Juli 1976

[25] Hein, H.W.: A system for understanding continuous German speech. In: Siekmann, J.
(ed.): Proc. of GWAI-81, Informatik-Fachberichte, Berlin, Heidelberg, N.Y.:
Springer 1981

[26] Hendrix, G.G.: Future prospects for computational linguistics. In: Proc. of the
18th annual meeting of the Association for Computational Linguistics,
Philadelphia 1980

[27] Jameson, A., Hoeppner, W., Wahlster, W.: The natural language system HAM-RPM as
a hotel manager: some representational prerequisites. In: Proc. der 10.
Jahrestagung der GI, Saarbrücken, Informatik-Fachberichte 33, Berlin,
Heidelberg, N.Y.: Springer 1980

[28] Kalgren, H., Walker, D.E.: Economic impact of research on natural language.
Vervielf. Vortragstext, Kopenhagen 1980

[29] Kaplan, S.J.: Cooperative responses from a portable natural language data base
query system. Stanford Univ., Heuristic Programming Project, Report HPP-79-
19, 1979

[30] Kolvenbach, M., Loetscher, A., Lutz, H.D. (eds.): Künstliche Intelligenz und
natürliche Sprache. Sprachverstehen und Problemlösen mit dem Computer.
Tübingen: Narr 1979

[31] Lenders, W.: Linguistische Datenverarbeitung - Stand der Forschung. In: Deutsche
Sprache, 3, S. 213-264, 1980

[32] Liebisch, G.: Das Konzept der natürlich-sprachlichen Datenbankschnittstelle NATAN.
In: Krallmann, D.: Dialogsysteme und Textverarbeitung. Essen 1980

[33] Metzing, D.: Tools for a procedural dialog model and some problems of application.
In: Hägglund, S., Hein, U. (eds.): Proc. of the International Workshop on
Models of Dialogue: Theory and application, Linköping Univ., 1981

[34] Ott, N.: Das experimentelle auf natürlicher Sprache basierende Informationssystem
USL. In: Nachr. für Dokumentation , 30, 3, S. 129-139, 1979

[35] Proceedings of the AISB-80 Conference, Amsterdam, Juli 1980

[36] Proceedings of the first annual national conference on artificial intelligence.
Stanford Univ., August 1980

[37] Proceedings of the first international workshop on natural language communication with computers. Univ. Warschau, Inst. für Informatik, Sept. 1980

[38] Proceedings of the second workshop on theoretical issues on natural language processing, Urbana-Champaigne, Illinois, Juli 1978

[39] Proceedings of the 8th International conference on Computational linguistics, Tokio, 1980

[40] Proceedings of the 18th annual meeting of the Association for Computational Linguistics, Philadelphia, 1980

[41] Rollinger, C.-R., Schneider, H.-J.: Inferenzen in natürlichsprachlichen Systemen der Künstlichen Intelligenz. Berlin: Einhorn 1980

[42] Sacerdoti, E.D.: A structure for plans and behavior. N.Y .: Elsevier 1977

[43] Sacerdoti, E.D.: Language access to distributed data with error recovery. In: Proc. of the 5IJCAI, Cambridge, Ma., S. 196-202, 1977

[44] Searle, J.S.: Speech acts: an essay in the philosophy of language. Cambridge, Ma. 1969

[45] Sridharan, N.S., Smith, D.: Design for a plan hypothesizer. In: Proc. of the AISB/GI Conference on artificial intelligence, Univ. Hamburg, S. 315-323, 1978

[46] Schefe, P.: Arten von Wissen und Inferenzen in natürlichsprachlichen Systemen. In: Rollinger, C.-R., Schneider, H.-J. (eds.): Inferenzen in natürlich-sprachlichen Systemen der Künstlichen Intelligenz. S. 1-36, Berlin: Einhorn.

[47] Schmidt, A., Schneider, H.-J.: Natürlich-sprachliche Frage-Antwort-Systeme - Bedeutung, Realisierung, Ausblick. In: Krallmann, D.: Zur Lage der Linguisti-schen Datenverarbeitung. Essen 1978

[48] Thompson, B.H.: Linguistics analysis of natural language communication with com-puters. In: Proc. of the 8th international conference on computational linguistics, S. 190-201, Tokio 1980

[49] Wahlster, W.: Die Repräsentation von vagem Wissen in natürlichsprachlichen Systemen der Künstlichen Intelligenz. Univ. Hamburg, Fachbereich Informatik, Bericht IFI-HH-B-38/77, 1977

[50] Waltz, D.L.: Natural language interfaces. In: SIGART Newsletter, 61, 1977

[51] Waltz, D.L.: An english language question answering system for a large relational database. In: CACM, 21, 7, 526-539, 1978

[52] Weiner, J.L.: BLAH - A system which explains its reasoning. In: AI, 15, 1, S. 19-48, 1980

[53] Wilensky, R.: Meta-Planning: Representing and using knowledge about planning in problem solving and natural language understanding. U.C. Berkeley, EECS Dept., Memo No. 80/33, 1980

[54] Winograd, T.: Understanding natural language. N.Y.: Academic 1972

[55] Witschas, W., Zänker, F., Helbig, H.: FAS-80 - A natural language information system. In: Proc. of the first international workshop on natural communica-tion with computers. Univ. Warschau, Inst. für Informatik, S. 120-124, 1980

[56] Woods, W., Kaplan, R.M., Nash-Webber, B.: The lunar sciences natural language in-formation system. BBN Report No. 2378, Cambridge, Ma. 1972

SWYSS - A Natural Language question-answering System for Scene-Analysis

Peter Schefe, Bernd Pretschner

The adequate representation of a universe of discourse in a computational system may be tested by introducing a sensory channel to the "real world". SWYSS ("Say-what-you-see-system") is a natural language system connected to a TV-camera gathering snapshots analysed by a scene analysis component. Since there is a continuum of object shapes and other property values, the uncertainty of definitions becomes a main problem of communication. It is described, how representations of natural language inputs and pictorial input are computed and tied together. At present, the system is focussed on the processing of natural language queries containing vague descriptors and imprecise quantifiers. The answers of SWYSS are in elaborate German as well as the questions.

1. Introduction

Interfacing a scene analysis program with a natural language system offers some opportunities for testing the strengths and weaknesses of both. A natural scene should be recognized by a program in terms meaningful enough to allow a description that can be used in a natural language description. On the other hand, success in referring to objects in natural scenes using natural language terms will depend on the linguistic adequacy of the system's model.

This was the guiding idea, when the project started off in 1977. The ground was prepared by a scene-analysis system designed by B. Neumann [8], and a natural-language system developed by P. Schefe [11]. In this paper, we will give an overview of the system's architecture, its performance, and some design considerations. SWYSS ("Say-what-you-see-system") is able to handle questions about two-dimensional static scenes (sketches), the answers being in elaborate German as well as the questions.

SWYSS is connected to the "real world" by a TV-camera. Snapshots are digitized and stored in memory for further analysis. A typical 2D-scene is depicted in FIG. O. Similar approaches are pursued by the HAM-RPM group [1], and Waltz [13] who designed a system for visual analog representation from input English sentences. Because SWYSS is conceived of as an instrumental question-answering system, not a dialogue modelling system, we will not discuss here similarities and differences in detail.

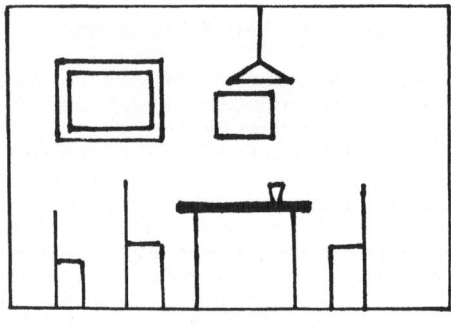

FIG. O

2. System's overview and implementation

Roughly speaking, SWYSS is conceived of as a sequence of modules
mostly interfaced by databases. The modules have access to different
sources of knowledge required for achieving their task:

(1) a dependency parser using a grammar and a lexicon, and yielding
the dependency structure of the natural language input [7, 11].

(2) a transformational component using transformation rules, and translating the dependency structure into a semantic representation
('deep structure').

(3) a translator translating the deep structure into a database query
in LISP/FUZZY [6].

(4) an evaluation component comprising a retriever that uses a semantic
net of linguistic definitions as well as the scene database, and a
subcomponent that transforms geometric descriptions into linguistic
ones, thus yielding an answer (or indicating its lack of knowledge)
by modifying the deep structure.

(5) a scene analysis component using a model database and the picture
database of edges, yielding (or updating) the scene database of geometric descriptions of objects [8].

(6) a generator using a special generative grammar, and the semantic
net, and generating a natural language output from the modified deep
structure.

SWYSS - overall structure

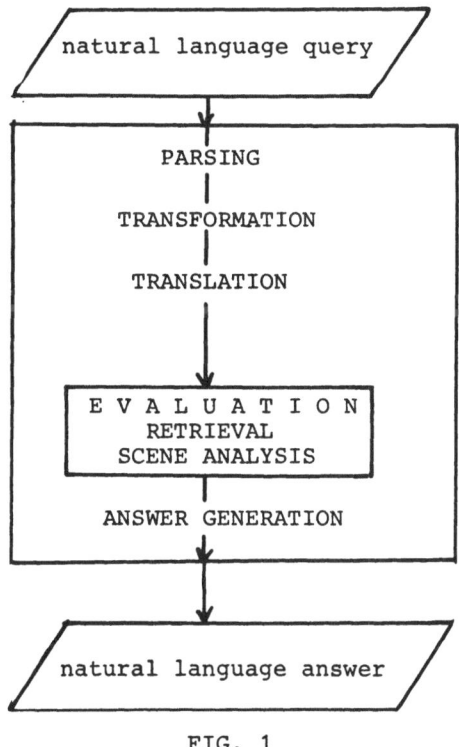

natural language query

PARSING

TRANSFORMATION

TRANSLATION

E V A L U A T I O N
RETRIEVAL
SCENE ANALYSIS

ANSWER GENERATION

natural language answer

FIG. 1

At present, SWYSS is not running as a full-fledged dialogue system. Each module listed above has been implemented more or less completely, if completeness is an achievable goal at all, but not all modules can be run at the same time yet. Primarily, the natural language component has been developed (especially by B. Pretschner and P. Schefe) and implemented in LISP/FUZZY. A special submodule deriving linguistic descriptions from pictorial data has been implemented by K.-J. Hanssmann [2] at a considerable level of detail. However, it cannot be run together with the rest being implemented in LISP/FUZZY, partly because the interface with the scene analysis component being written in SAIL has not been completed yet.

2.1 Input analysis and transformation

The input sentence is treated as a string of words without any punctuation. The syntactic analysis is done by a dependency grammar parser providing with one or more dependency structure descriptions or indicating the lack of lexical or syntactic rules which would account for a given input. E.g., the sentence:

> (Hat der Tisch der unter einer weißen Lampe steht eine dicke
> Platte)
> (Has the table which is standing beneath a white lamp a thick
> top)

is described by the structure:

```
(S Teil(NPN Tisch(DETN d
                  RELS stehen (RELPRO d
                               POBJ unter(NPD Lampe(UDETD e
                                                    ADJ weiss))))
            NPA Platte(UDETA e
                       ADJ dick)))
```

This "surface structure" is well suited for transformation into a
"deep structure" indicating more semantic relations instead of syntactic
ones in that it exhibits the following properties:

(1) It is morphologically and lexically standardized to some extent,
e.g., 'hat' → 'Teil', 'der' → 'd', etc.

(2) Mainly, the important syntactic dependencies are present, e.g.,
case - main verb, relative sentence - noun, etc., but not structural
information as embedded in rules like S → NP + VP. The parser uses
contextfree grammars attributed with priorities and general rules for
priority computation.

A new dependency parser using an attributive grammar augmented with
syntactic and semantic features has partly been implemented and may
replace the current one in the future.

The dependency structure is recursively translated into a "deep
structure" using a set of transformation rules according to the
following syntax:

```
      <rule>::=<syntactic category> =- <arcs>
      <arcs>::=<arc>/<arcs><arc>
       <arc>::=(<attribute><value>)
  <attribute>::=ISA/BEZUG/Q/GENER/KOP/INHALT/DEF/H/FRAG/PRAEZ
      <value>::=(<characterstring>)/*/S
<synt.categ.>::=<characterstring>
```

with (,), *, =-, S and all capital letter strings being terminal
symbols; e.g.

```
    PAJ=-(KOP S)(INHALT  )
WDETPA=-(Q (ALLE))(FRAG   )
```

The second production rule suggests to the translator to add two arcs
to the pending node of the deep structure with attribute 'Q'(uantifier)
and 'FRAG'(question), and values 'ALLE' and '*'(indicating the content
of the current node of the dependency structure with syntactic category WDETPA, a wh-question determiner in plural), say 'WELCH' (which),
respectively. Initially, the translator creates two nodes, 'SUBJECT'
and 'PRAEDIKAT', to which the corresponding descriptions are attached.

For every BEZUG and EIG, the translator generates new substructures
indicated by parentheses, e.g., in the 'deep structure' of our above
example:

```
(SUBJEKT ISA Tisch
        DEF Singular
        EIG(EIGOO1 INHALT unter
                   KOP stehen
                   BEZUG(OBJoo2 ISA Lampe
                          EIG(EIGOO3 INHALT weiss)))
 PRAEDIKAT EIG(EIGOO4 INHALT Teil
                      BEZUG(OBJOO5 ISA Platte
                            EIG(EIGOO6 INHALT dick))))
```

The substructures can be considered functional expressions representing
either 'objects' (OBJ-nodes, analogous to SUBJEKT node) or 'properties'
(EIG-nodes, analogous to PRAEDIKAT node). This "representation language"
bears some similarities with that of HAM-RPM [3] , and there will be a
simple algorithm for most structures of both devices to be translated
into its target structure. We hesitate to call such a representational
device a "language", because its semantics is hidden in its interpreter or may be implemented in an ad hoc manner. In any case, there
is no formal semantics specified. We suggest that only a family of
languages and metalanguages can account for the semantic 'operations'
involved, some of which will be described in the next sections. From
a deep structure, a FUZZY retrieval procedure is derived by a translation component using special rules for translation of hedges and
vague quantifiers.

FIG. 2 gives an overview of the modules described so far.

2.2 Databases and the linguistic interpretation of scenes

The 'semantics' of the system is spread over several databases and
their interpreters, including extensional and intensional information.
An overview of the evaluation procedure is depicted in FIG. 3. dis-
playing the (partly implemented) flow of control through the different
components of this module, which carries out the computed FUZZY
retrieval procedure. The resulting information is used by the answer
generation module.

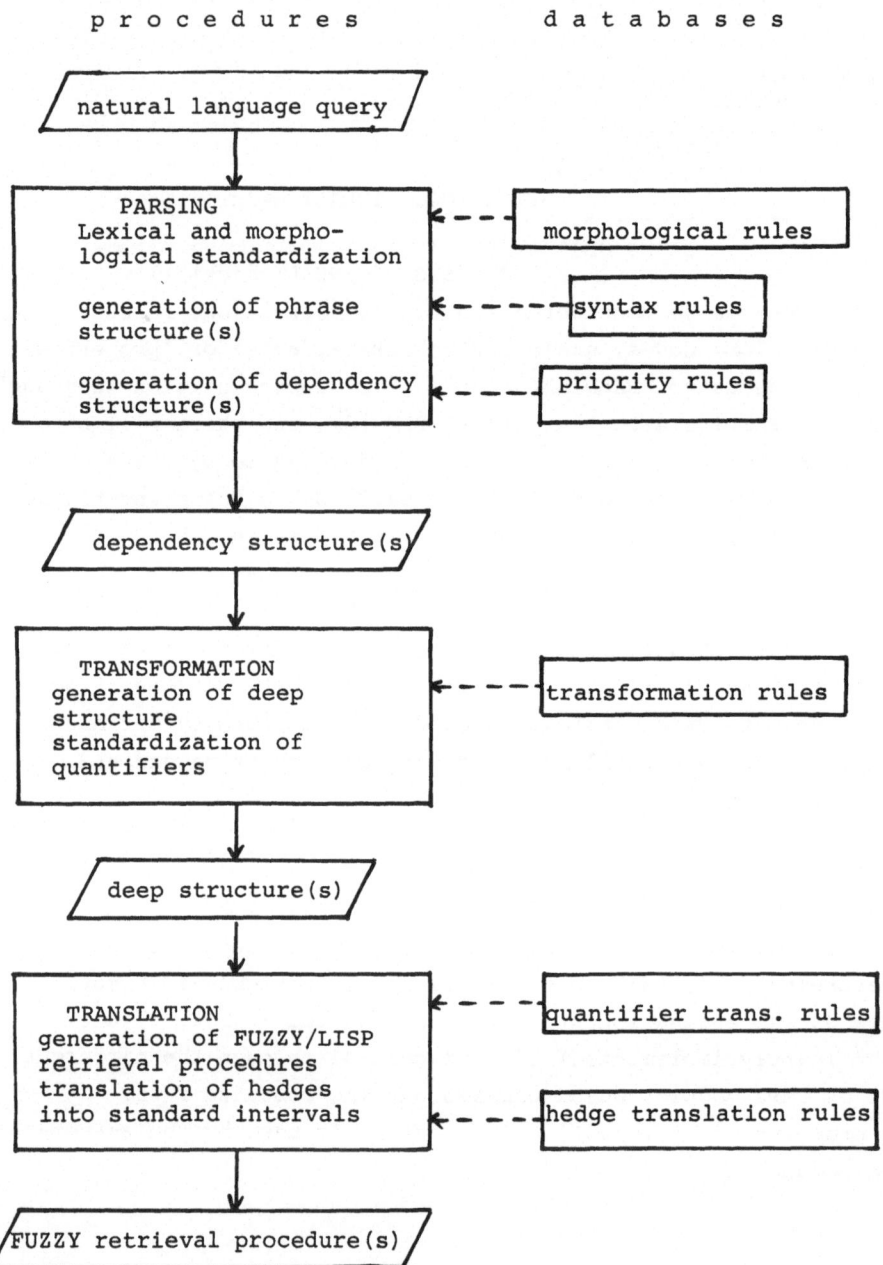

SWYSS - input analysis and translation

p r o c e d u r e s   d a t a b a s e s

natural language query

PARSING
Lexical and morpho-
logical standardization

generation of phrase
structure(s)

generation of dependency
structure(s)

morphological rules

syntax rules

priority rules

dependency structure(s)

TRANSFORMATION
generation of deep
structure
standardization of
quantifiers

transformation rules

deep structure(s)

TRANSLATION
generation of FUZZY/LISP
retrieval procedures
translation of hedges
into standard intervals

quantifier trans. rules

hedge translation rules

FUZZY retrieval procedure(s)

FIG. 2

SWYSS retrieval and scene analysis

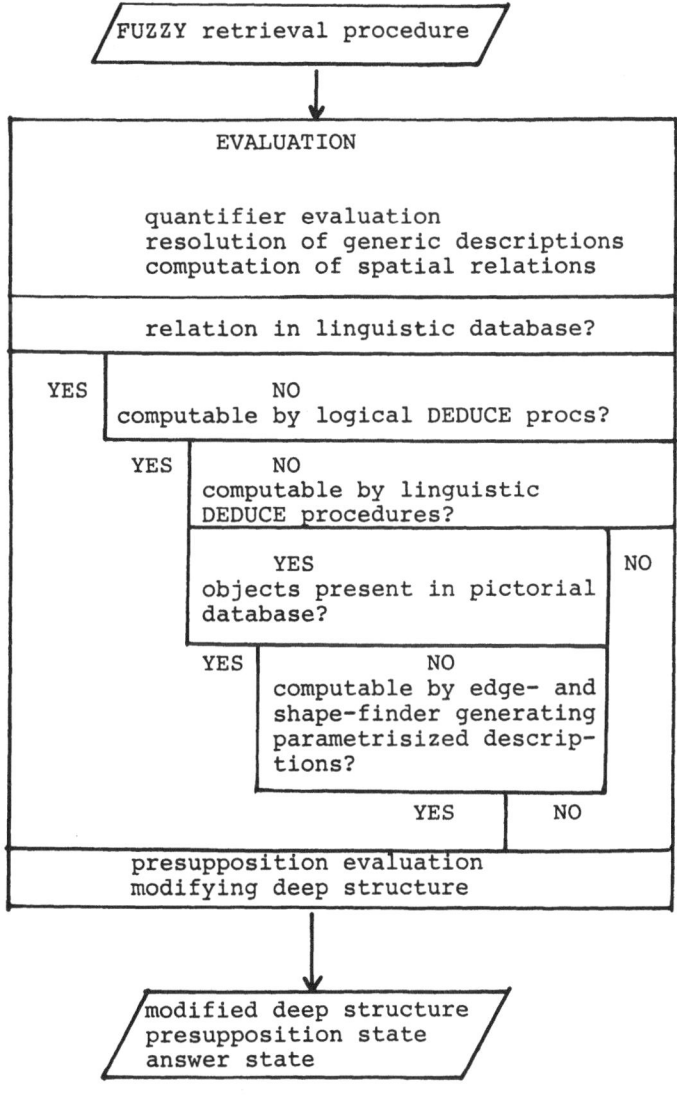

FIG. 3

2.2.1 Pictorial databases

The model database [8] contains knowledge about shapes of objects represented by lists of edges   . An object is described by
reference to one of the model shapes, and three parameters, translation
rotation, and scaling. The scene database thus contains descriptions of
objects by reference to model data, i.e., a name, and parameter values.
This framework of scene analysis is well suited for the recognition of

industrial products which have normed shapes with objective probabilistic variations, but not for the recognition of 'fuzzy' objects which vary considerably according to a subjective probability [12], e.g., the uncertainty as to what is comprised by the general concept of a 'chair'. On the other hand, as far as we know, there is no object recognition system coping with the fundamental linguistic uncertainty so far, except for some character recognition systems. This is one of the main limitations of SWYSS.

2.2.2 Linguistic interpretation of pictorial data

Beyond the crucial assignment of a name to an object, there are lots of 'fuzzy' problems as to the linguistic representation of a natural scene. Namely, spatial properties of natural objects, e.g., height orientation etc., and spatial relations as expressed in natural language prepositions, e.g., "beside" "near" "above" etc. are vague.

Vagueness of spatial properties and relations is due to the lack of an explicit precise definition which would be of no use for natural language partly because of the huge variety of contexts. However, even if the context could be fixed, it would be still impossible to escape the fundamental uncertainty of the definition of vague predicates. An appropriate approach to this indeterminism can only be an indeterministic model itself. In SWYSS, several approximation techniques may be used. There is no space here to go into the details.

2.3 Vague quantifiers and the evaluation of database queries

The evaluation of the query starts with the transformation of the deep structure (see 2.1) into a FOR-statement in LISP/FUZZY. This statement is evaluated by the LISP/FUZZY-interpreter and produces a so called 'search tree'. The search tree is a structured list of objects which were fetched or deduced from the database. It is the base for the natural language answer.

Vague quantifiers are divided into four groups according to the algorithm for computing   intervals:

```
1) some, several etc.   -   fixed intervals
2) almost every etc.    -   a percentage of all
3) about 10 etc.        -   e.g., from 8 to 12
4) few, many etc.       -   different intervals,
                            depending on the context
```

For further information about the evaluation and the representation of vague quantification see Pretschner [10].

3. Concluding remarks

SWYSS can be considered a system with natural language access to a database representing the description of a scene.

Accordingly, the questions and answers are mainly concerned with spatial properties and relations. A specialty of SWYSS is the processing of vague natural language terms and quantifiers. The system handles a lot of wh-questions (W-Fragen). Among these are welch- (which-), was fuer- (what kind of-), wieviel- (how many-), wie + Adjektiv- (how + adjective-), wozu- (to which-), worueber- (where above-), etc. The system clearly distinguishes between the violation of a presupposition and the indication of a negative answer. Answers are generated using object specifications with minimally discriminating properties. Internally, recognized objects are represented by their 2D-shapes, such that most linguistic properties and relations can be computed as required. Once computed, they can be accessed directly. To achieve this, the system uses the retrieval and deductive mechanisms of the FUZZY language.

SWYSS has been conceived of as an interactive aid for a scene analysis system for static natural scenes, initially.

Our first step in this direction is the modelling of question-answering behaviour involving vague descriptions. For this purpose, the system itself should be able to use vague natural language terms in its answers adjusting the meaning to changing semantic and - possibly - pragmatic contexts.

4. Some sample questions and answers

Wieviele Moebel gibt es?
(How many pieces of furniture are there?)
Die Szene enthaelt 34 Moebel.
(There are 34 pieces of furniture)

Steht die Vase auf einem Tisch?
(Is the vase standing on a table?)
Die Szene enthaelt mehr als eine Vase.
(There is more than one vase.)

Was fuer einen Rahmen hat das grosse Bild?
(What kind of frame does belong to the large painting?)
Das grosse Bild hat einen grauen Rahmen.
(A grey frame belongs to the large painting.)

Etliche Lampen haengen ueber einem Tisch?
(A lot of lamps are hanging above a table?)
Nein, nur einige Lampen haengen ueber einem Tisch.
(No, only a few lamps are hanging above a table.)

References

[1] VON HAHN, W., HOEPPNER, W., JAMESON, A., WAHLSTER, W. (1979). The anatomy of the natural language system HAM-RPM. Project Simulation of Natural-Language understanding. Universitaet Hamburg, Germanisches Seminar, Ber. Nr. 12, 1979

[2] HANSSMANN, K.-J. (1980). Sprachliche Bildinterpretation fuer ein Frage-Antwort-System. Universitaet Hamburg, Fachbereich Informatik: Mitteilung Nr. 74, IFI-HH-M-74/80, 1980.

[3] JAMESON, A., HOEPPNER, W., WAHLSTER, W. (1980). The natural language system HAM-RPM as a hotel manager: some representation prerequisites. Project Simulation of Natural-Language understanding. Universitaet Hamburg, Germanisches Seminar, Ber. Nr. 17, 1980

[4] LAKOFF, G. (1975). Hedges: A study in meaning criteria and the logic of fuzzy concepts. In HOCKNEY, D., HARPER, W., FREED, B. (Eds.), Contemporal research in philosophical logic and linguistic semantics. Reidel: Dordrecht, Boston, 1975

[5] LEFAIVRE, R.A. (1974). The representation of fuzzy knowledge. New Brunswick: Rutgers University, Dept. Comp. Sci., DCS-TR-33., 1974

[6] LEFAIVRE, R.A. (1977). FUZZY reference manual. New Brunswick: Rutgers University, Dept. Comp. Sci., 1977

[7] MITTELSTEIN, M., NEBEL, B., PRETSCHNER, B., SCHEFE, P. (1976). HASY - ein Programm zur syntaktischen Analyse natuerlicher Sprachen. Hamburg: Universitaet, Fachbereich Informatik, Mitteilung Nr. 36, IFI-HH-M-36/76, 1976

[8] NEUMANN, B. (1978). Interpretation of imperfect object contours for identification and tracking. IJCPR-78, Kyoto, Japan, 691-693, (1978)

[9] PEPPER, S., PRYTULAK, L.S. (1974). Sometimes frequently means seldom: Context effects in the interpretation of quantitative expressions. Journal of Research in Personality, 8, 95-101, (1974)

[10] PRETSCHNER, B. (1980). Die Behandlung natuerlichsprachlicher Quantifizierungen in Frage-Antwort-Systemen. Universitaet Hamburg, Fachbereich Informatik, Diplomarbeit, 1980

[11] SCHEFE, P. (1977). Theoretische und hochschuldidaktische Aspekte der Integration von Phrasenstrukturgrammatik und Dependenzgrammatik. Linguistik und Didaktik 29, 36-50, (1977)

[12] SCHEFE, P. (1980). On foundations of reasoning with uncertain facts and vague concepts. Int. J. Man-Machine Studies 12, 35-62, (1980)

[13] WALTZ, D.L. (1979). Visual analog representation for natural language understanding. IJCAI 1979, 926-934.

Acknowledgement

SWYSS started off as a "Project-Seminar" at the Fachbereich Informatik der Universitaet Hamburg in 1977 initiated by B. Neumann, B. Radig, and P. Schefe. Contributors to early design considerations are A. Jameson, K. Morik, B. Nebel, and H. Rasche.

NATURAL LANGUAGE INQUIRIES ABOUT MOTION
IN AN AUTOMATICALLY ANALYZED TRAFFIC SCENE

Heinz Marburger, Bernd Neumann
Hans-Joachim Novak

Fachbereich Informatik
Universitaet Hamburg

ABSTRACT

This contribution is concerned with natural language dialogue about
scenes with moving objects. Two systems are connected, a natural
language dialogue system originally conceived for static scenes and an
emerging scene analysis system for real-world TV-frame sequences. The
latter produces time dependent object descriptions which serve as a
referential database for inquiries. The time intervals relevant for
answering the questions are determined from domain specific
parameters, the context of the dialogue, the tense of the verbs and
time adverbials. For checking the correspondence between a verbally
specified motion and a trajectory, predicates are evaluated which can
be deduced from the verb's case-frame.

OVERVIEW

The system described in this paper is designed to answer yes/no
questions about moving objects in a real-world scene which has been
recorded and analyzed earlier. The scene analysis system works
bottom-up on a sequence of TV-frames and determines for each frame the
coordinates and properties of the objects using conceptual knowledge
about object models and shape as well as physical knowledge in form of
procedures. The trajectory of an object is expressed in terms of the
sequence of coordinates of its center of gravity as well as shape and
size information in each single TV-frame. We call this level of
representation, being scene dependent, referential knowledge.

Questions are asked in natural German language. For the purpose of
testing the performance of the system we assume the following
pragmatic dialogue situation: we telephone with another person which
is standing at a window, and ask questions about the traffic seen from
this person's point of view. The natural language system tries to
answer a question using the referential knowledge provided by the
scene analysis system. It also accesses conceptual knowledge which is
stored in a semantic net and consists of relations between concepts
underlying language.

Our aim is to answer questions like (1) and (2).

(1) Hielt ein Auto an?
     (Did a car stop?)

(2) Fuhr das gelbe Auto an?
     (Did the yellow car start?)

Most related research efforts differ from our approach in that they derive verbalizations bottom-up. For example the work of BADLER [4] which is further developed by TSOTSOS [5] offers motion conceptualizations which can be generated from image sequences and permit a crude verbalization by simple translation of concepts into words. Similarily the systems of OKADA [6] or TSUJI ET.AL. [7] do not attempt to relate truly natural language expressions to the analyzed movements.

In our system the use of HAM-RPM as a question-answering system provides the possibility to ask questions in natural German language. We emphasize a top-down approach where verbalizations are processed in order to decide whether or not they properly describe a given image sequence. The parsing component uses case-frame structures of verbs and selectional restrictions. The possible meanings of the verbs used in the question can be reduced due to the restricted context of a traffic scene. We feel that this domain and the above mentioned pragmatic situation of questioning a stationary observer provide a sufficiently rich setting without precluding performance testability.

After a brief overview of the system architecture we discuss motion specific problems which arise from the tense of verbs and time adverbials as well as possibilities for verifying verbally specified motion by evaluating predicates about object trajectories.

SYSTEM ARCHITECTURE

The architecture of the system has been strongly influenced by two independent investigations at the University of Hamburg. The scene analysis subsystem is being developed as part of a research effort towards understanding real world scenes with motion [1]. Current work concentrates on separating moving objects from static background and determining 3D-shape and trajectory of these objects. The dialogue subsystem is adapted from HAM-RPM [2,3] which works with a static

world of discourse and has a large amount of linguistic capabilities
at its disposal, e.g. pronoun resolution, handling of elliptical
expressions, spatial relations, quantifiers and restrictive clauses as
well as the capability to initiate clarification dialogues.

Both systems share a conceptual knowledge base which contains general
knowledge common for a language understanding system, as well as
information relevant for visually recognizing the objects in a scene,
e.g. object shape descriptions. As a result of the scene analysis
process specific object descriptions are entered into a referential
database which serves as the main communication channel between the
two subsystems.

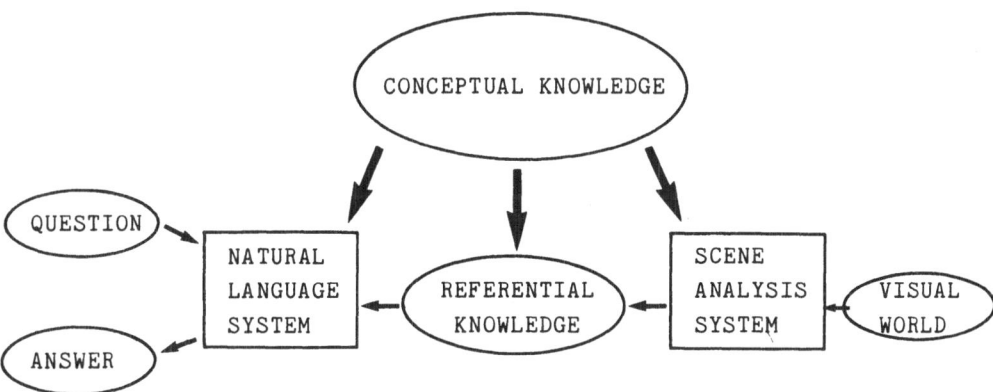

Figure 1: System overview

ISA-vertices are established between referential tokens and the
corresponding conceptual entities, also properties are instantiated.
A single token is used for objects found to be identical in successive
frames. For two frames T1 and T2 the referential database might
contain the entries shown in Fig. 2. Note that a real number between
0 and 1 (a Z-value in the programming language FUZZY) is used to
express the confidence in the factual truth of a database entry.

Since our system deals with traffic scenes we only consider motion in
two dimensions, i.e. in the ground plane. Typical scenes extend over
a time span of up to 20 sec. and are observed from a stationary
TV-camera.

T1:

```
        •

        •

    ((ISA AUTO1 VW-AUTO). 1.0)              "AUTO1 is a VW"
    ((REF AUTO1 ROT). 0.8)                  "colour red"
    ((ISA MANN1 MENSCH). 1.0)               "MANN1 is a man"
    ((ORT AUTO1 (15.0 20.0 0.5)). 0.7)      "center of gravity"
    ((SHAPE AUTO1 (<description of enclosing polyhedron>)). 0.8)

        •

        •
```

T2:

```
        •

        •

    ((ORT AUTO1 (15.5 20.2 0.5)). 0.7)

        •

        •
```

Figure 2: Entries in the referential database

TENSE AND TIME

In contrast to dialogue systems dealing with static scenes like
SWYSS [8], dialogues in our system refer to a sequence of images
ordered along an axis which we denote the time of scene, to be
distinguished from the time of dialogue which is given by the sequence
of questions. We make the following assumptions regarding scene and
dialogue times:

1. t0 and tn denote the beginning (first frame) and the end (last
   frame) of the scene, respectively.
2. Within these boundaries a time of speech ts can be arbitrarily
   chosen. It synchronizes the time of scene and the time of
   dialogue.
3. The system does not have any knowledge about the development of the
   scene beyond ts.
4. Although in reality each question takes some time, we assume that
   questions are always asked at ts, i.e. neither the time of
   dialogue progresses nor the time of scene.

Not quite consistent with the last assumption the notion of
progressing dialogue time is held upright solely for the purpose of
modelling dialogue context. In particular, a record of reference is

kept about previous questions to support the pronoun-resolution component of the natural language system HAM-RPM (see [2]).

We call the sequence of images which has to be regarded to answer a question, the (time) <u>interval</u> <u>of</u> <u>consideration</u>. In the absence of time adverbials the interval of consideration is determined by the tense of the verb. For present tense questions the interval boundaries are given by the parameters $tpr1$ and $tpr2$, where $tpr2$ is taken to be ts in our system. For present perfect and simple past the corresponding parameters are $tpa1$ and $tpa2$, where the latter is taken to be $t0$. Colloquial German does not necessitate a distinction between these tenses. Fig. 3 shows the intervals of consideration (together with the actual event intervals) for the following questions:

> (3) Faehrt der VW an?
>   (Does the VW start?)

> (4) Hielt das blaue Auto an?
>   (Did the blue car stop?)

> (5) Bog das rote Auto vorher ab?
>   (Before this, did the red car turn off?)

Question (3) will be negated since the event ´VW starts´ is not contained in the time of consideration.

```
     red car turns off    blue car stops    VW starts
                  ___                ___            __
¦------¦--------¦----------¦---¦---------¦--¦-----¦----¦ time of scene
t0    ti1     ti2        tj1 tj2      tk1 tk2    ts   tn

                                          ¦--¦        IC for (3)
                                        tpr1 tpr2

¦----------------------------------------------------¦  IC for (4)
tpa1                                          tpa2

¦------------------------¦                            IC for (5)
```

Figure 3: Intervals of consideration (IC) for questions (3) to (5)

Natural language utterances in time dependent domains usually imply a <u>time</u> <u>of</u> <u>reference</u> which may in some cases be identical with the time of speech. This is the case in (3) and (4) where the time of reference is ts. In question (5) the adverbial 'vorher' ('before this') implies another time of reference which is defined by the previously mentioned event. Here the resulting time of consideration extends from t0 to tj1. The effect of several adverbials can be described as restricting the interval of consideration with respect to a time of reference. They correspond to the category ADVe introduced by BAEUERLE [9]. We have selected the following subset: 'vorher', 'davor', 'dann', 'nachher', 'spaeter', 'danach' ('previously', 'before this', 'then', 'afterwards', 'later', 'after that').

Other time adverbials specify the interval of consideration referring always to the time of speech as a special time of reference. They are summarized in the category ADVs. We only work with those adverbials of the category ADVs which put the interval of consideration close to the time of speech, namely 'jetzt', 'nun', 'gerade', 'gegenwaertig', 'im Moment', 'eben', 'soeben' ('now', 'at present', 'just', 'just at the moment', 'just now'). This excludes adverbials like 'kuerzlich' ('recently').

Apart from the tense of the verbs and time adverbials, the length of the interval of consideration is also influenced by the domain (what the scene is about, which motions can be observed) and the course of dialogue. To handle these influences in our system the above mentioned parameters can be modified by domain and discourse dependent scaling factors.

After parsing a question about motion, the system determines the interval of consideration by first looking for adverbial clues. If none are present it resorts to the default values implied by the verb tense. We are aware of the fuzzy nature of the boundaries of the intervals of consideration and plan to extend our system accordingly if necessary.

LOCOMOTION VERBS

We investigate only questions involving verbs which denote a location change of the actor in the sentence. For a positive answer the trajectory of the actor, as recorded by the scene analysis system, must satisfy certain requirements or predicates implied by the verb. Closer inspection reveals that these predicates depend on the verb

itself as well as the deep-case structure which is extracted by the
parsing component. For locomotion verbs we use the following case
slots: AGENT, LOCATION, SOURCE, GOAL, PATH, OBJECTIVE. The
predicates also depend on which of the slots in the case-frame are
filled and which are not. Consider the case where only the AGENT slot
is filled:

(6) Hielt das Auto an?
    (Did the car stop?).

Here the two primitive predicates 'moving' and 'stationary' have to be
applied to the ACTOR trajectory over the interval of consideration.
They can be easily computed from the object positions for each
instance of the sequence. Four basic situations can be distinguished
by these primitives as illustrated in Fig. 4.

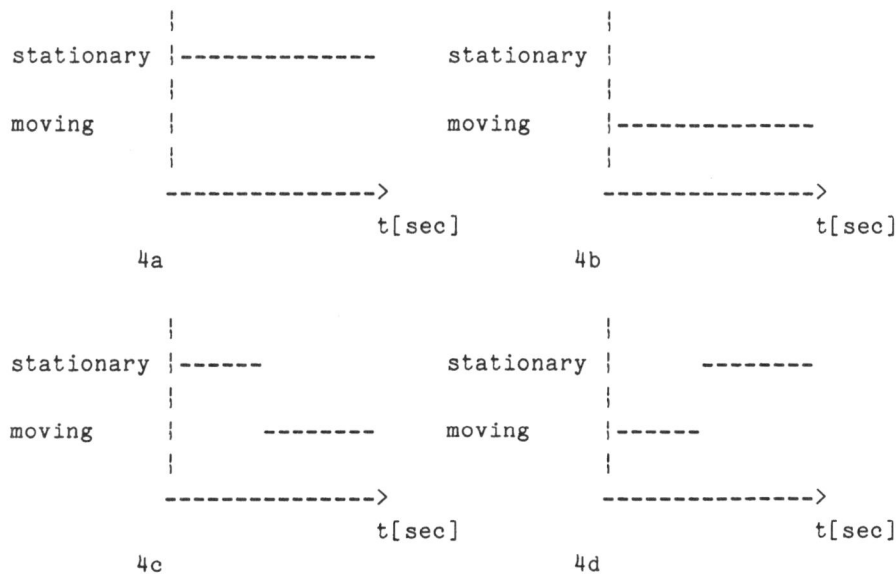

Figure 4: Primitive predicates for object trajectories

As we are analyzing locomotion verbs we neglect situation 4a. The
last three possibilities represent verb inherent features, namely the
manners of action: durative, inchoative and resultant. Some examples
of verbs which can be analyzed using the above predicates are 'fahren'
('drive'), 'gehen' ('walk'), 'anfahren' ('start'), 'losgehen' ('start
walking'), 'stoppen' ('stop'). Verbs like 'abbiegen' ('turn off') or
'wenden' ('turn') imply trajectories with more detailed properties.

Predicates involving the change of direction of a trajectory will be required, none of which have as yet been accurately designed.

Finally, we consider the situation where slots are filled besides the AGENT slot. This may be due to prepositional clauses (see (7) and (8)) or transitive verbs.

(7) Bog das Auto von der Schlueterstrasse in die Hartungstrasse ab?
    (Did the car turn off Schlueterstrasse into Hartungstrasse?)

(8) Haelt es auf der Hartungstrasse vor dem Theater an?
    (Does it stop on Hartungstrasse in front of the theater?)

In example (7) the slots SOURCE and GOAL are filled by von Schlueterstrasse´ and ´in Hartungstrasse´, respectively. The system not only checks whether there is a trajectory with the specified shape within the interval of consideration but also requires this trajectory to satisfy the spatial constraints imposed by the contents of the slots. Similarily, in example (8) the LOCATION slot is filled by ´in Hartungstrasse vor Theater´ (´in Hartungstrasse in front of theater´). It should be clear that deriving constraints from fuzzy spatial relations like ´vor´ (´in front of´) is a problem in itself. Presently, we use simple approximations and leave a sophisticated treatment to the future.

CONCLUSION

A natural language dialogue system and a scene analysis system for image sequences are being connected to explore the possibility of natural language communication with image understanding systems in general, and verbal description of motion in particular. A symbolic scene description in terms of time dependent object locations (and some additional properties) has been proposed as a level of representation suitable to serve as a referential database for inquiries. Answering yes/no questions about motion is viewed as a top-down process aiming at verifying certain trajectory properties. Three types of constraints on a trajectory can be distinguished. First, the interval of consideration as a temporal constraint, second, trajectory shape in space and time, third, spatial constraints on the location of a trajectory. It has been shown for some examples, how these constraints can be extracted from a question. The reported work is currently being implemented.

ACKNOWLEDGEMENTS

We wish to thank Walther v. Hahn, the head of the HAM-RPM project, for his helpful counsel in linguistic matters. We also gratefully acknowledge discussions with Hans-Hellmut Nagel who initiated this project.

REFERENCES

[1] Nagel, H.-H., Analyzing Sequences of TV-Frames, IJCAI-77, p.626, 1977.

[2] v.Hahn, W., Hoeppner, W., Jameson, A., Wahlster, W., The Anatomy of the Natural Language System HAM-RPM, in: Natural Language Based Computer Systems (Bolc, ed.), Hansa Verlag, Muenchen, 1980.

[3] Jameson, A., Hoeppner, W., Wahlster, W., The Natural Language System HAM-RPM as a Hotel Manager: Some Representational Prerequisites, HAM-RPM Bericht 17, Germanisches Seminar, Universitaet Hamburg, 1980.

[4] Badler, N.I., Temporal Scene Analysis: Conceptual Descriptions of Object Movements, University of Toronto, TR-80, 1975.

[5] Tsotsos, J.K., A Prototype Motion Understanding System, University of Toronto, TR-93, 1976.

[6] Okada, N., SUPP: Understanding Moving Picture Patterns Based on Linguistic Knowledge, IJCAI-79, p.690-692, 1979.

[7] Tsuji, S., Morizono,A., Kuroda, S., Understanding a Simple Cartoon Film by a Computer Vision System, IJCAI-77, p.609-610, 1977.

[8] Schefe, P., Pretschner, B., SWYSS - A Natural Language Question Answering System for Scene Analysis, 5. German Workshop on AI, Bad Honnef, 1981.

[9] Baeuerle, R., Tempus, Adverb, temporale Frage, in: Wortstellung und Bedeutung, Akten des 11. Ling. Koll. Pavia, Bd. 1, Tuebingen, 1977.

Christopher Habel / Claus-Rainer Rollinger

Aspekte der rechnergestützten Generierung von Inferenzregeln durch
Regelschemata

Abstract:
One of the main problems in designing Natural-Language-Systems depends
on the question "Where do all the inference rules come from?". In this
paper we describe a subsystem of the NL-QAS BACON supporting the task
of writing inference rules. The domain inference rules are seen as
transformations from logical expressions to logical expressions. The
inferential process is controlled by the operators in the domain of the
expression to be transformed. For any operator exists a set of relevant
rules. A relevant class of inferential rules depends on "semantic relations between words". A set of basic concepts of such relations is
introduced. Each of these concepts is paird to a rule-schema by which
it is possible to generate special inference rules for the operators of
the semantic representation language. The inferential component and the
rule-generating process (checking some types of inconsistencies) are
described. The problem is discussed from different viewpoints: the system designer's developing an AI-system and the cognitive scientist's
interested in the basic cognitive concepts of humans.

1. Einordnung

Die vorliegende Arbeit beschreibt eine Komponente des innerhalb des Projekts "Automatische Erstellung semantischer Netze" (TU Berlin) entwik-
kelten natürlich-sprachlichen (experimentellen) Frage-Antwort-Systems
BACON (Berlin Automatic COnstruction of Semantic Nets). In BACON, das
hier nur skizziert werden kann (vgl.[1]), herrscht eine strikte Trennung zwischen "Fakten-Wissen" und "Regel-Wissen", die sich physisch in
der getrennten Abspeicherung in einer "Wissensbasis" (WB) für Fakten-
Wissen und einem "Regellexikon" (RL) für das Regelwissen niederschlägt.

Während der Aufbau des Fakten-Wissens natürlich-sprachlich vorgenommen
werden kann, erfolgt die Formulierung der Regeln in einer speziellen
Regelrepräsentationssprache (RRL). Das natürlich-sprachlich ausgedrückte
Fakten-Wissen wird durch ein entsprechendes Interface in Formeln der
"logischen" Wissensrepräsentationssprache MSRL (vgl.[1]) überführt und
in der WB abgespeichert. Fragen werden analog über die Auswertung der
WB beantwortet. Das im Regellexikon abgespeicherte Wissen greift in
beide Prozesse ein. Bei der Eingabe neuer Fakten (readtime) werden (einige) Beziehungen zu den bekannten Fakten inferentiell aufgedeckt, bzw.
(einiges) implizites Wissen wird expliziert; bei der Beantwortung von
Fragen (questiontime) wird (gegebenenfalls) versucht, die Antworten vermittels inferentieller Prozesse zu beantworten.

Da MSRL eine logische Sprache ist (eine symbolische Sprache zur Beschrei-
bung formaler Theorien), ist RRL entsprechend ebenfalls eine logische
Sprache, die Inferenzen über MSRL als Transformationsregeln zwischen
MSRL-Ausdrücken beschreibt (siehe[2]).

Die folgenden Ausführungen befassen sich mit dem Problem des rechnergestützten Aufbaus der Regelmengen, wobei daran gedacht ist, allgemeine
Regelschemata zur Verfügung zu stellen, die die Formulierung von Regeln
vereinfachen und beschleunigen, und Verfahren zu implementieren, die die
Konsistenz der Regeln (untereinander und bzgl. des Fakten-Wissens) auf-
decken können. (Ähnliche Mechanismen existieren zum Teil in "frame-
Sprachen" bzw. Systemen, z.B. in AIMDS [3]).

2. Inferenzen in BACON

Während der Inferenzprozesse (Readtime und Questiontime) werden Regeln
mit beliebiger (hoffentlich kleiner) Anzahl von Prämissen auftreten.
Ein grobes Schema des Verhaltens des Inferenzsystems zur Readtime gibt
die folgende Abbildung.

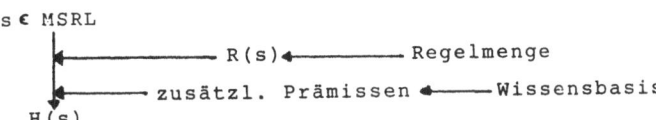

Abb. 1:   Der Inferenzprozess zur Readtime

Die Menge der für den Inferenzprozeß relevanten Regeln R(s) wird über
die in s auftretenden Operatoren angesteuert. In MSRL haben z.B. auch
Prädikatsnamen den Status von Operatoren; man denke etwa an Bedeutungspostulate, die offensichtlicherweise an den entsprechenden Prädikaten
festgemacht werden.

In den Regeln geforderte weitere Prämissen werden über der Wissensbasis
verifiziert, wobei (wenn es sich um Entscheidungsfragen handelt), unter
Umständen der Question-Time-Inferenzprozeß angestoßen wird (siehe [4]).

Die Inferenzregeln können im wesentlichen in zwei Klassen eingeteilt
werden, zum einen in solche, die Eigenschaften des Operators (per se)
wie Reflexivität, Symmetrie etc. beschreiben, zum anderen in solche, die
einen Operator inferentiell zu anderen Operatoren in Beziehung setzen;
diese definieren die Semantik der Operatoren im Sinne von Bedeutungspostulaten. Die Semantik eines prädikativen Konzepts (hier Operators)
wird auch über die erstere Klasse von Regeln bestimmt, dadurch, daß den
Operatoren diese Eigenschaften zu- oder abgesprochen werden, sowie über
das dem Operator zugeordnete Argument-Typ-Raster, wodurch festgelegt
wird, über welchen Objekten welcher Sorte der Operator operieren darf.

Diese Aspekte der Definition der Semantik prädikativer Konzepte macht
innerhalb der inferentiellen Komponente von BACON den wesentlichen Be-
standteil aus, und damit auch den größten Aufwand bei der Erstellung
der Regellexika. Um diesen Aufwand zu verringern und um die Adäquatheit
und Korrektheit der Regeln zu sichern, ist eine rechnergestützte Er-

stellung von Inferenzregeln ein geeignetes Mittel.

Die Frage, wo die Regeln herkommen, ist hierbei nicht berücksichtigt worden. Es dürfte klar sein, daß vor der Formulierung der Inferenzregeln ein großer Analyse-Aufwand getrieben werden muß. Zu analysieren ist die Wort- und Satzsemantik des Weltausschnitts, den man modellieren möchte, das Weltwissen über diesen Bereich geht in das Regelwissen ein.

3. Inferenzen - Einige kognitive Aspekte

Die in diesem Abschnitt skizzierten kognitiven Aspekte basieren auf den (hier nicht weiter erläuterten) Entitäten: Satz-Konzepte (SK), prädika- tive Konzepte (PK) und lexikalische Konzepte (LK), die im Sinne G. Mil- lers [5] verwendet werden. "Konzept" kann hier informell als die kogni- tive Entität (bzw. kognitive Entsprechung) für Sachverhalte (-> SK), Beziehungen zwischen Objekten (-> PK) und Worte/Lexeme (-> LK) angesehen werden. Als Darstellungsmittel für SKs können daher Formeln einer "logi- schen" Repräsentationssprache wie MSRL verwendet werden.

Die Beziehung LK ist jedoch nicht evident (etwa durch eine einfache Gleichsetzung), vielmehr ist davon auszugehen, daß die Wortsemantik durch Eigenschaften lexikalischer Konzepte und durch Beziehungen zwischen le- xikalischen Konzepten bestimmt wird. Für die Beschreibung derartiger Eigenschaften und Beziehungen bieten sich inferentielle Darstellungsme- thoden an. Wenn an dieser Stelle von Inferenzregeln gesprochen wird, ist es notwendig zu klären, welchen Status diese Regeln besitzen, d.h. "von was auf was inferiert wird". Wird von einem lexikalischen Konzept auf ein anderes inferiert? (Und wenn ja, wie kann das interpretiert werden). Da der kognitive, aber auch logisch formale, Status der SK eher zu er- kennen ist, ist eine Zurückführung der Inferenz-Beziehung zwischen LKs auf eine zwischen SKs sinnvoll. Die konzeptuelle Inferenzbeziehung auf der SK-Ebene (dargestellt durch das Symbol C->) kann in der folgenden Weise (vgl. [5]) interpretiert werden:

sk1 C-> sk2 gndw: Die mentale "Überprüfung", ob sk1 eine Situation re- präsentiert, beinhaltet alle mentalen Prozeduren, die für die "Überprüfung der Repräsentation dieser Si- tuation durch sk2 erfolgen.

Ein einfaches Beispiel soll die Zurückführung der inferentiellen Bezie- hungen zwischen LKs auf solche zwischen SKs und die Interpretation des Konzeptuellen Entailments (C->) illustrieren: (Hierbei wird durch Prä- dikatsoperatoren (PO) der spezielle Typ von PKs bezeichnet, der ein PK auf ein neues abbildet.) PKs: rennen, bewegen; PO: schnell

Aus "rennen" folgt "schnelles bewegen"
Inferenz: rennen(x) C-> (schnell (bewegen)) (x)

Im Hinblick auf Konzeptuelles Eintailment besagt dieses Beispiel, daß
man nur dann von einer Situation sagen kann, daß "jemand rennt", falls
man festgestellt hat, daß "dieser jemand sich schnell bewegt". Vermittels derartiger inferentieller Beziehungen zwischen SKs lassen sich Bedeutungsbeziehungen zwischen Worten (bzw. Lexemen) beschreiben, etwa in
der Art der Carnap'schen [6] Bedeutungspostulate. Wir wollen einige
auf den ersten Blick einfache Beispiele untersuchen. So gehört etwa die
folgende inferentielle Beziehung zum Wissen eines Sprecher-Hörers:

(1)   älter(x,y) & älter(y,z) C-> älter(x,z)

oder in der für Relationen bekannten Terminologie "älter ist transitiv".
(Anm.: Die Vermutung, daß alle Komparative diese Eigenschaft besitzen,
erweist sich - siehe [7] - als falsch.) Diese Eigenschaft des prädikativen (bzw. lexikalischen) Konzepts "älter" nur als eine inferentielle
Beziehung zwischen SKs festzumachen (der Ansatz Millers) erscheint nicht
adäquat zu sein, es ist vielmehr davon auszugehen, daß zur kognitiven
Ausstattung des Menschen ein Wissen der Art

(2)   transitiv (älter)

existiert. Ein wesentliches Argument für die kognitive Realität von (2)
ist das Prinzip kognitiver Ökonomie, das auf diesen Fall angewendet besagt: es ist ökonomischer, ein Konzept der Transitivität zu besitzen
(bzw. zu entwickeln, s.u.), und dieses auf die jeweiligen PKs anzuwenden. Derartige Konzepte, die als Prädikatsattribute (PATT) bezeichnet
werden sollen, lassen sich in der üblichen logischen Schreibweise (jedoch mit anderem Variablentyp) formulieren:

(3)   Transitiv (p) : p(x,y) & p(y,z) C-> p(x,z)

Einem PK das Attribut "transitiv" zuzusprechen, bedeutet also, eine
spezielle Regel für Konzeptuelles Entailment gemäß des Schemas (3) für
dieses PK anzusetzen; nach diesem Verfahren ist offensichtlicherweise
(1) aus (2) und (3) generierbar.

Neben PATTs, die auf ein PK zutreffen (und die im weiteren noch ausführlicher dargestellt werden), existieren ähnliche Beziehungen zwischen
mehreren PKs, etwa durch die folgenden Repräsentationen dargestellt:

(4)   convers (jünger, älter)

(5)   convers (p,q) : p(x,y) C-> q(y,x) , q(x,y) C-> p(y,x)

(6)   jünger(x,y) C-> älter(y,x) , älter(x,y) C-> jünger(y,x)

Wieder wird die inferentielle Beziehung zwischen SKs (6) vermittels
eines Inferenzenschemas (5) aus einer Beziehung (Relation) (4) zwischen
LKs erzeugt. Die Schwierigkeiten, die Menschen (aber auch "intelligente
Systeme") mit derartigen PATT-Konzepten haben können, seien an der folgenden Konzeptzuschreibung erläutert:

(7) transitiv (westlich) , transitiv (östlich)
     convers (westlich, östlich)
     antisymm(westlich) , antisymm(östlich)

wobei "antisymm" das Inferenzschema

(8) antisymm(p) : p(x,y) C-> not p(y,x)

zugeordnet ist. Der "kognitive Konflikt" tritt offensichtlicherweise
dann auf, wenn die Anzahl bzw. Art der "Transitionen" derart ist, daß
ein Ort, der aufgrund der Transitivitätsannahme östlich liegen müßte,
an sich westlich liegt. Es ist zu beachten, daß der Konflikt auch für
"östlich" allein, d.h. ohne das konverse PK, auftritt. Da auch "älter"
und "jünger" antisymmetrisch sind, in diesem Fall ein entsprechender
Konflikt jedoch ausbleibt, ist zu untersuchen, wann die Konstellation
"transitiv und antisymmetrisch" zu Konflikten führen kann und wann nicht.
Der wesentliche Unterschied in den beiden Fällen "östlich" bzw. "älter"
kann - wenn auch informell - dadurch gekennzeichnet werden, daß im einen
Fall die Transitivität "global" (und somit unabhängig von der Art und
Anzahl der Transitionsschritte) gilt, nämlich für "älter", bei "östlich"
jedoch nur von lokaler Transitivität gesprochen werden kann. Zu untersuchen bleibt, welche Eigenschaften die Trägermengen des PATT jeweils
haben, wobei die Trägermenge eines PATT zu einem PK in der folgenden
Weise definiert werden kann:

PK pk verfügt über die Eigenschaft patt auf der Trägermenge
TR(patt,pk) falls das zu patt(pk) gehörige Inferenzschema vermittels
aller Variablenbelegungen in TR(patt,pk) gültig ist.

Erkenntnisse über den Umfang der Trägermenge für patt zum PK pk gehören
gerade zu den wesentlichen Informationen, die ein Mensch oder System,
das Sprache verarbeitet, besitzen muß. Das Beispiel des Attributs "transitiv" zum Konzept "östlich" zeigt, wie der Erkenntniszuwachs der Wissenschaft die Eigenschaften gewisser Konzepte verändern kann. Erst die
Ergebnisse der astronomischen Forschung und die hiermit verbundenen Än-
derungen im Weltbild (und spätere empirische Erfahrungen) machten den
Konflikt "transitiv und antisymmetrisch" für östlich deutlich.

Neben einigen Auswirkungen, die der hier skizzierte Entwurf von PATT-
Konzepten, auf eine Theorie des Lernens und maschineller Kreativität
haben kann (vgl. Abs. 6), sollen hier noch zwei Problembereiche kurz
erläutert werden. Zum einen ist eine Liste der PATT aufzustellen; wir
gehen davon aus, daß sich auch in diesem Bereich eine Reduzierung auf
einige Basiskonzepte wird durchführen lassen. (Auch hier dem Prinzip
der kognitiven Ökonomie folgend). Zum anderen ist eine Erweiterung bzw.
Übertragung der entsprechenden Konzepte für zweistellige PKs auf mehrstellige notwendig.

4. Die rechnergestützte Regelgenerierung

Ausgangspunkt für die rechnergestützte Regelgenerierung ist die oben erwähnte PK-Orientierung des Inferenzprozesses, die insbesondere zu einer Strukturierung der Regelmenge bezüglich der Operatoren führt. Entsprechend wird auch der Aufbau der Regelmenge an den "Hauptoperatoren" festgemacht. (Die Fälle von Regeln mit mehreren Prämissen und deren Zuordnung zu Regelklassen, die Unterscheidung Readtime/Questiontime-Inferenzen sowie der Bewertungsanteil der Regel, der den Inferenzprozeß steuert, muß hier unberücksichtigt bleiben).

In 2. haben wir darauf hingewiesen, daß wir zwei Klassen von Inferenzregeln unterscheiden. Die Unterscheidung besteht darin, daß entweder eine Eigenschaft (PATT) wie Transitivität eines Operators durch eine Inferenzregel expliziert wird, oder aber, daß die Beziehung eines Operators zu anderen Operatoren qualifiziert wird. In beiden Fällen werden Eigenschaften von einem (oder mehreren) Operatoren genannt. PATTs können als Operator-Operatoren aufgefaßt werden, somit als Eigenschafts-Operatoren, die wiederum Operatoren als Argumente verlangen. Die Menge der PATTs kann hinsichtlich der Stellenzahl der geforderten Argumente geordnet werden; entsprechend unserer obigen Einschränkung behandeln wir hier einstellige und zweistellige Operator-Operatoren. Das Attribut "transitiv" entspräche dann einem einstelligen Operator-Operator, während "konvers" ein zweistelliger Operator-Operator wäre, der die Beziehung zwischen zwei Operatoren kennzeichnet. PATTs mit mehr als zwei Argumenten sollen hier nicht ausgeschlossen werden, weisen aber mit zunehmender Stellenzahl eine umfangreichere und kompliziertere Semantik auf.

Eine erste vereinfachende Darstellung des Verfahrens ergibt sich aus dem folgenden Schema:

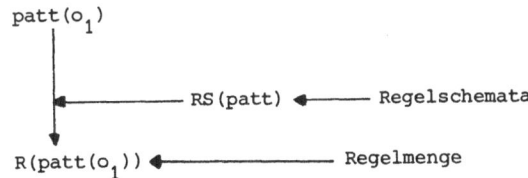

Abb. 2: Einfache Regelgenerierung

Dieses Schema beschreibt die Regelgenerierung für den einfachen Fall eines "beteiligten" Operators (o_1). patt ist als einstelliger Eigenschafts-Operator ein Attribut aus der Attributenmenge. Ist patt gleich der Symmetrie, dann muß o_1, über dem patt operiert, zweistellig sein, mit der zusätzlichen Bedingung, daß in dem Argumenttyp-Raster von o_1 beide Argumentstellen mit der gleichen Sorte ausgezeichnet sind.

Über patt wird aus einer Menge von Regelschemata das geeignete Regel-

schema ausgewählt und auf o_1 angewandt. Das Ergebnis ist die patt-Infe-
renzregel des Operators o_1 R(patt(o_1)), die nunmehr in die entsprechende
Regelklasse des Regellexikons eingetragen werden kann.

Das einem Eigenschaftsoperator zugeordnete Regelschema (es kann sich auch
um mehrere handeln!) hat auf dieser Ebene denselben Status wie die Inferenzregeln auf der in 2. beschriebenen Ebene. Es handelt sich um Transformationsregeln, die angewandt auf einen Operator unter Abprüfung der
geforderten Argumentstellenzahl und zugehörigen Sortenidentität Inferenzregeln generieren. Diese Regelschemata sind in einem speziellen Regel-
Schema-Lexikon abgespeichert und über die Eigenschaftsoperatoren zu Klassen zusammengefaßt.

Zur rechnergestützten Regelgenerierung gehört nicht nur der Transforma-
tionsprozeß, der Sätze aus RRL generiert, sondern auch ein Konsistenz-
check sowohl zwischen neuer Regel und alter Regelmenge, als auch zwischen neuer Regel und dem vorhandenen Faktenwissen.

Mit Aussagen wie patt(o_1) verfügen wir über Wissen über inferentielle
Eigenschaften der Operatoren. Wir können dieses Wissen in einer Wissensbasis (ähnlich der der Fakten) abspeichern. Durch eine Menge von Meta-
Regeln können wir die Beziehungen zwischen den inferentiellen Eigenschaften beschreiben. Ordnet man einem Operator (PK) eine neue inferentielle Eigenschaft (PATT) zu, kann nun mittels der Meta-Regeln überprüft
werden, ob diese neue inferentielle Eigenschaft mit den bekannten Eigenschaften des Operators verträglich ist oder nicht. Der Prozeß ist identisch mit dem des Eintragens neuen Faktenwissens in die Wissensbasis,
wo durch die Readtime-Inferenzen der gleiche konsistenzerhaltende Effekt
erzielt wird. Man verlagert lediglich die Forderung nach Widerspruchs-
freiheit aus der Menge der Inferenzregeln in die Menge der Meta-Regeln.
Darin liegen jedoch zumindest zwei Vorteile: Zum einen ist die Menge
der Meta-Regeln kleiner und überschaubarer als die der Inferenzregeln,
und zum anderen ist sie statisch, während die Menge der Inferenzregeln
dynamisch ist, in der Hinsicht, daß ein Erkenntniszuwachs über die Welt
sich auf die Menge der Inferenzregeln auswirken sollte, nicht jedoch
auf die Menge der Meta-Regeln.

Eine zweite Konsistenz-Überprüfung besteht darin, die inferentielle Eigenschaft des Operators in der Realität (hier in der Wissensbasis der
Fakten) zu überprüfen. Eine Möglichkeit zur Realisierung dieses Konzepts
besteht darin, die neue Regel auf das Faktenwissen anzuwenden. Werden
Widersprüche abgeleitet, ist entweder widersprüchliches Wissen in der
Wissensbasis, oder aber die Regel ist nicht adäquat. Der Prozeß ist einfach beschrieben: mit einer Ergänzungsfrage werden die Fakten der Wis-

sensbasis extrahiert, die bei der neuen Regel als Prämissen fungieren
können. Aus diesen leitet man die jeweilige Konklusio ab und untersucht
(mittels Readtime-Inferenzen), ob sich diese abgeleiteten Fakten wider-
spruchslos in die Wissensbasis integrieren lassen. Ist dies der Fall,
kann die Regel in das Regellexikon aufgenommen werden (siehe auch 5.)

Der Prozeß der rechnergestützten Regelgenerierung kann nun wie folgt
beschrieben werden:

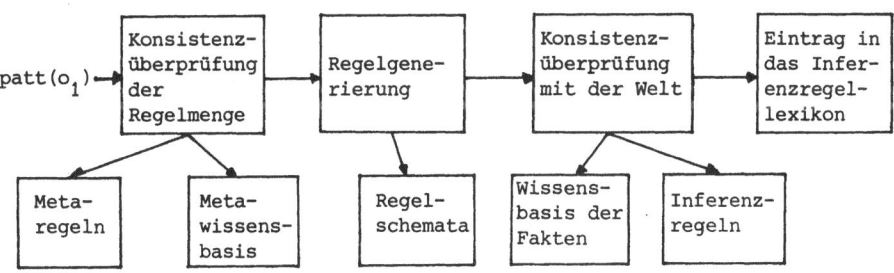

Abb. 3: Ablauf der rechnergestützten Regelgenerierung

5. Realisierung und Implementierung der rechnergestützten Regelgenerierung

Die im vorhergehenden Abschnitt erläuterte Konzeption einer rechnergestützten Regelgenerierung (vgl. insbes. Abb. 3) wird gegenwärtig implementiert und in das System BACON integriert. Der gesamte in Abb. 3 dargestellte Ablauf einer Regelgenerierung wird durch einen vorgelegten
Dialog gesteuert. Im folgenden werden die einzelnen Schritte (und verwendeten Systemkomponenten) skizziert:

Schritt 1: Durch einen Monitorbefehl wird dem System mitgeteilt, daß
eine Inferenzregel generiert werden soll. Hierdurch wird der Dialog ge-
startet. Der Benutzer wird gefragt, zu welchem Operator (PK) eine Inferenzregel generiert werden soll.

Schritt 2: Der Benutzer nennt den Operator (auch als natürlich-sprach-
liches Wort möglich). Das System sucht im Operatorenlexikon die für den
Generierungsprozeß relevante Information (Stelligkeit) und die Verweise
auf schon vorhandene Inferenzregeln (bzw. PATTs).

Schritt 3: Der Benutzer nennt das neue PATT zum aktuellen Operator. Eine
Liste der dem System bekannten PATTs und eine Beschreibung dieser Konzepte kann der Benutzer über eine Help-Funktion anfordern.

Schritt 4: Das neue PATT wird mit dem schon vorhandenen Wissen über den
aktuellen Operator verglichen. Hier ist vorerst nur eine Konsistenzprüfung vermittels explizit abgespeicherter Inkonsistenzbedingungen der Art
"INKONSISTENZ (symm.,antisymm.)" möglich. Falls Inkonsistenz entdeckt
wird, wird der Benutzer gefragt, welches der PATTs "korrekt"ist, das
neue, oder das hierzu inkonsistente.

Schritt 5: Falls die erste Konsistenzprüfung positiv verläuft, wird vermittels einer Transformationskomponente aus dem Inferenzschema zum PATT
die spezielle Inferenzregel des aktuellen Operators generiert und in
einem temporären Regelverzeichnis abgelegt.

Schritt 6: Die neugenerierte Regel wird auf Konsistenz zum Faktenwissen geprüft. Hierzu wird vorerst aus der Wissensbasis alles Wissen bzgl. des aktuellen Operators in eine temporäre WB übertragen. Anschließend wird über der temporären WB die inferentielle Hülle (H) bzgl. der neugenerierten Regel gebildet. Falls H(temp.WB) konsistent ist, wird die neue Regel ins Regelverzeichnis übernommen. Anderenfalls wird der Benutzer auf die Inkonsistenz aufmerksam gemacht und um eine Entscheidung gebeten (vgl. Schritt 4.)

Dieses gegenwärtig realisierte System stellt einen allerersten, in vielen Punkten noch unbefriedigenden, Anfang dar. Es ist auf die Unterstützung des Benutzers angewiesen und verlangt von ihm die wesentlichen Entscheidungen. Aus diesen Gründen ist es gegenwärtig nur als Hilfsmittel für den mit dem "Aufbau einer Welt" beschäftigten KI-Programmierer geeignet. Darüberhinaus werden bisher vom System wesentliche Inkonsistenzfälle nicht entdeckt. In den nächsten Systemversionen werden daher die folgenden Erweiterungen vorgenommen werden:

Schritt 2a: Es können in einem Systemdurchlauf auch die Beziehungen zwischen mehreren Operatoren behandelt werden, z.B. die Einführung der Beziehung "convers".

Schritt 3a: Bei der Konsistenzprüfung bzgl. der Regelmenge müssen vom System auch die Beziehungen zwischen mehreren Operatoren in Betracht gezogen werden. (Man denke daran, daß Inkonsistenz eventuell im Zusammenspiel zweier konverser Operatoren auftritt.) Hierzu soll ein entsprechend konzipiertes theorembeweisendes Subsystem eingesetzt werden. Zusätzlich sollen durch diese Komponente die Fälle, "in denen Inkonsistenz auftreten kann", ermittelt werden (etwa "transitiv und antisymmetrisch"). Der Benutzer soll dann auf die Gefahr einer Inkonsistenz aufmerksam gemacht werden.

Schritt 6a: Bei der Konsistenzprüfung bzgl. des Faktenwissens werden vermittels von Ergänzungsfragen die für die Inkonsistenz "gefährlichen" Fakten in die temporäre WB überführt und dort einer Konsistenzprüfung vermittels der bekannten und der neugenerierten Regel unterzogen. (Für das Auffinden der "gefährlichen Fakten" müssen geeignete Verfahren entwickelt werden.)

6. Ausblicke und abschließende Bemerkungen

Im folgenden werden einige Erweiterungen der bisher dargestellten Überlegungen skizziert werden:

Es soll ein Basisinventar von PATTs (sowohl für zwei- als auch für mehrstellige Operatoren) erstellt werden. Hierbei ist die Entwicklung von Konzepten der Art "2-3-transitiv" für mehrstellige Operatoren notwendig. Darüberhinaus sollen komplexe Inferenzbeziehungen, wie sie etwa im Beispiel "rennen - schnelles bewegen" (und allgemein bei Bedeutungspostulaten) auftreten, auf die Existenz von Beziehungskonzepten untersucht werden. Neben dem Grundlageninteresse, das hier für die Kognitionswissenschaft besteht, würde ein derartiges Basisinventar von Beziehungskonzepten den Aufbau inferentieller Systeme erheblich erleichtern, insbesondere, da Seiteneffekte (bzgl. Inkonsistenz) leichter erkennbar wären.

Für konsistente Inferenzregeln stehen zwei Typen der Verwendung zur Verfügung: einmalige Generierung und Abspeicherung im Regellexikon oder die Generierung bei Bedarf, d.h. Aktualisierung aufgrund des PATTs. Dieses Problem ist sowohl aus kognitiver Sicht (Welches Verfahren verwendet der Mensch?), als auch "System-Sicht" (Welches Verfahren ist effizienter?) zu untersuchen, und zwar durch Experimente bzgl. der (kognitiven) Ökonomie. Vermutlich ist eine Mischlösung, abhängig von der Kombination der PKs und PATTs, am geeignetsten.

Der vorgeschlagene Ansatz soll im Bereich "Erkennen von PATTs" verwendet werden. Über der WB werden Verfahren eingesetzt, die prüfen, ob die empirischen Daten mit der Hypothese gewisser PATTs übereinstimmen, etwa ob ein gewisser Operator transitiv sein könnte. Bei hinreichender Evidenz kann das entsprechende PATT dem Operator "probeweise" zugesprochen werden.Einige Probleme in diesem, äußerst spekulativen, Bereich sind: Wann liegt hinreichende Evidenz vor? Wann und warum werden Daten bzgl. eines PATTs ausgewertet? (regelmäßig?) Wie reagiert man auf spätere Widerlegungen der Hypothese? Untersuchungen hierzu können relevante Aufschlüsse über das kognitive Verhalten des Menschen erbringen (vgl. in 3. "östlich") und zu einer, wenn auch eingeschränkten, Kreativität von KI-Systemen führen.

Anm.: Die vorliegende Arbeit entstand im Rahmen des vom BMFT geförderten Projekts "Automatische Erstellung semantischer Netze". Wir danken den Teilnehmern der GI-Fachtagung über Künstliche Intelligenz für die ergiebige Diskussion, außerdem unseren Kollegen H. Gust und N. Klein, denen wir wesentliche Teile der Implementierung verdanken.

7. Literatur

[1] Habel, Ch. / Rollinger, C.-R. / Schmidt, A. / Schneider, H.-J. "A logic-oriented approach to automatic text understanding" in: Bolc, L. (ed.) : Natural language based computer systems . 57-117. München, Hanser, 1980

[2] Gust, H. / Habel, Ch. / Rollinger, C.-R.:Valuating transformations and inferences . Fachbereich 20-Informatik-Bericht : 80-6, Techn. Universität Berlin, 1980

[3] Sridharan, N.S. (ed.) : AIMDS - User manual - Version 2. Dept. of Computer Science, Rutgers University, New Brunswick, NJ. 1978

[4] Rollinger, C.-R. "Readtime Inferenzen für semantische Netze" in: Rollinger, C.-R./Schneider, H.-J. (Hrsg) : Inferenzen in natürlich-sprachlichen Systemen der KI. 115-150. Berlin, Einhorn-Verlag, 1980

[5] Miller, G. "Semantic relations among words" in: Halle, M./Bresnan, J./Miller, G. (eds.) : Linguistic theory and psychological reality. 60-118. Cambridge, Mass, MIT-Press, 1978

[6] Carnap, R. "Meaning postulates" . Phil. Studies 3. 65-73, (1952)

[7] Habel, Ch. / Rollinger, C.-R. "Zur rechnergestützten Generierung von Inferenzregeln / Inferenzen und Wortsemantik" . SNP-Report, Technische Universität Berlin, in Vorbereitung.

Expert Systems:
State of the Art and Future Prospects

Peter Raulefs

SEKI-Projekt
Institut fur Informatik III
Universitat Bonn
Postfach 1220
D-5300 Bonn 1, West Germany

1. Introduction

Knowledge-based systems, and expert systems in particular, have recently. gained significant economic and scientific importance because of
- ¤ a rapidly increasing demand for expert consultancy.
- ¤ tremendous cost reductions following the mechanization of expertise otherwise only available from highly trained specialists.
- ¤ accomplishments of advanced expert systems.

Furthermore, it becomes increasingly apparent that knowledge-based systems constitute an evolving tool for mechanizing fields in science and engineering that primarily rely on judgmental, experiental, and heuristic knowledge, and have so far been repugnant with mechanization, yet experienced slow growth in comparison with other fields.

This paper is intended to give a brief and introductury survey on the present state of knowledge engineering and future trends. In its present state of infancy, knowledge engineering withholds textbook expositions. The field consists of a growing number of expert systems. Apart from pattern-directed representation and search, there are hardly any general techniques for constructing expert systems. A thorough presentation of the field would therefore require a detailed and comparative analysis of various expert systems. As this is far beyond the scope of this paper, we merely try to work out some basic and unifying issues: Section 2 analyzes objectives for developing expert systems, followed by a sample of expert systems in Section 3. In Section 4, an attempt is made to work out some basic design principles for expert systems, as well as criteria for evaluating them. Summarizing conclusions are compiled in Section 5.

Notation. XP stands for (human) expert(s).
XPS stands for expert system(s).

2. Objectives of Expert Systems

There are primarily two objectives for developing XPS:
- ¤ To mechanize the activities of human experts.
- ¤ To have representations of fields of science amenable to mechanical manipulation.

This section analyzes these objectives and establishes criteria for determining the demand for XPS.

2.1. Consultancy Systems

XPS are intended to at least partially mechanize the activities of a (human)XP. The objectives for designing an XPS therefore derive from how we caracterize a human XP.

[XP] A (human) XP is a specialist for a distinguished **area of expertise**, and is **competent in consulting** a client by applying facts and techniques of the area of expertise. An XP is therefore characterized by
consulting competence consisting of the abilities to
  ◇ **understand** a client's problems which often arise outside the area of expertise of the XP.
    recognize from the queries of a client where applying own expertise may contribute to solve the client's problems.
  ◇ **transform** a client's problems into a model of the own area of expertise.
  ◇ **solve** a client's problems.
  ◇ **communicate** solutions to a client.
  ◇ **explain** the reasoning resulting in a solution to the client.
  ◇ help the client to **apply and integrate** solutions.

An XPS is a computer system mechanizing to some extent the activities of an XP. A **consultancy system** consists of a client conversing with an XP, with the XP aided by an XPS. There is a great variety in the extent to which an XPS may mechanize the activities of an XP. Total mechanization of an XP by an XPS requires mechanizing both expertise (i.e. knowledge and skills) and consulting competence. In most applications, however, it will only be possible or cost-effective to partially mechanize expertise and consulting competence.

The extent to which mechanizing consulting competence is desirable very much depends on the client. A client who is quite familiar with the area of expertise of an XP/XPS may ask only for a minimum of consulting competence, in contrast to a client who doesn't even know in which way knowledge and skills in the area of expertise may affect his own problems.

Mechanization introduces an additional difficulty: Mechanical systems operate on machine-oriented representations. Clients converse in natural or somewhat formalized technical language. To achieve the abilities comprising consulting competence, an XPS must therefore have the following capabilities:

◻ **Language Comprehension Capability: Understand** client's queries, **transform** them into internal representation, and **recognize** approaches to apply own expertise.
◻ **Solution Capability:** Solve client's problems where own expertise applies.
◻ **Answer Construction Capability: Construct answer** which explains solution to the client so that the client can understand and apply it.
◻ **Solution Explanation Capabiltity: Explain reasoning** resulting in the answer to the client so that the client may judge the reliability of the solution given by the XPS.
◻ **Solution Application Capability:** Help client in **applying and integrating** solution.

[Summary]. The activities of an XP aided or mechanized by an XPS
cannot be viewed in isolation. Instead, an XP/XPS together with a
client form a **consultancy system,** where they cooperate in finding,
evaluating, and applying solutions to problems arising from the
client's queries.

2.2. Determining the Demand for Expert Systems

   To determine demand and necessity for developing XPS, we con-
sider three criteria:
[**Economic Criterion**]   The cost-gains relationship.
[**Scientific Criterion I**]   Amount   of   new   insights   and   and
                                  techniques for mechanizing intellectual
                                  activities (**contributions to A I**).
[**Scientific Criterion II**] Benefits of having representations of
                                fields of science.

   This paper will not pursue the [Economic Criterion], but concentrates on the [Scientific Criteria]. In particular, justifying
[Scientific Criterion II] requires further explanation. We will
argue that the most substantial contributions of XPS will consist in
XPS substituting textbook expositions for both exposing fields of
science, and for being instrumental in their application and further
development. We start from four observations on the evolution of a
particular variety of fields of science. Our conclusions justifying
[Scientific Criterion II] will be based on these observations.

[**Observation 1**] In the history of science, those fields have developed most rapidly which allow the formation of theories to
represent the body of knowledge of such a field. Theory formation is
the most effective way of making knowledge both available and
applicable ("Am praktischsten ist eine gute Theorie" - A.Einstein).

[**Observation 2**] There are fields which are adverse to theory formation, as
¤ they comprise a large amount of isolated chunks of knowledge which
  are difficult to structure and cannot be abstracted s.t. they
  occur as instances of a few general principles.
¤ they typically employ heuristic techniques for reasoning and
search.
We call such a field a **diffuse field** of science in contrast to **well-
structured fields** allowing extensive theory formation.

[**Observation 3**] As knowledge of diffuse fields cannot be condensed
in theories, competence in a diffuse field cannot be acquired by
short and systematic training, but it is typically obtained after
extensive professional activity ("gathering experience").

[**Observation 4**] Many supposedly well-structured fields have diffuse sub-fields.
Examples: (1) Number theory is supposedly well-structured. But the
              sub-field of expertise about how to find proofs in
              number theory is diffuse.
          (2) The chemistry of large organic molecules is supposedly
              well-structured. But the sub-field of expertise on how
              to determine the structure of large organic molecules
              is diffuse.

From these observations, we conclude the following facts:
¤ Most fields of science contain diffuse sub-fields.
¤ Diffuse fields cannot be condensed in theories.
¤ Acquiring expertise in a diffuse field is extremely expensive.
  It is difficult to judge the reliability of expertise on a diffuse
  field.
  The development of diffuse fields is slow compared to the growth
  of well-structured fields.
  Developing applications of the expertise of a diffuse field is
  much more difficult than applying knowledge and skills belonging
  to a well-structured field.
  Human XP require extremely expensive training and perform worst on
  diffuse fields.

There are three main consequences for the demand for XPS:
I.   XPS should be developed for providing expertise and consulting
      competence on diffuse fields.
II.   XPS constitute instruments to further develop and apply diffuse
      fields.
III. The benefits of XPS increase with the accumulation of expertise
      which is both rapidly accessible and rapidly applicable.

3. Accomplishments of Expert Systems

To give an impression what can be achieved by XPS, we give a brief survey of successful XPS. This survey is by no means intended to be exhaustive.

Fields of Competence	Expert System	Area of Expertise	References
Medicin	MYCIN	bacteria identification & antibiotics therapy	[SHO 76]
	Digitalis Therapy Advisor		[SWA 77]
	PUFF	lung test interpretation	[KUN 78]
	INTERNIST	internal medicine diagnosis	[PMM 77]
	VM	iron-lung control	[FAG 78]
Chemistry	DENDRAL	identification of chemical compounds	[BF 78] [STE 78]
	CRYSALIS	structure of protein molecules	[ET 79]
	MOLGEN	molecular genetics	[FRI 79]
	SECS	design of organic synthesis	[WIP 74]
Mechanics	MECHANO	solving mechanics problems	[BUN 78]
	SACON	structural analysis consultant (for bridges, houses,etc.)	[BCEM 78]
Geology	PROSPECTOR	mineral prospecting oil prospecting	[HDE 78]
Plant diseases	Diagnosis of plant diseases		[MC 79]
Electric Circuits	EL	electric circuit analysis	[SS 77]
Programming	PECOS	automatic programming	[BAR 79]
	APE		[BOR 81]

4. Design Principles for Expert Systems

As it turns out in Sect.4.1, it is hardly avoidable to design an XPS as a **pattern directed inference system (PDIS)**. Therefore, this Section is actually a survey on how to design a PDIS. Very often,

the core of a PDIS is a **production system.** Production systems are
described in Sect.4.2, while Sect.4.3 mentions alternative
mechanisms for implementing PDIS. Finally, Sect.4.4 develops
criteria for evaluating the design of PDIS.

4.1. Basic Considerations

By our analysis of Sect.3, there are three requirements to consider when designing an XPS:
[RQ 1] XPS are intended to manipulate vast quantities of poorly
structured knowledge and skills. Hence, XPS require a
representation of knowledge and skills (=expertise) which
supports
  ○ rapid detection of expertise from situations where the expertise is immediately applicable towards achieving goals.
  ○ the acquisition of large amounts of new knowledge.
[RQ 2] XPS should incorporate all domain-specific reasoning
mechanisms and problem solving skills belonging to the
respective area of expertise.
[RQ 3] XPS should have capabilities for comprehending client's
queries, and for constructing, explaining, and applying solutions.
In this paper, we concentrate on design principles intended to meet
requirements [RQ 1,2].

Abstraction is the most effective method for representing large
amounts of knowledge. The two most important abstraction techniques
are **schematization** and **axiomatization.**

Schematization. A schema, or **pattern,** is a syntactic object to which
applying a substitution results in an instance of the pattern.
Hence, a pattern is a description of the set of all of its instances, called the **extension** of the pattern. In other words, **a
pattern is an abstraction of its extension.**

To illustrate the significance of abstraction achieved by
patterns we quote an example from [MIC 80] about chess end games.
Decisions for sequences of winning moves are based on **diagnostic
patterns** characterizing typical situations on the chess board. This
table compares the search space for small sub-domains with the
number of diagnostic patterns which suffice to decide on winning
moves.

Situation	Search Space	No. of caracterising patterns
King, Rook us. King	40 000	10
King, Pawn vs. King	100 000	20
King, Knight vs. King, Rook	2 000 000	30

Axiomatization. An area of knowledge is axiomatized by a **formal system** consisting of
- **axioms,** i.e. chunks of knowledge considered to be primitive.
- **deduction rules,** i.e. rules specifying how chunks of knowledge may be derived from each other.
- **meta-rules,** i.e. rules specifying how deduction rules may be applied, or altered and applied to achieve deductions in a goal-oriented way.

Pattern-directed inference systems (PDIS) integrate schematization and axiomatization, and form the core constituent of almost any XPS.

4.2. Production Systems
    Production systems are the most commonly occurring constituents of PDIS. We give a short and condensed survey on design principles of production systems.

4.2.1. Architecture. A production system consists of
¤ a **data base,** i.e. a system of syntactically uniform encodings **(data)** of chunks of knowledge.
¤ a **production base,** i.e. a system of **production rules;** a production rule is a pair <situation> -> <action>, where <situation> is a pattern, and the effect of applying a production rule is determined by the interpreter of the production system.
¤ an **interpreter** consisting of
  ◇ a **pattern matcher** matching data of the data base to <situation>-patterns of productions in the production base.
  ◇ an **executor** for executing <action>s, possibly changing data and production base.
  ◇ a **control** to select production rules to be considered by the pattern matcher and executor.

4.2.2. Recognize-Act-Cycle. A production system operates according to a recognize-act-cycle:
(1) **recognize:** determine a production rule from the production base which is **applicable,** i.e. the state of the data base is in the extension described by the <situation>-part of the production rule. The outcome of the recognize-phase consists of
  - an indication of an applicable production rule;
  - possibly bindings to match variables occurring in both <situation>- and <action>-part of the production rule.
(2) **act:** execute the <action>-part of the production rule determined in the recognize-phase, using bindings to match variables established in that phase.
The recognize-phase is carried out by control and pattern matcher, the act-phase by the executor of the interpreter.

    Often there are several applicable production rules. If the recognize-phase proposes several applicable production rules, the interpreter control has to decide which rule is to be executed (see

4.2.5)

4.2.3. Direction of derivations. Production systems may work in **forward or backward direction.**

In the forward direction, production rules are applied whenever the <situation>-part is satisfied, regardless whether effects of the <action>s are desirable or not. The danger of this forward reasoning strategy is that production rules may generate new data added to the data base, although such data are irrelevant to reach an intended goal state.

Backward reasoning first considers a goal situation of the data base, and determines which production rule(s) appear(s) to be most suitable to approach this goal given the current state. Having decided on such a rule, applying this rule now requires that the data base satisfies the <situation>-part of the rule. If this is not so, we obtain a **subgoal** and backward reasoning again is applied to reach this subgoal. Upon having reached an applicable production rule, the reverse of the sequence of rules that have been selected so far constitutes a **plan** s.t. executing the plan achieves the intended goal.

Backward reasoning has the advantage of being **goal-oriented,** i.e. it avoids littering the data base with irrelevant data that forward reasoning might produce. Another advantage of backward reasoning is that it is a strategy to avoid applying failing sequences of production rules in derivations with data base states where several production rules apply. A disadvantage of backward reasoning is that it constitutes a rather inflexible control mechanism. In practise, one often chooses a **mixed strategy** using both forward and backward reasoning.

4.2.4. Structure of the Data Base. The simplest way of constructing a data base consists of assembling a collection of encodings of chunks of knowledge. Such a collection may be implemented in a standard way, e.g. providing quick access using hash coded keys. However, structuring a data base may itself be part of knowledge representation. As an example, data items may be stored at nodes of trees s.t. access to data requires traversing the tree along paths starting at the root; the ancestor relationship of data items may then be used for representing semantic properties.

4.2.5. Control. The control part of the interpreter, i.e. the mechanism for controlling the application of production rules, is of crucial influence on the performance of a production system. There are two basic problems to solve when designing the control of an interpreter:
¤ **selection** of production rules to be processed by the recognition-act-cycle.
¤ **conflict resolution,** i.e. deciding which rule is to be applied after several rules have been recognized to be applicable.

4.2.5.1. Selection mechanisms. The main objective of selecting production rules for processing by the recognize-act-cycle is to avoid the inspection of inapplicable production rules. The rule selection phase may present just one, or a possibly structured collection of production rules to the recognize-act-cycle.

A coarse way of avoiding unwanted inspection of production rules consists in **decomposing the production base into several production bases,** and control access to a production base as a function of the current state of the production system. This technique often arises from decomposing the area of expertise s.t. each production base becomes a **domain expert.** If the effects of different domain experts are either independent of each other, or are reasonably coordinated, putting interpreters on different processors results in a system of **communicating production systems.**

If in a single production base several production rules are applicable, If in a single production base several production rules are applicable, there are three basic strategies to proceed:
(1) **First-encounter-strategy:** Select the production rule which happens to be the first being encountered when testing for applicability. For this strategy, production rules are often implemented as a lifo-stack {resp. lifo-queue} s.t. the most recently applied production rules will be inspected first {last} **(attention focussing)**
(2) **Conflict-resolution:** Collect all applicable production rules and employ some explicit conflict-resolution technique for making a choice.
(3) **Try all:** Execute all applicable production rules, resulting in several states which need to be worked on independently. Clearly, this srategy can only be pursued if a combinatorial explosion of paths can be avoided.

A production system **terminates** iff no production rule is applicable. Important properties of production systems ar **finite** and **unit termination.** If production rules are **term rewriting rules,** there are formal methods to check for these properties [HO 80].

An important species of production systems are those employing **fuzzy reasoning.** Here, data items are tagged with a "certainty factor", and producdtion rules compute such certainty factors for all new data they produce. The <situation>-patterns of production rules will contain match variables qualified with requirements on certainty factors of the data to be matched. Executing different sequences of production rules all starting from the same state of the of the production system may result in asserting different data, each of them to some degree of probability. Deriving a datum by several sequences of production rules may be taken to be an indication for increased evidence, while deriving conflicting data may be viewed as diminishing the evidence of such data. From these considerations we see that for fuzzy reasoning, the Try-all-section-strategy goes along with a mechanism of **evidence amplification/diminuation.** An example of such a system is MYCIN [SHO 76]; other mechanisms for evidence amplification/diminuation are investigated in [WAH 80].

4.2.5.2. Conflict resolution techniques. If several applicable production rules have been determined, and the Try-all-strategy is not employed, a decision for selecting one of the conflicting rules must be made. One typically collects all such production rules in an

agenda, and applies a seperate **conflict resolution mechanism** to the agenda, resulting in a rule to be executed.

There are three classes of conflict resolution techniques:
(1) **Rule-ordering.** This technique assigns each rule a **priority value** s.t. applicable rules become linearly ordered w.r.t. priority value. Quite often, the following priority measures are applied:
 ¤ generality order:
     more "specific" rules are assigned a higher priority; here, a rule <sit 1> -> <act 1> is more specific than rule <sit 2> -> <act 2> iff (under forward reasoning) the extension of <sit 1> {backward reasoning:<act 1>} is included in the extension of <sit 2> {<act 2>}.
 ¤ recency order:
     rule R1 has a higher priority than rule R2 iff R1 has been applied more recently (corresponds to attention focussing).

(2) **Data-controlled conflict resolution.** Priority values are attached to items of the data base. A rule of the agenda is selected iff the sum of all priority values of matching data items is maximal.

(3) **Meta-rules.** Meta-rules operating on the production rules of the agenda decide which production rule is to be executed next.

4.3. Alternative Techniques for Realizing Pattern Directed Inference Systems

Because of its central importance, different techniques for realizing pattern directed inference have emerged independently from various sub-fields of AI. The following is a list of some such techniques:
(1) **Horn-clause deductions.** A Horn clause L <= L1 & L2 & ...& Ln consists of literals (atomic predicate calculus formulas) forming an implication with a conjunction of literals being the premise, and a single literal being the conclusions. In disjunctive form, the above Horn clause is -L or L1 or Ln. Such a Horn clause can be interpreted as a production rule with premise and conclusion [WAR 77] employ resolution theorem-provers to interpret Horn clauses with backward reasoning.

(2) **PLANNER consequent/antecedent theorems** [HEW 72] are procedural implementations of predicate calculus implications interpreted as production rules.

(3) **Augmented Transition Networks** [WOO 70] consisting of states as nodes, and having production rules attached to the edges can be utilized as a control mechanism s.t. traversing an ATN consists of executing state transforming production rules attached to the edges being traversed.

(4) **Agents** [FRV 81] provide a way of realizing systems of communicating concurrent production systems.

4.4. Criteria for Evaluating Pattern Directed Inference Systems

Which mechanisms support the development of PDIS at minimal

cost, yet achieving maximal performance? This section discusses such mechanisms and criteria to evaluate them.

4.4.1. Constructive criteria. High performance while minimizing development costs is primarily achieved by adhering to the following constructive criteria.

¤ **Performance.**
   (1) **Completeness** of results produced by a PDIS depends on
      (1.1) the completeness of the knowledge base. To achieve this is a problem of **knowledge acquisition** and **knowledge base validation.**
      (1.2) the completeness of the deductive machinery, e.g. production rules and control of a production system. Techniques for achieving this so far only exist for logical calculi and term-rewriting systems.
   (2) **Correctness** of results produced by PDIS
      (2.1) depends on the correctness of the knowledge base, again a problem of **knowledge acquisition** and **knowledge validation.**
      (2.2) depends on the correctness of the deductive machinery (see comment under (1.2)).
      (2.3) is supported by the **transparency** of the I/O-behavior of a PDIS from inspecting its knowledge base and deductive machinery.
   (3) **Efficiency** is especially affected by
      (3.1) efficient pattern matching.
      (3.2) **knowledge organization** in the data base s.t. unsuccessful search is excluded as much as possible.
      (3.3) the quality of rules and control, again a problem of **knowledge acquisition.**

¤ **Development costs.**
   (1) **Knowledge acquisition** is the overwhelming fraction in the development of a PDIS.
   (2) **Modularity** is the degree of separation of functional units, s.t. changes, deletions, and additions do not entail modifications of other functional units. As system development proceeds incrementally, lack of modularity greatly increases development costs.
   These constructive criteria imply the technical criteria discussed next.

4.4.2. Technical criteria. The above constructive criteria are met if the following technical criteria are satisfied: modularity, transparency, and support of knowledge acquisition.

¤ **Modularity.** The following observations provide guidelines for achieving modularity in production systems:
   (1) Modularity is increased the more chunks of knowledge are represented in single production rules resp. data items. The amount of knowledge represented in such chunks is often referred to as **granularity.** There is often a trade-off between granularity and effiency.
   (2) Backward reasoning supports modularity better than forward reasoning. This is due to the fact that conflict resolution can be better modularized for backward reasoning.
   (3) Modularity decreases the more control mechanisms are coded

into production rules. It is preferable to seperate control as e.g. in meta-rules, ATNs, agent-systems.

¤ **Transparency.** The transparency of production systems is usually low. The reason is that transparent I/O-behavior is achieved by stamping control structures on state changing actions (as higher programming languages do). Again, a cure for this deficiency of production system consists in introducing modular explicit control mechanisms as in meta-rules, ATNs, and agent-systems.

¤ **Knowledge acquisition.** There are several reasons for the fact that knowledge acquisition constitutes by far the most expensive part in the development of an expert system:
(1) Human expert knowledge is primarily heuristic knowledge with hardly any explicit documentation being available.
(2) Human expert knowledge is efficiently available whenever there is a need to apply it. This implies that acquiring such knowledge is best done by observing an expert when applying his knowledge. This is done by a **knowledge engineer** interrogating the expert and transforming answers and observations on answers into representations for the XPS.
Hence, knowledge acquisition requires heavy participation of human experts and knowledge engineers. There are two techniques for **mechanizing resp. supporting knowledge acquisition:**
 ¤ **Inductive inference,** as done in e.g. grammatical inference +BIE 766 program synthesis from examples and forming cartesian covers.
 ¤ **XP-dialogue in a generate- and test-cycle:** A PDIS generates examples and presents them to an XP for judgment. If the XP declines, the PDIS explains its reasoning to the XP, and XP and PDIS cooperate in correcting the PDIS. This technique is realized e.g. in TEIRESIAS [DAV 79] and APE [BOR 81].

5. Conclusions and Future Trends

5.1. Satisfying Demand
(1) Cost-profit analyses have not been made so far.
(2) XPS provide the only mechanized support for mastering diffuse fields. An XPS constitutes both a theory of a diffuse field and a tool for mechanizing the application of expertise. Given the slow development of diffuse fields, we expect XPS to inroduce a major thrust towards speeding up the rate of innovations in such fields.
(3) Measured in terms of performance, XPS belong to the most successful AI-systems.
(4) XPS contribute mechanisms towards mechanizing the following intellectual activities:
 ⋄ knowledge-acquisition.
 ⋄ abstraction.
 ⋄ knowledge-representation.

5.2. Current State
(1) Current XPS provide mechanized consultance for expert clients. They are not capable of consulting non-experts reliable.
(2) Advanced XPS exhibit competence on small , well-confined fields which exhibits that of human specialilsts.
(3) The expense for developing competent, advanced XPS is of the order of men-decades.

(4) XPS command representing and making available large amounts of small, isolated chunks of knowledge.
(5) Unsolved problems are:
  ○ knowledge acquisition.
  ○ techniques for making XPS cooperate with exparts and clients efficiently.

5.3. Future Trends
(1) XPS require vast and fast memories. XPS are less processor-intensive and more memory-intensive.
(2) Technologies for data bases and information systems become a sub-area of knowledge engineering. There is a danger that this will be recognized by research funding agencies too late.
(3) A next step in the evolution of XPS will be concurrently cooperating pattern-directed inference systems realized on multicomputers.

6. Bibliography

[BAR 79]   Barstow, D.R. An experiment in knowledge-based automatic programming.A J. Artificial Intelligence: 12(1979)73-119.
[BCEM 78]   Bennet,J., Creary,L., Englemore,R.S., Melosh,R. SACON: a knowledge-based consultant for structural analysis. Memo HPP-78-28/Stan-CS-78-699. Stanford Univ., Dept. of Computer Sci., 1978.
[BF 78]   Buchanan,B.G., Feigenbaum,E.A. DENDRAL and META-DENDRAL: Their applications dimensions. J. Artificial Intelligence: 11(1978).
[BIE 76]   Bierman,A.W. Approaches to automatic programming, in Advances in Computers (eds. Yovits, Rubinoff), Vol.15. Academic Press, 1976.
[BOR 81]   Bartels,U., Olthoff,W., Raulefs,P. APE: An expert system for automatic programming from abstract specifications of data types and algorithms. Memo SEKI-BN-81-01. Univ.Bonn, Inst. f. Informatik III, 1981.
[BUN 78]   Bundy,A. Will it reach the top? Prediction in the mechanics world. J. Artificial Inteligence, 1978.
[DAV 79]   Davis,R. Interactive transfer of expertise. J.Artificial Intelligence:12(1979)121-157.
[ET 79]   Engelmore,R., Terry,A. Structure and function of the CRYSALIS system. Proc. 6th IJCAI-79, Cambridge, 1979.
[FAG 78]   Fagan,L. M. Ventilator management: a program to provide on-line consultative advice in the intensive care unit. Memo HPP-78-16. Stanford University, Dept. of Computer Sci., 1978.
[FEI 80]   Feigenbaum,E.A. Expert Systems - looking back and looking ahead. Proc. 10.GI-Jahrestagung (Saarbrucken 1980), Springer Informatik-Fachberichte vol.33.
[FRI 79]   Friedland,P. Knowledge-based hierarchical planning in molecular genetics. Ph. D. Thesis, Stanford Unif., Computer Sci. Dept., 1979.
[FRV 81]   Fischer,H.L., Raulefs,P., Voss,H. CSSA: Design and implementation model for a programming language for asynchronous concurrent processes. SEKI-Memo. Univ. Bonn, Inst. f. Informatik III, 1981.
[HDE 78]   Hart,P.E., Duda,R.O., Einavdi,M.T. A computer-based consultation system for mineral exploration. Tech.Rept., SRI International (1978).
[HEW 72]   Hewitt,C. Planner: A language for ... Tech.Rept. TR-258.

M.I.T.A.I.-Lab., 1972.

[HO 80]   Huet,G., Oppen,D.C. Equations and rewrite rules: a survey. Tech.Rept.CSL-111, SRI International (1980).

[KUN 78]   Kunz,J. A physological rule-based system for interpreting pulmonary function test results. Memo HPP-78-19. Stanford University, Dept. of Computer Sci., 1978.

[MC 78]   Michalski,R.S., Chilansky,R. Knowledge-acquisition by encoding expert rules versus computer induction from examples. Int. J. for Man-Machine Studies (1979).

[MIC 79]   Michie,D.E. (Editor). Expert Systems in the Microelectronic Age. Edinburgh Univ.Press 1979.

[MIC 80]   Michie,D.E. Knowledge-based systems. Tech.Rept. UIUDCS-R-80-1001. Univ. of Illinois (Urbana), Dept. of Computer Science, 1980.

[PMM 77]   Pople,M.E., Myers,J.D., Miller,R.A. DIALOG: a model of diagnostic logic for internal medicine. Proc.5th IJCAI-77, Cambridge 1977.

[SHO 76]   Shortliffe,E.H. Computer-Based Medical Consultations: MYCIN. Elsevier/North-Holland Publ. Co., 1976.

[SS 77]   Stallman,R.M., Sussman,G.J. Forward reasoning and dependency-directed backtracking in a system for coputer-aided circuit analysis. J. Artificial Intelligence: 9(1977)135-196.

[STE 78]   Stefik,M. Inferring DNA structures from segmentation data. J. Artificial Intelligence:11(1978)85-114.

[SWA 77]   Swartout,W.R. A Digitalis Therapy Advisor with explanta-tions. Tech.Rept. MIT/LCS/TR-176, M.I.T., 1977.

[WAH 80]   Wahlster,W. Theorie, Entwurf und Implementation einer Erklarungskomponente fur approximative Inferenzprozesse in naturlichsprachlichen Dialogsystemen. Dissertation. Univ. Hamburg, Fachbereich Informatik, 1980.

[WAR 77]   Warren, D.H.D. Pereira,C.M., Pereira,F.C.N. Prolog- the language and its implementation compared with Lisp. Proc.ACM Symp. on AI and Programming Languages, Roches-ter, 1977.

[WHR 78]   Waterman,D.A., Hayes-Roth,F. (Editors). Pattern-Directed Inference Systems. Academic Press, 1978.

[WIP 74]   Wipke,W.T. Computer-assisted 3-dimensional synthetic analysis, in Computer Representation and Manipulation of Chemical Information, eds. Wipke, Heller, Feldmann and Hyde. Wiley Interscience, 1974.

[WOO 70]   Woods,W.A. Transition Network Grammars for Natural Language Analysis. CACM:13(1970)591-606.

An Expert System
for Implementing Abstract Sorting Algorithms
on Parameterized Abstract Data Types

Ulrich Bartels, Walter Olthoff, and Peter Raulefs

SEKI-PROJEKT
Institut für Informatik III
Universität Bonn
Postfach 2220
D-5300 Bonn 1, West Germany

and

Institut für Software-Technologie
Gesellschaft für Mathematik und Datenverarbeitung mbH
Schloss Birlinghoven, D-5205 St.Augustin 1, West Germany

Abstract

The APE (Automatic Programming Expert) system constructs executable and efficient programs from
- algebraic specifications of abstract data types, and
- abstract algorithms given as conditional term-rewrite-rule-systems with terms built up from operation symbols of the abstract data types involved.

The APE is an experimental system devised to develop methods for codifying a rather broad extent of programming knowledge required to construct implementations of data types and algorithms.

For data type specifications, the APE admits hidden operations, conditional axioms, and parameterized data types. The APE automatically implements algebraic specifications of all commonly known data types in terms of clusters of INTERLISP-functions. The APE constructs executable implementations of a variety of sorting and searching algorithms.

As an experimental prototype, the APE demonstrates that a **knowledge-based programming paradigm** provides a useful tool for partially automating an important phase of software development.

Keywords and Phrases. Abstract data types, automatic programming, codification of programming knowledge, expert systems, knowledge representation, production systems.

1. Introduction

A standard paradigm of software design is to start with abstract specifications, and to gradually expand, refine, and transform them to an appropriate level to obtain efficient implementations. This approach factors software design into the constructions of abstract specifications, and the development of more concrete representations. Such a factorization entails a corresponding structuring of design, validation, adaption, and maintenance of software systems.

We present the APE system (Automatic Programming Expert) which consists of two subsystems:
- ADTCOMP codes algebraic specifications of abstract data types as executable INTERLISP-programs.
- ALGCOMP constructs executable INTERLISP-programs from abstract algorithms given in terms of conditional term-rewrite rules with terms made up from operation symbols of abstract data types being implemented by ADTCOMP.

Section 2 surveys the structure of the APE. The specification language for abstract algorithms is outlined in Section 3. This paper concentrates on the ALGCOMP subsystem. The way the ALGCOMP works is explained in Sections 4, illustrated by a detailed walk through the implementation of an abstract program. The accomplishments of the APE in its present state of development are summarized in Section 5.

Further details on the ADTCOMP subsystem are given in [EKRT 80a,80b]. The APE is implemented in INTERLISP and is fully operational. The system with detailed documentation (in German) is available from the third author.

2. System Structure

The structure of the APE is summarized in the following illustration:

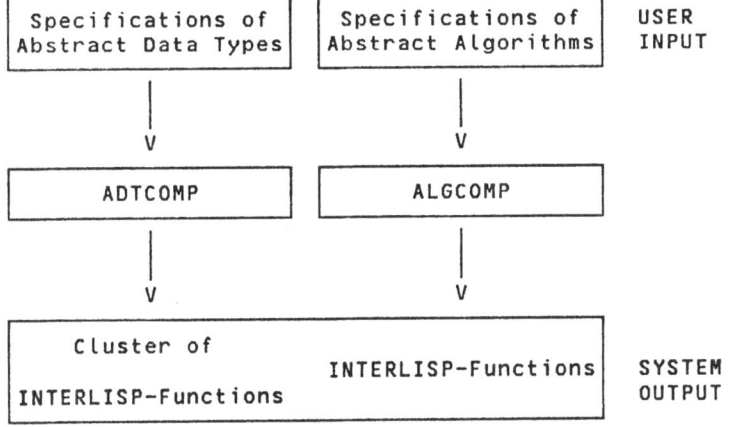

In both ADTCOMP and ALGCOMP, programming knowledge is codified in terms of production rules. Both subsystems contain **rule manipulation packages** providing an extensive interface for interactive experiments and modifications of the production bases. As has been experienced in the development of other expert systems, knowledge acquisition is the most serious problem. As we do not see a feasible way of acquiring programming knowledge automatically, an extensive dialogue and editing support turned out to be of crucial importance in the evolution of our system.

A **production system** consists of
- a **production base** containing **production rules**
- a **production control** guiding the selection of production rules.
- a **data base** to which production rules are applied.
Production rules operate on a data base. A production rule is of the form <test> -> <action>.
<test> is evaluated to a predicate which is satisfied or not by the data base. If the <test> is satisfied by the data base, the rule is **applied** by executing <action> on the data base. The effect of <action > is to possibly alter the data base. In many production systems , production rules may also change the production base (e.g. by adding/deleting production rules), or the production control. In APE, however, production rules only affect the data base.

The production control selects production rules to be checked for applicability and subsequent application. In the simplest form of a production system, the production base is just a list of production rules. and the production control moves through the list from one rule to the next. Initially, our production control used **agendas**. An agenda is a control program for sequencing the order of considering production rules, e.g. a regular expression of names of production rules and intermediate tests for branching. In the evolution of our system, however, more and more "control knowledge" in agendas was transferred to the organization of production bases, and our present system does not use agendas at all any more.

3.Specification of Abstract Algorithms

Specifications to the APE consists of
- **algebraic specifications** of all data types involved, and
- a set of production systems each of which specify an **abstract algorithm** .
The production rules of an abstract algorithm consist of terms and assertions built from operation symbols and sorted variables of the algebraic data type specification together with operation symbols denoting the algorithm and auxiliary algorithms being specified.

Abstract algorithms are specified in terms of the following syntax:

```
<abstract-algorithm> ::= <header><prod-system><comment>
<header>             ::= abstract algorithm
                         <fcn-name><formal-params-dcl>
                         { relations <relation> }
                         { preconditions <assertion> }
                         { external <fcn-name> }
<prod-system>        ::= prodsystem
                         <fcn-name><formal-params-list> =
                         set-of-<production-rule>
<production-rule>    ::= <assertion> -> <term>
<comment>            ::= (some explanatory text)
```

<header> introduces
* the name of the algorithm (a function name)
* declarations for formal parameters consisting of a sort name, an
  identifier, and an optional initial value. Formal parameters are
  partitioned into
  - user accessible parameter positions (must be supplied with
    actual parameters)
  - internal parameter positions (for internal recursive calls)
    which must not be supplied with actual parameters in a user call
    (internal initialization)
* preconditions on actual parameters (for user accessible parameter
  positions only)
* references to the external algorithms invoked in this algorithm.

A <prod-system> is a production system consisting of a set of production rules, i.e. test/action-pairs where tests are boolean terms,
and actions are terms s.t. all terms are constructed from formal
parameters and operation/function symbols of any of the abstract
data types involved, the name of the abstract algorithm (a recursive
application) and names of external algorithms.

4. The Automatic Implementation of Abstract Algorithms

The second subsystem of the APE is called ALGCOMP, and constructs
LISP-implementations of abstract algorithms given in terms of a
syntax as outlined in section 3.2. Just like ADTCOMP, ALGCOMP is an
expert system with programming knowledge being codified in terms of
production systems. In this section, we give an overview of the
structure of the system, and then explain how ALGCOMP works by
giving a detailed walk through the implementation of the selection
sort algorithm. Note that abstract algorithms are production systems
using terms constructed from operation symbols of abstract data
types. Implementations generated by ALGCOMP are based on implementations of all abstract data types involved, as produced by ADTCOMP.

4.1. System Structure

An abstract algorithm input is processed by ALGCOMP in three phases:

INPUT-Phase: The abstract algorithm is parsed and trans-

lated into an internal form. A user is supported in debugging syntax errors.

IMPLEMENTATION-Phase: This phase constructs a LISP-LAMBDA-form implementing the abstract algorithm.

LISP-Phase: The output of the previous phase is extended
by an interface according to the data given in
the <header>-section of the abstract algorithm
specification. The result is a definition of a
LISP-function which can be invoked by supplying data to the user accessible parameter
positions.

Only the IMPLEMENTATION-Phase incorporates specialized programming
knowledge in terms of production systems. This phase proceeds in six
successive steps:

STEP-1: The test-expressions constitute the left-hand-sides of the
productions of the abstract algorithm. Each test-expression
is decomposed to a disjunction or conjunction of literals,
i.e. atomic tests.
STEP-2: Each literal is converted to a LISP-form.
STEP-3: The outcomes of **STEP-1** and **STEP-2** are combined to produce
LISP-forms for all left-hand-sides.

The remaining STEP-4 to STEP-6 apply to the right-hand-sides (actions) of the production rules.

STEP-4: General observations about the structure of right-hand-sides
are made. Particularly, all **copying** decisions are made. This
is necessary because arguments in different parameter positions are independent of each other in the abstract specification. For example, if POP(s) and s (with s denoting a
stack) occur in different parameter positions, applying the
operation POP to s has no influence on the stack s at the
other parameter position. If, however, s is implemented as a
specific stack object, POPping this object may result in
encountering the POPped stack object, when coming across the
object implemented for s at the second parameter position.
One possibility to avoid such unwanted side-effects consists
in maintaining different copies of data objects at different
positions. To avoid unnecessary copies, the necessity for
making copies, resp. working with references without copying
is established in **STEP-4.**
STEP-5: Recursive calls to the algorithm are processed. In
particular, this involves substitutions and making copies as
established in **STEP-4.**
STEP-6: The results of all previous steps are assembled to construct
a LAMBDA-form implementing the algorithm.

4.2. A Walk through the Automatic Implementation of the Selection-Sort Algorithm

We consider the following input specification of the Selection-Sort
algorithm:

```
abstract algorithm SELECTION-SORT;
parameters          user OPENLIST[INT] OL;
                    internal OPENLIST[INT] OL1 :=
                            (INIT OL1 OPENLIST[INT]),
                            OPENLIST[INT] OL2 :=
                            (INIT OL2 OPENLIST[INT]);
external            MAXLIST, APPEND;
prodsystem SELECTION-SORT(OL,OL1,OL2) =
(1) { read(OL,1) = UNDEF ——> OL2;
(2)    read(OL,1) ≠ MAXLIST(OL)
       ——>   SELECTION-SORT(remove(OL,1),
                            add(OL1,1,read(OL,1)),OL2);
(3)    read(OL,1) = MAXLIST(OL)
       ——>   SELECTION-SORT(APPEND(OL1,remove(OL,1)),
                            EMPTY-OBJECT,add(OL2,1,read(OL,1))) }
comment SELECTION-SORT obtains the maximum of OL, adds this
        value to OL2 and removes it from OL.
        Then, SELECTION-SORT is recursively applied to OL
        until OL is empty.
        OL2 then contains the resulting sorted list!!
```

Omitting the conversion of the abstract algorithm to an internal representation in the **INPUT-phase**, we describe how the **IMPLEMENTATION-phase** generates a LAMBDA-form implementing SELECTION-SORT.

STEP-1. This step applies to left-hand-sides (lhs) of productions only. There is only one applicable rule which observes that all left-hand-sides are literal boolean expressions. It is also noted that the lhs of rule (2) contains a ≠-relation.

STEP-2. First, each lhs-expression is decomposed and searched for applications of external algorithms:

```
S2-1.    if lhs matches <*REL,*LEFT,*RIGHT>,
            and *LEFT invokes the agorithm
                being implemented,
            and *RIGHT invokes an external algorithm
         then
            L PREDICATE
                    ((REL *REL)(LEFT *LEFT)(RIGHT *RIGHT)

S2-1:Result. L2 PREDICATE ((REL ≠)
                           (LEFT read(OL,1))
                           (RIGHT MAXLIST(OL)))
```

A second rule S2-9 determines that ≠ is implemented as NEQ in LISP, yielding

```
S2-9:Result. L2 PREDICATE (FORM.(NEQ read(OL,1)
           MAXLIST(OL)))
```

Notation. Li resp. Ri denote the left- resp. right-hand-side of rule
i.

STEP-3. (No significance in this example).

The subsequent steps apply to the rhs of the productions of the
algorithm only.

STEP-4.
In its simplest form, a rhs is just an atom. This is detected by
rule 4-2:

```
S4-2.     if rhs matches <*ATOM>
          and *ATOM is a formal parameter
        then invokation of the algorithm evaluates to *ATOM.

S4-2:Result. R1 FORM       (OL2)
             R1 EVALUATES (PARAMETER)
```

Rule S4-1 observes that (2) and (3) contain recursive calls to the
algorithm:

```
S4-1.     if rhs matches <*ALGNAME(...)>
          then rhs contains a recursive call to the algorithm.

S4-1:Result. R2 EVALUATES (RECURSIVELY)
             R3 EVALUATES (RECURSIVELY)
```

ALGCOMP attempts to convert recursive to iterative structures. When
modelling a recursive call by an iteration, values corresponding to
parameters being passed in a call have to be determined. Very often,
data objects representing such values need to be copied to prevent
unwanted side-effects. In our example, in (2) and (3) a copy of OL
must be supplied as an argument of the operation read, as the remove
operation changes OL.

```
S4-51.     if a subexpression of rhs matches
              <*PARAM ... (*PARAM ... >
           and *PARAM is a formal parameter
         then replace the second occurrence of *PARAM
              with a copy.

S4-51:Result. R2 COPIES (OL)
              R3 COPIES (OL)
```

Finally, rule S4-9 prepares arguments of recursive calls for STEP-5:

```
S4-9:Result. R2 ARG1    (EXPR.(remove(OL,1))
             R2 ARG2    (EXPR.(add (OL1,1,read(OL,1))))
             R3 ARG3    (EXPR.(OL2))
             R2 ARGLIST (ARG1 ARG2 ARG3)
```

STEP-5. We now consider the arguments of recursive calls. Rule S5-1
applies to the simplest case that such an argument is an atom, and
this is true for ARG3. The action of rule S5-1 consists in attaching
the form (SETQ *FP *ATOM) to the corresponding argument, where *FP
matches the appropriate formal parameter, and *ATOM the argument itself.

```
S5-1:Result. R2 ARG3 (EXPR.(SETQ OL2 OL2))
```

However,in our case S5-1 results in a dummy assignment, and there is
a rule S5-2 deleting such assignments:

```
S5-2:Result. R2 ARG3 (FORM.)
```

Rule S5-1 also applies if the specification requires assigning the
empty object of the corresponding data structure. Then, rule S5-9
obtains the empty data object of the data structure, i.e. (OPENLIST
DO) in our example:

```
S5-1:Result. R3 ARG2 (EXPR.(SETQ OL1 EMPTY-OBJECT))
S5-9:Result. R3 ARG2 (FORM.(SETQ OL1(OPENLIST[INT] DO)))
```

Productions (2) and (3) contain recursive calls to SELECTION-SORT
which would generate procedure instances if the algorithm were implemented as a recursive procedure. This is detected by rule S5-31
and results in

```
S5-31:Result. R2 ARG1 (EXPR.(SETQ OL remove(OL,1)))
              R3 ARG3 (EXPR.
                             (SETQ OL2 add(OL2,1,read(X3,1))))
```

However, the recursive calls change OL resp. OL2 so that no assignment is necessary . S5-8 removes the assignment introduced by S5-31:

```
S5-8:Result. R2 ARG1 (FORM.remove(OL,1))
             R3 ARG1 (FORM.add(OL2,1,read(X3,1)))
```

Considering the other arguments, rules S5-31 and S5-8 also apply to
ARG2 of R2:

```
S5-31.    if call corresponds to a recursive instantiation
          and rhs has property COPIES with value *P
      then replace *P with X2.
```

```
S5-31:Result. R2 ARG2
              (EXPR.(SETQ OL1 add(OL1,1,read(X2,1))))
```

```
S5-8:Result. R2 ARG2 (FORM.add(OL1,1,read(X2,1)))
```

Calls to external algorithms are rewritten by rule S5-4:

```
S5-4:Result. R3 ARG1
             (EXPR.(SETQ OL (APPEND OL1 remove(OL1,1))))
```

STEP-6. The right-hand-sides are now assembled according to the
result of STEPs-4,5. For (1), STEP-4 has observed that R1 is just an
atom , so R1 is kept unchanged:

```
S6-2:Result. R1 FINAL (OL2)
```

For R2, and R3, forms for evaluating the arguments have been generated already. In addition, the decissions about copying arguments
need to be implemented now, and recursive calls to the algorithm are
coded by rule S6-1:

```
S6-1:Result.
R2 FINAL ((COPY OL X2)(remove(OL,1))
                      (add(OL1,1,read(X2,1)))
                      (SELECTION-SORT OL OL1 OL2))
R3 FINAL ((COPY OL X3)(SETQ (APPEND OL1 remove(OL,1)))
                      (SETQ OL1 (OPENLIST[INT] DO))
                      (add(OL2,1,read(X3,1)))
                      (SELECTION-SORT OL OL1 OL2))
```

Finally, left-and-right-hand-sides are compiled to an LAMBDA-form:

LISP-Phase. The LISP-Phase establishes an interface for calling the
implementation of the algorithm, following data and requirements
given in the <header>-section. In particular, the implementation
successively clears LISP-stacks s.t. garbage copies of parameters
are deleted. The result is that at run-time the function stack of
the LISP-system contains a top-level call to the algorithm implementation, together with just one copy of the COND-form independent of
the extent of the file to be sorted and the corresponding number of
recursive calls.

Notation: For reasons of easier internal use calls to data type
operators are converted into a LISP-executable form, e.g. read(OL,1)
is converted to (OL READ 1).

APE   4.Automatic Implementation of Abstract Algorithms

Result of the LISP-Phase:

```
<SELECTION-SORT
 <LAMBDA (OL OL1 OL2)
    (COND
     ((EQ (QUOTE OPENLIST[INT])
          (GETP OL (QUOTE PARAMETER)))
      (COND
       ((GETD (QUOTE APPEND))
        (COND
         ((GETD (QUOTE MAXLIST))
          (COND
           ((GETD (QUOTE COPY))
            (INIT OL1 OPENLIST[INT])
            (INIT OL2 OPENLIST[INT])
            <RPLACA (QUOTE SELECTION-SORT)
              (DSUBST OL (QUOTE OL)
                (SUBST <QUOTE (RETEVAL
                               (STKPOS (QUOTE SELECTION-SORT) -1)
                               (QUOTE (SELECTION-SORT NIL>
                      (QUOTE (SELECTION-SORT OL OL1 OL2))
                      (GETP (QUOTE SELECTION-SORT)
                            (QUOTE ALGORITHM>
            (APPLY SELECTION-SORT NIL))
           (T (PRINT "***ERROR*** AUXILIARY FCN" (QUOTE COPY)
                     "UNDEFINED")))
         (T (PRINT "***ERROR*** EXTERNAL" (QUOTE MAXLIST)
                   "UNDEFINED")))
       (T (PRINT "***ERROR*** EXTERNAL" (QUOTE APPEND)
                 "UNDEFINED"))))
     (T (PRINT "***ERROR***" OL "NOT OF TYPE OPENLIST[INT]")>>
```

Result of automatic coding:

```
        <LAMBDA NIL
            (COND
              ((EQ (OL READ 1)
                   (QUOTE UNDEF))
               OL2)
              ((NEQ (OL READ 1)
                    (MAXLIST OL))
               (COPY OL X2)
               (OL REMOVE 1)
               (OL1 ADD 1 (X2 READ 1))
               (SELECTION-SORT OL OL1 OL2))
              ((EQ (OL READ 1)
                   (MAXLIST OL))
               (COPY OL X3)
               (SETQ OL (APPEND OL1 (OL REMOVE 1)))
               (SETQ OL1 (OPENLIST[INT] DO))
               (OL2 ADD 1 (X3 READ 1))
               (SELECTION-SORT OL OL1 OL2))
              (T (ERROR 10>
```

THE FOLLOWING RULES HAVE BEEN APPLIED:
(S1-1 S2-1 S2-9 S3-1 S4-1 S4-2 S4-51 S4-52 S4-9 S5-1 S5-31 S5-4 S5-8
S5-9 S6-1 S6-2)

5. Accomplishments

In its present state of development, the programming expertise incorporated in the APE enables the system to automatically implement
a large amount of algebraic data type specifications, and some of
the standard algorithms in sorting and searching.

Data types. THE ADTCOMP-subsystem automatically implements all
algebraic specifications we could get hold of from the literature,
and many more in addition.
This includes
- open and bounded lists, queues, and stacks;
- sequential file structures;
- arrays and records of fixed and variable length resp. number of
  fields;
- tree structures.

In our experiments, ADTCOMP has successfully implemented 76
algebraic specifications of abstract data types. As illustrated in
the open list example, ADTCOMP admits **hidden operations** , **conditional axioms** , and **parameterized data types**. However, there are two
restrictions:
- ADTCOMP requires that all objects of a data type to be implemented
  are inductively constructed from elementary objects. For example,
  ADTCOMP cannot implement the ring abstraction.
- For parameterized data types, ADTCOMP does not check requirements
  imposed on actual parameter types (see [EH 81], [HR 81]).

Algorithms. So far the ALGCOMP-subsystem has successfully implemented the following sorting and searching algorithms (see [KN 73]):
- straight-selection sort;
- straight-insertion sort;
- bubble sort;
- merge sort;
- quick sort;
- Fibonaccian search;
- binary search;
- sequential search.

ALGCOMP is also successful in implementing some numerical algorithms
such as the greatest-common-divisor, least-common-multiple, and
factorial algorithm.

In applying this expertise, the APE is capable of generating systems
of programs which are implementations of abstract specifications. A
successful example is a management system for processing files of
personel data.

6. Final Remarks and Conclusions.

6.1 Interactive System Development and Theory Formation. The devel-
opment of the APE has been evolutionary, driven by considering more
and more examples, and feeding the programming knowledge necessary
to implement the examples into the production bases. To support
codifying and incorporating programming knowledge, APE has an extensive interactive user interface. This interface helps a user to find
out why APE failed, coding new rules and experimenting with them,
and finally changing meta-rules and the production control unit after inserting new rules into the production bases. The userinterface
is extremly important for upgrading the production bases: whenever a

new portion of programming knowledge has been fed to APE, it is usually in order to condense rules into fewer and more general rules.
Rule condensation actually contributes to the formation of a **theory
of programming** , and we expect such a theory to eventually evolve
from our investigation.

6.2. Accomplishments. Previous systems start at a much more concrete
level of data structures such as sets, collections, etc., and implement them at the somewhat more "concrete" level of lists, arrays,
etc. APE generates code from representation-free **axiomatizations** of
all structures previous systems could implement, and in addition
succeeded for about 70 other axiomatizations. APE generates clusters
of routines which may be mutually recursive. Previous systems could
not introduce recursions.

6.3. A Successful Paradigm. Considering the amount of work which has
been invested in its development so far, the APE is still in its infancy. Demonstrated accomplishments and experiments have shown that
with incorporating additional programming knowledge, the APE will
become a powerful tool in software development. Given the limited
success of the program synthesis paradigms (e.g.
[BI 79], [BS 77], [MW 79]) after a decade of work, we claim that the
knowledge-based programming paradigm supported by the APE is the
only approach which is likely to provide tools for substantially
automating phases of the industrial software development cycle. In
fact, we think that program synthesis and knowledge-based programming complement each other: Program synthesis (as in
[BI 79], [MW 79]) should produce abstract algorithms from non-
algorithmic specifications. Then, a system such as ours brings in
the expertise to produce efficient programs.

7. References

[EH 81]   Ehrig, H. Algebraic theory of parameterized specifica-
            tions with requirements.
            Proc. 6th CAAP, Genova 1981, Springer-Verlag (in press).

[EKRT 80a] Eigemeier, H., Ch.Knabe, P.Raulefs, K.Tramer. Automatic
            implementation of algebraic specifications of abstract
            data types.
            Memo SEKI-BN-79 (Nov.79), Univ. Bonn, Inst. f. Informatik
            III and Proc. AISB-80 Conf. on Artificial Intelligence.

[EKTR 80b] Eigemeier, H., Ch.Knabe, P.Raulefs, K.Tramer. An expert
            system for automatic coding of abstract data type speci-
            fications.
            Proc. 10th Annual GI-Conf., Springer Informatik-
            Fachberichte 33,1980, pp. 431-441.

[HR 81]   Hornung, G., P.Raulefs. Initial and terminal algebra
            semantics of parameterized abstract data type specifica-
            tions with inequalities.
            Proc. 6th CAAP, Genova 1981, Springer-Verlag (in press).

[KN 73]   Knuth, D.E. The Art of Computer Programming.
            Vol.3, Addison-Wesley, 1973

CONTEXT DIRECTED TRANSLATION

Werner Dilger
University of Kaiserslautern
Computer Science Department
D-6750 Kaiserslautern

Summary

The translator of the natural language information system PLIDIS is
described. It transduces natural language sentences into expressions
of the internal representation language KS. Some general problems with
natural language translation, mainly word ambiguity, are discussed and
the solutions for them within the PLIDIS translator are described.
Suggestions for further improvements are made.

0. Introduction

There are mainly two approaches to the translation of natural language
(NL) sentences into expressions of the internal representation language
of a system. The first one performs translation in one step which comprises syntactic and semantic processing. The second one partitions
translation into several steps, whereof the first step in general is
the syntactic analysis of the sentence. The first approach is mostly
used in text understanding systems (e.g. cf. [LR 80],[RS 79],[SL 79]),
whereas the second approach is preferred in question answering systems
(cf. [BB 80],[BK 80],[HH 80],[HR 80],[ND 80]).

In this paper I will deal with some problems and solutions for them in
a translation of the second type and compare them to the first type. I
will use as a representative for the second type the translation component of the NL information system PLIDIS (cf. [BK 80]). To make the
examples of the paper understandable I shall explain a few details of
the PLIDIS mini-world. This is the control of water pollution in some
region of the Federal Republic of Germany. Twice or three times a year
samples of polluted water are taken from the purification plants of the
firms in that region. These samples are analysed by chemical laboratories and the concentration of certain pollutants in the samples are
determined. The resulting data can be evaluated under several aspects.

1. A survey of the PLIDIS translator

The PLIDIS translator proceeds in three steps: parsing, translation by means of translation rules, and transformation by means of meaning postulates. These steps, together with their respective inputs and outputs are shown in fig. 1. The structure of the PLIDIS translator is similar to that of typical compilers for high level programming languages.

Of course, the translator differs from a compiler in details. To begin with the third step, this is a transformation step rather than a translation step, because syntax and semantics of intermediate KS and target KS are the same. KS is a predicate calculus language with sorts and λ-abstraction (cf. [DZ 78],[Zi 79]). To understand the examples of this paper it is not necessary to know the details of KS, it is enough to know first order predicate calculus. The two levels of KS differ from each other by the definition of single predicates. In general, the intermediate KS - expressions make a more extensive use of the syntax and semantics of KS, they are surface oriented and therefore contain some redundancies. Transformation into target KS - expressions is a kind of reduction which eliminates the redundancies (cf. [Zi 80]). The

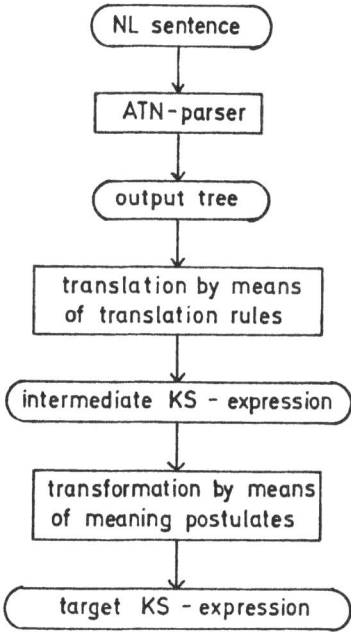

figure 1

meaning postulates may be viewed as production rules, the left hand
sides of which consist of patterns which are to be matched against the
intermediate KS - expressions, and the right hand sides consist of
patterns as well, in which all slots have to be related to some slots
of the corresponding left hand side patterns.

There is another difference between the PLIDIS translator and a compiler
in the output tree of the parser. This is a slightly modified parse tree,
therefore called "output tree". That means, the parse tree is modified
by some (in most cases only one) transformations in the sense of transformation grammar.

In the rest of the paper I will deal with the second translation step,
which yields an intermediate KS - expression starting from the output
tree, and which is in some sense the core of the PLIDIS translator. To
see how the translation rules work, let us first have a look on the
form of a typical output tree. Then we will discuss a special problem
with NL translation, namely the ambiguity of words. Hereafter we are
ready to define the translation rules and to sketch an algorithm for
the evaluation of the output tree by means of the rules, which yields
the intermediate KS - expression.

2. Output trees

Let us take as an example a question about the PLIDIS mini-world.

Welche Betriebe in Stuttgart hat Zimpel im Jahr 1979 geprüft?
Which plants in Stuttgart has Zimpel checked in 1979?

The question presupposes that Zimpel is a sampler, i.e. a man who takes
samples of polluted water from any firms, and it asks if Zimpel has
taken samples from any plants of firms in Stuttgart in 1979. The PLIDIS
parser produces the output tree of fig. 2 for this sentence. This is a
typical output tree of the PLIDIS parser. It has only height 3, i.e.
it is rather flat. Almost all words of the sentence are labels of nodes
which have the same depth. In fact, the parser only decomposes the sentence into a sequence of noun groups and prepositional noun groups and
puts the infinitive form of the main verb to the front of it. In a few
cases the height of the output tree increases, mainly if noun groups
or prepositional noun groups contain terms like

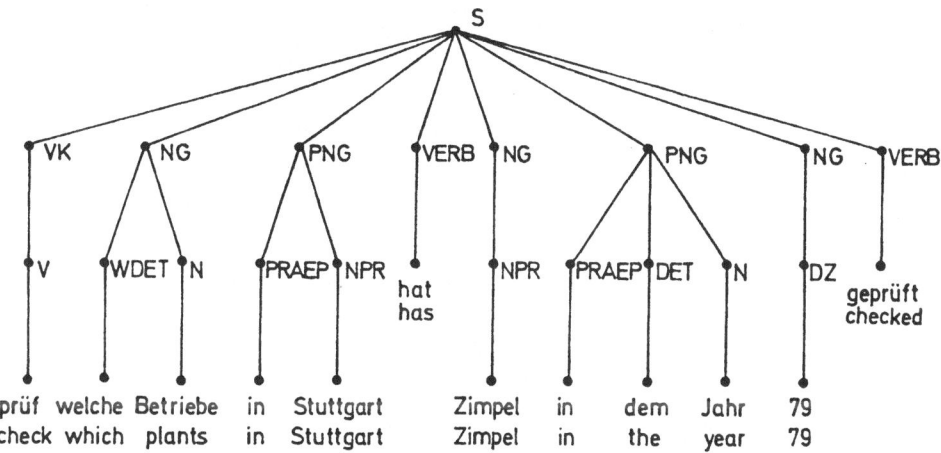

figure 2

the samples taken by Zimpel
the samples which Zimpel has taken

But such terms do not affect the general working method of the parser.

Compared with other parsing strategies the PLIDIS parser performs a rather coarse parsing. It has the advantage to be very efficient. A lot of sentences are parsed with linear amount of time. One could presume that the translation process starting with such a tree will become complicated and time consuming and would be more efficient if we had a richer syntactic structure. But the efficiency of the translation does not only depend on the syntactic structure produced by the parser. It depends also on how we overcome the problem of word ambiguity.

3. Word ambiguity

Ambiguity is a typical feature of NL words and even in such a small section of the real world as the PLIDIS world we have to cope with this problem. We will illustrate this by an example. The word "prüfen" (check) has in the world of polluted water among others the following two meanings:

(a) einen Betrieb prüfen ≙ eine Probe von einem Betrieb nehmen
    check a plant   ≙ take a sample from a plant

(b) eine Probe prüfen ≙ eine Probe analysieren
    check a sample   ≙ analyse a sample

At a first glance, to find out the meaning of "prüfen" we have to search
for the words "plant" or "sample" in the sentence. But this is not
sufficient. Compare the following questions:

(1) Welche Firmen in Stuttgart hat Zimpel geprüft?
    Which firms in Stuttgart has Zimpel checked?
(2) Wurde Lauxmann von Zimpel geprüft?
    Was Lauxmann checked by Zimpel?
(3) Welche Betriebe in Stuttgart hat die CLUA geprüft?
    Which plants in Stuttgart have been checked by the CLUA?

The first question asks of which firms Zimpel has checked any plants
and the second asks whether Zimpel has checked any plants of the firm
Lauxmann. In both questions "prüfen" has the first meaning. In the
third question "prüfen" has the second meaning because "CLUA" is the
name of a chemical laboratory and the question asks from which plants
the CLUA has analysed any samples. These examples show that some amount
of syntactic and semantic information is needed for the disambiguation
of word meanings.

4. Translation rules

From these observations it follows, that the translation rules should
contain syntactic and semantic conditions which are to be checked
against the sentence in order to obtain the correct translation of a
word. In fact, the PLIDIS translation rules contain such conditions. A
great part of the syntactic conditions are"structural conditions", i.e.
they ask for relations between the labels of nodes in the output tree
and are therefore tree structure-like patterns. In the PLIDIS translation rules the structural conditions are defined by means of the
"structural conditions" or "filters" of transformation grammar (cf.
[Pa 76],[Br 77],[Wu 79]). Another, equivalent, way would be to establish
them by means of "local constraints" (cf. [JL 77],[JL 80]).

The semantic conditions ask mainly for the sorts of the translations
of single words, noun groups, or prepositional noun groups. The sorts
become known as soon as these parts of the sentence are translated
(remember that the internal representation language KS is a sorted cal-

culus). This has an important consequence for the translation algorithm.

Now assume the sentence satisfies all conditions contained in a translation rule. Then we expect the rule to yield a translation for the
actual word. Indeed it does so, but this translation is not yet complete,
except it is a KS-constant. In general, it is a pattern containing
terminal and nonterminal symbols of the KS-syntax and a set of slots.
We will denote an arbitrary KS-pattern containing the slots $s_1, \ldots, s_n$
as $P(s_1, \ldots, s_n)$. To get a complete translation of the actual word, we
have to fill the translations of other parts of the sentence in the
slots. Therefore, for each slot there is defined a "filler rule" which
determines the translation of some part of the sentence which is required. This is done by the evaluation of syntactic and semantic conditions which have the same form as those in the translation rules. In
most cases the filler rules contain a default value, which is in general
a KS-variable. Though the conditions of translation rules and filler
rules have the same form, they are used differently. In a translation
rule they are used as predicates, i.e. if they are satisfied, the rule
yields a KS-pattern for the actual word. In a filler rule they are used
beyond that as a function which yields the translation of a node in the
output tree and has to be filled in the slot to which the filler rule
belongs. Now we will give a coarse syntax for the translation rules:

```
<translation rule> := (<translation statement list>)
<translation statement list> ::= <translation statement>|
                                 <translation statement>;
                                     <translation statement list>
<translation statement> ::= <condition> → <conditional pattern>
<conditional pattern> ::=  P(s₁,...,sₙ) (<filler rule list>)
<filler rule list> ::= <filler rule> | <filler rule>
                                       <filler rule list>
<filler rule> ::=  (<filler statement list>)
<filler statement list> ::= <filler statement> | <filler statement>;
                                <filler statement list>
<filler statement> ::= <condition> → <expression> | <expression>
```

By <condition> we mean the syntactic and semantic conditions of the
rules, <expression> is an expression containing terminal and nonterminal
KS-symbols, but no slots.

Let us consider as an example some part of the translation rule for
"prüfen". If the rule is evaluated in the context of our example question

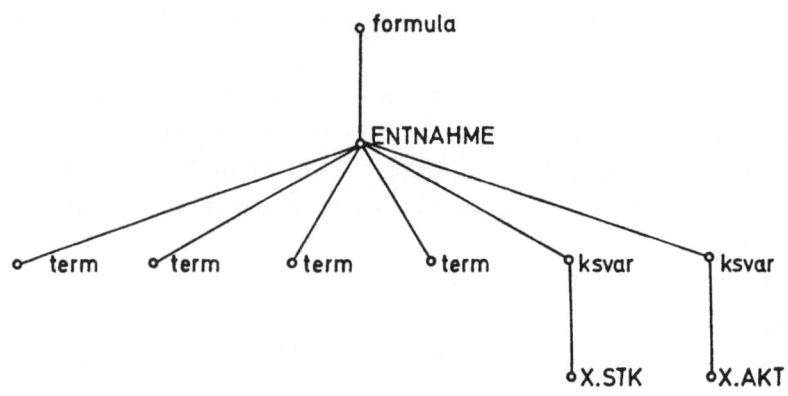

figure 3

we get a conditional pattern which is shown in fig. 3 as a tree-like structure. The KS terminal symbols are written in upper case letters, the nonterminal symbols in lower case letters. There are four filler rules belonging to the four nodes labelled "term", in turns:

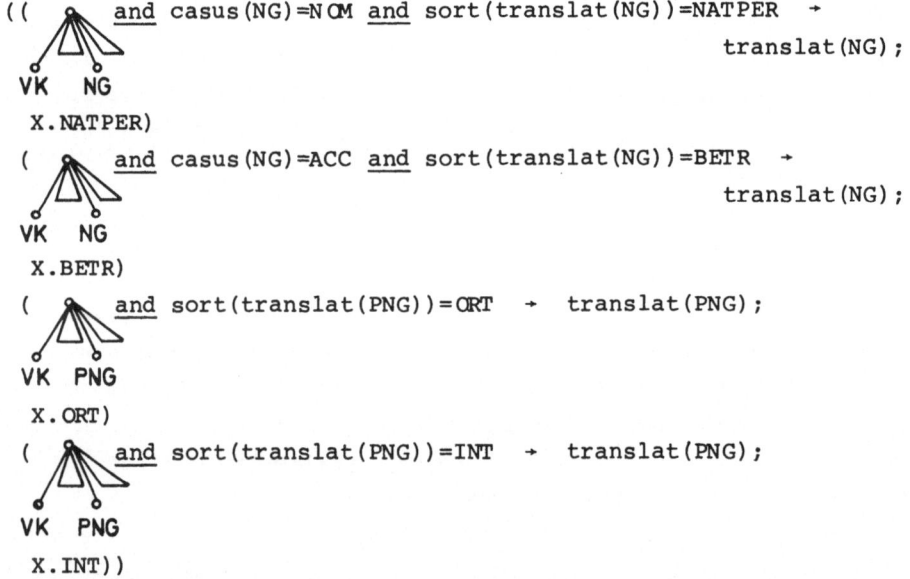

Each of the four filler rules contains a default value. The function "translat" yields the translation of a node and "sort" asks for the sort of that translation. The small diagrams represent structural conditions, where the triangles denote arbitrary subtrees. The amount of time for the evaluation of the conditions depends heavily on the evaluation of the structural conditions, and this, in turn, depends on the height of the output tree. This is another reason why the flat output trees increase the efficiency of the whole translation.

5. The translation algorithm

The main task of the translation algorithm is to evaluate the conditions of the translation rules. As we have seen, there is often needed the translation of another part of the sentence to complete the translation of the actual word. If the algorithm demands the translation of another node calling the function "translat", it may happen that this translation has not been determined yet. In the PLIDIS translator the output tree is evaluated from right to left and bottom up in order to minimize such cases. But they cannot be excluded in general, therefore the translation algorithm must be able to determine the translation of a node if needed during the translation process. For this purpose it has to be called recursively. But this leads to the problem of circular evaluation. That means, it may happen during the evaluation of the tree that for the translation of a node n_1 there is needed the translation of a node n_2 and for the translation of n_2 there is needed that of n_1 in turn. The same difficulty occurs within attribute grammars which are usually defined for programming languages. In fact the translation rules describe in a more global manner similar relations between the nodes of a tree as do the attributes and semantic functions of an attribute grammar locally. The attribute grammars are a quite general framework, therefore the PLIDIS translator can also be described within this framework, cf. [Di 80]. Now for the attribute grammars algorithms are known which detect circularities in the evaluation process a priori (cf. [Bo 76]), so that they can be eliminated in advance. These algorithms can be adopted after an appropriate modification for the PLIDIS translation rules.

Because recursive calls of the translation algortihm cannot be excluded, we propose another strategy for the translation, namely the opposite direction: top-down and left-to-right. Processing this way, the algorithm consequently obeys the principle to determine the translation of a node only when and only if it is needed. This strategy has the advantage that possibly some of the nodes of the output tree are never evaluated, because they contain redundant information even for the intermediate KS-level, and the translation rules are able to detect such superfluous nodes. This would further increase the efficiency of the translation. If the algorithm proceeds in this way, it passes through the example output tree of fig. 2 in a way which is sketched in fig. 4.

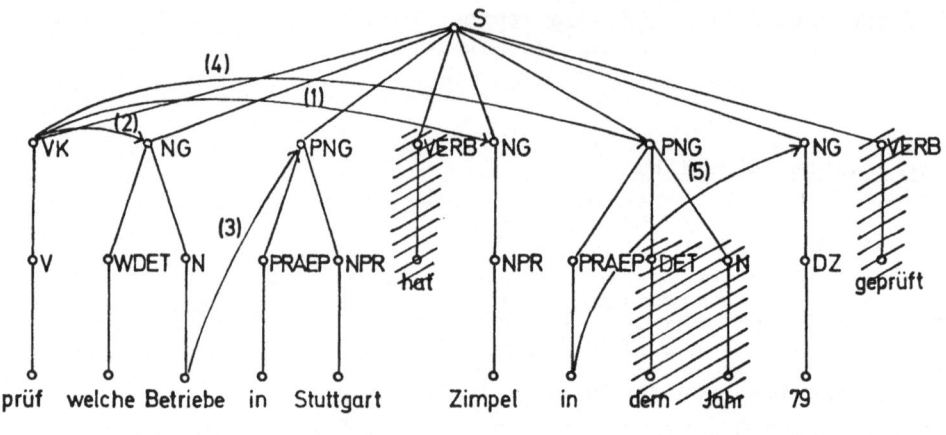

figure 4

The hatched parts of the tree were not used for the translation and were therefore not evaluated.

6. Comparison with other approaches

The PLIDIS translation rules are quite similar to Riegers and Smalls "word experts" (cf. [RS 79]) except that the word experts are defined as procedures. The starting point of Riegers and Smalls investigations is the same problem as that we had with the definition of the translation rules, namely word ambiguity. So Rieger and Small decided to direct the translation entirely by the word experts. These contain a minimum of syntactic and semantic conditions about the sentential context of a word and yield patterns which are incomplete translations, together with some questions, which require answers from the facts mentioned in the sentence, thus completing the translation of the word. This corresponds to the slots and filler rules in the translation rules. Rieger and Small suggest a translation in one step. There syntactic analysis of any parts of the NL sentence is performed only if it is needed for the translation. I suppose that in reasonably large translation systems based on word experts the total amount for syntactic analysis is nearly the same as in PLIDIS. At least separation of noun groups and prepositional noun groups as it is done e.g. in the system described by Schank, Lebowitz, and Birnbaum (cf. [SL 79]) will be needed. And this is essentially what the PLIDIS parser does. The advantage of the PLIDIS translator is its greater modularity and its more extensive use of the syntactic information.

References

[BB 80] Bronnenberg W.J.H.J./Bunt H.C./Landsbergen S.P.J./Scha R.J.H./
Schoenmakers W.J./ van Utteren E.P.C., The question-answering
system PHLIQA1
Bolc (ed.), Natural language question answering systems
München, Hanser, 1980, 217

[BK 80] Berry-Rogghe G.L./Kolvenbach M./Lutz H.-D., Interacting with
PLIDIS, a deductive question answering system for German
Bolc (ed.), Natural language question answering systems
München, Hanser, 1980, 137

[Bo 76] Bochmann G.V., Semantic evaluation from left to right
CACM 19, 55 (1976)

[Br 77] Bresnan J., A realistic transformational grammar
Halle/Bresnan/Miller (eds.), Linguistic theory and psychological
reality
Cambridge, Mass., MIT Press, 1977

[Di 80] Dilger W., Automatic translation with attribute grammars
Proceedings of the 8th International Conference on Computational
Linguistics, Tokyo 1980, 397

[DZ 78] Dilger W./Zifonun G., The predicate calculus-language KS as
query language
Gallaire/Minker (eds.), Logic and data bases
New York, Plenum Press, 1978, 377

[HH 80] von Hahn W./Hoeppner W./Jameson A./Wahlster W., The anatomy of
the natural language dialogue system HAM-RPM
Bolc (ed.), Natural language based computer systems
München, Hanser, 1980, 119

[HR 80] Habel C.U./Rollinger C.-R./Schmidt A./Schneider H.-J., A logic-
oriented approach to automatic text understanding
Bolc (ed.), Natural language based computer systems
München, Hanser, 1980, 57

[JL 77] Joshi A.K./Levy L.S., Constraints on structural descriptions:
Local transformations
SIAM J. Comput. 6, 271 (1977)

[JL 80] Joshi A.K./Levy L.S., Phrase structure trees bear more fruit
than you would have thought
Philadelphia, Ps, 1980
Abstract in Proceedings of the 18th ACL-Conference,
Philadelphia, Ps, 1980, 41

[LR 80] Laubsch J.H./Roesner D.F., Active schemata and their role in
semantic parsing
Proceedings of the 8th International Conference on Computational
Linguistics, Tokyo 1980, 364

[ND 80] Nishida T./Doshita S., Hierarchical meaning representation and
analysis of natural language documents
Proceedings of the 8th International Conference on Computational
Linguistics, Tokyo 1980, 85

[Pa 76] Pause E., Zur Theorie transformationeller Syntaxen. Generative
Kraft - Entscheidbarkeit - Analyse
Linguistische Forschungen 14
Wiesbaden, Athenaion, 1976

[RS 79] Rieger C./Small S., Word expert parsing
Proceedings of the 6th International Joint Conference on
Artificial Intelligence, Tokyo 1979, 723

[SL 79] Schank R.S./Lebowitz M./Birnbaum L., Parsing directly into
knowledge structures
Proceedings of the 6th International Joint Conference on
Artificial Intelligence, Tokyo 1979, 772

[Wu 79] Wulz H., Formalismen einer Übersetzungsgrammatik
Forschungsberichte des Instituts für deutsche Sprache Mannheim
46
Tübingen, G. Narr-Verlag, 1979

[Zi 79] Zifonun G., Formale Repräsentation natürlichsprachlicher
Äusserungen
Kolvenbach/Lötscher/Lutz (eds.), Künstliche Intelligenz und
natürliche Sprache. Sprachverstehen und Problemlösen mit dem
Computer
Tübingen, G. Narr-Verlag, 1979, 93

[Zi 80] Zifonun G., Levels of representation in natural language based
information systems and their relation to the methodology of
computational linguistics
Proceedings of the 8th International Conference on Computational
Linguistics, Tokyo 1980, 202

GLP: A Linguistic Processor

G. Görz, Univ. Erlangen-Nürnberg

GLP is a linguistic processor for the analysis and generation of natural language [1] which will be integrated into a speech unterstanding system [2]. GLP is an extension of the General Syntactic Processor [3], which implements a multiprocessing scheme. To quote Kay, it uses two central data structures, an agenda of tasks to be carried out, and a chart. The chart is a directed graph consisting of edges and vertices which represents the utterance being analyzed or generated together with its constituents etc. Both encapsulate completely the state of the entire processor at any moment during tis operation. The whole processing is controlled by a monitor which generates and administrates tasks. Tasks are selected according to scheduling rules, which implement the processing strategy, and carried out by an interpreter. They are generated out of the rules of the grammar which is a procedural one similar to an ATN. It can be seen as a directed graph in which the permissible transitions between states are represented by arcs. To each arc operations are attached which determine the applicability of the transition and cause side effects. The typical task is an attempt to apply an arc of the grammar to an edge in the chart. In the case of success, new information will be added to the chart. In order to process input data containing gaps and erros as it is the case in the analysis of continuous speech it is useful to introduce the concept of direction-independent island-parsing. The analysis starts at a word hypothesis with a high quality rating inside the utterance, and is continued by trying to expand this island on both sides by making predictions on words and word categories. To conduct these steps efficiently the grammar has bo be preprocessed into a certain inverted form. All edges in the chart, which are representing word and phrase hypotheses, carry a quality measure. A special category is introduced to represent gaps in the utterance which are to be filled later an via requests to the word hypothisizer. A constitutive characteristic of GLP's processing strategy is the close tying of syntactic and semantic analysis: First islands are constructed bottom-up; when a "semantic focus" is reached, case frames are applied to generate semantic hypotheses on phrase level. In a third step these hypotheses are evaluated syntactically in a top-down manner. Special tasks establish a connection to the inference processor (FRL) to conduct contextual inference.

[1] Görz, G., Beckstein, C., GLP: Ein linguistischer Prozessor IAB-125 (Tech. Rept.), RRZE, Erlangen 1980
[2] Hein, H.-W., Contribution in this volume
[3] Kay, M., Syntactic Processing and the Functional Sentence Perspective, TINLAP-1, p. 6-9, Cambridge, Mass. 1975

AI LANGUAGES AND AI MACHINES: AN OVERVIEW

Harold Boley

Universitaet Hamburg

Abstract

An overview of programming languages and machine architectures for
artificial intelligence is given. Five key very-high-level features of
AI languages are described in their relation to underlying high-level
features.   The realization of these language features by corresponding
modules of AI machines is discussed.

1. INTRODUCTION

Like other fields AI stimulated -- and was stimulated by -- the
development of programming languages and machine architectures tailored
to its specific needs. While languages for AI research, called
AI languages, are a long-established subfield of AI ([8], [10], [14],
[27], [34], [37]) the special interest in machines for AI research,
called AI machines, has arisen more recently, mainly for efficiency
reasons ([7], [11], [17], [28]). Of course, there is an intimate
relationship between languages and machines: When building a physical
or virtual machine one has to invent a command language to use it
(minimum: {ON, OFF}); for the implementation of a programming language
one must construct a physical or virtual machine with this language as
its command language. Furthermore, to realize a machine one can program
a piece of software in a language to interpret the machine commands;
alternatively one can microprogram a piece of firmware or build a piece
of hardware to interpret these commands. Often there are several layers
of languages and machines until a hardware machine is reached. It is
thus becoming more and more difficult to distinguish sharp layer
boundaries in computer systems (as it has always been in brains).
Therefore it is advantageous to treat AI languages and AI machines
together in a joint AI subfield, which may be called
AI languages and AI machines (or AI languages & machines), as initiated
in the KI-Rundbrief [11].

Since AI is a very programming-intensive field the subfield of AI
languages & machines is a very important one: Language tools with the
right expressive power and their efficient machine support are a
conditio sine qua non for AI. The need for special AI languages &
machines stems from the fact that many AI systems touch the limits of
computational tractability. It is therefore important to exploit the
entire spectrum of possibilities for improving their efficiency.   In
particular, the often neglected lower-level parts of this spectrum must
be dealt with systematically. In other words, the base components of AI
systems must consist of efficient AI languages & machines.

The area of AI languages & machines is of course related to other AI
subfields and to further computer science fields. Examples in AI
include 1. representation of knowledge (in particular: pattern-action
rules, knowledge bases) since AI languages can be regarded as
representation languages   and   2. problem solving (in particular:
heuristic search, expert systems) because AI machines can be regarded as
programmable problem solvers. Examples in computer science are
1. programming languages (in   particular: non-numeric   languages,

functional programming) which is a superfield of AI languages and
2. computer architecture (in particular: non-von Neumann architectures,
language-directed computers) which is a superfield of AI machines.

For the following discussion we will use the symmetric and exhaustive
scale (exemplified with five programming languages used in AI)

```
          lower-level      |          |       higher-level
/----------------^---------\ |        | /----------^---------------\
very-low-level | low-level | medium-level | high-level | very-high-level
CADR Microcode | Macrocode |      C       |    LISP    |     FUZZY
```

for language and machine levels. AI languages are mostly higher-level
languages, often very-high-level ones. In particular, PLANNER-like AI
languages [27] such as FUZZY are typical very-high-level languages.
However, very-high-levelness is not a necessary condition for AI
languages because, e.g., the AI language LISP ([3], [34], [52]) is
high-level and the LISP implementation languages C [21], CADR Macrocode
[29], and CADR Microcode [29] are medium-level, low-level, and
very-low-level, respectively; nor is it a sufficient condition for AI
languages because there are very-high-level languages which are at the
periphery of AI languages, such as symbolic manipulation languages like
MACSYMA [45] and there are other very-high-level languages which are
non-AI languages, such as set-oriented languages like SETL and business
languages like BDL [33].

In the following sections we will restrict ourselves to higher-level AI
languages. To characterize this class of languages we will use the five
interrelated features data structures, decomposition method, data bases,
program specification, and control structures. First we will
characterize high-level AI languages as programming languages using
sect.2: list data structures (decomposed by selectors), sect.3: property
list data bases, and sect.4: functional programs (with recursive control
structures). Building on these, we will then characterize
very-high-level AI languages as programming languages additionally using
sect.5: collection data structures,   sect.6: pattern matching
decomposition,   sect.7: associative assertion data bases,
sect.8: pattern-action rule programs,   and   sect.9: non-deterministic
control structures.

The five characteristic features of very-high-level AI languages can be
viewed as extensions and implementation bases of corresponding
high-level AI language features, as indicated by the rows of the
following table:

language features	high-level	very-high-level
data structures	sect.2: lists	sect.5: collections
decomposition method	sect.2: selectors	sect.6: pattern matches
data bases	sect.3: prop. lists	sect.7: ass. assertions
program specification	sect.4: functions	sect.8: pat.-act. rules
control structures	sect.4: recursion	sect.9: non-determinsim

Along with this characterization of AI languages we will characterize
higher-level AI machines as machines for the realization of the
corresponding language features: virtual machine modules for their
software implementation (mainly by LISP function definitions,
exemplified by traces using ´evaluates to´ arrows like "=>") and
physical machine modules for their hardware implementation (mainly by
non-von Neumann features, such as associative memories and
multiprocessors).

Although we may have under-emphasized some features (e.g. frames) and over-emphasized other ones (e.g. collections) we think that this characterization describes a basic, coherent kernel of AI language & machine features in which most of the remaining ones can be easily implemented and which can be regarded as a more precise (but still preliminary) explication of the AI language & machine concept. The reason for treating high-level and very-high-level AI language & machine features in an integrated manner (with the trade-off that some features have to be omitted) is the feeling that there is a need to bring together in one paper some of the AI language & machine material scattered throughout the literature.

2. HIGH-LEVEL DATA STRUCTURES: LISTS

Most AI languages -- beginning with IPL-V and further developed in LISP -- use lists as their basic data structure built from atoms ([3], [34], [52]). A list is a ´parenthesized´ sequence of elements, which can be thought of as a 1-dimensional array 1. of dynamically alterable length, 2. whose elements can have heterogenous types, namely atoms (numbers and symbols) and recursively embedded lists, 3. which is composed by means of constructor functions like CONS rather than through assignments to array elements, 4. which is decomposed by means of selector functions like CAR and CDR rather than through a position index. In the following we will use expressions, i.e. lists and atoms, as our only data type.

A flat list such as L = (1 LIST WITH 5 ELEMENTS) does not contain embedded lists, hence is directly isomorphic to a string. Lists like L can be composed by a constructor CONS as in (CONS 1 ´(LIST WITH 5 ELEMENTS)) => L (in ambiguous situations we use the ´quote´ prefix "´" to ´passivate´ expressions; here "´" prevents LIST from being interpreted as a constructor) and can be decomposed by selectors CAR and CDR as in (CAR L) => 1 and (CDR L) => (LIST WITH 5 ELEMENTS). In general, for arbitrary non-empty lists l there holds the mathematical relationship (CONS (CAR l) (CDR l)) = l. A nested list such as M = (1 (NESTED LIST) WITH (2 (OF ITS 5) ELEMENTS) EMBEDDED) contains embedded lists such as (NESTED LIST) and (2 (OF ITS 5) ELEMENTS). Lists are isomorphic to ordered trees. For example, M is isomorphic to the tree (note that we use ´stretched nodes´, i.e. depict nodes as horizontal lines from which the branches depart as vertical lines):

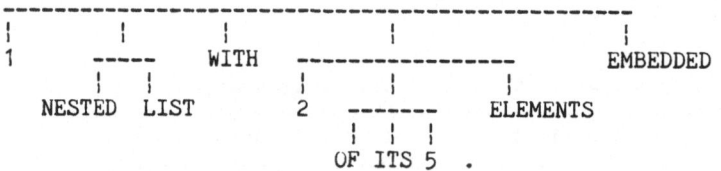

The implementation of lists is normally done by sets of pointer pairs. The pairs may consist of two consecutive words or two half words of a single word. The first (CAR) element of each pair points to an element of a list (pictorially, downward from a stretched node), while the second (CDR) points to the remainder of the list (pictorially, to the right inside a stretched node). The CDR of the last pair of a list is a dummy pointer to the empty list, (), identified with NIL. In this way pairs are linked to binary trees isomorphic to stretched node trees. For example, M is implemented as the following 26-pointer binary tree (pairs become CAR/CDR boxes containing "*" pointer tails; the CAR/CDR pointers continue as "|"/"-" shafts and end with "v"/">" heads, except for NIL pointers whose shafts and heads coincide with their "*" tails):

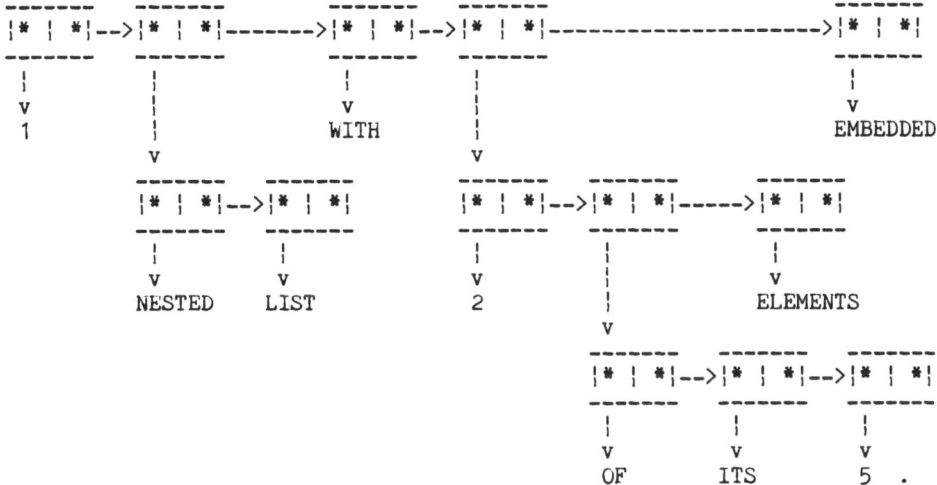

In a storage-saving technique which in the CADR LISP machine is called "CDR-coding" ([7], [24], [41]), array-like tuples of more than 2 consecutive pointers are used. These are pointers to list <u>elements</u> (CARs) only; the <u>remainders</u> (CDRs) of a list are stored in consecutive storage words (halving the pointer consumption). Thus the previous example can be compacted to the 13-pointer n-ary tree (trivially isomorphic to stretched node trees):

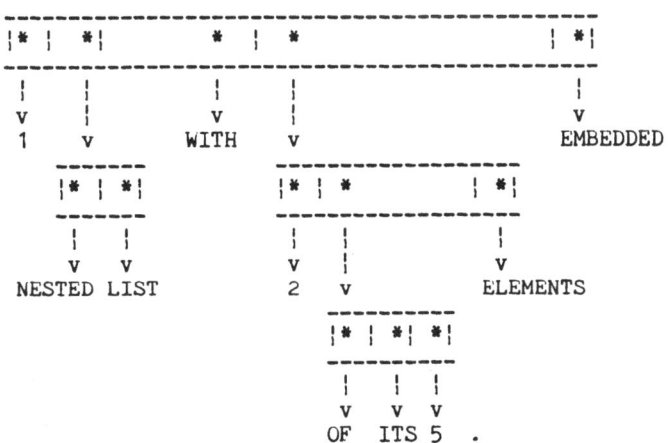

A "CDR-code" field (not ⸏ ⸏wn here) indicates whether a machine word is a final list element or whether its consecutive word is a CAR pointer (compacted representation) or a CDR pointer (ordinary representation). Some part of a compacted list which has to be modified by LISP's RPLACA-like functions [52] can be 'decompacted' to an ordinary list without changing the other parts by using "invisible pointers" [41].

List modifying functions often produce 'garbage' words, which are not pointed to by any pointer. These are periodically recollected for further use by an automatic garbage collector. Garbage collectors often use complicated algorithms and have posed the main problems in LISP implementations. There has been much work in improved garbage collectors recently, including algorithms that exploit the potential concurrency between garbage consumers and producers. Some of these new ideas have already been implemented in recent LISP machines. The CADR machine, for example, uses the real-time, incremental, compacting collector described in [6], which, however, seems to require a lot of main memory. Instead of thinking about ever new refinements of garbage collectors we should perhaps think about ways to more or less get rid of the very need for garbage collection in the future. An 'environment enlargement' approach would rely on storages and address spaces which are so large that the garbage scattered throughout them would hardly matter (the CADR machine, for example, can run approximately one day without garbage collection); in [50] something along these lines is motivated with the anticipation of very large and cheap "write-once" memories. An 'environment protection' approach would avoid the use of list modifying functions that create garbage or at least restrict their operation to special storage areas (related to the "areas" of the CADR machine); the replacement of list modifying functions by list copying functions is also desirable for reasons of program clarity and security [52]. The efficiency to be gained by not doing garbage collection would be paid for by some efficiency loss through copying. However, special copying hardware and cheap, fast memories may make this loss very small.

An even more radical deviation from classical list storage organization would be to abandon the usual pointer representation of lists (not only getting rid of the CDR pointers as in CDR-coding but also getting rid of the CAR pointers). The motivation is that the fixed size of address spaces will always be a problem, no matter how large they are: While the current generation of 16 address bit stand-alone minicomputers is interesting for rudimentary AI applications, mostly for getting experience with LISP [44], not much serious AI research can be done with a total of just 64 K words. The PDP-10, which for a long time was the principal AI computer, had 18 address bits (256 K words) which where completely exhausted by large systems such as MACSYMA [45] and KRL programs [9]. The CADR machine has 24 address bits (16 M words), a 64-fold increase which is estimated to be sufficient for the coming generation of knowledge-based AI systems. However, AI machines of the future may need address spaces as large as 32 address bits (e.g. VAX-11) or more. This permanent need for address space expansions in pointer-based systems has obvious disadvantages: It makes AI machines non-extensible because each expansion requires redesigns of the basic architectures; it hinders the construction of truly self-organizing, learning, and growing AI systems; finally the address space size can never be optimized for all kinds of programs (for some it will be too small, for some it will be unnecessarily large). Therefore instead of the usual pointer organization of list storage, pointerless (address space-less) list representations based on associative memories (see section 7) or (binary) tree-structured memories may become preferable.

3. HIGH-LEVEL DATA BASES: PROPERTY LISTS

Classical AI languages such as IPL-V and LISP are integrated with a symbol-oriented data base in the form of "description lists" (IPL-V) or "property lists" (LISP). These are used to characterize a symbol with an arbitrary (and dynamically varying) number of 'properties'. Each property is a pair consisting of an attribute and a value, like <COLOR GREEN>. The property list describing a symbol s with the attribute-value pairs <a1 v1>, <a2 v2>, ..., <aN vN> can be written as [s <a1 v1> <a2 v2> ... <aN vN>]. For example, a property list describing the symbol CAT could look like [CAT <ISA MAMMAL> <FEAR DOG> <CHASE MOUSE>]. A standard application of property lists in LISP is to store function definitions under distinguished attributes of function names (cf. section 4). Property lists can be regarded as associating an individual <u>s</u> with binary relations <u>a1</u>, <u>a2</u>, ..., <u>aN</u> in an object-oriented manner, in contrast to the relation-oriented grouping of n-ary relationships in the relational model for data banks. However, property lists can be generalized to "relation lists" [12] to permit an object-oriented grouping of n-ary relationships too, thus fully complementing the relational model. Instead of attribute-value pairs, relation lists use ´relation-arguments´ tuples, like <EXCHANGE US-DOLLAR DEUTSCH-MARK>. The relation list describing a symbol <u>s</u> with the relation-arguments tuples <<u>r1</u> <u>a11</u> ... <u>a1m1</u>>, <<u>r2</u> <u>a21</u> ... <u>a2m2</u>>, ..., <<u>rN</u> <u>aN1</u> ... <u>aNmN</u>> can be written [<u>s</u> <<u>r1</u> <u>a11</u> ... <u>a1m1</u>> <<u>r2</u> <u>a21</u> ... <u>a2m2</u>> ... <<u>rN</u> <u>aN1</u> ... <u>aNmN</u>>]. For example, a relation list describing the symbol DOG could look like [DOG <ISA MAMMAL> <CHASE CAT> <BARK> <BETWEEN CAT PONY> <BITE MAN LEG>]. Some AI languages use features which can be regarded as further generalizations of property lists, namely "frames" as in KRL [9] or FRL [52] and "classes" as in object-oriented programming [49].

The set of symbols with property lists constitutes a data base which can be accessed by means of functions for storage/update (PUT), retrieval (GET) and removal (neglected here). The call (PUT <u>s</u> <u>v</u> <u>a</u>) stores <<u>a</u> <u>v</u>> in the property list of <u>s</u>, superseding a possible previous value under <u>a</u>. The call (GET <u>s</u> <u>a</u>) retrieves the value under <u>a</u> of <u>s</u>. For example, to store the attribute-value pair <COLOR BLACK> in the CAT property list one calls (PUT CAT BLACK COLOR), to update <CHASE MOUSE> to <CHASE DOG> one calls (PUT CAT DOG CHASE), and to retrieve the value of the attribute FEAR one calls (GET CAT FEAR).

In LISP a property list for the symbol <u>s</u> is implemented as the even-length list (<u>a1</u> <u>v1</u> <u>a2</u> <u>v2</u> ... <u>aN</u> <u>vN</u>) associated with <u>s</u> via hash-coding (note that for general relation lists such an omission of the "<>" brackets would result in ambiguities). For this a hash function can be used which maps an arbitrarily-sized symbol to a fixed-sized number (the address of the property list) in a ´random´ manner, where the distribution of the numbers should be regular [30]. Since the calls of a hash <u>function</u> for the same symbol must always yield the same number, property list addresses can be found uniquely from their symbols (however, more than one symbol may map to the same address, so that the correct property list must sometimes be searched linearly among a -- usually small -- set of property lists). The data base functions PUT and GET first look up the property list of their <u>s</u> argument (using the hash function) and then process this list (using list processing functions).

4. HIGH-LEVEL PROGRAMS: FUNCTIONS

Functions are one of the most important language concepts in higher-level languages. In high-level AI languages such as LISP functions are even the only language concept, on which everything else must be built. A functional programming style is also becoming more and more popular in non-AI languages [5]. A first example of a function was the selector CAR presented in section 2; the application (CAR L), in short CAR:L, returned the first element, 1, of L (for 1-argument functions we will use an ´apply´ infix ":" to save a pair of parentheses). Often, however, functions as used in AI languages are applicable to varying numbers of arguments (for example, the addition function PLUS can be used in applications like (PLUS 5 7) and (PLUS 5 7 3)) and may not only return values but also yield side-effects (for example, the assignment function SETQ as used in (SETQ X 2) returns the value 2 and has the effect of binding X to 2). Function applications may be nested as in (CAR (CDR L)), in short CAR:CDR:L, which via (CAR

´(LIST WITH 5 ELEMENTS)) returns the second element, LIST, of L.

Transformation functions are used to transform expressions into other expressions. Predicate functions are used to test expressions for their properties, returning ´true´ if the property holds and ´false´ otherwise (in LISP-like systems the truth-value ´false´ is often represented by the empty list ´NIL´ and the truth-value ´true´ by the atom ´T´ or any other non-NIL expression). Special functions are used to evaluate expressions in non-standard ways. There are ´primitive´ transformation functions like CAR, CDR, CONS (see section 2), predicate functions like ATOM (for distinguishing atoms from other expressions), EQ (for discriminating equal from different atoms), NULL (for testing for the empty list), AND (for conjunction), and OR (for disjunction), and special functions like SETQ (for assignments) and COND (for conditional branches, using one ´clause´ argument (condition action) interpreted as ´if condition then action´, which is followed by zero or more such clause arguments interpreted as ´else if condition then action´). Based on these, more complicated named functions can be defined by putting a LAMBDA expression (for anonymous functions consisting of formal arguments and bodies) under the attribute EXPR of the symbol to be used as the function name (cf. section 3). Often, such definitions are recursive, i.e. the function to be defined calls itself in certain branches of the defining body, using ´smaller´ arguments. High-level AI languages such as LISP are characterized by their frequent use of recursion, even in situations where iterative constructs such as WHILE would be sufficient in principle. The reasons for this are the uniformity achieved by using only one control construct and the greater conciseness of recursive definitions.

As a first example we define a transformation function *APPEND (a standard LISP function) with two list arguments L and M; it transforms them into a single list which is the concatenation of L and M. Thus (*APPEND ´(A B) ´(1 2 3)) should return (A B 1 2 3). *APPEND´s LISP implementation is:

```
(PUT *APPEND
 (LAMBDA (L M)
  (COND (NULL:L M) (T (CONS CAR:L (*APPEND CDR:L M)))))
 EXPR) .
```

In English the COND body of this definition may be described as follows: If L is empty -- NULL:L -- the value of M is returned; otherwise -- T -- a list is constructed from the CAR of L and a recursive call of *APPEND with the CDR of L as its new L and the unchanged value of M.

The evaluation of a call like (*APPEND ´(A B) ´(1 2 3)) can be understood most easily by using substitution semantics, i.e. successively replacing (sub)expressions by their values (subexpressions to be replaced are underlined):

(*APPEND ´(A B) ´(1 2 3))   (A B 1 2 3)
         v
(CONS A (*APPEND ´(B) ´(1 2 3)))   (CONS A ´(B 1 2 3))
              v
(CONS A (CONS B (*APPEND ´() ´(1 2 3)))) > (CONS A (CONS B ´(1 2 3))).

More implementation-oriented semantics (still much simplified if compared with actual LISP implementations [3]) use a stack of function calls, where replacements of calls by their values take place at the upper part of the stack only, thereby pushing down older, uncompleted calls (nestings are marked by "\#\" placeholders; stack parts to be replaced are underlined):

```
---------------------------          ---------------------------
| (*APPEND '(A B) '(1 2 3)) |        | (A B 1 2 3)             |
---------------------------          ---------------------------
            v                                    ^              \
---------------------------          ---------------------------
| (*APPEND '(B) '(1 2 3))   |        | '(B 1 2 3)              |
| (CONS A \#\)              |        | (CONS A \#\)            |
---------------------------          ---------------------------
            v                                    ^
---------------------------          ---------------------------
| (*APPEND '() '(1 2 3))    |        | '(1 2 3)                |
| (CONS B \#\)              |   >    | (CONS B \#\)            |
| (CONS A \#\)              |        | (CONS A \#\)            |
---------------------------          ---------------------------
```

The left-hand sides of the evaluation traces show the growing of the
expression/stack with recursive function calls and the right-hand sides
show the corresponding shrinking with returned values. The traces
illustrate that recursive evaluations sometimes may need much storage
(and time) because the maximal growth expansion $g(f,a1,...,aN)$ of a
function f is dependent on f and its arguments $a1, ..., aN$. In the
still well-behaved *APPEND example g is linearly dependent on the length
of the list L, i.e. $g(*APPEND,L,M) = 1+length(L)$.

As a second example (which will be generalized in section 6) we define a
predicate function EQUAL with two expression arguments L and M; it
tests whether L and M are equal (returning T) or different (returning
NIL). For example, (EQUAL '(A 2 A (2 4 E) 4) '(A 2 A (2 4 E) 4)) should
return T, (EQUAL '(A 2) '(A B)) should return NIL. EQUAL's LISP
implementation is (we avoid using ATOM for NIL and EQ for lists):

```
(PUT EQUAL
 (LAMBDA (L M)
  (COND ((AND NULL:L NULL:M) T)
        ((OR NULL:L NULL:M) NIL)
        ((AND ATOM:L ATOM:M) (EQ L M))
        ((OR ATOM:L ATOM:M) NIL)
        (T (AND (EQUAL CAR:L CAR:M) (EQUAL CDR:L CDR:M)))))
 EXPR) .
```

In English this definition may be paraphrased as follows: If both L and
M are empty the truth value returned is T; else if either L or M is
empty the value returned is NIL; else if both L and M are atoms the
value is T if they are EQ; else if either L or M is an atom the value
is NIL; otherwise the value is the conjunction of recursive calls of
EQUAL for the CARs and for the CDRs of L and M.

Since recursive functions are so important in AI languages it is clear
that AI machines should make their evaluation as efficient as possible.
Normally, the stack used for such evaluations is a 'software stack',
i.e. is programmed by means of one register (top element of stack) and
ordinary machine words (other stack elements). Instead of this, one can
use a 'hardware stack', i.e. a very fast cache-like hardware buffer
(for some number of upper stack elements) possibly supplemented by
ordinary machine words (for remaining stack elements). Hardware stacks
have already been used for a long time in ALGOL-oriented stack computers
[16] and are now also being used for LISP machines. For example, the
CADR machine uses a stack buffer of 1 K words, accessible in the cycle
time of 180 nano seconds [24].

Even more dramatic improvements of the efficiency of recursive function evaluation can be expected from exploiting the possibility of evaluating side-effect-free subexpressions in parallel (cf. section 9). For example, the subexpressions (EQUAL CAR:L CAR:M) and (EQUAL CDR:L CDR:M) of the AND in the last clause of the EQUAL definition could be evaluated in parallel (although LISP´s AND semantics evaluate left-right). There is a great deal of work in this area (cf. e.g. [22], [25]), often under the heading of "data-flow architectures" [1].

5. VERY-HIGH-LEVEL DATA STRUCTURES: COLLECTIONS

In very-high-level languages not only lists but also other data structures should be available, e.g. sets, bags, and strings. In QA4/QLISP [51] and FIT [10] ´self-normalizing´ data structures are used for this which may be called ´collections´. These can all be represented using lists: The first element of a list is distinguished as a data type indicator, e.g. CLASS for sets, BAG for bags, and STRING for strings (´CLASS´ is an ersatz term introduced in the LISP-based QLISP language, because ´SET´ was already occupied for assignment). For example, a set {e1, e2, ..., eN} becomes (CLASS e1 e2 ... eN).

The interesting thing about collections is that the data type indicator is also defined as a constructor function which normalizes the remaining elements of the list (mainly by duplicate removal and reordering), returning the entire list (including the type indicator itself) in the normalized form. For example, (CLASS C E A C B D A E E) normalizes to (CLASS A B C D E) since sets are idempotent and commutative, so that repeated elements and the order of the elements carry no information. Similarly (STRING A (STRING 1 2 3) B (BAG B A (STRING C A) B) A) normalizes to (STRING A 1 2 3 B (BAG A B B (STRING C A)) A) since strings are associative and bags are commutative. Eight ´basic collections´ (TUPLE, STRING, COMMUNE, ACOMMUNE, BAG, ABAG, CLASS, HEAP) are obtained by systematic variation of the three binary characteristics commutativity, idempotence, and associativity [10]. An important advantage of self-normalization is the automatic reduction of collection equality (the testing of which is often inefficient) to list equality (the testing of which is efficient), e.g. (EQUAL (BAG A B A) (BAG B A A)) => (EQUAL (BAG A A B) ´(BAG A A B)) => T. The selectors CAR and CDR for lists can be generalized to generic selectors HEAD and TAIL for collections. For example, HEAD:(TUPLE A B C) would return the first tuple element A but HEAD:(CLASS A B C) would return some set element A, B, or C, non-deterministically. Apart from basic collections various other collections, e.g. a DRLH collection for generalized semantic nets [12], can be defined using list functions.

The machine realization of collection normalization can be done by implementing the type indicators as functions working on lists. For example, in LISP the constructor function CLASS can be defined as

```
(PUT CLASS
 (LAMBDA (%L) (CONS ´CLASS (SORT (MAPCAR ´EVAL %L) ´LEXORDER ´NODUPS)))
 FEXPR) .
```

CLASS is defined as a FEXPR [3] to permit a varying number of actual arguments which are made to one list bound to the single formal argument %L ("%" marks L as a ´unique´ identifier). The arguments are then explicitly evaluated by repeating EVAL for all %L elements using MAPCAR [52]. After this, they are sorted lexicographically with duplicates deleted by the UCILISP function SORT (the NODUPS argument of SORT reflects the idempotence of sets and would be omitted in the definition of non-idempotent bags). Finally, the atom CLASS is CONSed again to the list of evaluated and sorted set elements.

The sorting which is done in the normalization of commutative collections could be performed by hardware as in [46].

6. VERY-HIGH-LEVEL DECOMPOSITION: PATTERN MATCHING

The concept of pattern matching is central to very-high-level AI languages because it is needed for explicit structure decompositions, which are also used implicitly for associative retrieval (section 7) and pattern-action rules (section 8). A MATCH function for matching a pattern L to an instance M can be developed from the EQUAL predicate (section 4) for testing the equality of expressions L and M.

First we permit a "don't care" symbol ´ID´ which matches arbitrary expressions, not just occurrences of itself. Thus, (MATCH ´(A ID A ID 4) ´(A 2 A (2 4 E) 4)) would return T because the first ID occurrence matches the atom 2 and the second ID occurrence matches the list (2 4 E). The choice of ´ID´ as the don't care symbol is justified by the fact that it can be regarded as the identity function [10]. This first MATCH version can be implemented as the following trivial extension of the EQUAL function:

```
(PUT MATCH
 (LAMBDA (L M)
  (COND ((EQUAL L ´ID) T)
        ((AND NULL:L NULL:M) T)
        ((OR NULL:L NULL:M) NIL)
        ((AND ATOM:L ATOM:M) (EQ L M))
        ((OR ATOM:L ATOM:M) NIL)
        (T (AND (MATCH CAR:L CAR:M) (MATCH CDR:L CDR:M)))))
 EXPR)
```

Only one clause has been added at the beginning of the COND; it returns T if L is equal to the atom ID, no matter what M is.

The MATCH function can be generalized so that it can handle a "multiple dont't care" symbol ´#ID´ which matches any number (0, 1, 2, ...) of expressions. Thus, (MATCH ´(A #ID 4) ´(A 2 A (2 4 E) 4)) would return T because #ID matches the sequence 2 A (2 4 E). The choice of ´#ID´ as the multiple don't care symbol is justified by the fact that it can be regarded as a Kleene-like repetition (#) of the identity function (ID), also usable for constants (both in (MATCH ´(A #ID 4) ´(A 2 A (2 4 E) 4)) and in (MATCH ´(A #2 4) ´(A 2 2 2 4)) the # operator would cause repetitions which yield the semantically equivalent matches (MATCH ´(A ID ID ID 4) ´(A 2 A (2 4 E) 4)) and (MATCH ´(A 2 2 2 4) ´(A 2 2 2 4)), respectively [10]. A second MATCH version thus becomes:

```
(PUT MATCH
 (LAMBDA (L M)
  (COND ((EQUAL L ´ID) T)
        ((AND (OR NULL:L (EQUAL L ´(#ID))) NULL:M) T)
          . . .
        ((EQUAL CAR:L ´#ID)
         (OR (MATCH CDR:L M) (MATCH L CDR:M)))
        (T (AND (MATCH CAR:L CAR:M) (MATCH CDR:L CDR:M)))))
 EXPR) .
```

The second clause has been expanded to make (MATCH '(#ID) NIL) return T.
Before the last clause another clause has been inserted which is
triggered by #ID. Its OR simulates a rudimentary form of backtracking
control (cf. section 9): The first OR argument tries to match L
without the #ID atom to M, returning T if it succeeds; otherwise a
'backtrack' to the second OR argument takes place, which tries to match
L to the CDR of M. Since the second possibility keeps the #ID atom in L
the recursive MATCH call again falls through to the same clause (unless
the expanded second clause applies); since it shortened M, new
possibilities are tried in this round.

This MATCH version can be used for a very specific kind of pattern
matching which is more appropriately called 'keyword matching' or
'substring searching'; it uses only 'flat' patterns of the form (#ID
keyword #ID), where keyword is a sequence of letters. For example,
(MATCH '(#ID A D A #ID) '(P A D A D A L)) would return T because the
first #ID occurrence matches P, the keyword A D A matches the first A D
A occurrence, and the second #ID occurrence matches D A L;
alternatively the first #ID occurrence matches P A D, the keyword A D A
matches the second A D A occurrence, and the second #ID occurrence
matches L (however, the simple MATCH function above would stop after
having found the first alternative). The example shows that keyword
matching may be non-deterministic. Nevertheless there are very
efficient (linear) algorithms for finding all keyword occurrences in a
string [2]. Since in AI systems -- except in ELIZA-like ones -- nested
lists (trees) are more important than flat lists (strings) the role of
keyword matching in AI languages is limited.

Another generalization of MATCH is to permit variables, represented as
"?" prefixed atoms, which match corresponding M elements if these
elements are identical for identical variables, so that the variables
can be bound to these elements in a consistent manner (to deal with
variables we interpret "?" prefixed atoms ?atom as lists (? atom)).
For example, (MATCH '(?X 2 ?X (2 4 E) ?Y) '(A 2 A (2 4 E) 4)) should
return T and bind X to A and Y to 4. The third MATCH version, then,
becomes:

```
(PUT MATCH
 (LAMBDA (L M)
  ((LAMBDA (B) (COND ((MATCH1 L M) (SETPAIRLIST B) T) (T NIL)))
   NIL))
 EXPR)

(PUT MATCH1
 (LAMBDA (L M)
  (COND . . .
        ((AND ATOM:L ATOM:M) (EQ L M))
        (ATOM:L NIL)
        ((EQUAL CAR:L '?)
         ((LAMBDA (A)
           (COND (A (EQUAL CAR:CDR:A M))
                 (T (SETQ B (CONS (LIST CAR:CDR:L M) B)) T)))
          (ASSOC CAR:CDR:L B)))
        (ATOM:M NIL)
        (T (AND (MATCH1 CAR:L CAR:M) (MATCH1 CDR:L CDR:M)))))))
 EXPR) .
```

The new MATCH main function uses a LAMBDA application to create a local
environment in which a binding list B is initialized with NIL. If the
workhorse function MATCH1 returns T the bindings generated by it are
globalized with a SETPAIRLIST function (whose simple definition is not
shown) and T is returned; otherwise NIL is returned.

MATCH1 is a generalization of the first MATCH version. The clause returning NIL for the disjunction (OR ATOM:L ATOM:M) has been split into two clauses for its two disjuncts. Between these a new clause for pattern variables has been inserted. It uses a LAMBDA application to locally bind A to the value of ASSOC [52] applied to the variable (without "?") and to the binding list B (ASSOC returns a corresponding variable-value pair list from B, or NIL if there is none): If A is non-NIL the variable already has a value in B and this value, CAR:CDR:A, must be EQUAL to M; otherwise the variable is paired with M using LIST and is put into the B list and T is returned.

Note that "?" variables correspond to ID in that both match exactly one element. Similarly, we can use ">" variables which correspond to #ID in that both match 0 or more elements. For example (MATCH ´(>X A 2 >X A (>Y) >Z) ´(A 2 A (2 4 E) 4)) would return T and bind X to the empty sequence, Y to the sequence 2 4 E, and Z to 4. Furthermore, not only for lists but also for collections match definitions can be provided [12]. For example, (MATCH ´(BAG ?Y ?Y A) ´(BAG A B B)) would return T and bind Y to B. Finally, not only the L but also the M argument of the MATCH function could be permitted to be a pattern containing variables, yielding a unification matcher [14], needed for "logic programming" [31] and useful for "pattern-directed procedure invocation" (section 8). For example, (MATCH ´(?X 2 A (2 ?Y E) 4) ´(A 2 ?X (2 4 ?Z) ?Y)) would return T and bind X to A, Y to 4, and Z to E. For simple kinds of unification matching linear algorithms are available [39]. If, however, unification matching is coupled with multiple ">" variables or with certain collections (mainly strings) it becomes a non-trivial decidability question [40]. All AI languages implemented thus far have therefore confined unification matching to simple cases.

There are proposals for hardware matchers [36] which can be used to speed up frequently needed kinds of elementary matching.

7. VERY-HIGH-LEVEL DATA BASES: ASSOCIATIVE ASSERTIONS

Newer AI languages such as SAIL and PLANNER are integrated with an associative data base in the form of associative assertions [8].

Assertions are related to symbols with property lists (cf. section 3). An assertion can be constucted from a sequence of values extracted from the attribute-value pairs of a property list (so that the attributes are made implicit in the order of the sequence); the value sequence is put into an (ADD-prefixed) list directly after the symbol instead of associating attribute-value pairs with the symbol. For example, instead of the property list [CAT <ISA MAMMAL> <FEAR DOG> <CHASE MOUSE>] we can use the assertion ADD:(CAT MAMMAL DOG MOUSE), where the values MAMMAL, DOG, and MOUSE correspond to the attributes ISA, FEAR, and CHASE in that order. This can be regarded as a trivialized property list [((CAT MAMMAL DOG MOUSE) <TRUTHVALUE T>] associated with the list (CAT MAMMAL DOG MOUSE) instead of with the symbol CAT. In the relational model this assertion could be interpreted as an instance of a relation CAT with the domains ISA, FEAR, and CHASE. In general, assertions can be arbitrary nested lists as in CONNIVER [43] or collections as in QA4/QLISP [51]. QA4/QLISP even permit non-trivial property lists to be associated with such expressions.

The set of assertions constitutes an associative data base which can be accessed by means of functions for storage (ADD), retrieval (FETCH), and removal (neglected here). The call ADD:expression stores expression in the data base. The call FETCH:pattern associatively retrieves an expression matched by <u>pattern</u> from the data base, where <u>pattern</u> specifies arbitrary parts of the contents of an expression by its constants (leaving other ones unspecified by don´t cares) and retrieves the remaining ones as values of its variables. An illustration of storage has already been given through our introductory ADD example. Examples of retrieval are FETCH:(CAT >X), which finds (as the value of X) the entire value sequence MAMMAL DOG MOUSE, and FETCH:(?S MAMMAL ?Y MOUSE), which finds all symbols S (here: CAT) which are mammals and chase mice, no matter which things Y (here: DOG) they fear.

Associative assertions are often implemented by a kind of file inversion technique, called "coordinate indexing" in QA4 (see also "discrimination nets" [14]). The basic principle can be best understood by regarding assertions as property lists again. To index a property list [<u>s</u> ... <<u>a</u> <u>v</u>> ...] we generate for each attribute <u>a</u> an ´inverse´ attribute (´coordinate´) <u>a-1</u> and put <u>s</u> as a value under the attribute <u>a-1</u> of <u>a</u> -- possibly new -- property list for <u>v</u>, obtaining [<u>v</u> ... <<u>a-1</u> <u>s</u>> ...]. For example, the assertions/property lists

```
ADD:(CAT MAMMAL DOG MOUSE)   [CAT <ISA MAMMAL> <FEAR DOG> <CHASE MOUSE>]
ADD:(DOG MAMMAL MAN CAT)     [DOG <ISA MAMMAL> <FEAR MAN> <CHASE CAT>]
ADD:(MAN MAMMAL MAN MAMMAL)  [MAN <ISA MAMMAL> <FEAR MAN> <CHASE MAMMAL>]
```

through these inverse attributes become (´CHASE-1´ is read ´is chased by´ etc.; for CLASS see section 5)

```
[MOUSE <CHASE-1 CAT>  ]
[CAT <CHASE-1 DOG>   <ISA MAMMAL> <FEAR DOG> <CHASE MOUSE>]
[DOG <FEAR-1 CAT>    <ISA MAMMAL> <FEAR MAN> <CHASE CAT>]
[MAN <FEAR-1 (CLASS DOG MAN)>   <ISA MAMMAL> <FEAR MAN> <CHASE MAMMAL>]
[MAMMAL <ISA-1 (CLASS CAT DOG MAN)> <CHASE-1 MAN>  ] .
```

Now, for example, all property lists of the form [?X ... <ISA MAMMAL> <FEAR MAN> <CHASE ?Z>] are retrievable by a call FETCH:(?X MAMMAL MAN ?Z) by using the inverse attributes ISA-1 and FEAR-1 of MAMMAL and MAN, respectively. More precisely, the intersection of the symbols which are found under the attribute ISA-1 of MAMMAL and under the attribute FEAR-1 of MAN is formed: (INTERSECTION (GET MAMMAL ISA-1) (GET MAN FEAR-1)) => (INTERSECTION (CLASS CAT DOG MAN) (CLASS DOG MAN)) => (CLASS DOG MAN). The result (CLASS DOG MAN) means that the property lists/assertions for the symbols DOG and MAN have been retrieved. The former binds X to DOG and Z to CAT; the latter binds X to MAN and Z to MAMMAL. In most PLANNER-like languages these two solutions would be yielded non-deterministically.

Hardware implementations of associative retrieval have already been proposed for quite a long time in the form of associative or content-addressable memories [30]. However, software techniques for simulating such memories on conventional von Neumann computers as described above have been preferred until recently, because hardware associative memories were so expensive that they could only be used for small buffer and control stores. Gradually, though, associative memories are becoming more attractive as hardware is becoming more cheap and flexible because of new technologies such as VLSI and magnetic bubble memories. Not only AI ([17], [23]) but also other areas are getting increasingly interested in associative memories, often as part of "data base machines" [18], e.g. for relational data banks in weather forecasting systems and air navigation systems.

The specific problem with hardware associative memories for AI is the following: The assertions to be stored in such memories are not fixed-length records but variable-length expressions. Therefore the

standard method of organizing an associative memory by using fixed
memory matrices, where the rows are records and the columns are
associative access paths, cannot be used directly. Some expressions
will be shorter than the row-length, wasting part of the associative
access capability; other expressions will be longer than the
row-length, having a not associatively accessible ´tail´. A partial
solution of this problem is to divide expressions exceeding the
row-length into parts which fit into a row, store these parts into
consecutive rows, and use a corresponding number of retrievals to find
entire assertions. For a presentation of further methods of coping with
the ´variable-length problem´ see [32].

8. VERY-HIGH-LEVEL PROGRAMS: PATTERN-ACTION RULES

Pattern-action rules (cf. [37], [48]) are transformation rules
pattern -> action which decompose expressions with their left-hand side
(invocation) pattern and reconstruct them to new expressions with their
right-hand side action. To evaluate an expression a "pattern-directed
procedure invocation" mechanism [27] selects a rule with a matching
left-hand side and replaces the expression with the corresponding
right-hand side. Pattern-action rules can often be used to define
very-high-level programs in a manner which is more modular, concise, and
readable than corresponding (LISP) function definitions.

A program called name which for the patterns formargs1, ..., formargsN
is defined by the bodies body1, ..., bodyN, respectively, becomes a set
of N = 1, 2, ... pattern-action rules (name formargs1) -> body1, ...,
(name formargsN) -> bodyN. In principle, a call (name actargsI) of the
program name with the actual arguments actargsI is evaluated by a rule
(name formargsI) -> bodyI whose pattern matches the call, binding the
variables in formargsI to the constants matched in actargsI; then bodyI
is instantiated with these bindings and evaluated itself.

For example, the *APPEND function of section 4 becomes the single
pattern-action rule (*APPEND (>LS) (>MS)) -> (LIST LS MS). On the
left-hand side the sequences of list elements LS and MS are extracted
from the two argument lists; on the right-hand side LS and MS are just
written into the context of the list constructor LIST. An evaluation of
the call (*APPEND ´(A B) ´(1 2 3)) can be illustrated by

(*APPEND (>LS)   (>MS))   -> (LIST LS   MS)
          ^   ^   v   v
(*APPEND ´(A B) ´(1 2 3)) => (LIST A B 1 2 3) => (A B 1 2 3) .

The *APPEND pattern is matched to the *APPEND call binding LS to A B and
MS to 1 2 3 as indicated by the "^" arrows; then the LIST action is
evaluated with these bindings as indicated by the "v" arrows, returning
the appended list.

As a second example the EQUAL function of section 4 can be defined as a
set of two trivial rules, (EQUAL ?X ?X) -> T, (EQUAL ?X ?Y) -> NIL,
because the invocation match tests for the equality of the two X
occurrences (if the third MATCH version of section 6 is used for the
invocation match, the EQUAL occurring there must not be defined by the
above pattern-action rules to avoid circularity). If a call like (EQUAL
´(A 2 A (2 4 E) 4) ´(A 2 A (2 4 E) 4)) is matched by more than one
pattern-action rule, the conflict resolution strategy of using the rule
with the most specific pattern can be applied. In particular, a pattern
like (EQUAL ?X ?X) with two identical variables is more specific than a
pattern like (EQUAL ?X ?Y) with two different variables. Therefore in

this case the first rule is used which correctly returns T.

A set of rules may also define a program corresponding to several functions, e.g. to MAMMAL (non-trivial) and CAT (trivial) as in

```
(MAMMAL ?X) -> (CAT X)
(CAT TOM) -> T .
```

With these rules we can evaluate (MAMMAL TOM) => (CAT TOM) => T.

Our previous pattern-action rules have all implicitly been <u>backward</u> rules, i.e. they reduce goals into other goals. This can be made explicit by rewriting non-trivial rules as so-called <u>servants</u> (a term used in KRL. For example, the non-trivial rule above would be defined as the servant (SERVANT (MAMMAL ?X) GOAL:(CAT X)). If now (MAMMAL TOM) is demanded by GOAL:(MAMMAL TOM) the servant is invoked and instead performs GOAL:(CAT TOM) to demand (CAT TOM) (the latter goal would succeed if the trivial rule above had been rewritten as the assertion ADD:(CAT TOM)). A complementary kind of pattern-action rules are <u>forward</u> rules, i.e. they augment assertions with other assertions. These can be explicitly written as so-called <u>demons</u> (a term made popular by Charniak). For example, to complement the previous servant we could define the demon (DEMON (CAT ?X) ASSERT:(MAMMAL X)). If now (CAT TOM) is stored in the data base by ASSERT:(CAT TOM) the demon is invoked and additionally performs ASSERT:(MAMMAL TOM) to store (MAMMAL TOM) in the data base. Below we will explain basic GOAL and ASSERT statements.

A call GOAL:<u>expr</u> first tries to look up <u>expr</u> in the data base of assertions with FETCH:<u>expr</u>. Only if <u>expr</u> cannot be found there the servants with a matching invocation pattern are retrieved from the data base and some of their bodies are evaluated with the bindings obtained by the invocation match (usually giving rise to new GOALs, recursively). The evaluation tries the servant bodies in turn until it finds a successful one (i.e. applies a trivialized conflict resolution strategy), causing a depth-first tree traversal (cf. section 9).

Extending our servant example let us assume that the data base contains

```
(SERVANT (ANIMAL ?X) GOAL:(MAMMAL X))
(SERVANT (ANIMAL ?X) GOAL:(BIRD X))
(SERVANT (MAMMAL ?X) GOAL:(CAT X))
ADD:(CAT TOM) .
```

Then GOAL:(ANIMAL TOM) evaluates thus (numbers show the tree traversal):

```
                    GOAL:(ANIMAL TOM)=>FETCH:(ANIMAL TOM)
                    1 v                      3 v
GOAL:(BIRD TOM)=>FETCH:(BIRD TOM)   GOAL:(MAMMAL TOM)=>FETCH:(MAMMAL TOM)
        2 v                                    4 v
      failure                       GOAL:(CAT TOM)=>FETCH:(CAT TOM)
                                              5 v
                                          (ANIMAL TOM) .
```

Since (ANIMAL TOM) is not in the data base of assertions the two servants with the matching invocation pattern (ANIMAL ?X) are retrieved. We assume that the instantiated body GOAL:(BIRD TOM) of one of them is tried first (1): it fails because (BIRD TOM) is neither asserted nor matched by the invocation pattern of any servant (2). Therefore a backtrack occurs and the instantiated body GOAL:(MAMMAL TOM) of the other one is tried (3): (MAMMAL TOM) is not asserted but is matched by the invocation pattern (MAMMAL ?X) of a servant (4). The instantiated body GOAL:(CAT TOM) of this servant succeeds because (CAT TOM) is asserted, so that the original goal is proved (5).

A call ASSERT:<u>expr</u> stores <u>expr</u> in the data base with ADD:<u>expr</u>. Furthermore, the demons with a matching invocation pattern are retrieved from the data base and all of their bodies are evaluated with the bindings obtained by the invocation match (usually giving rise to new ASSERTs, recursively). The evaluation uses the demon bodies simultaneously (i.e. needs no conflict resolution strategy), causing a kind of breadth-first tree traversal (cf. section 9).

Extending our demon example let us assume that the data base contains

```
(DEMON (CAT ?X) ASSERT:(MAMMAL X))
(DEMON (CAT ?X) ASSERT:(PET X))
(DEMON (MAMMAL ?X) ASSERT:(ANIMAL X))
```

Then ASSERT:(CAT TOM) evaluates thus (numbers show the tree traversal):

$$ASSERT:(CAT\ TOM)=>ADD:(CAT\ TOM)$$

```
                         1 v                         1 v
ASSERT:(PET TOM)=>ADD:(PET TOM)   ASSERT:(MAMMAL TOM)=>ADD:(MAMMAL TOM)
                                                    2 v
                                  ASSERT:(ANIMAL TOM)=>ADD:(ANIMAL TOM) .
```

After (CAT TOM) has been added to the data base the two demons with the matching invocation pattern (CAT ?X) are invoked. Their instantiated bodies ASSERT:(PET TOM) and ASSERT:(MAMMAL TOM) are evaluated simultaneously (1). One of them adds (PET TOM) to the data base. The other one adds (MAMMAL TOM) to the data base and causes the demon with the matching invocation pattern (MAMMAL ?X) to be invoked (2). The instantiated body ASSERT:(ANIMAL TOM) of this demon adds (ANIMAL TOM) to the data base.

Servants need not use instances as in our previous GOAL:(ANIMAL TOM) -- corresponding to the closed question "Is Tom an animal?" -- but may also use patterns as in GOAL:(ANIMAL ?ETY) and GOAL:(?PTY TOM) -- corresponding to the open questions "Which entities are animals?" and "What properties does Tom have?", respectively. While closed goals try to prove the truth of their instance, open goals try to find variable values that make their pattern true. As in associative retrievals the pattern variables become bound to the values found. In the above examples ETY would be bound to TOM and PTY to CAT, MAMMAL, or ANIMAL, non-deterministically.

Pattern-action rules are related to computation rules used in non-von Neumann architectures. In particular, the two kinds of pattern-action rules used in AI languages, demons and servants, correspond to data-driven and demand-driven computations, respectively, as used in multiprocessors [47]. It will therefore be a promising possibility to build AI pattern-action rules directly into hardware. This would amount to an extended associative memory machine, in which the rows -- corresponding to left-hand side patterns of rules -- are associated with right-hand side actions (cf. [30], [32]).

9. VERY-HIGH-LEVEL CONTROL: NON-DETERMINISM

The three preceding subsections dealing with pattern matching, associative retrieval, and pattern-action rules have already indicated the ubiquity of non-deterministic control in many AI languages.

Indeed, the allowing of non-deterministic programs is perhaps the most important feature of very-high-level AI languages. Non-determinism is a powerful method of abstracting from unnecessary detail, and abstraction is one of the few ways of successfully coping with complex systems. As the existential quantifier of logic permits the abstraction from explicit disjuncts only one of which need hold true, non-deterministic control permits an abstraction from a set of computations, only one of which need succeed, while the other ones may fail. Starting with Floyd's original paper [20] interest in non-deterministic programs has been increasing continuously in computer science ([4], [10], [13], [26], [38]). This development is very encouraging for AI researchers who for a long time have used non-deterministic control. On the other hand, from the beginning AI's problem-solving applications have been a major application area for non-determinism (as early as in [20] the example used was the 8-queens problem).

Although non-deterministic control structures are convenient for the programmer to work with, they appear to be inconvenient for physical machines to execute. Most combinatorial problems cause the degree of non-determinism to grow exponentially with the length of the input data. This 'combinatorial explosion' is one of the most urgent 'practical' problems in AI because it can slow down ordinary machines in an extreme manner. We discuss two approaches toward a solution of this problem.

Heuristic search: Non-deterministic alternatives can be processed 'from left to right' in a depth-first manner: If the evaluation always using the left-most alternative succeeds its value is taken; if it fails the remaining alternatives are recursively evaluated in the same manner (see the GOAL evaluation tree in section 8). Non-deterministic alternatives can also be processed 'simultaneously' in a breadth-first manner: All alternatives are repeatedly evaluated one step, always throwing away failing alternatives; the value of the first successful alternative is taken (cf. the ASSERT evaluation tree in section 8). Depth-first search has the advantage that it can by chance find a solution quickly; it has the disadvantage that it may diverge into an infinite subtree although a solution exists somewhere in the search tree (another disadvantage of "chronological backtracking" has been discussed in [43]). Breadth-first search has the advantage that it always finds a solution if one exists somewhere in the search tree; it has the disadvantage that it is slow if the solution is deep inside the tree. In a kind of synthesis of the advantages of depth-first and breadth-first search non-deterministic alternatives are processed under a heuristic schedule in a best-first manner: The alternative is always taken which is both estimated to be closest to success and is as far left as possible. The estimation is done by a heuristic function which analyzes the alternatives to score their distance from successful termination. To do this, it must often use specific knowledge about the problem domain ([14], [37]).

Multiprocessors: Non-deterministic alternatives can also be viewed as processes which can be executed in parallel by a multiprocessor. This has certain advantages over the heuristic search approach described above. The difficulty of finding heuristics for problems for which no specific knowledge is available is avoided. In particular, the user need not worry about providing heuristics for the symbolic/combinatoric computations at the domain knowledge-free implementation basis of a non-deterministic programming language (e.g. for pattern matching). Multiprocessors constitute one of the must intensively studied subareas in computer architecture today ([1], [5], [18], [19], [22], [25], [42], [46]). Although this work is most interesting for AI three possible flaws of parallelism have been mentioned in the literature which we'll discuss in the following:

1. A parallel exploration of programs with many conditional branches wastes almost all processing power, except that for the single path which happens to correspond to the execution path a sequential processor would take. Minsky [35] therefore conjectured that the speed-up through n parallel processors is often not n but just log(n) or less. Fortunately, this flaw does not arise for non-determinism because an exploration of several non-deterministic branches is not avoidable by any physical machine. However, here a multiprocessor shows its true advantage over a monoprocessor: The former can explore many branches at once, while the latter must explore them one after the other.

2. The organization of the communication between parallel processors can become so difficult and time-consuming that the resulting overhead is hardly compensated for by the speed gained through parallelism. Perhaps this flaw is also avoided when realizing non-determinism through parallelism, because non-deterministic parallel processes don't communicate with each other in a horizontal manner; they are just created by father processes and give their results back to them in a hierarchical manner. This very non-cooperativeness of non-determinism prevents the complications and efficency loss that arise with horizontal communication. For cooperative "actor"-like forms of parallelism the communication problems can be minimized by well-designed communication networks ([28], [42]) and message passing methods ([19], [27]).

3. The number of parallel processors cannot catch up with the number of processes which may grow as an exponential function of the input. Therefore any fixed number of processors will for certain inputs be exceeded by the number of processes. One solution of this problem is to schedule the excess processes on certain processors in a quasi-parallel manner (as on todays monoprocessor systems). Furthermore, the forthcoming VLSI technology may permit a multiplicative expansion of processors just as today's technology permits a multiplicative expansion of memory; although each multiplication will only permit increasing the exploration of the search tree by one additional step this increase may become critical for solving previously unsolved combinatorial problems.

Altogether, the ideal solution seems to be a combination of heuristic search and multiprocessors: Having n processors, a heuristic scheduling function would then select the n most promising non-deterministic alternatives and the processors would process them in parallel.

10. CONCLUSIONS

While our attempt to structure the web of characteristic AI language & machine features in this paper may be a necessary first step toward a theory of AI languages & machines, much more work is required before a more formal (but practically relevant) theory can emerge. This could be a part of a more general language & machine theory.

A theoretical integration of language and machine aspects is needed because practical AI languages & machines are reaching a state in which not only AI languages give rise to AI machine architectures but also AI machines give new impulses to AI languages. This is exemplified by the CADR machine, an AI machine which is oriented toward the AI language LISP but which also inspired the ´LISP machine LISP´ extension of LISP.

In summary, the further development of AI languages & AI machines would benefit by more communication and cooperation across the boundaries of 1. AI, programming languages, and computer architecture, 2. Computer hardware, software, and operational semantics, and 3. LISP machines, associative memories, and multiprocessors. More ´interdisciplinary´ research projects and conferences might be a good way to achieve this.

REFERENCES

Due to space limitations we often cite only the newest publication of projects. For more references see e.g. the ´incremental´ bibliography started in [11].

[1] Ackerman, W.: Data flow languages. 1979 National Computer Conference, AFIPS Conf. Proc., Vol. 48.

[2] Aho, A. & Corasick, M.: Efficient string matching: An aid to bibliographic search. CACM 18(5), June 1975.

[3] Allen, J.: Anatomy of LISP. McGraw-Hill, New York, 1978.

[4] Anderson, B.: Programming languages for artificial intelligence: The role of nondeterminism. School of Artificial Intelligence, Univ. of Edinburgh, Experim. Progr. Reports No. 25, March 1972.

[5] Backus, J.: Can programming be liberated from the von Neuman style? CACM 21(8), August 1978.

[6] Baker, H.: List processing in real time on a serial computer. CACM 21(4), April 1978.

[7] Bawden, D. & Greenblatt, R. & Holloway, J. & Knight, T. & Moon, D. & Weinreb, D.: The LISP machine. In: Winston, P. & Brown, R. (Eds.): Artificial intelligence: an MIT perspective. Vol. 2. The MIT Press, Cambridge, Mass. 1979.

[8] Bobrow, D. & Raphael, B.: New programming languages for artificial intelligence research. Computing Surveys 6(3), 1974, 153-174.

[9] Bobrow, D. & Winograd, T. & The KRL Research Group: Experience with KRL-0 - One cycle of a knowledge representation language. Proc. 5th IJCAI, 1977.

[10] Boley, H.: Five views of FIT programming. Univ. Hamburg, FB Inform., IFI-HH-B-57/79, Sept. 1979.

[11] Boley, H.: A preliminary survey of artificial intelligence machines. KI-Rundbrief, Nr. 20, April 1980. AISB Quarterly, Issue 37, May 1980. SIGART Newsletter, No. 72, July 1980.

[12] Boley, H.: Processing directed recursive labelnode hypergraphs with FIT programs. Univ. Hamburg, FB Inform., IFI-HH-M-81/80, Sept. 1980.

[13] Broy, M. & Pepper, P. & Wirsing, M.: On relations between programs. Proc. Fourth International Symp. on Programming, Paris, April 1980, Springer-Verlag, Berlin, Heidelberg, New York, 1980.

[14] Charniak, E. & Riesbeck, C., & McDermott, D.: Artificial intelligence programming. Lawrence Erlbaum Associates, Hillsdale, N.J., 1980.

[15] Conference Record of the 1980 LISP Conference. Stanford University, August 1980.

[16] Doran, R.: Architecture of stack machines. In: Chu, Y. (Ed.): High-level language computer architecture. Academic, New York 1975.

[17] Fahlman, S.: Design sketch for a million-element NETL machine. Proc. 1st NCAI-80, Stanford University, August 1980.

[18] Fifth Workshop on Computer Architecture for Non-numeric Processing. SIGIR 15(2), SIGMOD 10(4), March 1980.

[19] Fischer, H. & Raulefs, P.: Design rationale for the interactive programming language CSSA for asynchronous multiprocessor systems. Univ. Bonn, Inst. f. Inform. III, Memo SEKI-BN-79-09, Nov. 1979.

[20] Floyd, R.: Nondeterministic algorithms. JACM 14(4), October 1967.

[21] Foderaro, J.: The FRANZ LISP manual. UC Berkeley, 1980.

[22] Friedman, D. & Wise, D.: Aspects of applicative programming for parallel processing. IEEE Trans. Computers 27(4), April 1978.

[23] Goto, E. & Ida, T. & Hiraki, K. & Suzuki, M. & Inada, N.: FLATS, a machine for numerical, symbolic and associative computing. Proc. 6th IJCAI, 1979.

[24] Greenblatt, R. & Knight, T. & Holloway, J. & Moon, D.:   LISP Machine Progress Report. The LISP Machine. MIT, Artificial Intelligence Laboratory, no date.

[25] Guetschow, K. & Stecher, R.: Entwurf eines Multiprozessor-Systems zur Auswertung rekursiver Funktionen. Univ. Hamburg, FB Inform., Mai 1980.

[26] Harel, D. & Pratt, V.: Nondeterminism in logics of programs. MIT, Laboratory for Computer Science, MIT/LCS/TM-98, February 1978.

[27] Hewitt, C.: How to use what you know. Proc. 4th IJCAI, 1975.

[28] Hewitt, C.: The Apiary network architecture for knowledgeable systems. In: [15].

[29] Knight, T. & Moon, D. & Holloway, J. & Steele, G.: CADR. MIT, AI Memo 528, June 1979.

[30] Kohonen, T.: Content-addressable memories. Springer-Verlag, Berlin, Heidelberg, New York, 1980.

[31] Kowalski, R.: Logic for problem solving. North-Holland, 1979.

[32] Lea, R.: Associative processing of non-numerical information. In: Boulaye, G. & Lewin, D. (Eds.): Computer architecture. Reidel Publ. Comp., Dordrecht, Boston, 1977.

[33] Leavenworth, B. (Ed.): ACM SIGPLAN symposium on very high level languages. March 1974, SIGPLAN Notices 9(4).

[34] McCarthy, J.: LISP - Notes on its past and future. In: [15].

[35] Minsky. M.: Form and content in computer science. JACM 17(2), 1970.

[36] Mukhopadhyay, A.: Hardware algorithms for nonnumeric computation. Proc. 5th Ann. Symp. Computer Architect., SIGARCH 6(7), April 1978.

[37] Nilsson, N.: Principles of artificial intelligence. Tioga, 1980.

[38] Nivat, M.: Non deterministic programs: An algebraic overview. Proc. IFIP 1980.

[39] Paterson, M. & Wegman, M.: Linear unification. 8th Ann. ACM Symp. on Theory of Computing, May 1976.

[40] Raulefs, P. & Siekmann, J. & Szabo, P., & Unvericht, E.: A short survey on the state of the art in matching and unification problems. Inst. f. Inform. I, Univ. Karlsruhe, SEKI 3-78, 1978.

[41] Schoichet, S.: The LISP machine. Mini-micro systems, June 1978.

[42] Sullivan, H. & Bashkow, T.: A large scale, homogeneous, fully distributed parallel machine, I. Proc. 4th Ann. Symp. Computer Architecture, SIGARCH 5 (7), March 1977.

[43] Sussman, G. & McDermott, D.: Why conniving is better than planning. MIT AI Laboratory, AI Memo No. 255A, April 1972.

[44] The Lisp Company: The TLC-LISP documentation. Box 487, Redwood Estates, CA 95044, 1980.

[45] The Mathlab Group: MACSYMA Reference Manual. Version Eight. MIT, Project MAC, November 1975.

[46] Thompson, C. & Kung, H.: Sorting on a mesh-connected parallel computer. 8th Ann. ACM Symp. on Theory of Computing, May 1976.

[47] Treleaven, P. & Brownbridge, D. & Hopkins, R.: Data driven and demand driven computer architecture. The University of Newcastle upon Tyne, Computing Laboratory, July 1980.

[48] Waterman, D. & Hayes-Roth, F. (Eds.): Pattern-directed inference systems. Academic, 1978.

[49] Weinreb, D. & Moon, D.: Flavors: Message passing in the Lisp machine. MIT, AI Lab., AI Memo No. 602, November 1980.

[50] White, J.: Address/memory management for a gigantic LISP environment or, GC considered harmful. In: [15].

[51] Wilber, M.: A QLISP Reference Manual. Technical Note 118, AI Center, SRI, March 1976.

[52] Winston, P. & Horn, B.: LISP. Addison-Wesley, 1981.

A CONCURRENT CHART PARSER

Peter Raulefs and Hans Siebenbach

SEKI - PROJEKT
Institut für Informatik III
Universität Bonn
Bertha-von-Suttner-Platz 6
D-5300 Bonn 1, West Germany

- SUMMARY -

Abstract. A *Concurrent Chart Parser* (CCP) implemented in the programming language CSSA [FRV 81] for societies of agents to be realized
on multicomputers is described. The CCP is based on the model of
generalized augmented transition networks (gATNs) presented in [KERP 79],
continuing work by A. Kay and T. Winograd [KAY 78, WINO 75]. As a
CSSA-implementation on a multicomputer is not available yet, the CCP
has been realized in a simplified CSSA-version which is executed on a
sequential system simulating multicomputer structures. The simulation
system permits performance measurements allowing to draw rough conclusions about favorable multicomputer architectures for doing concurrent chart parsing.

1. A Short Survey of CSSA

1.1. *Agents.* CSSA-computations are done by <u>agents</u>. An agent consists of
a *cluster of operation-capabilities* that can be activated by sending a
message to the agent. A *message* contains (1) a symbol naming a specific
operation-capability of the target agent, and (2) an *envelope* to be
decoded by pattern match by the recipient agent.

1.2. *Communication among agents.* A communication from an agent A to an
agent B is effected by A sending a message to B. Hence, a communication
requires that (a) the agent A is *acquainted with* the agent B, and
(b) agent A is in possession of the name identifying the operation-
capability of which an activation is requested of from target agent B.

Executing (an instance of) an operation-capability is *indivisible*
and may result in any finite number of messages *concurrently* transmitted to agents the sending agent is acquainted with and has access-
rights to. Conceptually, we assume that transmission times for messages
between agents are *positive, finite,* but *indefinite*. Hence, (a) all
messages eventually arrive at recipient agents, and (b) if an agent

concurrently sends several messages to a target agent, there is no way of knowing which message arrives first.

We obtain an *agent net* when representing agents as nodes and drawing a directed edge labelled with access-rights (operation names) from each agent to all agents it is acquainted with. An agent net represents potential flow of information. Agent nets may dynamically change due to (1) transmitting agent acquaintances in messages, (2) generating new agents, and (3) terminating agents.

1.3. *Scripts*. *Scripts* are agent schemata s.t. agents are generated from scripts by supplying appropriate bindings as result of a pattern match (*creation match*). The *type* of an agent is the script it had been generated from.

1.4. *Facetting*. When executing an operation-capability, an agent may replace the current cluster of operation-capabilities by another cluster. A cluster of operation-capabilities is called a *facet*.

1.5. *Selection of received messages*. Agents collect all incoming messages in a *mailbox*. An agent not busy executing an operation-capability incessantly inspects its mailbox for messages to process. Processing a message is *enabled* if (a) its operation-identifier names an operation-capability provided by the current facet of the agent, and (b) its envelope-part can be successfully matched against the entry-pattern associated with the respective operation-capability.

2. Model of a Concurrent Chart Parser

Our model of a CCP consists of a system manipulating three network structures:

2.1. *Chart-Networks*. Words of an input sentence are the nodes of a chart. Three types of edges emanate from nodes in a chart-network:
- a CONSTIT-edge leads to the set of all <u>constituents</u> of the word (i.e. directory entries).
- a PP-edge leads to a list of PUSH-arcs with preactions as generated from context-dependent ATN-networks.
- a P-edge leads to a list of PUSH-arcs without preactions as generated from context-independent ATN-networks.

2.2. *CATN-Networks*. A CATN-network (concurrent ATN-network) consists of several ATN-networks, each containing CAT-, WRD-, JUMP-, POP-, PUSH-, and VIR-edges (see [KERP 79, KAY 78, WINO 75]).

2.3. *State-Sequence Networks.* A state-sequence networks compiles parses through a CATN-network.

A CCP manipulates such network structures by applying operations defined in terms of transitions among parse-triples. A parse-triple (c,r,e) consists of edges in the chart-, CATN-, and state-sequence network, respectively.

3. CSSA-Implementation of a CCP

The CSSA-implementation of the CCP consists of a system of agents which we can decompose into a static and a dynamic component consisting of agents belonging permanently to the system, resp. agents being generated and destructed throughout the course of a CSSA-computation.

3.1. *Static component.* Permanent agents of the CCP are:
   (1) DIRMGR, the directory manager providing access to a directory
       of a part of the German language (we are using the directory
       of the PLIDIS-project [IDS]).
   (2) RULEMGR, the rule manager, administrates one or several ATN-
       grammars.
   (3) SENTENCE, an agent primarily performing two tasks:
       (3.1) constructing chart-networks.
       (3.2) initiation and termination of parses.

3.2. *Dynamic components* of the CCP are:
   (1) a chart-network consisting of chart-agents.
   (2) consumer agents "applying" edges in the CATN-network to edges
       in the chart-network.

4. Multicomputer Architectures

We have investigated CCP-simulations for various multicomputer architectures. Their basic characteristic is the way of clustering processors to form tree, ring, star, and mixed structures.

5. Performance Measurements

Performance measurements with our simulated CSSA-implementation of the CCP have been made to obtain rough guidelines for answers to the following problems:
- Which multicomputer architecture is most favorable for a CCP in terms
  of turnaround time and processor utilization (CSSA-implementations
  are intended to support both multiprogramming and multiprocessing).

- How many processors are required for parsing typical German sentences efficiently.

- What is the reduction of turnaround time for ATN-parsing achievable
  with our CCP over conventional ATN-parsers.

6. References

[FRV 81]   H.L. Fischer, P. Raulefs, H. Voss. The CSSA Programming
             Language for Asynchronous Parallel Computation on Multi-
             computer Systems. SEKI-Projekt, Univ. Bonn (in preparation).
             A preliminary survey is given in
             "CSSA: Arbeitsbericht 1979-1981". Memo SEKI-BN-81-03,
             SEKI-Projekt, Inst. f. Informatik III, Univ. Bonn, 1981.

[IDS]   Arbeitsgruppe MasA. Ein Lexikon für die maschinelle Sprach-
             analyse des Deutschen. Forschungsberichte des Instituts für
             deutsche Sprache, Bd. 19, 1974.

[KAY 78]   A. Kay. Morphological and syntactic analysis and linguistic
             structures processing. in A. Zampolli (ed.), Fundamental
             Studies in Computer Sciences 5, 1978.

[KERP 79]   A. Kerp. ATN's: Überlegungen zu einem neuen Formalismus,
             einem parallelen Interpreter und anderen Anwendungsgebieten.
             in Christaller, Metzing (eds.), Augmented Transition Net-
             work-Grammatiken, Einhorn Verlag Berlin, 1979.

[WINO 75]   T. Winograd. Language as a Cognitive Process. Draft, Oct. 75.

A Parallel Connection Graph Proof Procedure

Günter Hornung, Anfried Knapp, Ulrike Knapp
Institut für Informatik III
Postfach 2220
D-5300 Bonn

Abstract. A parallel connection graph proof procedure is described which is going to be implemented in CSSA, a new language for asynchronous multiprocessor systems.

0. Introduction

The interactive programming language CSSA for asynchronous multiprocessor systems is currently being implemented at Bonn University (/FR 80/). It is based on the concept of a dynamically changing system of asynchronously working processes (called *agents*). Agents have their private memories; they can never share memory. Agents communicate by message passing. The transmission time of messages is assumed to be positive and finite but indefinite. Thus communication between agents is nondeterministic but fair. Agents can change the agent system by creating new agents or by terminating themselves.

As computing time is crucial in automatic theorem proving *parallel algorithms* could bring an advance in this area. Among the various proof methods Kowalski's *connection graph proof procedure* (/Kow 75/) seems to be most appropriate for parallelization. It works on a modular data structure, the connection graph, and concentrates at a time only on local parts of the graph.

1. The Parallel Algorithm

The connection graph algorithm is a *resolution based* proof procedure. In the beginning, the axioms and the negated theorem are transformed into clausal form. Each occurrence of a literal in an input clause or a factor of it becomes a node in the initial connection graph. Links of the same clause are grouped together. Two nodes are connected by a link, if they can be made complementary. The links are labelled by the most general complementing substitution. They mark possible resolution steps. When resolving on a link, a new resolvent clause is generated. Its literals and links can be computed from the two parent clauses. The theorem is proved, if the empty clause can thus be derived from the initial connection graph.

In our model, clauses are implemented by agents. These *clause agents* know about their literals, their links and the most general complementing substitutions. They can communicate with the clause agents they are linked to.

A *supervisor agent* is responsible for building up the initial connection graph by creating the clause agents and for keeping a model of the current connection graph in his local memory. He is acquainted with all clause agents, who inform the

supervisor about "good" links according to local link selection criteria (see
/ESSUW 80/ for examples of such heuristics).

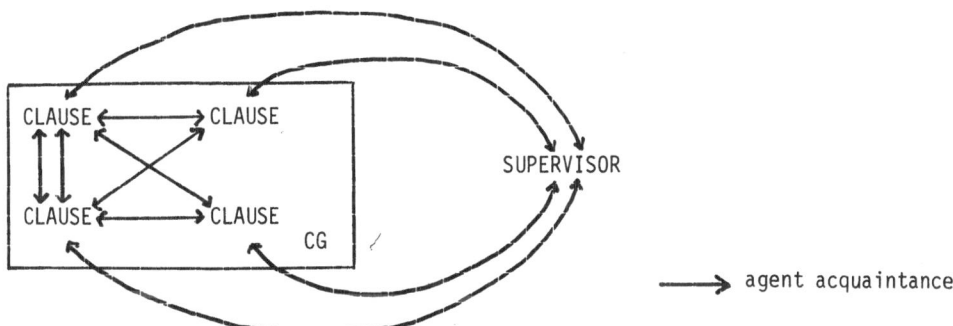

Fig. 1.1 The connection graph implementation

There are several *pruning operations* cutting down a connection graph without
affecting the satisfiability of the set of clauses. A clause can be deleted from the
graph if it is a tautology or if it contains a "pure literal" i.e. a literal with no
links. A link departing from literal L1 can be deleted if all links of a literal L2
in the same clause are incompatible with that link i.e. the corresponding substitutions
cannot be unified. All these operations and computations can be executed asynchronously
in a decentralized way by the clause agents.

On the other hand, *resolution* is coordinated by the supervisor. He selects one or
several links to be resolved upon. Two neighbouring links, however, must not be
resolved concurrently. When a link is resolved, the parent clause agents compute the
links to be handed over to the new resolvent clause. They then "introduce" the new
resolvent to their neighbours. Only when all neighbours have "accepted" the resolvent
can that new clause agent act on his own. After some pruning operations he creates
all factors of himself with their links and finally informs the supervisor that the
resolution step has been successfully finished.

In the following chapters we present our algorithm in more detail.

2. The Initialization Phase

Execution is started with a phase of initialization during which the initial
connection graph is built up.

We assume there are n clauses which are read in by the supervisor who then creates
the CSSA-agents CA1,...,CAn representing these clauses. They are active subjects
who can generate their connecting links all by themselves and in parallel.

The initialization procedure is the following programm:

a) requests of clause agent CAi:

   CAi sends messages to all agents CAj with j<i informing them of his
   clause text. The clauses CAj search for complementary literals, try to unify and

insert a link if they have been successful.

b) answer to clause agent CAi:

Every clause agent CAj gives the clause agent CAi the number of inserted links (even if it is zero) and information about these links.

c) terminate:

Having read in n clauses the supervisor informs all clause agent of that number n. Now a clause agent CAi can tell the supervisor that he has finished his link computations when the following situation occurs :

1) CAi has generated links to n-i agents

2) CAi has received i-1 messages about the number of inserted links from other agents and has received the corresponding number of link information messages

Thus, the initialization phase is finished as soon as the supervisor has received n answers from the clause agents.

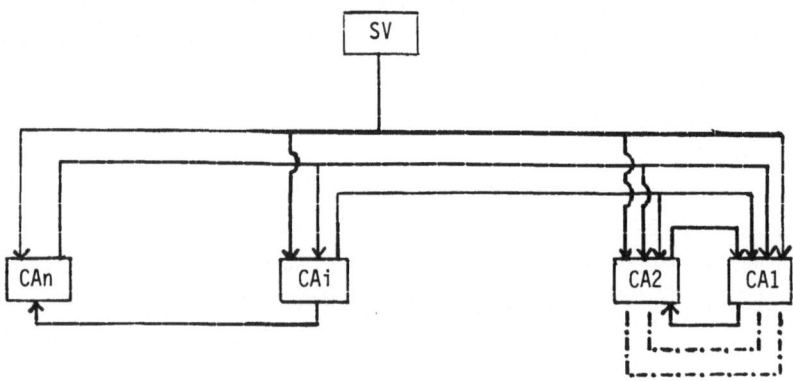

Fig. 2.1 Snapshot of the initialization phase
⟶ messages; —·—·— links

Now it is obvious that some clause agents may have finished their tasks earlier than others. Since they should not be idle if some intelligent work remains to be done there are several local operations which can be executed by the agents in parallel. These operations are of course restrained in the initialization phase because the agents may not yet know the full set of their links.

3. Local Operations

Best_Links

If we use local information in order to select a link for resolution every clause can evaluate his best links on his own. They may be asked for by the supervisor or automatically sent to him.

Make_Factor

Since we use binary resolution it is necessary to supplement the resolution operation with a factoring operation,which merges potentially identical links in the same clause. An instance $C\theta$ of a clause C is called a factor of C if θ is a most general unifier of some subset of literals in C.

Delete_A_Link

This is an operation affecting also an acquainted agent. If a clause agent determines to delete a link he must inform his linked partner about this decision. Apparently his partner agent has to delete the registration for the same link.

Delete_A_Clause

This is another operation affecting acquainted agents. When a clause agent terminates,all his neighbours - linked clause agents - must delete their links to the literals of that clause agent.

Pruning Operations: Tautology_Check

                 Purity_Check

                 Incompatibility_Check

If a clause is a tautology or contains a pure literal the clause can be deleted from the graph (operation Delete_A_Clause).

A much more complex operation is the check for incompatible links. For every link there exists a compatibility table.

L1	L2	....	Li	....	Ln	
m	n				/	test order
m,s_m	p,s_p q,s_q n,s_n				j,s_j $1,s_1$	(index of compatible link, substitution)

Fig.3.1 Snapshot of the compatibility table for $link_k$ for literal Li

The columns in the table correspond to the literals L1,...,Ln of the considered clause agent. The k-th link for literal Li can be deleted if we find that all links for a literal Lj ($j\neq i$) are incompatible with $link_k$. This means on the other hand that we may stop the incompatibility-check for a literal Lj at the first compatible link of that literal. The number of that link is then entered into the compatibility table as test order of the corresponding literal. See e.g. column 1: we mark our having searched until $link_m$ for literal L1 and add m together with the unifying substitution s_m to the set of indices of compatible links. Since compatibility is symmetric,the analogous information (k,s_k) is entered into the compatibility table for $link_m$ for literal L1. But no test order can be added because we do not know anything about the links indexed from 1 to k-1.

Thus we are able to state for some literal class at time t:

tested links $\cong$ {1..test order} $\cup$ M

incompatible links $\cong$ {1..test order} - M

where M is the set of indices of compatible links at time t

The unifying substitution entered together with a compatible link in the table is computed during the compatibility check. It is later needed in the resolution process. Thus we need not generate it twice.

4. Parallel Resolution

In a resolution step new clause agents are generated and links are inherited by these agents. The supervisor decides if, when and where resolution takes place in the connection graph. He administrates a data base of possible resolution candidates (links). Clause agents locally select these resolution candidates from their links using heuristic functions and hand them to the supervisor. From this subset of all links the supervisor selects one or several links which will in fact be resolved. However, not more than one link of a clause agent may be resolved upon at a time. Having determined a link for resolution the supervisor generates a resolvent clause agent in an initial facet. Then the parent clause agents are requested to resolve.

During the first phase of *resolution* only messages from the partner clause agent are accepted (realization by change of the facet). Now every parent clause agent can compute the information to be transmitted to the resolvent. First the substitution of the link is applied to the literals of the clause agent. The new links are transmitted to the resolvent. Finally the parent clause agents send a message to those neighbours which have to register the new resolvent informing them about the inherited link and the associated substitution. Links from the resolvent to parent clause agents are directly evaluated.

All neighbour clause agents have to *acknowledge* the acquaintance to the new resolvent to the parent clauses. In order to receive and handle these acknowledgements the parent clause agents enter a facet in which all messages are acceptable. In this facet the parent clause agents keep in mind that their resolvent is possibly unknown to the sender of some message and has to receive the information as well. The most relevant problem is the prevention of the *loss of a link* in parallel resolution. As is illustrated beneath the loss of a link may occur if resolvents are generated inheriting links without knowing about each other.

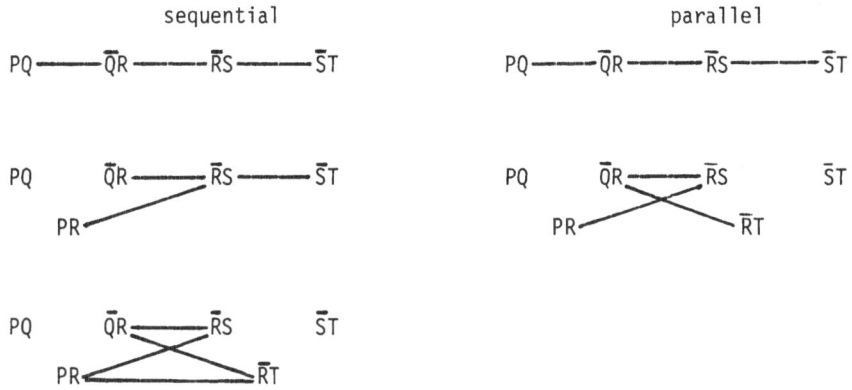

Fig. 4.1 Loss of a Link in a Parallel System

To avoid this, we must guarantee that a resolution will be finished only when all neighbours know the new resolvent, particularly those neighbours the parent clause agents were not conscious of when starting resolution. Only then may the parent clauses activate the new resolvent agent and finish resolution with a reply to the supervisor. Now the parent clause agents are ready to be selected for a new resolution by the supervisor.

As in parallel resolution both resolvents - here we regard only two ones - are treated equally it may happen that the same link between the resolvents is evaluated and inherited twice. But these *twofold links* can easily be found by a local test on the level of the resolvent: two links connecting the same literals are equal and are allowed to merge into one link.

The second problem is: a resolution may last indefinitely long if only enough new clauses are generated in the neighbourhood of the resolvent - taking into account CSSA message passing.

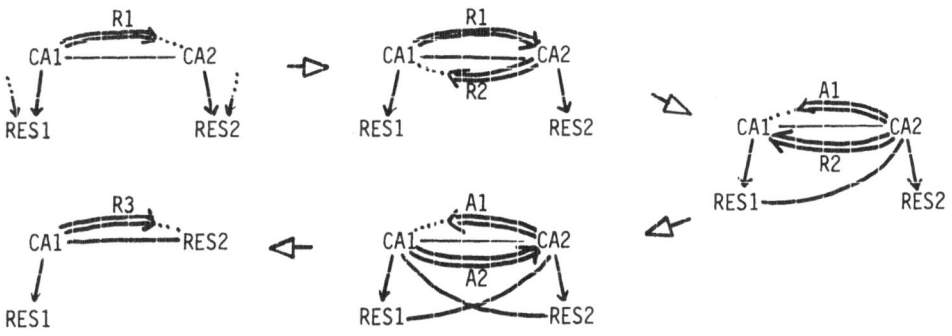

Fig. 4.2 Illustration of never-ending resolution

R$\Rightarrow$ request message; A$\Rightarrow$ acknowledgement message; ——link

A certain amount of time is required for working upon these new neighbours (until they have sent their acknowledgements), in which several new neighbours may possibly be created. Global control by the supervisor can avoid this deadlock.

Inheritance of links between parent clause agents and resolvent is not realized by the acknowledgement mechanism of course. The parent clause agents locally evaluate these links and hand them directly to the resolvent. There are possibly some pseudo links within a parent clause agent - if there are complement literals - which are never resolved but inherited.

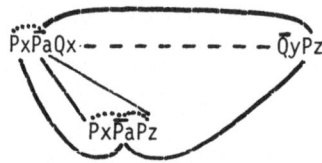

Fig. 4.3 Pseudo links in a clause agent
········ pseudo link

As soon as the *resolvent* gets its local information from one parent clause agent the compatibility operation can be started (unification of substitutions). Deletion of links is not possible at this moment because not all links are known. Having received the information from the other parent clause agent the local operations compatibility check, tautology check, check for twofold links are performable. New links are only added by inheritance of existing links. The global actions of the resolvent clause are administered by the parent clause agents until the resolvent agent is integrated into the connection graph. The resolvent becomes a self responsible clause agent after the parent clause agents have finished resolution. Then the first step of the resolvent will be evaluating his factors which means generating new factor clause agents and inserting them into the connection graph analogous to the mechanism of resolution but with only one parent clause agent concerned. Having completed this step the resolvent and possibly his factor clause agents give an acknowledgement to the supervisor and then are real clause agents.

Exception Handling

Breaking off a started resolution

There is a purity check during the evaluation of the resolvent's contents and its links by the parent clause agents which may result in breaking off the resolution. The supervisor is informed about that action. If the neighbour clause agents already know the resolvent a breaking off e.g. after a tautology check done by the resolvent has to be treated like the deletion of a clause agent.

Addressing a non-existing link

It is guaranteed that by using the operation Delete_A_Link also the partner clause agent respectively the supervisor are informed about the deletion. Therefore this

case can only occur if the messages Address_A_Link and Delete_A_Link overlap. The
message of link deletion will be interpreted as an answer to the attempt of
addressing a link which no longer exists.

Communication exception

A target error is caused when a terminated clause agent is addressed later. Here
the acknowledgement-request message crosses with the deletion message which can
also be interpreted as above.

Non-controllable communication exceptions

mailbox-overflow, port-overflow

5. Further Prospects

In our approach we want to study in how far the connection graph proof procedure
can be parallelized. Our algorithm is not yet implemented. So we do not know whether
we can really get a net speed-up or whether there will be a synchronization and
communication overhead. We expect that at least the deletion strategies will work
quite well asynchronously. On the other hand it is not quite sure whether concurrent
execution of resolution steps is really effective.

By the construction of our system - local resolution, but global link selection -
we are able to incorporate both *local* and *global* resolution strategies and heuristics,
as in (/ESSUW 80/).

6. References

/FR 79/

H.L. Fischer - P. Raulefs, "Design Rationale for the Interactive Programming
Language CSSA for Asynchronous Multiprocessor Systems", Memo SEKI-BN-79-09,
Institut für Informatik III, Universität Bonn, 1979

/Kow 75/

R. Kowalski, "A Proof Procedure Using Connection Graphs",
JACM 22(1975), 572-595

/ESSUW 80/

N. Eisinger - J. Siekmann - G. Smolka - E. Unvericht - Chr. Walther,
"The Markgraf Karl Refutation Procedure", Proceedings of the AISB-80 conference,
Amsterdam 1980

Integrated, Knowledge-based Information Manipulation Systems

Heinz-Dieter Boecker and Gerhard Fischer
Institut fuer Informatik, Universitaet
Azenbergstrasse 12, D-7000 Stuttgart

The Problem

The personal computer of the future will offer its user an Information Manipulation System (IMS). An **IMS** will allow the user to do almost all of his work (design specifications, plans, programs, documentations, reports, memos, reference notes as well as communication with others) on-line (FISCHER and LAUBSCH 1980).

Our current research activity concentrates on the development of a program understanding system as part of an **IMS** to support the development, understanding and modification of programs by humans. From a more traditional point of view it may be described as a **knowledge-based programming environment.**

The current **"sofware-crisis"** is basically caused by our human limitations to deal with the complexity of our software artifacts which steadily increased during the last twenty years. Problem solving with the computer has matured and the original main activity of carrying out **single well-specified tasks** (ie algorithms) has been replaced by the need for **complex systems** which fit an environment of needs. There is enough empirical evidence that a variety of support mechanims and design aids is needed to cope with the different problems of the two domains. **Fig.** 1 characterizes the differences between algorithms and systems in terms of some general principles.

Fig. 1: "Algorithms" versus "Systems"

	Algorithms	Systems
examples	Factorial, Fibonacci numbers	text processing systems, expert systems (MACSYMA, Dendral)
specifi- cations	precise, complete; do not change over time	not precise; incomplete; change over time; evolve over time
use	small building block; in general only useful within larger systems	real world systems; to fit an environment of needs
local transparency	intricate logic; highly optimized, require proof	locally transparent; complexity is based on a large number of interactions between modules
classificat. in PS terms	well-structured problem, abstract problem	ill-structured problem, problem in semantically rich domain
design criteria	efficiency, correctness	modifiability, transparancy uniformity, reliability
semantics	intrinsic	extrinsic

IMS can be seen as prototypes of systems which try to fight the complexities of large software systems in the following way: the computer and the human cooperate to produce software more quickly and more reliably than either of the two could do working alone (see GOLDSTEIN and BOBROW 1980; MASINTER 1980; RICH, SHROBE and WATERS 1979). The original meaning of "programming" as the art of finding and coding of algorithms is too restricted to cover the many possible uses of a computer by a human being. We believe that programming has to be studied as a human activity (comparable to writing) that is concerned primarily with design processes, explication and representation of knowledge and understanding.

The Implementation

The current system is one step towards our long range research goal to develop the fundamental principles behind an **IMS**; it serves as a testbed to construct prototype systems which meet many of our evolving design criteria.

The system provides a programming environment (FABIAN 1981) to the user that supports as many steps of the problem solving- and information manipulation processes as possible. Whereas most of the computer systems and programming environments currently in use only support the implementation and execution phase of a program, our system is meant to support the earlier steps (with corresponding weaker methods) of problem formulation and global design as well as the test, debugging and documentation phases following the implementation and execution step of a typical systems programming task (in the sense discussed above).

The system may be best described as a multiple window system (BAUER, BOECKER and FISCHER 1981) providing uniform, direct interactive facilities to the user. It is based on our belief that **a program is not its listing;** what we really need is a collection of multiple (eg textual or graphical) representations; particular properties of systems/devices/objects can often be seen better from particular viewpoints. We regard a program as a complex information structure, only parts of which are of interest to the programmer at a certain time.

The knowledge base (simultaneously compiled by our system while the user is working with it) can be inspected via a multiple window system, that is used for the generation of multiple perspectives and representations of the program under development. The knowledge base is organized in extended property list structures which bear some resemblance to frames. In LISP-like languages, the functions are the basic units in which most of the knowledge about a program is accumulated. The knowledge frame may contain knowledge about static and dynamic aspects of a function, eg its history of development, its behavior in time and space, its control and data structures and its relation to other functions - to mention just a few. A basic knowledge unit above the level of the functions is the package concept which is primarily used for documentation and debugging purposes.

Fig. 2 shows the system in action: the **printstructure** window (as an example of a "perspective" of a program) displays the static calling structure of the program edited in parallel in the **edit** window.

Fig. 2: A system of multiple overlapping windows

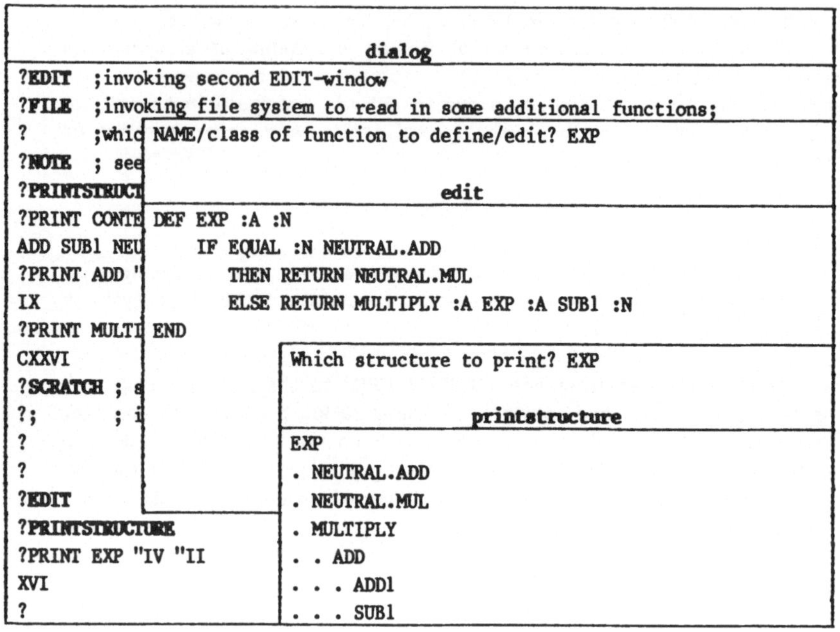

```
                              dialog
?EDIT    ;invoking second EDIT-window
?FILE    ;invoking file system to read in some additional functions;
?        ;whic NAME/class of function to define/edit? EXP
?NOTE    ; see
?PRINTSTRUCT                   edit
?PRINT CONTE DEF EXP :A :N
ADD SUB1 NEU    IF EQUAL :N NEUTRAL.ADD
?PRINT ADD '        THEN RETURN NEUTRAL.MUL
IX                  ELSE RETURN MULTIPLY :A EXP :A SUB1 :N
?PRINT MULTI END
CXXVI             Which structure to print? EXP
?SCRATCH ; s
?;       ; i                   printstructure
?                 EXP
?                 . NEUTRAL.ADD
?EDIT             . NEUTRAL.MUL
?PRINTSTRUCTURE   . MULTIPLY
?PRINT EXP "IV "II  . . ADD
XVI                . . . ADD1
?                  . . . SUB1
```

References

Bauer, J., H.-D. Boecker and G.Fischer (1981): "Entwurf und Implementation eines Systems multipler Fenster", in Notizen zum Interaktiven Programmieren, Heft 4, Oldenburg

Fabian, F. (1981): "Rechnerunterstuetztes Entwickeln, Implementieren und Dokumentieren von Software Sytemen", Master Thesis, Institut fuer Informatik, Universitaet Stuttgart

Fischer, G. and J. Laubsch (1980): "LISP-basierte Programmentwicklungssysteme zur Unterstuetzung des Problemloesungsprozesses", in Heft 4 der Notizen zum Interaktiven Programmieren, Fachausschuss 2 der Gesellschaft fuer Informatik, Darmstadt, Maerz 1980, pp 100-112

Goldstein, I. and D. G. Bobrow (1980): "Descriptions for a Programming Environment", Proceedings of AAAI, pp 187-189, Stanford

Goldstein, I. and D.G. Bobrow (1980): "Extending Object-oriented Programming in Smalltalk", Proceedings of the LISP conference, Stanford

Masinter, L.M. (1980): "Global Program Analysis in an Interactive Environment", PhD thesis, Stanford

Rich, C., H. Shrobe and R. Waters (1979): "Computer Aided Evolutionary Design for Software Engineering", MIT AI Memo 506, Cambridge, Ma

MATINGS IN MATRICES

Wolfgang Bibel

Technische Universität München

Abstract

This paper gives an overview over the connection method in Automated Theorem Proving, developed earlier by the author. Its prominent features are illustrated with a number of examples. These features provide it with provable advantages over any standard proof method. Some of them also have been obtained by Andrews in an independent approach using matings. The relationship between these two methods is clarified.

1. INTRODUCTION

A prominent feature of human thinking is the ability to logical reasoning. Everyone uses this ability all the time, mostly in an unconscious way. It was this particular feature which eventually led to man's scientific activity. Therefore it is not surprising that over a period of 2000 years man has reflected upon the very nature of this feature. He has modelled it within natural language and isolated general rules which somehow are applied in the brain according to common experience. These rules have been abstracted from natural language and expressed within formal languages which model natural language in the sense that they keep the logical structure (characterized by the rules) unchanged. These formal languages together with the rules are called *formal (logical) systems*.

There are many such formal systems to date, developed under a variety of aspects. These aspects include some of a purely technical nature and others referring to the particular fields of application. For instance, logical rules involving beliefs may be essential for modelling common sense reasoning, for proving theorems in strict mathematics, however, they are certainly inappropriate; hence to date for these two particular applications one might use different formal systems.

Among these formal systems those of first-order logic certainly play a dominant role. On one hand, their rules are so fundamental that probably any (existing or future) sytem of practical importance will have incorporated them in some form. This, for instance, is true with systems for higher-order or modal logic which simply are extensions of first-order logic. On the other hand, first-order logic is both natural and powerful enough for modelling much of our reasoning in a natural satisfactory way. Therefore we will focus our attention now to first-order logic (fol) keeping in mind that this is an artificial but reasonable restriction for the time being.

Although the present paper is written with a particular formal system for fol in mind - let us denote it by FOL - we will not specify it in detail in this paper. No trouble will arise from that for readers familiar with the basic concepts of fol. In FOL we have the class of (*well-formed*) *formulas* as usual which correspond to syntactically correct pieces of text in natural language.

The most fundamental problem in FOL like in any other formal system is the development of a (hopefully efficient) procedure which for any such formulas $F_0, ..., F_n$, $n \geq 0$, decides whether F_0 is a consequence of $F_1, ..., F_n$ according to the rules in FOL or not. Such a procedure is called a *decision procedure*. In this most general form this problem in fact has no solution according to a result by Gödel except when the F_i's, $i = 0, ..., n$, are taken from certain (practically important) subclasses of formulas. For arbitrary F_i's there are only so-called *semi-decision* or *proof procedures* which are guaranteed to give a result in the affirmative case only and in the negative case may give an answer or run forever. This is the type of procedures we are going to study in this paper.

If we could develop an *efficient* such procedure this would have enormous practical impacts for may kinds of applications in science because of the general nature of fol discussed before. Some of these applications are described in 15 . According to results in complexity theory, it might be (the relevant problems are still open) that such procedures cannot be efficient for *arbitrary* formulas F_i, in principal. But even if this would turn out to be the case, it would not say very much on the feasability of proof procedures *in practice* because of the worst-case nature of such general complexity results. Therefore the development of efficient proof procedures does remain a challenging and extraordinarily promising research goal.

This is not to say that current proof procedures are not efficient at all. On the contrary, running deductive systems have proved rather deep mathematical theorems automatically, have even solved a number of open mathematical problems (none of the famous ones, of course) for which a human proof was never achieved before, and are in daily use as programming assistants by generating or verifying pieces of programming code. The interested reader is referred to the proceedings of the Conferences on Automated Deduction 8 and 13 for more information in this context. These achievements in many respects are still modest, however, if they are compared with human performances.

The reasons for their deficiencies seem to be of two different kinds. On one hand, human beings seem to quickly adapt powerful strategies which speed up the search. Research is just beginning to study the mechanisms which guide this process. On the other hand, the existing systems are based on proof procedures which apparently are working in such a redundant way that it is even amazing that they are successful at all. Even at a point in the course of a proof where a mathematician would say "It is now obvious ...", they would proceed to fill the memory space with many more formulas. Researchers (like all people) tend to a monotheistic attitude in such a situation expecting the cure from solving *one* of these two kinds of problems. We, however, believe that necessarily *both* kinds of deficiencies have to be removed in order to substantially enhance the performance of running systems.

For reasons near at hand the present paper is concerned with one of these kinds of deficiencies only, notably that of redundancy which plagues any of the popular proof procedures in use. They include those based on the resolution principle introduced by Robinson in 1965 [16], but also most of those based on a natural-deduction-like approach [9].

In the last decade, there have been two mostly independent but closely related developments, however, which provide a remarkable improvement in that direction. One was carried out by Andrews (under the keyword "matings") the other by the present author ("systematic proof procedure", "complementary matrices", "spanning sets of connections"). The results have been published in a number of papers of a rather technical nature (see [1] - [5] for the most recent ones). Therefore the present paper attempts to provide a more illustrative overview over this kind of method which incidentally is probably less redundant than any other known proof method. In the course of this introduction we also point out the similarities and differences in the work of these two authors, and occasionally compare it with standard proof methods.

It is hoped that the presentation is such that not only an expert in the field will be able to quickly find out the essence of this method but also a non-expert with a little familiarity with fol will get a feeling for the enhancement achieved by its prominent features which are summarized in the last section 8. On the other hand, our presented examples necessarily will be rather trivial and academic due to the restrictions in available space. The many details of a complicated technical nature for more complex problems have to be left to the computer. Although both authors and their associates earlier have realized such implementations, the implementation of the most advanced version described in this paper, however, is not yet completed but is currently in progress (project "Beweisverfahren" supported by the Deutsche Forschungsgemeinschaft).

2. THE BASIC CONCEPTS FOR THE CONNECTION METHOD

As our first example we choose an instance of a very old syllogism saying that the man Socrates is mortal since every man is mortal. The logic of such a statement in

natural language is often ambiguous. For this reason the formal first-order language
has been developed in order to express the statement in the following logically equivalent but unambiguous way (see ch. 4 in [13] for an informal introduction).

A1: ∀x (MANx → MTLx)   : "every man is mortal"

A2: MANsocrates   : "Socrates is a man"

TH: MTLsocrates   : "Socrates is mortal"

With these partial statements the whole statement says: from (the *axioms*) A1 and
A2 we may infer (the *theorem*) TH. In fact we may express the whole statement as
the single formula A1 ∧ A2 → TH wherein A1, A2, and TH abbreviate the respective formulas above. Note the usage of the convention that ∧ binds more than → in
order to save parentheses (such obvious conventions will not be mentioned any more).
For purely didactic reasons in this formula the implication sign → is substituted
equivalently by negation ¬ and disjunction ∨ and the scope of each occurrence of
¬ is achieved to be atomic, by applying well-known equivalence rules. The resulting
formula then reads

    F: ∃x (MANx ∧ ─ MTLx) ∨ ¬ MANsocrates ∨ MTLsocrates.

The original inference from A1 and A2 to TH is a valid one if and only if F
is a *valid* formula or a *theorem* in the sense of fol (or FOL) without non-logi-
cal axioms. The problem is how to test the validity of F (and of other theorems) as
quickly as possible.

For the following it is very illustrative to display such a formula in a 2-dimensional
format by listing the parts connected by ∨ from left to right, and within each such
part the subparts connected by ∧ from top down. F represented in this way reads

$$\exists x \left\{ \begin{matrix} MANx \\ \neg\ MTLx \end{matrix} \right\} \quad \{\neg\ MANsocrates\} \quad \{MTLsocrates\} .$$

Without the quantifier ∃x this structure is called a *matrix in normal form* which
in general is a set of sets of *literals* or shortly a set of *clauses*. In this particular example we have a set of three clauses listed from left to right, the literals
in each clause listed top-down. If you cross such a matrix in 2-dimensional format
from left to right thus visiting exactly one literal in each clause you obtain a good
illustration for what is called a *path through* the matrix. Doing this with our matrix also denoted by F, only the first clause gives us a choice whether to visit the
top or the bottom literal. Hence there are exactly two paths through F.

        {MANx, ¬ MANsocrates, MTLsocrates}

and   {¬ MTLx, ¬ MANsocrates, MTLsocrates} .

An unordered pair of literals such as {MANx, ¬ MANsocrates} with one and the same predicate symbol - here MAN -, one literal unnegated the other negated, and both contained in some path through a matrix is called a *connection* in that matrix. A set of connections is called *spanning* for a matrix if each path through it contains such a connection (as a subset). Obviously, there are exactly two connections in F which in fact are spanning for F and are illustrated by

$$\exists x \left\{ \begin{array}{l} \text{MANx} \\ \neg \text{ MTL} \end{array} \right\} \quad \{\neg \text{ MANsocrates}\} \quad \{\text{MTLsocrates}\} \; .$$

Now, according to results of Andrews and the author F in fact is a theorem if and only if there is a substitution of some term for the variable x such that after this substitution each of the two spanning connections consists of two *complementary* literals, i.e. a literal L and its negated form ¬ L. This obviously is the case if we substitute socrates for x; hence F in fact is a theorem or, in other words, MTLsocrates is a logical consequence of the two axioms A1 and A2.

It was pointed out before that the elimination of the implication sign serves didactical purposes only. We now can see why it does not affect the essence of the method at all. We have just to redefine the crucial notion of a spanning set of connections for arbitrary formulas via the equivalence rules relating logical connectives, a simple exercise indeed. For our original formula we thus obtain

$$\forall x \; (\text{MANx} \rightarrow \text{MTLx}) \; \wedge \; \text{MANsocrates} \quad \rightarrow \quad \text{MTLsocrates.}$$

This demonstrates that it is a negligible technical detail whether we prefer to work with the originally given formula or the equivalent 2-dimensional display. In this paper we mostly prefer the latter since it displays the paths, the connections and the spanning properties in a much more illustrative way.

Let us be sure that among all these comments and definitions we do not miss the crucial message of this discussion: For establishing the proof for our theorem F all we have to do is (i) locating the two spanning connections within F and (ii) testing the existence of an appropiate substitution. It is important to notice that this does not require any storage for copies of parts of the given formula, which for this method is true in general not only with this trivial example.

For comparison it is interesting to have a look at the popular resolution method [16]. For reasons, which today may be regarded as historical ones, the whole given formula first is negated. The resulting formula is transformed into *clausal form* similar to what we did with F above. From the resulting set of clauses (or matrix)

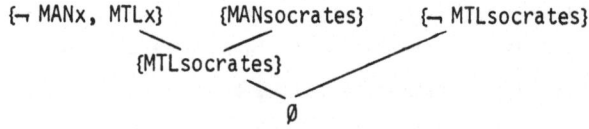

Figure 1. The resolution proof for F

the empty set (or clause) is derived by two applications of the resolution rule as shown in figure 1.

If we now recall our previous proof it becomes obvious that each resolution step resolving upon two literals corresponds exactly to locating the connection between these two literals in the given formula and vice versa. The empty set is derived as soon as the set of connections thus obtained becomes spanning and vice versa. As a difference, we first notice that in the clausal form of resolution the negation signs occur at the opposite end of the connections due to negating the original formula. Less trivial is the fact that in the course of the resolution proof a new clause, namely {MTLsocrates}, has been generated. Since in general no clauses may be deleted this not only requires additional memory space but also increases the search space since we may resolve any two old or new clauses. A lot of research efforts have been invested into resolution in order to avoid these drawbacks (keywords are "structure sharing" and "refinements of resolution") which may become disastrous in more realistic problems where tens of thousands of generated clauses are not unusual. In our approach these problems have not to be eliminated since they just do not arise at all.

Under these aspects, then, our method appears as a clever representation of resolution avoiding some of its drawbacks. That it is more than just that will become clear as we proceed with more examples. Perhaps at this point it might therefore be appropriate to introduce some name for this new method. Over the years the author used to call it the *systematic* method to stress the point that it pursues a more systematic proof search than other methods. This is not a very distinctive name, however, since all these methods are more or less systematic. In view of the fact that locating connections in the formula may be regarded as its characteristic activity as we have already seen, *connection principle* or *method* sounds like a better name which will be used in this paper.

The connection method as described up to this point is identical with Andrews' *general matings* method except for the following notational differences. Following the resolution tradition Andrews starts with negating the given formula. This does not do any difference worth mentioning; but why then add this step even if it is a tiny one? Consequently, his paths run top-down rather than left-right in the matrix. Incidentally, he refers to a formula like the one explicitly named F above as in *negation normal form* where the scope of each explicit or implicit (via →, e.g.) negation is atomic.

A set of connections in his terminology is a *potential mating*. A set of connections such that there is a substitution making all connected pairs of literals complementary is called a *mating*. If additionally it is spanning which is p-*acceptable* in his notation then he calls it a *refutation mating*. A single connection (the literals therein) are called *potential mates* (*with respect to the empty mating*). More substantial differences between the two methods than these merely notational ones will emerge as we proceed with further examples.

3. GENERATING SPANNING SETS OF CONNECTIONS

The previous section demonstrated that a proof with the connection method requires two things, namely a spanning set of connections and an appropriate substitution. Although a realistic proof procedure will not perform these two tasks separately, a separate discussion will certainly be helpful for the reader. Therefore let us abstract within the present section from all aspects related with the substitution. This can be achieved by assuming that the appropriate substitution has been determined in advance. The formula F from the previous section in matrix form would then read

$$\left\{ \begin{array}{l} \text{MANsocrates} \\ \neg \text{ MTLsocrates} \end{array} \right\} \quad \{\neg \text{ MANsocrates}\} \quad \{\text{MTLsocrates}\} \ .$$

By abbreviating MANsocrates by L and MTLsocrates by K, and deleting the braces we obtain simply $\begin{array}{l} L \\ \neg K \end{array} \neg L \ \ K$. In this case, where the literals are simply (possibly negated) propositional variables our basic question whether F is a theorem reduces to that whether this matrix in propositonal logic (sometimes called the *ground level*) is a tautology. As before this is the case if and only if each of its paths contains a connection. We are now going to describe an algorithm which decides exactly that. Let us call it SSC for "spanning set of connections". Since our matrix is a little too simple for illustrating its behaviour we add four more literals and thus consider the matrix $\begin{array}{cc} L & \neg L \\ \neg K & M \end{array} \neg M \ \ K \ \begin{array}{c} L \\ K \end{array}$.

Initially, SSC chooses any clause, say the left-most one, and in it any literal, say L. It is easy to design a data-structure for storing the whole matrix such that a clause containing the negation of the chosen literal can be determined immediately, for instance by looking it up in a table which contains all occurring literals in a determined order together with a reference to those clauses in which they occur. Do-

ing this establishes a first connection in our matrix $\rightarrow \begin{array}{cc} \overline{L} & \neg L \\ \neg K & M \end{array} \neg M \ \ K \ \begin{array}{c} L \\ K \end{array}$. At

same time a marker is set in the first clause (the little arrow in the picture) noting that L has been processed but the rest of the clause - in this case just ¬ K - yet has to be processed. This completes the first step of SSC in which all paths containing this connection {L, ¬ L} - only two in this particular example but obviously there may be many more in general - have been checked and will *never be considered any more* by SSC.

The paths yet to be processed may be partitioned into those which contain L (but not ¬ L) from the first connection and those which do not contain L. SSC proceeds with the first ones while the second ones have been stored on a stack simply by the reference illustrated with the marker above. The situation now is the same as initially after a clause had been chosen which is now the second to the left clause marked with a vertical arrow. SSC chooses any literal except ¬ L in it. In the present example this must be M since this is the only one left. As before any clause from the *remaining* ones (to the right of the vertical arrow) is determined which contains

¬ M thus establishing the second connection as shown in $\rightarrow \neg\,K \begin{smallmatrix}L\\ \end{smallmatrix} \neg\begin{smallmatrix}L\\M\end{smallmatrix} \neg\,M \; K \begin{smallmatrix}L\\K\end{smallmatrix}$.

Would there have been more literals in the second clause this would have provided a new entry on the stack as illustrated with the second horizontal arrow pointing to nothing in this particular example. After this second step all paths containing both connections have been checked.

SSC still is in the course of processing those paths containing L (but not ¬ L, and not M, ¬ M any more). Among these the same partition may be made with respect to M as before with respect to L thus proceeding with a third step as before in the second step, and so forth. Note that such a chain is never longer than there are clauses in the whole matrix since new clauses in this process are always selected from those not already involved in the present chain. Due to the particular situation of this example there is no such third step, however, since all paths containing L also contain both selected connections. SSC notices this since the third clause does not contain any other literal than ¬ M. In such a situation it backs up by considering the topmost (non-empty) entry on the stack which is illustrated by the leftmost horizontal arrow thus starting a new chain from the situation illustrated by

$\neg\,K \begin{smallmatrix}L\\ \uparrow\end{smallmatrix} \neg\begin{smallmatrix}L\\M\end{smallmatrix} \neg\,M \; K \begin{smallmatrix}L\\K\end{smallmatrix}$.

As before SSC selects any literal in the actual clause marked by the vertical arrow, which has not been processed before, and any clause containing its complement, thus

establishing a third connection as shown in $\rightarrow \neg\,K \begin{smallmatrix}L\\ \uparrow\end{smallmatrix} K \neg\begin{smallmatrix}L\\M\end{smallmatrix} \neg\,M \; \begin{smallmatrix}L\\K\end{smallmatrix}$ where the reordering of the clauses has been performed only for illustrative reasons, of course. Note the new horizontal arrow with respect to the general case. Again the new chain after this step has already been completed. Since the stack is empty SSC terminates with

success. The three selected connections, which incidentally have not to be stored explicitly, are in fact spanning for this matrix. The rightmost clause and any connections containing its literals had not to be used at all.

This completes the description of algorithm SSC testing any matrix for a set of
spanning connections. Already in the previous section we have stressed the point
that no extra storage for copies of the parts of the given formula is required. Only
the markers directing the chaining through the formula have to be stored in addition
to a single copy of the formula and something like the table (of the size of the formula) mentioned further above. Although we have described SSC only in its simplest
form with a trivial example this is true also in its full version for abitrary formulas.

In fact, this full version, which has been developed in [4], is of a rather complicated nature in order to avoid certain redundant steps arising in special situations.
It has been demonstrated in [4] that this full version may simulate any known refinement of resolution with less or equal steps (and less storage) where the amount
of work for performing a single step is about the same for the resolution and the connection method: Since there are formulas for which SSC requires *strictly less*
steps we see that the connection method provides a real (and provable) advantage over
known resolution methods *in addition* to the representational advantage mentioned
several times before. There is one more major advantage to be discussed in later sections. As a warning in the opposite direction we mention that determining a spanning
set of connections is known as a hard problem in general (actually co-NP-hard); hence
no miracles should be expected for the worst case.

It should be mentioned that the full version in fact may deal with *arbitrary* formulas or matrices not only those in normal form which we have considered thus far. For
instance, any literal (e.g. M) in the previous matrix might be substituted by a whole
(non-normal form) matrix; SSC still would be able to process such a matrix as before
and without any change of its structure. The reason for this generalization lies in
the fact that the characterization of tautologies via connections in each path which
was mentioned before holds for arbitrary formulas (see theorem 1.3 in [3]). Andrews
has illustrated the damaging effect of the transformation to clausal form, which is
required for resolution, with several examples. For instance, in [1] it has been
demonstrated that the simple mathematical statement $f(S \cup T) = f(S) \cup f(T)$ for a
function f and two sets S and T after elimination of the defined operations
(like $\cup$ but not $\leftrightarrow$) leads to a formula with 12 literals compared to 104 literals
in the corresponding clausal form. Now imagine the effect when the proof *searches*
among 104 rather than among 12 literals!

It might be helpful for the reader to consider SSC as a proof rule rather than an
algorithm. Namely, for any given matrix, say A, SSC in each step essentially adds

a single connection w to the set   W of those connections obtained in previous
steps; hence the rule is   (A, W) ⊢ (A, W ∪ {w}) . Note that the formula A does
not change in contrast to any other logical rules. Initially, W = ∅ and the termination criterion for a derivation is the spanning property of W for A.

4. UNIFICATION

In section 2 we have seen, that a proof of a theorem involves the two subproblems of

(i)   determining a spanning set of connections such that

(ii) there is a substitution of terms for variables which makes the connected liter-
      als complementary

In the previous section we have described the basic idea of an algorithm SSC for
solving (i) on the ground level. Obviously, such an algorithm is applicable also
on the *general* level, i.e. in fol, by simply neglecting the terms in the literals.
Therefore we now take the existence of such an algorithm for granted and ask for a solution of subproblem (ii).

Since the test for (ii) may be performed fast (which will be discussed now) and a potential failure might be detected after any step of SSC, it is preferable to check
for (ii) after each step of SSC. For example, after the first step of SSC applied to the matrix F from section 2 we would have to test whether there is a
substitution, say σ_1, which makes MANx and ¬ MANsocrates complementary. Of
course, σ_1 = {x ← socrates} provides the solution and thus is kept for the following steps. After having obtained the second connection in the second step subproblem (ii) now requires a substitution σ_2 such that the two literals ¬ MTLx and
MTLsocrates after application of σ_1 and then σ_2 become complementary. Obviously
σ_2 = ∅ since σ_1 alone is sufficient in this particular case thus completing the
proof.

In general, we proceed this way considering in the n-th step two literals L_1 and L_2
and the composition $\sigma_{n-1} \sigma_{n-2} \ldots \sigma_1$ of the substitutions obtained in the previous
steps (substituting terms for variables) and test for a substitution σ_n such that
$\sigma_n L_1' = \sigma_n \neg L_2'$ where $L_i' = \sigma_{n-1} \ldots \sigma_1 L_i$ for i = 1,2. This problem of determining
σ_n is known as the *unification* problem [16] which has been well explored with
fast solutions (running in linear time) for the general case. We will not discuss any
of these unification algorithms in detail assuming that the reader grasps somewhat of
their nature from further examples. But we have to point out that they are subject
to an essential restriction.

Consider any predicate Q with two arguments and the formula $\forall c \exists x (Qcx \rightarrow \overline{Qxc})$.

Applying the connection method this turns out to be a theorem since the substitution $\sigma_1 = \{x \leftarrow c\}$ solves subproblem (ii). Let us now exchange the two quantifiers to yield $\exists x \, \forall c \, (Qcx \rightarrow Qxc)$. Simply by reading the formula as a statement with his natural language, the reader will see that this cannot be a true statement for arbitrary Q's although our method, as described thus far, would result in the same proof with $\sigma_1 = \{x \leftarrow c\}$. Of course, σ_1 cannot be a correct solution since according to the formula the existence of object x is claimed *independent* of the choice for c while σ_1 would suggest a *dependent* solution.

Standard proof methods take care of that by introducing so-called *Skolem functions* for each $\forall$-quantifier with the dominating $\exists$-quantified variables as arguments. In the present example, $\exists x$ dominates $\forall c$ in the (tree-) structure of the formula which is expressed shortly by $x < c$; hence, c is substituted by fx to yield $\exists x \, (Q(fx)x \rightarrow Qxfx)$. Obviously, this prevents the two connected literals to be unified since for no substitution can x and fx yield the same term.

As an alternate solution to this one may regard $c = \sigma_1 x$ as a tree-ordering relation $c <\cdot x$. Such a substitution is then called *acceptable* if the transitive closure $\triangleleft$ of $< \, \cup <\cdot$ has no cycles. In this sense σ_1 for our present example is not acceptable since $c <\cdot x < c$ obviously leads to the cycle $c \triangleleft c$. Thus all we have to do is restricting unification to acceptable substitutions only which has several technical advantages over the solution via Skolem functions. Namely, some fast unification methods, after having introduced Skolem functions, construct $\triangleleft$ from them - hence their introduction is in fact redundant - and test for cycles anyway (e.g. Huet's method). Further, our solution elegantly fits to what will be discussed in later sections.

We complete the description of the most basic aspects of the connection method by pointing out that it crucially requires (selective) backtracking whenever an acceptable substitution does not exist like in $\forall b \, \exists x \, \forall c \, (Q(fcx)x \rightarrow Qxc \lor \exists y \, Qyb)$. Here, the dotted connection has no acceptable substitution. Hence SSC has to back up and consider the alternate (fully lined) connection which yields the proof with the acceptable substitution $\{x \leftarrow b, \, y \leftarrow fcx\}$.

At this point it is appropriate to continue the comparison with Andrews' work. Like the standard resolution methods he still uses Skolem functions. Further the advanced development of SSC is due exclusively to the present author as well as the avoidance of explicit amplification and the optimal splitting feature to be discussed in the next two sections.

5. IMPLICIT AMPLIFICATION

Consider the formula

$$\text{fac0} = 1 \land \forall xy \ (\text{facx} = y \to \text{fac}(x+1) = y\cdot(x+1)) \ \to \ \exists z \ \text{fac2} = z \ .$$

It claims the existence of a value for the factorial function for the argument 2 which obviously is a valid statement. As before, we prefer the matrix representation which is

$$\lnot \ \text{fac0} = 1 \qquad \exists xy \left\{ \begin{array}{l} \text{facx} = y \\ \lnot \ \text{fac}(x+1) = y\cdot(x+1) \end{array} \right\} \qquad \exists z \ \text{fac2} = z \ .$$

An attempt to prove this theorem with the connection method as described in the previous sections will fail, however. The reason for this failure is the fact that we must allow for an arbitrary number of independent copies of any $\exists$-quantified part in the matrix. Adding further such copies is called *amplification* by Andrews. For the connection method it is not necessary, that these copies are generated *explicitly* which is illustrated in the following picture.

The three connections are spanning in a generalized sense to provide for more than one copy of a $\exists$-quantified clause. These copies are distinguished by numbering the endpoints of the connections in an obvious way. The corresponding acceptable substitution is $\{x^1 \leftarrow 0, y^1 \leftarrow 1, x^2 \leftarrow 1, y^2 \leftarrow 1, z^1 \leftarrow 2\}$ providing the expected answer for z. Hence the picture shows the whole proof for this theorem.

Introducing a self-explanatory notation and returning to the original formula this proof for general input $n \geq 1$ reads

It represents both the natural specification of the problem to compute the value of the factorial for input n and a proof respectively a program determining how to compute this value efficiently. Such a program may be compiled automatically as usual to run as efficient as any conventional program computing $\text{fac}(n)$.

This close connection of (this kind of) proofs and of programs has been discussed by the author as early as 1974. For this and further information concerning predicate logic as a suitable programming environment see [7] and the references therein.

6. SPLITTING BY NEED

Consider the formula $\forall x$ ILLx → ILLpat ∧ ILLbob presented together with its proof

along the lines discussed in the previous section. This looks like a satisfactory solution but has in fact a major drawback. Imagine the three literals to be substituted
by matrices of considerable size with many more required connections. Then the implicit generation of a second copy of the matrix to the left of the implication certainly
may increase the search space for appropriate connections in a substantial way since
in particular connections between the two copies have to be taken into consideration
as the previous example has demonstrated. The second copy, however, is not actually
required (not even implicitly) since the two conclusions are independent from each
other because of the separating conjunction; hence the proof may take advantage of
what is called *splitting* in conventional methods.

In these methods, however, splitting is applied in a preprocessing step thus destroy-
ing the structures of the formula also in cases where in the course of proof no need
arises for it. In order to avoid this the author has proposed an alternate form of
splitting by need which incidentally is more general than previous splitting methods (for an example see below) and elegantly fits into the connection method. It extends the relation <· and with it ◄, which have been introduced in section 4, to
include occurrences of conjunction symbols and then to allow for independent unification. For instance, in the present example it would relate ∧ <· x to express that
the occurrence of ∧ dominates that of ∀x. Thus we have ∧ < x. Whenever we have
two connections with their ends being separated by an ∧ and raising the need for a
substitution of non-compatible terms like pat and bob with one and the same variable like x then this substitution is still acceptable if ∧ < x holds or may be
established. In this sense the following proof is to be regarded as a simpler one than

that given before: $\forall x$ ILLx → ILLpat ∧ ILLbob   with ∧ <· x .

The merits of this sophisticated technique become more visible in more complicated
problems which is illustrated in the figures 2 and 3 with an example that (for reasons of space) is still artificially elaborated but shows an effect that may well occur
in complicated theorems. Figure 2 shows the 4-step proof with the connection method
involving no search at all. Figure 3 shows an optimal 8-step proof with resolution.
For resolution fans it is a healthy exercise to elaborate it by hand *before* looking

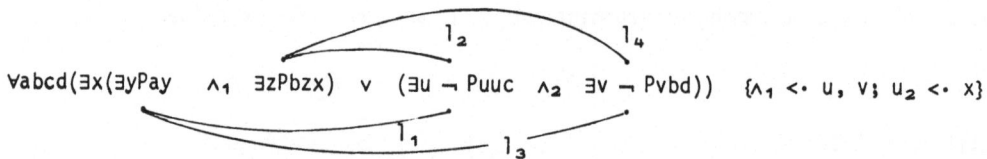

$\forall abcd(\exists x(\exists y Pay \quad \wedge_1 \quad \exists z Pbzx) \quad v \quad (\exists u \neg Puuc \quad \wedge_2 \quad \exists v \neg Pvbd)) \quad \{\wedge_1 <\cdot u, v; u_2 <\cdot x\}$

Figure 2. A theorem and its proof with the connection method

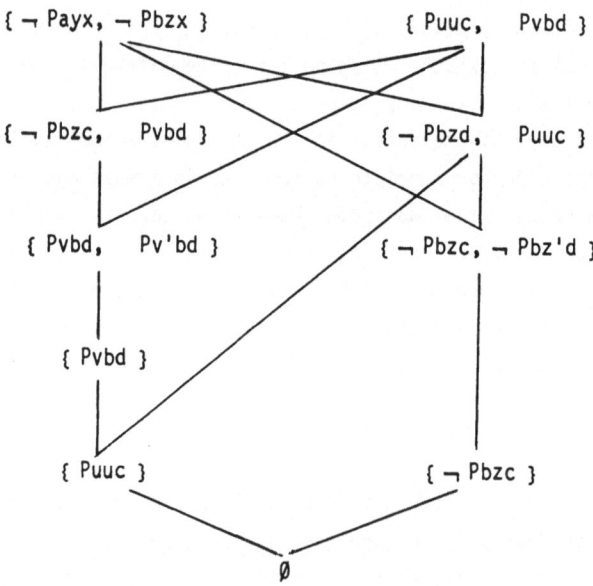

Figure 3. The resolution derivation of the theorem in figure 2.

into the picture since in relation to the small size of the problem it involves considerable search. The comparison is fair since for resolution splitting may be pre-
vented by a slight change in the example which has no effect for the connection meth-
od: $\exists x w (\exists y\ Payxw \wedge \exists z\ Pbzxw)\ v\ \exists s\ (\exists u \neg Puucs \wedge \exists v \neg Prbds)$.

Remember the proof rule introduced for the connection method in section 3. In the
present section and in section 4 we have seen that each step not only adds a connection w to formula A but possibly also extends the relation $<\cdot$ to $<\cdot'$ say,
which initially is empty. Hence its complete form is $(A, W, <\cdot) \vdash (A, W \cup \{w\}, <\cdot')$,
where A never changes.

7. NATURAL DEDUCTION PROOFS

The results reported in this paper were initiated by a thorough study of natural deduction proofs [11]. It is not surprising then that the connection proofs described

in this paper are closely related to natural deduction proofs which may even be print-
ed out immediately once the connection proof has been achieved. In this transformation the resulting relation <· provides the information on the sequence of the deduction steps and the connections encode both the instantiated terms (via unification)
and the property qualifying the formulas at the leaves of the deduction tree as axioms. This is demonstrated in figure 4 with the natural deduction proof corresponding in this way to the connection proof for the first example of the previous
section. Note that the ∧-splitting is performed prior to the instantiation of the
terms pat and bob for x due to the information given by ∧ <· x which reveals the proper nature of this relation. For the natural deduction proof obtained
from the proof in figure 2 see figure 3 in [5].

In section 2 we have already pointed out the close relation of the connection method

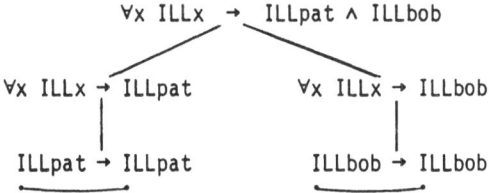

∀x ILLx → ILLpat ∧ ILLbob

∀x ILLx → ILLpat   ∀x ILLx → ILLbob

ILLpat → ILLpat   ILLbob → ILLbob

Figure 4. The natural deduction proof obtained from the

connection proof   ∀x ILLx → ILLpat ∧ ILLbob,   ∧ <· x   .

with resolution and its refinements which has been studied in [4] in detail as mentioned in section 3 above. Here we now see on the other hand the close relation with
natural deduction proofs. This justifies that the connection method may be regarded
as a *higher level* proof method providing a deeper insight into the characteristic
features of theorems (versus formulas) than do the resolution or the natural deduction
proof method.

8. SUMMARY

In this paper we have given an overview over a proof method for theorems in first-order
logic called the *connection method*. With a number of examples we have illustrated
its prominent features summarized as follows:

(i) It may be regarded as a higher level proof method providing deeper insight
       into the characteristic features of theorems (versus formulas) than do
       conventional proof methods (see section 7).

(ii) It operates exclusively on a single copy of the very given formula (see section 3, 5, and the proof rule at the end of section 6);

(iii) in particular, no transformation into any normal form of the given formula is required which allows to use any standard logical connectives and to speed up search by antiprenexing (see section 2);

(iv) not even Skolem functions have to be introduced, i.e. only the terms in the original formula have to be unified (see section 4).

(v) Unification is generalized to include an optimal splitting by need (see section 6).

(vi) Amplification is accomplished by a systematic indexing without violating feature (ii) (see section 5).

(vii) A connection proof can easily be transformed into a natural, thus immediately comprehensible deduction of the given formula (see section 7).

All of these features have been developed by the present author in a number of technical papers (see [3] - [5] and their references). More recently some of them have been obtained by Andrews in an independent approach with *matings* (see [1] and [2] and their references). The present paper has clarified this relationship.

Due to its intended nature the paper has not provided any technical details such as precise definitions, theorems, proofs or other justifications, and algorithms. For these details the interested reader is referred to the references mentioned before.

REFERENCES

[1] P.B. Andrews, Theorem Proving via General Matings, Journal of the ACM (to appear).

[2] P.B. Andrews, Transforming matings into natural deduction proofs, Proc 5th Conf. on Autom. Deduction (W. Bibel, R. Kowalski, eds.), LN in Comp. Sc. 87 (Springer, Berlin, 1980), 281-292.

[3] W. Bibel, On matrices with connections, Journal of the ACM (to appear).

[4] W. Bibel, A comparative study of several proof procedures, Artificial Intelligence Journal (to appear).

[5] W. Bibel, The complete theoretical basis for the systematic proof method, Bericht ATP-6-XII-80, Institut für Informatik, TUM (1980). Submitted to Journal of the ACM.

[6] W. Bibel, Automated theorem proving (book in preparation to appear in Vieweg Verlag, Wiesbaden).

[7] W. Bibel, Syntax-directed, semantics-supported program synthesis, Artificial Intelligence Journal 14 (1980) 243-261.

[8] W. Bibel and R. Kowalski (eds.), 5th Conference on Automated Deduction, LN in Computer Sc. 87 (Springer, Berlin, 1980).

[9] W.W. Bledsoe, Non-resolution theorem proving, Artificial Intelligence 9 (1977) 1-35.

[10] C.-L. Chang and R.C.-T. Lee, Symbolic logic and mechanical theorem proving (Academic Press, New York, 1973).

[11] G. Gentzen, Untersuchungen über das logische Schließen I, Mathemat. Zeitschrift 39, (1935) 176-210.

[12] J. Herbrand, Recherches sur la Theorie de la Demonstration, Traveaux de la Sosietê des Sciences et des Lettres de Varsovie, Classe III sciences mathematiques et physiques, 33 (1930).

[13] W. Joyner (ed.), 4th Workshop on Automated Deduction (Austin, Texas, 1979).

[14] D.W. Loveland, Automated theorem proving (North Holland, Amsterdam, 1978).

[15] N.J. Nilsson, Principles of artificial intelligence (Tioga, Palo Alto, 1980).

[16] J.A. Robinson, Logic: form and function, Edinburgh University Press (1979).

Subsumption and Connection Graphs

Norbert Eisinger

Department of Computer Science
University of Maryland
College Park, MD

Abstract: A subsumption test based on the principal idea of Kowalski's connection graph proof procedure is developed. In contrast to the standard test this new test is sufficiently efficient to permit the unrestricted use of the subsumption rule in practice. The test is not limited to the connection graph proof procedure, but most naturally embedded into it. In the latter case the unrestricted combination of subsumption with other deletion rules is shown to be inconsistent.

1. Introduction

R. Kowalski's connection graph proof procedure [K75] represents a set of logical formulae not as a set but as a graph like structure. Inference rules such as resolution and factoring are expressed as operations on that graph. In addition to these operations, which usually expand the graph, the procedure also provides for deletion operations that remove certain components from the graph. Other approaches based on graphs have been proposed by [SI76], [SH76], [AN79].

One of the striking properties of the connection graph proof procedure is that application of a deletion operation can result in the applicability of further deletion operations, thus potentially leading to a snowball effect which rapidly reduces the graph. The probability of this effect rises with the number of deletion rules available.

A very powerful deletion rule for resolution based systems is the subsumption rule ([L78], chapter 4). Unfortunately a test for subsumption is very expensive and is usually implemented only for restricted cases. In this paper a test for subsumption based on the principal idea of the connection graph proof procedure is developed, which in contrast to the standard test ([L78]) is sufficiently efficient to permit unrestricted subsumption in practical cases. Though not limited to it, the test is most naturally embedded into the connection graph proof procedure, but unrestricted combination of subsumption, tautology, and purity deletion is shown to make the connection graph proof procedure inconsistent.

2. Definitions and Notations

The paper is based on the first order predicate calculus with the usual
notational conventions for constants, variables, terms, atoms, literals,
and clauses. The number of literals in a clause C is denoted by $|C|$.
The empty clause is denoted by ▫. The elements in a set of clauses are
always assumed to be variable disjoint.

A _substitution_ is a mapping σ from variables to terms identical almost
everywhere. It is extended to mappings on terms, atoms, literals, and
clauses by the usual homomorphism. A _unifier_ for two terms (or literals)
s, t is a substitution σ for which $\sigma(s) = \sigma(t)$. If for any other
unifier θ for s, t there is a θ' with $\theta = \theta' \circ \sigma$, we say σ is a _most
general unifier_ (mgu) for s and t. Two literals are called σ-
complementary, if they are of opposite sign and σ is an mgu for their
atoms. Two substitutions σ, θ are strongly compatible, if for each
variable v $\sigma(v) \neq v \wedge \theta(v) \neq v \Rightarrow \sigma(v) = \theta(v)$. Note that for a set of
pairwise strongly compatible substitutions their functional composition
is commutative.

A _connection graph_ is a pair (C, L) for which
1) C is a set of clauses
2) Let LIT = $\bigcup_{C \in L} C$ be the set of all literals occuring in the clauses
   of C.
   Then $L \subseteq C \times \text{LIT} \times C \times \text{LIT}$ is a relation such that

   a) $(C,L,C',L') \in L \Rightarrow C \neq C'$, $L \in C$, $L' \in C'$, L and L' are σ-complementary
   b) $(C,L,C',L') \in L \Leftrightarrow (C',L',C,L) \in L$

The graph is said to be _total_, if condition 2a) also holds in the
opposite direction. A literal L in a clause C is _pure_, if there are no
C', L' such that $(C,L,C',L') \in L$. The elements of L are called _links._
They connect σ-complementary literals in different clauses, thus
indicating possible resolutions.

The connection graph proof procedure defined in [K75] processes a set
C of clauses in the following way: first all possible links within C
are computed, i.e. a total graph (C, L) is constructed. This graph is
then reduced by some deletion rules yielding another total graph. Next
a link is selected and its resolvent created and incorporated into the
graph together with all its factors. Then the link resolved upon is
deleted from the graph and again the reduction rules are applied. The

next link is selected and so on until ▫∈C or L = ∅.

Incorporating a new clause into the graph means creating all links
between its literals and the rest of the graph. A literal in a resolvent
or factor has to be connected to all those places in the graph to which
at least one of its parent literals is connected by a link. Thus the
links are simply inherited. In addition to these inherited links all
links between a resolvent (or factor) and its parent clauses have to
be explicitly computed, or, more efficiently, derived from "autolinks"
between complementary literals in self resolving clauses ([B75]).

The reduction rules contribute both to the *practical* attractivity and
the *theoretical* difficulties of the connection graph proof procedure.
The original rules are: delete a clause if it contains a pure literal
and delete a clause which is a tautology. Further possible rules
indluce: delete a link if its resolvent is a tautology [WA81], delete
a clause if it is subsumed by another clause in the graph, delete a
link if its resolvent is subsumed by another clause in the graph. Note
that each deletion may cause a purity to arise, thereby causing further
deletions. It is not yet known as to which combinations of these
deletion rules preserve the completeness of the procedure.

3. Subsumption and the S-link Test

Let C and D be clauses. C σ-subsumes D, if $|C| \leq |D|$ and σ is a
substitution such that σ(C) ⊆ D. Throughout this paper the terms
subsumption and σ-subsumption will be used interchangeably, though
usually subsumption is defined more generally than σ-subsumption (see
[L78]).

The standard test for σ-subsumption works as follows: given C and D,
first make sure that $|C| \leq |D|$ and that D is not a tautology. Then
negate D and change variables in D to constants, yielding a set $\mathcal{D}$ of
ground unit clauses. C σ-subsumes D iff ▫ is derivable from {C} ∪ $\mathcal{D}$.
(Details can be found in [Cl73] and [L78].)

The positive aspect of this subsumption test is that it uses the same
mechanism which underlies the entire deduction system, i.e. resolution.
But from a practical point of view this turns out to be a disavantage.
Normally one has to check for subsumption as soon as a new clause is
generated, i.e. after each resolution step. This means that each
"major" resolution step is followed by several "minor" resolution steps
for the subsumption test, thus multiplying the overall expense. Yet
even worse, given a resolvent C there is no hint as to which clauses

potentially subsume or are subsumed by C. So the test, already
expensive in itself, has to be performed within an iteration over all
elements of the given set of clauses. In practice, of course, one would
first make sure that the predicates are in common, so that the test is
not performed during each iteration step.

The resulting cost is such that for practical systems only restricted
versions of subsumption are implemented, e.g. only for cases where the
subsuming clause is a unit. Omitting subsumption, on the other hand,
can cause considerable redundancies.

The central problem for a subsumption test consists in efficiently
finding out which literals in which clauses are unifiable. Disregarding
the signs of the literals this corresponds to the very same problem
that arises when two clauses have to be selected for the next resolution
step. In both cases comparing all literals of all clauses is a possible
but inefficient solution.

In the resolution case the connection graph procedure provides for a
more efficient alternative. The literals of a set of clauses are
compared with each other once and forever when the initial graph is
constructed. Subsequently the necessary information is directly
available in the form of the links. Because of the inheritance mechanism
for links the new literals in resolvents and factors need not go through
any search process either. Thus the problem of finding two resolvable
clauses is reduced to simply picking a link.

This basic idea can be applied to the subsumption problem by introducing
links of a new type that connect unifiable literals. Formally we define
a subsumption graph (S-graph) as a pair (C, S) such that

1) C is a set of clauses

2) Let LIT = $\bigcup_{C \in L} C$ be the set of all literals occuring in the clauses
    of C. Then $S \subseteq C \times \text{LIT} \times C \times \text{LIT}$ is a relation such that

    a) $(C,L,C',L') \in S \Rightarrow C \neq C'$, $L \in C$, $L' \in C'$, L and L' are unifiable

    b) $(C,L,C',L') \in S \Leftrightarrow (C',L',C,L) \in S$

The S-graph is said to be S-total, if condition 2a) also holds in the
opposite direction. A literal L in a clause C is S-pure, if there are
no C', L' such that $(C,L,C',L') \in S$. The elements of S are called S-links.

Given a set of clauses to be refuted, we initially compute all possible
S-links between literals in these clauses. When a new resolvent or
factor is derived, the S-links are inherited from the parent clauses in

the same way as are the resolution links in the connection graph proof
procedure. But in contrast to resolution links (R-links) S-links are
never deleted, unless one of the parent clauses is removed from C. It
can be shown easily that under these circumstances the S-graph remains
S-total throughout the entire computation (see [E80]).

In order to develop a subsumption test using S-graphs we need some
further definitions:
Let (C, S) be a S-graph, $C \in \mathcal{C}$ a clause and $L \in C$ a literal.
We define $con(C,L) := \{D \in \mathcal{C} \mid \exists K \in D \ (C,L,D,K) \in S\}$ as the set of all
clauses connected to L in C by S-links.

Further let $sub(C) := \bigcap_{L \in C} con(C,L)$ be the set of all clauses connected
to every literal in L by S-links.

For $L \in C$ and another clause $D \in \mathcal{C}$ we define
$uni(C,L,D) := \{\sigma \mid \exists K \in D \ (C,L,D,K) \in S \wedge \sigma(L) = K\}$ as the set of all matching
substitutions mapping L onto some literal in D. Finally let $U_1, \ldots, U_n$
be sets of substitutions. Then $merge(U_1, \ldots, U_n) := \{(\sigma_1, \ldots, \sigma_n) \in U_1 \times \ldots \times U_n \mid$
the σ_i are pairwise strongly compatible$\}$
is the subset of their cartesian product, for which the functional
composition of the components yields a unique substitution regardless
of their order.

The subsumption test is provided by the following theorems:

Theorem 1

Let (C,S) be an S-total subsumption graph and $C = \{L_1, \ldots, L_n\} \in \mathcal{C}$
a clause, $n \geq 1$. Then for $D \in \mathcal{C}$
$C \ \sigma$-subsumes D iff $|C| \leq |D| \wedge D \in sub(C) \wedge$
$$merge(uni(C,L_1,D), \ldots, uni(C,L_n,D)) \neq \emptyset.$$

Theorem 2

Let (C,S) be an S-total subsumption graph and $D = \{K_1, \ldots, K_m\} \in \mathcal{C}$
a clause, $m \geq 1$. Then for $C \neq \square$
$C \ \sigma$-subsumes D only if $C \in \bigcup_{i=1}^{n} con(D,K_i)$.

Detailed proofs can be found in [E80].

The following example illustrates the principle of a test based on
Theorem 1. Assume the set of clauses $\mathcal{C} = \{C, D_1, D_2, D_3, D_4\}$ with
$C = \{Pub, Quv\}$, $D_1 = \{Pxy, Qya\}$, $D_2 = \{Pzb, Pab, Qab\}$, $D_3 = \{Pww, Rw\}$,
$D_4 = \{Qaa, Rb\}$. We want to find all clauses subsumed by C. In this case
only S-links connected to C are relevant, so for reasons of clarity
all other S-links are omitted in the S-graph for C:

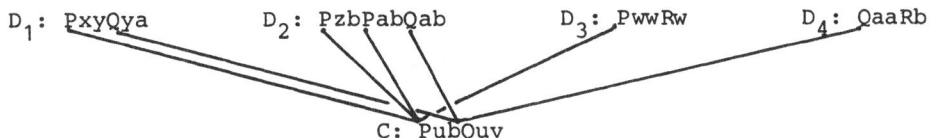

D_1: PxyQya D_2: PzbPabQab D_3: PwwRw D_4: QaaRb

C: PubQuv

Now $|C| \leq |D_i|$ for all i and sub(C) = $\{D_1,D_2\}$, because D_3 and D_4 are each connected to only one literal of C. We have to associate with each literal of C a set of matching substitutions for each clause in sub(C). In this case uni(C,Pub,D_1) = Ø because there is no σ such that σ(Pub) = Pxy. Thus D_1 can be disregarded.

For D_2 we obtain uni(C,Pub,D_2) = {{u := z}, {u := a}} and uni(C,Quv,D_2) = {{u := a, v := b}}. The substitutions {u := a} and {u := a, v := b} are strongly compatible, thus C subsumes D_2 (but none of D_1, D_3, D_4).

The main point of the test is that the expensive unification is postponed until the function sub preselected a plausible subset of candidates for subsumption. In case we are looking for subsuming rather than subsumed clauses, this preselection process is slightly more complicated. By Theorem 2 we first determine all clauses connected by at least one S-link to the given clause D. Then from this set we ascertain those C for which $|C| \leq |D|$ and D∈sub(C) holds and only then the unification operations are performed.

In both cases this preselection and the fact that the literals to be unified are explicitly known, can save considerable time. On the other hand some effort has to be invested for the computation of all S-links in the initial graph. As with the connection graph proof procedure this advance cost can be heigher than a possible gain, if the set of clauses is only small. For more complex examples however, there is certainly a pay off. But of course any gain in time has to be paid for by additional storage needed for the S-links.

4. Refinements of the S-link Test

The inheriting mechanism for S-links can be optimized in the same way as described in [B75] for resolution links. Here the proofs are very simple because S-graphs are always total.

Another refinement results from the observation that for a clause C containing an S-pure literal sub(C) = Ø. That means that such a clause cannot subsume any other clause.

When computing the uni(C,L_i,D) we need to know which $K \in D$ are unifiable with L_i. As the definition of uni shows, these are exactly those literals we already had to consider for the computation of con and sub. The information obtained during the computation of con and sub should be stored in an appropriate data structure to avoid having to recompute it for uni.

Thus far the S-link test was developed without considering the underlying inference mechanism. Since they are based on the same principal idea as connection graphs, S-graphs appear to be combined most naturally with this inference method. We can modify the definition of a connection graph to be a triple (C,R,S) such that (C,R) is a connection graph (in the hitherto sense) and (C,S) is an S-graph. For such a graph we can define a new kind of subsumption: a clause <u>C subsumes an R-link</u> (D_1,K_1,D_2,K_2), if C subsumes the resolvent of (D_1,K_1,D_2,K_2). It is possible to extend the test to cover this kind of subsumption (see [E80]).

Deleting subsumed links has the effect as if all resolutions leading to subsumed resolvents were performed prior to other steps. This results in a stronger reduction of the graph as in the usual case were subsumptions occur only randomly. The difference is similar to the one between deleting tautology clauses and deleting tautology links in a graph [WA81].

5. Consistency of the Connection Graph Procedure with Subsumption

In [E80] the consistency of all deletion rules mentioned in the introduction is proven for α-derivations [SS80], using a proof technique introduced in [B79]. Unfortunately this technique is not suitable to arbitrary derivations, but results shown in [SS76] indicate that there is a translation between α-derivations and arbitrary ground case strategies. The respective proofs are very complex and hard to follow, but if extended to the case of subsumption they might ensure the consistency for the ground case.

In the general case, however, the connection graph proof procedure with unrestricted subsumption is inconsistent as the following example shows:

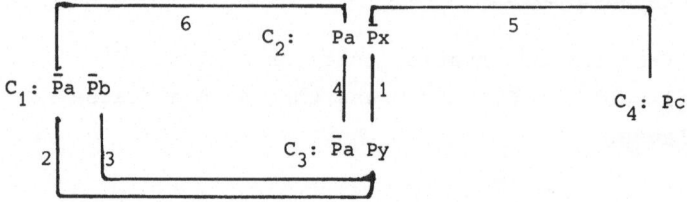

The resolvent of link 1 is a tautology, the resolvent of link 2 is subsumed by C_1, thus both links are deleted and the graph becomes

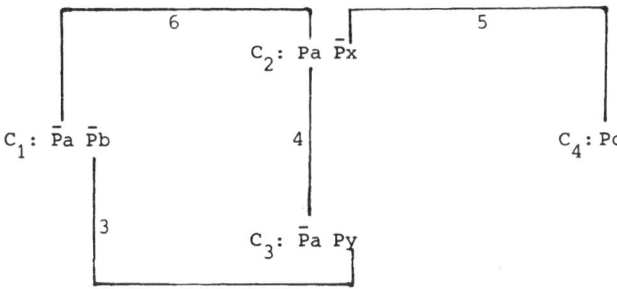

Resolution links 3, 5 and the successor of 6 (in that order) will yield the empty clause. If instead of that we select link 4 for the next step, the resolvent is $Pu\bar{P}v$ with link 3 and 5 inherited. This resolvent subsumes both C_2 and C_3, which are deleted. The resulting graph is

Now C_1 contains a pure literal and the subsequent deletions finally erase the entire graph.

This result demonstrates the necessity of restrictions for the deletion rules. It has yet to be shown which restrictions preserve consistency and completeness.

6. Practical Results

The S-link test has been implemented in the Markgraf Karl system at the University of Karlsruhe [ESSUW80], [SS80], [ESSW81]. Subsumption was restricted such that a resolvent may not be subsumed by its own parent clauses. The necessity of this restriction appears plausible, because a similar one applies to factors. No example for the inconsistency of the procedure with this restriction could be found thus far, but neither has there been a formal proof of its consistency.

On the average a graph has about the same number of S-links as it has R-links. This may seem an inappropriate increase in storage requirement. But in the actual implementation S-links need much less storage than R-links. Moreover, it is not the physical storage that is important, but the number of active R-links in the search space, and this number can be reduced considerably.

Practical tests indicate that the reduction of the graph caused by subsumption usually more than compensates for the storage used by the S-links. An example is P. Andrews' "challenge" proposed at the deduction workshop in Austin 1979: $(\exists xQx \equiv \forall yQy) \equiv (\exists x\forall y \; Qx \equiv Qy)$. Here subsumption reduces the initial graph by 89 % of the clauses and by 99,5 % of the R-links (which is however an extreme case).

In order to get some experience with more "natural" problems, a selection of examples from [MOW76] and [WM76] was run using the strategies basic resolution, set-of-support, and unit refutation, each with and without subsumption. The values compared are:

$$\text{G-penetrance} = \frac{\text{\# clauses in proof}}{\text{\# clauses generated}}$$

$$\text{D-penetrance} = \frac{\text{\# Resolvents/Factors in proof}}{\text{\# Resolvents/Factors totally deduced}}$$

$$\text{R-value} = \frac{\text{\# clauses deleted}}{\text{\# clauses generated}}$$

The results are compiled in the following table (- means that the system did not find a proof):

Name & strategy	G-penetrance no subs	subs	D-penetrance no subs	subs	R-value no subs	subs
Burstall						
BASIC	0,37	0,39	0,29	0,31	0,33	0,50
SOS	0,49	0,50	0,43	0,44	0,51	0,52
UNIT	0,45	0,48	0,38	0,42	0,39	0,42
Burstall-S						
BASIC	0,37	0,36	0,29	0,28	0,28	0,41
SOS	0,42	0,50	0,33	0,44	0,42	0,42
UNIT	0,42	0,45	0,34	0,38	0,32	0,35
Prim						
BASIC	0,87	0,81	0,86	0,86	0,35	0,43
SOS	0,57	0,71	0,46	0,63	0,34	0,43
UNIT	0,95	0,96	1,00	1,00	0,23	0,33
MOW						
BASIC	0,01	0,37	0,01	0,29	0,83	0,58
SOS	0,78	0,78	1,00	1,00	0,11	0,22
UNIT	-	-	-	-	-	-
EW3						
BASIC	0,77	0,89	0,77	1,00	0,27	0,95
SOS	-	0,94	-	1,00	-	0,94
UNIT	-	-	-	-	-	-
Hasparts-2						
BASIC	0,87	0,91	0,80	0,86	0,35	0,36
SOS	0,95	1,00	0,92	1,00	0,35	0,42
UNIT	-	-	-	-	-	-
LS-17						
BASIC	0,23	0,50	0,17	0,45	0,39	0,35
SOS	-	0,76	-	0,88	-	0,38
UNIT	0,15	0,41	0,09	0,33	0,22	0,41
LS-115						
BASIC	-	0,41	-	0,64	-	0,34
SOS	0,46	0,46	1,00	1,00	0,00	0,11
UNIT	-	0,41	-	0,64	-	0,12

The table shows that subsumption usually caused a considerable
improvement of the penetrances, i.e. fewer unnecessary steps were
performed. This demonstrates the reduction of the search space. Sometimes the system even found a proof where it did not without subsumption. The increase of the R-value indicates that subsumption infact
has a very strong impact on the size of the graph.

References

[AN79]   P. Andrews:
          Theorem Proving via General Matings, Carnegie Mellon
          University, Research Report 79-6

[B79]   W. Bibel:
          On Matrices with Connections, Universität Karlsruhe, 1979

[B75]   M. Bruynooghe:
          The Inheritance of Links in a Connection Graph,
          Report CW2, Katholieke Universiteit Leuven, 1975

[CL73]   C.L. Chang, R.C.T. Lee:
          Symbolic Logic and Mechanical Theorem Proving,
          Academic Press, New York, 1973

[E80]   N. Eisinger:
          Connectionsgraphen und Subsumptionsregeln,
          Diplom thesis, Institut für Informatik I, Universität
          Karlsruhe, 1980 (in German)

[ESSUW80] N. Eisinger, J. Siekmann, G. Smolka, E. Unvericht, C.Walther:
          The Markgraf Karl Refutation Procedure,
          Proceedings of AISB Conf., Amsterdam, 1980

[ESSW81] N. Eisinger, J. Siekmann, G. Smolka, C. Walther, P. Kursawe:
          The Markgraf Karl Refutation Procedure: USER MANUAL,
          Universität Karlsruhe, 1981

[ESW78]   N. Eisinger, J. Siekmann, G. Wrightson:
          Paramodulated Connection Graphs,
          Proceedings of the AISB/GI Conference, Hamburg, 1978

[H77]   G. Huet:
          Confluent Reductions: Abstract Properties and Applications
          to Rewrite Systems,
          IRIA laboria, Rapport de Recherche No. 250, 1977

[K75]   R. Kowalski:
          A Proof Procedure Using Connection Graphs,
          JACM vol. 22 No. 4, 1975

[LS75]   M. Livesey, J. Siekmann:
          Termination and Decidability Results for String Unification,
          Essex University Memo CSM-8-75, 1975

[L78]   D. Loveland:
          Automated Theorem Proving: A Logical Basis Fundamental
          Studies in Computer Science, North-Holland, 1978

[MOW76]   J. McCharen, R. Overbeck, L. Wos:
          Problems and Experiments for and with Automated Theorem
          Proving Programs, IEEE Trans. on Computers, vol C-25, No. 6,
          1976

[R65]   J.A. Robinson:
          A Machine-Oriented Logic Based on the Resolution Principle,
          JACM, vol 12, 1965

[SH76]   R.E. Shostak:
          Refutation Graphs, Journ. of Art. Intelligence, vol 7, No. 1,
          1976

[SI76]   S. Sickel:
          A Search Technique for Clause Interconnectivity Graphs,
          IEEE Trans. on Comp., vol C-25, No. 8, 1976

[SS76]   J. Siekmann, W. Stephan:
          Completeness and Soundness of the Connection Graph Proof
          Procedure, Interner Bericht 7/76, Institut für Informatik I,
          Universität Karlsruhe, 1976

[SS80]   J. Siekmann, G. Smolka:
          Selection Heuristics, Deletion Strategies and Terminator
          Configurations for the Connection Graph Proof Procedure,
          Universität Karlsruhe, 1980

[SS81]   J. Siekmann, W. Stephan:
          Completeness and Consistency of the Connection Graph Proof
          Procedure,
          to appear 1981

[WA81]   C. Walther:
          Elimination of Redundant Links in Extended Connection Graphs,
          Proc. of GWAI-81, Springer Fachberichte 1981

[WM76]   E. Wilson, J. Minker:
          Resolution, Refinements, and Search Strategies; A
          Comparative Study,
          IEEE Trans. on Computers, vol C-25, No. 6, 1976

Selection Heuristics, Deletion Strategies and N-Level Terminator Configurations for the Connection Graph Proof Procedure

J. Siekmann, G. Smolka
UNIVERSITÄT KARLSRUHE
Institut für Informatik I
Postfach 6380
D-7500 Karlsruhe 1

ABSTRACT: This report presents a quick overview of the Markgraf Karl Refutation Procedure, an automated theorem prover (TP) currently under development at the University of Karlsruhe, and then concentrates in detail on those parts of the system, which presently determine the choice of the deduction steps to be performed by the system.

The characteristic behaviour of the Karlsruher TP, whose hallmark is its

(i) display of an 'active' and directed behaviour in its striving for a proof, rather than the 'passive' combinatorial search through very large search spaces, which was the classical behaviour of the TPs of the past

(ii) and consequently its main feature, which is *not to generate* a search space of many thousands of clauses, but instead to find a proof with comparatively few redundant derivation steps,

is explained in terms of those features, whose evaluation determines the selection of each specific deduction step.

In particular the heuristic selection functions are discussed in detail and are evaluated with respect to their relative merit.

References:

J. Siekmann, G. Smolka:
Selection Heuristics, Deletion Strategies and N-Level
Terminator Configurations for the Connection Graph Proof
Procedure.
Universität Karlsruhe, Research Report, 1981.

N. Eisinger:
Subsumption and Connection Graphs.
Universität Karlsruhe, Research Report, 1981.

N. Eisinger, J. Siekmann, G. Smolka, E. Unvericht, C. Walther:
The Markgraf Karl Refutation Procedure (FALL 1980).
Universität Karlsruhe, Research Report, 1981.

N. Eisinger, P. Kursawe, J. Siekmann, G. Smolka, C. Walther:
The Markgraf Karl Refutation Procedure: USER MANUAL.
Universität Karlsruhe, Research Report, 1981.

C. Walther:
Elimination of Redundant Links in Extended Connection Graphs.
Universität Karlsruhe, Research Report, 1981.

ELIMINATION OF REDUNDANT

LINKS IN EXTENDED CONNECTION GRAPHS

Christoph Walther

Institut für Informatik I
UNIVERSITÄT KARLSRUHE
Postfach 6380
D-7500 Karlsruhe 1

Abstract:

The connection graph proof procedure [1, 2] allows us to remove a clause from the graph, if it is a tautology or a pure clause, i.e. if it is a clause which contains a literal which is not connected to any other literal in the graph.

This clause deletion rule can be transferred to links if we view a link as a potential clause: each link represents a potential factor, resolvent or para-modulant. Links which generate tautologies or pure clauses are called redundant links. Since non-redundant as well as redundant links are copied (i.e. inherited) in the process of a derivation, the elimination of redundant links as early as possible (i.e. immediately after their generation) prohibits their occasional exponential growth. We extend the connection graph proof procedure by several new types of links in order to formulate necessary and sufficient criteria that links are redundant. These criteria are used for an extension of the connection graph proof procedure by a reduction rule for redundant links which is currently being implemented and evaluated in the Markgraf Karl Refutation Procedure [4, 8]. These new links are also used to eliminate search on resolution-link inheritance [see 7]. The link-generation and inheritance rules for extended connection graphs are presented in [7].

Contents:

1. Introduction

In theorem proving by connection graphs, several attempts have been made to cut down the search space generated by the set of links in the graph:

- by computation of the value of a given link by means of heuristic estimates [3]

- by the transfer of strategies such as "set of support" or "unit refutation" to connection graphs [4]

- by a subsumption technique for connection graphs based on so-called s-links [5].

In contrast to the first two approaches, subsumption does not discriminate or favour certain *links*, but leads to a deletion of certain (i.e. subsumed) *clauses*. However, if we view a link as a potential clause, subsumption is applicable to links as well:

We say a link ℓ is subsumed by a clause C, if the clause R generated by ℓ is subsumed by C. In subsumed connection graphs, subsumed links (instead of subsumed clauses) are deleted (for details see [5]).

Obviously this idea is also useful for other clause-deletion rules:

The connection graph proof procedure [1] allows the deletion of a clause with all its links, if it is;

- a tautology

- a pure clause.

Links which generate a tautology or a pure clause (e.g. by resolution) are called *redundant links*. We can enlarge the clause deletion rule mentioned above to links, by removing all redundant links from the connection graph.

The advantage of this approach is not merely that we reduce the search space by a few redundant links, but that *we prevent the growth of the graph caused by the inheritance of redundant links*.

We shall start with a survey of basic notions used in theorem proving with para-modulated connection graphs [2]. Then we shall discuss the different ways a tautology can be generated in a connection graph. Based on this analysis new link types are introduced by which a criterion for links is formulated which is necessary and sufficient for tautology generation. From this criterion we can establish a deletion rule for links which generate tautologies and we can incorporate it into the connection graph proof procedure.

Purity clauses are dealt with in the same way [7].

The generation and inheritance rules for the newly defined link types are given in [7].

2. Basic Notions

We assume that the reader is familiar with the basic notions of theorem proving based on resolution [6], connection graphs [1] and paramodulated connection graphs [2]. We remind the reader however of some definitions which are essential for the subsequent sections:

A *connection graph* is a set of clauses together with several sets of links. The latter include

-F-LINKS, the set of factorisation links

-R-LINKS, the set of resolution links

-P-LINKS, the set of paramodulation links.

A *factorisation link*(F-link) is a pair $<C,\tau>$, where C is a clause and τ is a most general unifier (mgu) for $\tau L_0 = \tau L_i$ $(1 \le i \le n)$ where $\{L_0, L_1, \ldots, L_n\} \subset C$. If $\ell = <C,\tau>$ is an F-link, the clause τC is the *factor of C*, formed by ℓ.

The *absolute value* $|L|$ of an unnegated literal L is L. $|L|$ is L' if $L = \neg L'$.

We say that two literals L and K are *complementary equal*, if $L \neq K$ and $|L| = |K|$.

Two literals L and K are *complementary unifiable*, iff for all substitutions Θ $\Theta L \neq \Theta K$ and for at least one substitution τ $\tau |L| = \tau |K|$.

Two literals L and K are *unifiable*, iff for at least one substitution τ $\tau L = \tau K$.

Two literals L and K are *(complementary) unifiable with mgu* τ, iff τ is a mgu for $\tau L = \tau K (\tau |L| = \tau |K|)$.

A *resolution link*(R-link) ℓ is a 5-tupel $<C,M,D,N,\tau>$ where C and D are two distinct clauses and $M \in C$ and $N \in D$ are two complementary unifiable literals with mgu τ.

The *resolvent* R generated by the R-link ℓ is defined as

$$R = \tau(C-\{M\}) \cup \tau(D-\{N\}).$$

A *term access function* α is a partial mapping from the set of literals to the set of terms, such that, if a literal L is in the domain of α, then $\alpha(L)$ is a subterm of L.

If a literal L is in the domain of a term access function α, we say α *is admissible for L*.

We shall make use of the following proposition later:

Proposition 1:
If α is an admissible term access function for a literal L, then for each

substitution τ, α is admissible for τL and $\alpha(\tau L) = \tau\ \alpha(L)$.

Each term access function α induces an *equivalence relation* $\stackrel{\alpha}{=}$ on the set of literals:

$L \stackrel{\alpha}{=} K$ iff α is admissible for L and α is admissible for K implies

$\qquad\qquad$ L = K except for the subterms of L and K given by α

Example:
If L = P(xf(x)), K = P(xf(y)) and α selects the first argument of the second argument of each literal, i.e. $\alpha(L) = x$ and $\alpha(K) = y$, then

$\quad$ $L \stackrel{\alpha}{=} K.$

In the next sections we make use of the following proposition:

Proposition 2:
If L and K are literals and α is an admissible term access function for L and for K such that

$\quad$ (1) $L \stackrel{\alpha}{=} K$ and
$\quad$ (2) $\alpha(L) = \alpha(K)$
then   L = K.

A *paramodulation link*(P-link) ℓ is a 6-tuple $<C,M,\alpha,D,N,\tau>$ where C and D are two distinct clauses, M is a non-equality literal in C, N is a equality literal of the form s $\equiv$ t in D, α is an admissible term access function for M and τ is a mgu for

$$\tau\alpha(M) = \tau s.$$

The *paramodulant* P generated by the P-link ℓ is defined as follows:

$$P = \tau(C-\{M\}) \cup \tau(D-\{N\}) \cup \{\tau\hat{M}\}$$

where $\qquad\qquad$ $\tau\hat{M} \stackrel{\alpha}{=} \tau M$
and $\qquad\qquad$ $\alpha(\tau\hat{M}) = \tau t$.

$\tau\hat{M}$ is called the *paramodulated literal* and is obtained from τM by replacing the subterm $\tau\alpha(M)$ (which is equal to τs) by τt.

3. Tautologies

3.1 Tautology Generation

A clause is a *tautology*, iff

(1) it contains a literal of the form $t \equiv t$

   or

(2) it contains two complementary equal literals.

We classify tautologies by the way in which they are generated:

Type 1: A tautology is generated by an application of a substitution to a clause (this happens on factorisation, resolution and paramodulation).

Example:
The application of the factoring-substitution $\tau = \{x/a \quad y/a\}$ to the clause $C = <\neg Px, Py, Qxa, Qay>$ results in a factor of C $<\neg Pa, Pa, Qaa>$ which is a tautology.

Type 2: The two complementary equal literals in a tautology stem from distinct parent clauses and are made complementary equal by the application of a substitution to both parent clauses (this happens on resolution and paramodulation).

Example:
Resolution upon $\neg Qxa$ and Qay in the parent clauses $<Px, \neg Qxa>$ and $<Qay, Py>$ results in the resolvent $<Pa, \neg Pa>$ which is a tautology.

Type 3: The tautology is generated by replacing a subterm of a literal in a clause and by applying a substitution to the clause (this happens only on paramodulation).

Example:
Paramodulation upon $\neg P(f(f(a)))$ and $f(f(x)) \equiv x$ in the parent clauses $<\neg Pf(f(a)), Pa>$ and $<f(f(x)) \equiv x>$ results in the paramodulant $<\neg Pa, Pa>$ which is a tautology.

Type 4: The tautology is generated by inserting complementary equal literals in a clause which stem from two distinct clauses and are made complementary equal by subterm replacement and application of a substitution to both clauses (this happens only on paramodulation).

Example:
Paramodulation upon $\neg Pf(f(a))$ and $f(f(x)) \equiv x$ in the parent clauses $<\neg Pf(f(a))>$ and $<f(f(x)) \equiv x, Pa>$ results in the paramodulant $<\neg Pa, Pa>$ which is a tautology.

3.2 Tautology Detection

Next we shall analyze the different types of tautologies to develop criteria which prevent us from generating tautologies during the search for a proof.

Type 1 - Tautologies:

Tautologies that are generated in this way are detected using socalled Tautology Substitution Links:

(DEF) A *tautology substitution link* (TS-link) is a triple $<C,L,K>$ where C is a clause and L and K are complementary unifiable literals in C, or is a triple $<C,s,t>$ where s and t are unifiable terms and $s \equiv t$ is a literal in C.

(DEF) A connection graph is *fully TS-connected*, iff for each clause C and for each pair of complementary unifiable literals $L \in C$ and $K \in C$ (for each literal $s \equiv t \in C$), the TS-link $<C,L,K>$ ($<C,s,t>$) is in TS-LINKS, i.e. the set of all TS-links of a connection graph.

Subsequently we assume connection graphs to be fully TS-connected.

(DEF) A F-link $<C,\sigma>$ or a
R-link $<C,M,D,N,\sigma>$ or a
P-link $<C,M,\alpha,D,N,\sigma>$ or a
P-link $<D,N,\alpha,C,M,\sigma>$

is τ_1-*redundant* iff there exists a

TS-link $<C,L,K> \in$ TS-LINKS($<C,s,t> \in$ TS-LINKS)
such that

$$L \neq M, \qquad K \neq M \quad (s \equiv t \neq M)$$
$$\text{and} \quad \sigma|L| = \sigma|K|(\sigma s = \sigma t).$$

Lemma (τ_1-criterion)

If ℓ is a τ_1-redundant F-, R- or P-link in a connection graph then the factor, resolvent or paramodulant generated by ℓ is a tautology.

Proof:

Let C be the clause generated by ℓ. From the definition of factorisation, resolution, paramodulation and τ_1-redundancy we can infer that

$$\sigma L \in C, \quad \sigma K \in C \quad \text{and} \quad \sigma|L| = \sigma|K|.$$

Since L and K have opposite signs by definition of TS-links, C contains two complementary equal literals and hence is a tautology.

If the TS-link which makes ℓ τ_1-redundant is of the form $<C,s,t>$ where s and t are terms, C contains a literal of the form $\sigma s \equiv \sigma s$ and hence is a tautology.

□

Type 2 – Tautologies

Tautologies of this type are detected on the basis of socalled Tautology Resolvent Links:

(DEF) A *tautology resolvent link* (TR-link) is a quadruple $<C,L,D,K>$ where C and D are distinct clauses and $L \in C$ and $K \in D$ are complementary unifiable literals.

(DEF) A connection graph is *fully TR-connected*, iff for each pair of clauses C and D in the graph and for each pair of complementary unifiable literals $L \in C$ and $K \in D$ a TR-link $<C,L,D,K>$ is a member of TR-LINKS (the set of all TR-links of the graph), iff no R-link $<C,L,D,K,\tau>$ is in R-LINKS.

In a fully TR-connected connection graph each pair of complementary unifiable literals in distinct clauses is connected with exactly one TR- or R-link!

Subsequently we assume connection graphs to be fully TR-connected.

(DEF) A R-link $<C,M,D,N,\sigma>$ or a
P-link $<C,M,\alpha,D,N,\sigma>$ or a
P-link $<D,N,\alpha,C,M,\sigma>$

in a connection graph is τ_2-*redundant*, iff there is a

R-link $<C,L,D,K,\Theta> \in$ R-LINKS or a
TR-link $<C,L,D,K> \in$ TR-LINKS

such that

$$L \neq M, \quad K \neq N \quad \text{and} \quad \tau|L| = \tau!K|.$$

Lemma (τ_2-criterion)

If ℓ is a τ_2-redundant R- or P-link in a connection graph then the resolvent or paramodulant generated by ℓ is a tautology.

Proof:

Let C be the clause generated by ℓ. From the definition of resolution, paramodulation and τ_2-redundancy we infer that

$$\sigma L \in C, \quad \sigma K \in C \quad \text{and} \quad \sigma|L| = \sigma|K|.$$

Since L and K have opposite signs by the definition of R- and TR-links, C is a tautology.

□

Type 3 - Tautologies

We introduce another new link type to detect tautologies of this type:

(DEF) A *tautology paramodulant link* (TP-link) is a 5-tupel $<C,M,\alpha,D,s \equiv t>$ where C
and D are distinct clauses, M is a non-equality literal in C, $s \equiv t$ is an equality
literal in D and α is an admissible term access function for M, such that $\alpha(M)$ and
s are unifiable terms.

(DEF) A connection graph is *fully TP-connected*, iff for each pair of clauses C and
D in the graph and for each pair of a non-equality literal $M \in C$ and an equality literal
$s \equiv t \in D$ a TP-link $<C,M,\alpha,D,s \equiv t>$ is in TP-LINKS (the set of all TP-links in a
connection graph) iff no P-link $<C,M,\alpha,D,s \equiv t,\sigma>$ is in P-LINKS, where α is an
admissible term access function for M and $\alpha(M)$ and s are unifiable terms.

In a fully TP-connected connection graph each side of an equality literal is
connected to a subterm of a non-equality literal in another clause by exactly one P-
or TP-link, whenever the side of the equality and the subterm are unifiable!

Subsequently we assume connection graphs to be fully TP-connected.

(DEF) A P-link $<C,M,\alpha,D,s \equiv t,\sigma>$ in a connection graph is τ_3-*redundant*, iff there is
a P-link $<C,N,\alpha,D,t \equiv s,\Theta> \in$ P-LINKS or a
 TP-link $<C,N,\alpha,D,t \equiv s> \in$ TP-LINKS
such that
M and N have opposite signs and the same predicate symbol, $\sigma|M| \overset{\alpha}{\cong} \sigma|N|$ and $\sigma t = \sigma\alpha(N)$.

Lemma (τ_3-criterion)

If ℓ is a τ_3-redundant P-link, then the associated paramodulant contains two
complementary equal literals and hence is a tautology.

Proof:
If $\sigma\hat{M}$ is the paramodulated literal in the paramodulant P given by the P-link
$<C,M,\alpha,D,s \equiv t,\sigma>$, we have by the definition of paramodulation:

$$\sigma\hat{M} \overset{\alpha}{\cong} \sigma M$$

and $\quad\sigma\alpha(\hat{M}) = \sigma t$.

Hence by the τ_3-redundancy of link ℓ:

$$\sigma|M| \overset{\alpha}{\cong} \sigma|N|$$

and $\quad\sigma t = \sigma\alpha(N)$

we can infer that

$$\sigma|\hat{M}| \overset{\alpha}{\cong} \sigma|N|$$

and
$$\sigma\alpha(\hat{M}) = \sigma\alpha(N)$$

which gives us $\sigma|\hat{M}| = \sigma|N|$, i.e. $\sigma\hat{M}$ and σN are complementary equal literals. Since $\sigma\hat{M} \in P$ and $\sigma N \in P$, P is a tautology.

□

Type 4 - Tautologies

It is characteristic for tautologies of this type that the two complementary equal literals are the paramodulated literal and a literal stemming from the equality clause.

(DEF) A P-link $<C,M,\alpha,D,s \equiv t,\sigma>$ in a connection graph is $\tau_4\text{-}redundant$, iff there exists a literal $N \in D$ different from $s \equiv t$ such that
M and N have opposite signs and the same predicate symbol,
$\sigma|M| \overset{\alpha}{\cong} \sigma|N|$ and $\sigma t = \sigma\alpha(N)$.

Lemma ($\tau_4\text{-}criterion$)

If ℓ is a τ_4-redundant P-link, then the paramodulant P generated by ℓ contains two complementary equal literals and is therefore a tautology.

Proof:
If $\sigma\hat{M}$ is the paramodulated literal in the paramodulant P given by $<C,M,\alpha,D,s \equiv t,\sigma>$, we know from the definition of paramodulation:

$$\sigma\hat{M} \overset{\alpha}{\cong} \sigma M$$
and
$$\sigma\alpha(\hat{M}) = \sigma t.$$

Hence by the τ_4-redundancy of link ℓ:

$$\sigma|M| \overset{\alpha}{\cong} \sigma|N|$$
$$\sigma t = \sigma\alpha(N)$$

we can infer that

$$\sigma|\hat{M}| \overset{\alpha}{\cong} \sigma|N|$$
$$\sigma\alpha(\hat{M}) = \sigma\alpha(N)$$

which gives us $\sigma|\hat{M}| = \sigma|N|$.

Since $\sigma\hat{M} \in P$ and $\sigma N \in P$, P is a tautology.

□

Remark

The detection of type-4 tautologies involves a *search* for the literal $N \in D$. This problem could be solved by the introduction of a new class of links (similar to

P-links), which connect one side of an equality with a subterm of a literal *in the same clause*. Using these links the literal NED could be found without search. We reject this solution: As in the case of P-links, the number of those links in a connection graph would be very large, so that the cost of generating, inheriting and storing these links exceeds the cost of the search for a specific literal in a clause. Note that this argument does not hold for TP-links, since the number of TP-links compared to the number of P-links in a connection graph is very small indeed.

3.3 Tautology Redundant Links

In order to avoid the generation of tautologies, we shall introduce the notion of tautology redundant links:

(DEF) A F-, R- or P-link ℓ in a fully TS-, TR- and TP-connected connection graph is *tautology redundant* (τ-redundant), iff ℓ is τ_i-redundant for some $i \in \{1,2,3,4\}$.

Theorem 1

A clause generated by an F-, R- or P-link ℓ in a fully TS-, TR- and TP-connected connection graph is a tautology, iff ℓ is a τ-redundant link.

Proof:

"if": This is an obvious consequence of the τ_1-, τ_2-, τ_3- and τ_4-criteria.

□

"only if": Here we demonstrate the proof only for P-links and paramodulants. The proof for F-links, R-links, factors and resolvents is a subcase of the paramodulation case and worked out in the same way.

Suppose the paramodulant P generated by the P-link $<C,M,\alpha,D,s \equiv t,\sigma>$ is a tautology.

P is given as

$$\sigma(C-\{M\}) \cup \sigma(D-\{s \equiv t\}) \cup \{\sigma\hat{M}\}$$

where

$$\sigma M \overset{\alpha}{\cong} \sigma\hat{M}$$

$$\sigma\alpha(M) = \sigma s$$

and

$$\sigma\alpha(\hat{M}) = \sigma t.$$

Case 1:

Let us suppose $\sigma q \equiv \sigma r \in P$, where $\sigma q = \sigma r$. Since $\hat{M}$ is a non-equality literal we know

$$\sigma q \equiv \sigma r \in \sigma(C-\{M\}) \cup \sigma(D-\{s \equiv t\})$$

and hence $q \equiv r \in C \cup D$, $q \equiv r \neq M$.

Since q and r are unifiable, there exists a TS-link $<C,q,r>$ or $<D,q,r>$ in TS-LINKS because we work with fully TS-connected graphs.

Hence P-link ℓ is τ_1-redundant.

Case 2:

Let us assume we have two literals $\sigma L \in P$ and $\sigma K \in P$, which are complementary equal.

We can distinguish five cases depending on the membership of σL and σK in

$$\sigma(C-\{M\}), \quad \sigma(D-\{s \equiv t\}) \quad \text{and} \quad \{\sigma\hat{M}\}.$$

Case (i):
$$\sigma L \in \sigma(C-\{M\}) \quad \text{and} \quad \sigma K \in \sigma(C-\{M\}).$$

With L and K we have two complementary unifiable literals in C different from M. Since we work with fully TS-connected graphs there must be a TS-link $<C,L,K>$ in TS-LINKS. With $L \neq M$, $K \neq M$ and $\sigma|L| = \sigma|K|$, ℓ is a τ-redundant link by the definition of τ_1- and τ-redundancy.

Case (ii):
$$\sigma L \in \sigma(D-\{s \equiv t\}) \quad \text{and} \quad \sigma K \in \sigma(D-\{s \equiv t\}).$$

The proof is the same as for case (i).

Case (iii):
$$\sigma L \in \sigma(C-\{M\}) \quad \text{and} \quad \sigma K \in \sigma(D-\{s \equiv t\}).$$

With L and K we have two complementary unifiable literals in C and D different from M and $s \equiv t$. Since we work with fully TR-connected graphs there must be a R-link $<C,L,D,K,\Theta>$ or a TR-link $<C,L,D,K>$ with $L \neq M$, $K \neq s \equiv t$ and $\sigma|L| = \sigma|K|$.

Hence ℓ is a τ-redundant link by the definition of τ_2- and τ-redundancy.

Case (iv):
$$\sigma L \in \sigma(C-\{M\}) \quad \text{and} \quad \sigma K = \sigma\hat{M}.$$

By the definition of paramodulation we know
$$\alpha(\sigma\hat{M}) = \sigma t$$
and hence
$$\alpha(\sigma K) = \sigma t.$$

With $\sigma|L| = \sigma|K|$ we get

$$\alpha(\sigma K) = \alpha(\sigma L)$$

and so $\qquad\qquad\qquad \alpha(\sigma L) = \sigma t.$

Hence in a fully TP-connected graph there must be a

$$\text{P-link} \quad <C,L,\alpha,D,t \equiv s,\theta> \quad \text{ or a}$$
$$\text{TP-link} \quad <C,L,\alpha,D,t \equiv s> \; .$$

With $\qquad\qquad\qquad \sigma|L| \stackrel{\alpha}{\cong} \sigma|K|$

and $\qquad\qquad\qquad \sigma K \stackrel{\alpha}{\cong} \sigma M \; ,$

we have $\qquad\qquad\qquad \sigma|L| \stackrel{\alpha}{\cong} \sigma|M|$ which together

with $\qquad\qquad\qquad \alpha(\sigma L) = \sigma t$ establishes the τ_3-redundancy and hence the τ-redundancy of the given P-link.

Case (v):
$$\sigma L \in \sigma(D - \{s \equiv t\}) \quad \text{and} \quad \sigma K = \sigma \hat{M}$$

From $\qquad\qquad\qquad \sigma|L| = \sigma|K|$ we know

$$\sigma\alpha(L) = \sigma\alpha(K) \quad \text{and hence}$$

$$\sigma\alpha(L) = \sigma t \quad \text{by definition of paramodulation. Since } L\in D \text{ is}$$

different from $s \equiv t$, the given P-link is τ-redundant by the definition of τ_4- and τ-redundancy.

$\square$

3.4 Tautology Link Reduction

Theorem 1 gives us a necessary and sufficient condition to detect links which generate tautologies by means of TS-, TR- and TP-links.

In an implementation we use this information to avoid generation of tautologies: we extend the Connection Graph Proof Procedure by a socalled *τ-link reduction rule:*

(1) For each clause in the initial graph create all TS-links to guarantee the fully TS-connected property of the graph.

(2) After creation of the initial graph, remove each τ-redundant F-link from the graph. *Recolour* each τ-redundant R- or P-link to a TR- or TP-link to guarantee that the graph is still fully TR- and TP-connected.

(3) After generation of a factor, remove the associated F-link from the graph. After

generation of a resolvent or paramodulant, *recolour* the associated R- or P-link to a TR- or TP-link (R- and P-links must not be removed to guarantee the fully TR- and TP-connected property of the graph). In addition generate all TS-links for the factor, resolvent or paramodulant.

(4) After generation of a resolvent or paramodulant, remove each τ-redundant F-link from the graph, which is attached to the resolvent or paramodulant. After generation of a factor, resolvent or paramodulant, *recolour* each τ-redundant R- or P-link to a TR- or TP-link, which is connected to a literal in the factor, resolvent or paramodulant.

(5) After recolouring a R- or P-link, check the link's parent clauses for purity.

4. *Literature*

[1] R. KOWALSKI
     A Proof Procedure using Connection Graphs
     JACM, vol 22, no 4, Oct. 75

[2] J. SIEKMANN, G. WRIGHTSON
     Paramodulated Connection Graphs
     Acta Informatica, no 13, 1980

[3] J. SIEKMANN, G. SMOLKA
     Selection Heuristics, Deletion Strategies and Terminator Configurations for the
     Conncection Graph Proof Procedure
     Universität Karlsruhe, 1981

[4] N. EISINGER, J. SIEKMANN, G. SMOLKA, C. WALTHER
     The Markgraf Karl Refutation Procedure (FALL 1980)
     Universität Karlsruhe, 1981

[5] N. EISINGER
     Subsumption and Connectiongraphs
     Springer Fachberichte 1981 (this volume)

[6] D.W. LOVELAND
     Automated Theorem Proving:
     A Logical Basis
     North Holland Publishing Company, 1978

[7] C. WALTHER
     Elimination of Redundant Links in Extended Connection Graphs
     Interner Bericht, Universität Karlsruhe, 1981

[8] N. EISINGER, P. KURSAWE, J. SIEKMANN, G. SMOLKA, C. WALTHER
     The Markgraf Karl Refutation Procedure: USER MANUAL
     Universität Karlsruhe, 1981

TERM REDUCTION SYSTEMS AND ALGEBRAIC ALGORITHMS

Rüdiger Loos

Institut für Informatik I
UNIVERSITÄT KARLSRUHE
Postfach 6380
D.7500 Karlsruhe 1

Abstract

We give a short survey of results and applications of term rewriting systems. We show that common algebraic algorithms can be understood as reduction or completion procedures for equationally defined algebraic theories. Most naturally this can be done by proving algebraic reduction relations noetherian and confluent directly; however, important algebraic algorithms are instances of the Knuth Bendix completion procedure for term reduction systems.

> It is the common curse of all general and abstract theories that they have to be far advanced before yielding useful results in concrete problems.
>
> Hermann Weyl,
> Algebraic Theory of Numbers,
> Princeton University Press,
> 1940, p.124.

1. Introduction

Let $B = x_1^2 + x_2^2$ be an integral polynomial in the indeterminates x_1 and x_2. If we consider x_1 and x_2 as zeros of the polynomial $A \in \mathbb{Z}[x]$, $A = a_2 x^2 + a_1 x + a_0$ of degree 2 then B can be expressed in terms of a_0, a_1 and a_2, since $y_1 = x_1 + x_2 = -a_1/a_2$ and $y_2 = x_1 x_2 = a_0/a_2$. In order to rewrite B in the coefficients of A we compare B with y_1^2 and set $B-y_1^2 = -2x_1 x_2$ which we rewrite as $B - y_1^2 = -2y_2$ or $B = y_1^2 - 2y_2 = (a_1^2 - 2a_0 a_2)/a_2$. Algebraically speaking, we have the symmetrical polynomial B in x_1 and x_2 expressed by the elementary symmetrical functions y_1 and y_2 in x_1 and x_2. Gauß [1] has given an algorithm for carrying out systematically the rewriting process:

$$B* \leftarrow GAUSS(B)$$

[Input: $B \in \mathbb{Z}[x_1,\ldots,x_r]$, a symmetrical polynomial in $x_1,\ldots,x_r$.
Output: $B* \in \mathbb{Z}[y_1,\ldots,y_r]$ with $B*(y_1,\ldots,y_r) = B(x_1,\ldots,x_r)$ where the
y_i are the elementary symmetrical polynomials in $x_1,\ldots,x_r$.]

(1) [Initialize.] $B* \leftarrow 0$.

(2) [Rewrite.]

    while $B \neq 0$ do

       $\{$let $ax_1^{n_1} \ldots x_r^{n_r}$ be the leading term of B.

       set $b(y_1,\ldots,y_r) \leftarrow ay_1^{n_1-n_2} \ldots y_{r-1}^{n_{r-1}-n_r} y_r^{n_r}$, $B* \leftarrow B* + b(y_1,\ldots,y_r)$

         $b(x_1,\ldots x_r) \leftarrow b(y_1(x_1,\ldots,x_r),\ldots,y_r(x_1,\ldots,x_r))$,

         $B \leftarrow B - b(x_1,\ldots,x_r)\}$ ∎

The leading term of B is the term with the highest exponent vector
$n_1 \ldots n_r$ considered as a non-negative integer with a radix larger than
any occurring n_i. In $B-b$ the y_i are considered as terms in $x_1,\ldots,x_r$
whereas in $B*+b$ the y_i are indeterminates. The process terminates since
the set of exponent vectors is well founded and the leading term of B
cancels in $B-b$. In addition, the process terminates uniquely as was
proved by Gauß.

Another way to look at this algebraic algorithm is to consider, for
any fixed r, the equations

$$y_1 = x_1 + \ldots + x_r$$
$$y_2 = x_1x_2 + \ldots + x_{r-1}x_r$$
$$\vdots$$
$$y_r = x_1 \ldots x_r$$

as computation rules for a rewrite process. Let us attempt to do this
for $r = 2$: $y_1 = x_1 + x_2$, $y_2 = x_1x_2$. We set

        (1) $x_1 = - x_2 + y_1$

and get   (2) $x_2^2 = x_2y_1 - y_2$

after substitution of x_1. Next we interprete these equations as rewrite
rules from left to right. Then the term $x_1^2 + x_2^2$ is rewritten as

$$\xrightarrow[(2)]{} x_1^2 + x_2y_1 - y_2 \xrightarrow[(1)]{} x_2^2 - 2x_2y_1 + y_1^2 + x_2y_1 - y_2 \xrightarrow[(2)]{}$$

$$x_2y_1 - y_2 - 2x_2y_1 + y_1^2 + x_2y_1 - y_2 = y_1^2 - 2y_2.$$

The system (1), (2) is a complete term reduction system which reduces any term in a finite number of steps to a unique result. The reduction process is non-deterministic with respect to the order in which the rules are applied and with respect to the subterms to which they are applied. The process implies as a special case the given Gaussian algorithm.

Complete reduction systems were studied systematically by Knuth and Bendix [2] and found many applications in the algebraic definition of abstract data types and in some other cases, among them group theory. We will show that many and very fundamental algebraic algorithms are either special forms of Knuth-Bendix like completion algorithms or are directly special instances of the completion process given by Knuth and Bendix.

The importance of a complete reduction system stems from the fact that it provides a decision procedure for the equational theory, the axioms of which were used as starting point of the completion process. An equation can simply be decided by reducing both terms to their canonical forms which are checked for equality.

In Section 2 we give a short exposition of reduction systems following Huet [3] and Huet and Oppen [4].

In Section 3 we study in some detail Bergman's [5] algorithm as completion algorithm which generalizes two famous algebraic algorithms: Euclid's algorithm and the Gaussian elimination algorithm for linear systems.

2. Confluent Reduction Systems

Let E be any set. We want to characterize a binary relation on E, called <u>reduction</u> and denoted by $x \to y$, abstractly by axioms. Most important, the reduction relation is <u>confluent</u>, iff

$$\bigwedge_{x,y,z \,\in\, E} \{ \overset{*}{\swarrow} \overset{z}{\underset{x \quad y}{\searrow}} \overset{*}{} \to \bigvee_{u \in E} \overset{x \quad y}{\underset{u}{\searrow \swarrow}} \}$$

where $\overset{*}{\to}$ denotes the transitive reflexive closure of $\to$, namely zero or more reductions. Next, the reduction relation is <u>noetherian</u>, if there do not exist infinite reduction chains $x_0 \to x_1 \to x_2 \to \ldots$. The importance of these two concepts is based on the simple

Theorem

If a relation $\to$ over E is noetherian and confluent then for every element e of E there is a unique $\bar{e} \in E$ such that $e \overset{*}{\to} \bar{e}$.

The <u>proof</u> is based on two observations. Since $\to$ is noetherian, every $e \in E$ can be reduced into irreducible elements $e_1, e_2, \ldots$ (normal forms of e). Now assume $e_1 \neq e_2$ for any two such normal forms of e. We have $e \overset{*}{\to} e_1$ and $e \overset{*}{\to} e_2$ and by the definition of confluence there is an $\bar{e} \in E$ with $e_1 \overset{*}{\to} \bar{e}$ and $e_2 \overset{*}{\to} \bar{e}$, contradicting the irreducibility of e_1 and e_2. Therefore $e_1 = e_2$ ∎

<u>Example 1:</u> Let $E = \mathbb{N}$ and define $\to$ to be the subtraction in $\mathbb{N}$ by a fixed element $b \in \mathbb{N}$. Clearly, $\to$ is confluent since for all reductions $a \overset{*}{\to} a_1 = a - q_1 b$ with $q_1 \geq 0$ reduction steps and

$a \overset{*}{\to} a_2 = a - q_2 b$ with $q_2 \geq 0$ steps we have

$a_2 \overset{*}{\to} a_1 = a_2 - (q_1 - q_2)b$, if $q_1 \geq q_2$, and

$a_1 \overset{*}{\to} a_2 = q_1 - (q_2 - q_1)b$, if $q_2 \geq q_1$. In order to make $\to$ noetherian, we restrict b to be non-zero, therefore $a_1 \to a_2$ implies $a_1 > a_2$ and $\mathbb{N}$ is well founded. The unique normal form of a is a mod b in $\mathbb{N}$ ∎

For algebraic algorithms which can be understood as confluent and noetherian reductions the two properties have different weight. Although there are in general only sufficient but not neccessary conditions available to ensure finite termination, in the algebraic context termination is usually not the problem.For this reason we only refer the reader to the literature here for the problem of establishing termination [4, 6, 7].

A much more difficult problem is to establish confluence. A weaker

condition is <u>local confluence</u> which asserts for →, that for all x,y,z
with z → x and z → y there exists a u with x $\overset{*}{\to}$ u and y $\overset{*}{\to}$ u.

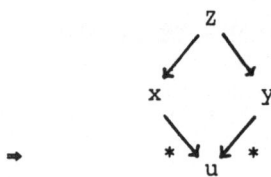

Clearly confluence implies local confluence but not vice versa as the
following example shows.

<u>Example 2:</u> Let E = {A,B,C,D} and → defined by A → B, A → C, B → A,
B → D. Then we get for all different pairs of E × E.

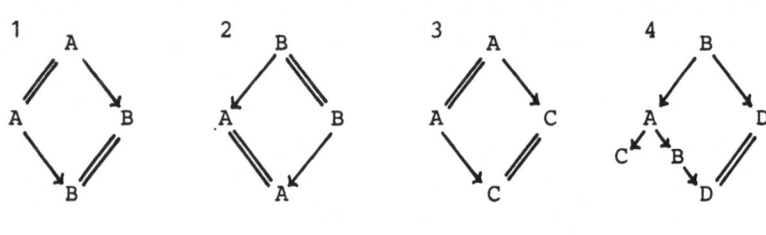

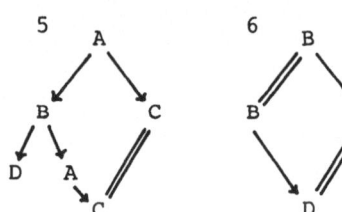

The diamonds 4 and 5 show that → is
local confluent, however the diamonds
4, 5 show also that → is not confluent,
since C and D are irreducible ▌

Also in the example we observe that → allows A → B → A → B → ... and
it may be conjectured that the lack of finite termination inhibits that
local confluence implies confluence. Indeed, we have the

<u>Lemma</u> (Newman 1942)

For a noetherian reduction relation confluence and local confluence
are equivalent.

An elegant proof based on noetherian induction [8] was given by Huet
[3].

In fact, removing A → B or B → A in the example leaves → noetherian,
but → is neither confluent nor locally confluent anymore. The constructive
progress by the Lemma consists in localizing the test for common

reduced instances of elements related by common ancestors to elements only which are related by a common father. Or considered in another way, the check for local confluence consists in showing that all ambiguities which can arise in single step reductions can be resolved by a common reduced instance of the two different elements.

The work of Newman [9] was inspired by a paper by Church and Rosser [10] saying that confluence implies the, now so called "Church Rosser", property: For all x,y $x \overset{*}{\leftrightarrow} y$ is equivalent to the existance of Z with $x \overset{*}{\to} z$ and $y \overset{*}{\to} z$. $\overset{*}{\leftrightarrow}$ means 0 or more reductions → or ← in any order. Newman's paper was written in the language of topology. It became the basis of Huet's work on term rewriting systems, but on the other hand, independent from Huet, it also became the basis of Bergman's [5] work on the diamond lemma in algebraic ring theory. Given the common ancestor of two independent developments, we are now trained to ask whether they can be reduced to a common instance.

The question of local confluence appears in Bergman's paper in the following way. Let X be a set of generators and X* the free monoid over X. In formal languages X is called an alphabet, in algebra X is called a set of indeterminates and X* is denoted by <X>. X is <u>not</u> a set of variables from a logical point of view, but rather a set of constants. A reduction system S consists of pairs $s = (l_s, r_s)$, where $l_s \in X^*$ and r_s are algebraic elements the precise meaning of which is deferred for the moment. An element w of X* is reducible iff there is an $s \in S$ such that l_s is a substring of w.

Now there are two kinds of ambiguities which can arise in reductions. An <u>overlap ambiguity</u> of S is a 5-tuple (s,s',A,B,C) with s,s' $\in$ S and A,B,C $\in X^+$, the free semigroup over X, such that l_s = AB and $l_{s'}$ = BC. Obviously, the monomial ABC can be reduced by single reductions in two essentially different ways:

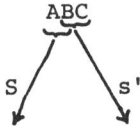

As a side remark we observe that the overlap condition violates one of the famous LL(k) conditions [11] in context free grammars, considering AB and BC as nonterminals on the right hand side of productions. The second ambiguity (s,s',A,B,C) with s ≠ s' $\in$ S and A,B,C $\in$ X* is called an <u>inclusion ambiguity</u> if l_s = B and $l_{s'}$ = ABC:

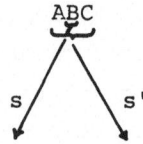

Bergman calls the ambiguities resolvable iff the reduction relation
defined by s is local confluent, since these are the only possible
ambiguities.

For the algebraic structures considered he can prove independently
Newman's Lemma and the confluence-Theorem. To this result we will return
in section 3.

Let T denote the set of terms over a signature Σ of operator symbols
of a fixed arity. We are interested in the first order language of T
over a set V of variables. T is closed by operators: for all $f \in \Sigma$ of
arity n, $n \geq 0$, and $t_1, \ldots, t_n \in T$ we have $f(t_1, \ldots, t_n) \in T$. A substitution
σ is an endomorphism of T leaving the variables $x = \sigma(x)$ fixed almost
everywhere and with $\sigma(f(t_1, \ldots, t_n)) = f(\sigma(t_1), \ldots, \sigma(t_n))$. We denote a
substitution σ by a finite set of assignments of terms to variables
$\{x_1 \leftarrow t_1, \ldots, x_n \leftarrow t_n\}$, $n \geq 0$.

T is ordered by the quasi-ordering $\stackrel{<}{=}$ of subsumption: t precedes or
equals t' iff there is a substitution σ with $t' = \sigma(t)$; t' is an
instance of (the pattern) t under (the match) σ. If we do not distinguish
terms which differ only by the names of variables and if we augment T
by a maximum element then the set of terms is a complete lattice. As a
consequence, any two terms having a common instance have also a unique
most general such instance, the least upper bound of them in the
lattice, and they are called unifiable. There are simple and efficient
algorithms known to decide and construct matches and most general
unifiers [12, 13].

A term reduction system R is a set of pairs (l,r) of terms such that
the variable set of r is contained in that of l. A term t is reducible
to t', if any subterm of t is an instance of any l in R, say with match
σ; t' is then t with the matched subterm replaced by $\sigma(r)$. The reduction
relation $\underset{R}{\rightarrow}$ is the smallest relation containing R compatible with
substitution and replacement.

Knuth and Bendix [13] discovered that local confluence of a finite
noetherian term reduction system can be decided by exhaustively
enumerating all least upper bounds of one left hand side of a rule (l,r)

with any subterm of any other left hand side. These least upper bounds
are terms which can be ambiguously reduced. To be more precise, we have
the

Definition   Let (l_s, r_s) and $(l_{s'}, r_{s'}) \in R$ and assume $l_{s'}$ variable -
disjoint from l_s without loss of generality.

If there exist a non-variable subterm t of l_s and a most general unifier
σ such that $\sigma(t) = \sigma(l_{s'})$ then $\sigma(l_s)$ is the superposition of rule s'
with rule s which gives rise to the critical pair (t_1, t_2):

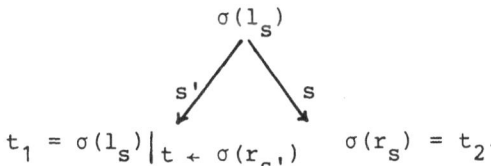

$$t_1 = \sigma(l_s)\big|_{t \leftarrow \sigma(r_{s'})} \qquad \sigma(r_s) = t_2.$$

Theorem   (Knuth-Bendix 1970)

The relation $\underset{R}{\rightarrow}$ is local confluent iff for all critical pairs (t_1, t_2) of
the reduction system R there is a u such that $t_1 \underset{R}{\overset{*}{\rightarrow}} u$ and $t_2 \underset{R}{\overset{*}{\rightarrow}} u$.

A proof not relying on termination of R was given by Huet [ ]. Clearly,
if R is finite there is only a finite number of critical pairs which
have to be tested for reducing to a common instance.

As a special case we consider ground term reduction systems, i.e. term
systems without variables. A reduction is then always a replacement
of equals by equals which is contained in the general case with empty
substitutions. Huet and Lankford have shown [14] that termination for
ground term reduction systems is decidable and as a consequence the
Knuth-Bendix confluence test can be applied, if the termination decision
is positive.

Next, let us consider reduction systems in their connection to equations.
A Σ-equation is a pair of terms t = t' over the signature Σ. A Σ-con-
gruence $\sim$ is a relation over Σ such that for all operators f and all
terms $t_1, \ldots, t_n, t_1', \ldots, t_n'$ with $t_1 \sim t_1', \ldots, t_n \sim t_n'$ we have also
$f(t_1, \ldots, t_n) \sim f(t_1', \ldots, t_n')$. The equality $=_E$ generated by a set E of
equations is the smallest Σ-congruence over T containing for all $t =_E t'$
also $\sigma(t) =_E \sigma(t')$ for any substitution σ. For any set E of axioms, $=_E$
describes the equational theory generated by these axioms. So far we
have considered terms as pure syntactical objects as they occur for
example in derivation or abstract syntax trees is language theory. If
we interpret the operators in Σ as denotations of the fundamental

operations of a (universal) algebra A and the variables in the terms as ranging over the carrier of A then a term equation has also a semantic in A, which we denote by $A = t = t'$ and which means that for all interpretations of the variables of t and t' in A both terms denote the same object of the carrier. A is said to be a model M of equation. Both notions of equality are connected by Birkhoffs [15] completeness

Theorem For all algebras A which are models of E

$$A \models t = t' \quad \text{iff} \quad t =_E t'.$$

In order to establish the validity in A we have to obtain t = t' from the equations in E by substitutions and replacements only in a pure symbolic manner. Now the connection to term reduction systems becomes apparent: if it is possible to read the equations t = t' as reduction rules, say t → t', then the pure syntactic reduction process suffices to solve the decision problem t = t' in A working only by substitutions and replacements.

The following example reveals that reading as reductions creates problems.

Example 3 Let us take (with variable x and constant 0) the equations

(E1) $x + (-x) = 0$,
(E2) $-0 = 0$

as axioms from abelian groups and read them as reductions

(R1) $x + (-x) \to 0$,
(R2) $-0 \to 0$.

If we now try to simplify 0 + 0 we realize quickly that the term is irreducible. The reason is that we would need (R2) also in the other direction 0 → -0 which leads to 0 +(-0) to which (R1) applied yields 0. The trouble is, however, that the two rules -0 → 0 and 0 → -0 are clearly not noetherian anymore ∎

It seems to be an unavoidable temptation to solve the problem of the lost uniqueness of reductions by restrictions on the reduction system of the reduction rules. A typical restriction in an algebraic manipulation system is not to allow "+" as the leading term operator on the left hand side of a rule. Other attempts are, fixing the evaluation order inside of the terms or the application order of the rules.

Mathematically speaking, we have replaced the symmetric relation "="
by the asymmetric relation "→" and destroyed hereby the equivalence
classes mod $=_E$. Therefore, the task is, to <u>extend</u> R to a complete
system, i.e. a system being noetherian and complete. The Knuth-Bendix
decision algorithm offers itself for extension: any critical pair not
being reducible to a common instance is clearly in $=_E$ and should therefore be added to the equations. If the finite termination is maintained
and the process of adding new pairs terminates an extended complete
system R is obtained where $t =_E t'$ is realized by $t \overset{*}{\underset{R}{\leftrightarrow}} t'$ and checked
by an u with $t \overset{*}{\underset{R}{\to}} u$, $t' \overset{*}{\to} u$. This is the Knuth-Bendix extension procedure.

3. Algebraic Reduction and Completion Algorithms

Let us consider first an example in order to understand the direction
we have to look for.

<u>Example 4</u>:   Given the equation

$$\sqrt{3} = \sqrt{8 + 2\sqrt{15}} \ - \sqrt{5}$$

which is to be proved. Working numerically over the reals does not
lead to a proof since there are no finite numerical representations of
the radicals but only approximations. Working algebraically we extend
the field of the rationals Q by the algebraic numbers $\sqrt{3}$ and $\sqrt{5}$ defined
as zeros of the equations

$$\text{(E1)} \qquad x^2 = 3$$
$$\text{(E2)} \qquad y^2 = 5$$

Now the algebra $A = Q(\sqrt{3}, \sqrt{5})$ is isomorphic to the residue class ring
$\mathbb{Z}[x,y]/(x^2-3, y^2-5)$ and we are able to express the given equation with

$$\text{(E3)} \qquad z^2 = 8 + 2xy$$
as $\qquad \text{(E4)} \qquad x = z - y.$

In order to check the equation (E4) we interpret (E1)-(E4) as a reduction
system and ask whether it is complete. Obviously, it is noetherian if
we order the indeterminates $x > y > z$ and according to the degree in
the single indeterminates. To see that it is confluent also, we form
all least upper bounds of the left hand sides which lead to critical
pairs: the only non-trivial term which can be reduced ambiguously is
x^2 which yields by rule (1) 3 and by rule (4) $x (z - y)$ and $(z - y)$
$(z - y)$ which after multiplying out to $z^2 - 2zy + y^2$ and applying (3)

gives $8 + 2xy - 2zy + y^2$ which allows the reduction by (4) again
$8 + 2(z - y)y - 2zy + y^2$ which simplifies to $8 - y^2$ and after reduction
by (2) to $8 - 5 = 3$ ∎

Typically in algebra one considers a structure defined by axioms, here
for example the ring $\mathbb{Z}[x,y]$ of polynomials over the integers, and
imposes restrictions in form of ground term equations. One works then
in the residue class ring modulo the ideal generated by the equations
which in our example has a complete reduction system such that any term
equation can be tested by reduction of the two terms to their canonical
forms. In this algebraic approach one can restrict oneself to ground
term reductions because the axioms involving (universally quantified)
variables ranging over the algebra are taken care of implicitly by
the algebraic simplifications like multiplication, cancellation of
polynomials in our example. So, the algebraic reduction process by
ground term equations relies on algebraic simplification which realizes
the axioms of the structure. An alternative approach would be to
formulate both the axioms and the equations defining the ideal by term
equations and to apply the Knuth-Bendix extension process explicitly.

Next we show that the collection algorithms [16, 17] for finite
soluble groups are reductions by a complete reduction system. For any
such group there exist generators $g_1,\ldots,g_n$ such that any element of G
can be expressed in canonical form ("normal words") $g_n^{e_n}\ldots g_1^{e_1}$ with
$0 \leq e_i < p_i$, $1 \leq i \leq n$, $\Pi_{i=1}^{n} p_i = |G|$. A collection algorithm R produces
for any element w of G its canonical form R(w). Let w_1,w_2 be any terms
in the generators of G. The group multiplication is then realized by
$R(w_1 \cdot w_2)$ and the inversion by $R(w_1^{-1})$. As usual in computer algebra,
one replaces the algebraic structure, here G, by the set of irreducible
elements, here G_{irr}, which is called ample set [18] and consists of the
canonical representation of the equivalence classes of terms denoting
the same algebraic object. Computationally one gains efficiency by
restricting also the inputs to R to be in canonical form.

How does R look like? In fact R is given by the power commutator
presentation of $G = \langle g_1,\ldots,g_n | g_i^{p_i} = g_{ii}, [g_i,g_j] = g_{ij}, 1 \leq i \leq n, i < j \leq n \rangle$.
Here the p_i are integers greater 1, $g_i^r \notin G_{i-1} = \langle g_1,\ldots,g_{i-1} \rangle$ for any
r less than p_i, $1 \leq i \leq n$, G_o is the identity subgroup of G and the g_{ij}
are words in the generators of $g_1,\ldots,g_{j-1}$. The symbol $[g_i,g_j]$ is the
commutator $g_i^{-1}g_j^{-1}g_ig_j$.

Theorem A power commutator presentation of a finite soluble group is a complete reduction system, where the rules are of the form $g_i^{p_i} \to g_{ii}$ or $g_i g_j \to g_j g_i g_{ij}$.

Proof The proof that the system is noetherian is identical with the termination proof of the collection algorithm.

The same is true, of course, for showing confluence, since the collection algorithm realizes a function. A complete reduction system defines for every term its canonical form and defines a function (and not only a relation). We use therefore the notation $R(t)$ for the function defined by a complete reduction system and applied to f. We elaborate nevertheless some points in the reduction terminology.

We note first that any term containing negative exponents can be replaced by a term in which only the generators have negative exponents by using the group axioms, then every term with $g_i^{e_i}$ and $e_i < 0$ can be replaced by $g_i^{e_i'}$ with $e_i' \equiv e_i$ mod $|g_i|$, the order of the generator g_i. All terms are then words of the monoid $\langle g_1, \ldots, g_n \rangle^*$ and there occur only overlap ambiguities in the sense of Bergman. However, they are all resolvable since every term possess a unique normal form $g_n^{e_n} \ldots g_1^{e_1}$, with $0 \leq l_i < p_i$. The order of the generators in this word can always be established by the commutator rules and the exponent conditions by the power rules. Therefore they are irreducible and any two different normal forms denote different elements of the group ∎

Example 5:

We take an example from [17]. The dihedral group of order 12 can be presented as

$$D_{12} = <a,b,c \mid a^3 = b^2 = 1, \ c^2 = a^2, \ [a,b] = a, [a,c] = 1, \ [b,c] = a^2>.$$

The reduction system is

(1) $a^3 \to 1$,   (4) $ab \to ba^2$,

(2) $b^2 \to 1$,   (5) $ac \to ca$,

(3) $c^2 \to a^2$,   (6) $bc \to cba^2$.

The overlap ambiguities are

Origin	lowest upper bound	different reductions		reduced to
(1), (4)	a^3b	b,	$a^2b^2a^2$	b
(1), (5)	a^3c	c,	a^2ca	c
(2), (4)	ab^2	a,	ba^2b	a
(2), (6)	b^2c	c,	b^2c	c
(3), (5)	ac^2	a^3,	cac	1
(2), (6)	bc^2	bc^2,	cba^2c	ba^2
(4), (6)	abc	ba^2c,	$a \, cba^2$	cba

It takes, for example, 15 reduction steps to check confluence for bc^2 from rules (2), (6)■

There are special interpreter generators described in [17] for
performing reductions in power-commutator representations. The operations
$*$ and $^{-1}$ are then implemented by $R(u*v)$ and $R(u^{-1})$, where u and v are
in canonical form. Here the reduction system R replaces the group
multiplication and inversion table.

To work in $\mathbb{Z}_n$ we represent the elements by O and strings $S^b(O)$, where
S^b stands for the successor function S repeated b times; we need only
a single equation $n = O$ in $\mathbb{Z}_n$ and interprete it as a complete reduction
system $S^n(O) \to O$, $n > 0$.

The canonical representative of any number $S^m(O) \in \mathbb{N}$ can then be found
by simple matches. For example we find in $\mathbb{Z}_2$ with $S(S(O) \to O$ for
$\mathbb{Z} = S(S(S(S(S(O))))) \to S(S(S(O))) \to S(O) = 1$.

More generally, taking two such equations $m = O$ and $n = O$, for $m, n \in \mathbb{N}$
denoted by terms constructed from O and S, the task of getting a
complete reduction system consists in finding least upper bounds, in
this case m, if $m \geq n$, which produces the new reduction rule $r_1 = m$
mod $n \to O$ by the method just shown, which in turn produces $r_2 = n$ mod
$r_1 \to O$ until the greatest common divisor of m and n is reached, so the
complete reduction system consists of the single rule $\gcd(m,n) \to O$.
and the algebraic structure we work in is $\mathbb{Z}_{\gcd(m,n)}$ which is isomorphic
to $\mathbb{Z}/(\gcd(m,n))$. The Euclidean algorithm for natural number m and n is
therefore a simple instance of the Knuth-Bendix extension procedure in
the special case of two ground term rules - an instance and not only
an analogue. There are no arithmetical operation required, the only
subalgorithm is the replacement of equals by equals.

Another algebraic algorithm which completes a reduction system is
Buchberger's algorithm for polynomial ideals. Let K be a field and
$K[x_1,...,x_n]$ the polynomial ring over K in the indeterminates $x_1,...,x_n$,
which are words in the commutative monoid $<x_1,...,x_n>^*$. Let $f_1,...,f_r \in$
$K[x_1,...,x_n]$ generate the ideal I corresponding to the equivalence by
$\equiv_E$ where E is the set of polynomial equations $f_i = 0$, $1 \leq i \leq r$. Based on
E Buchberger defines a reduction relation $\underset{E}{\to}$. The initial set of reductions
is then completed to a Gröbner basis E' for the ideal I such that $g \in I$
iff $g \underset{E}{\to} O$. Moreover, any polynomial $g \in K[x_1,...,x_n]/I$ can be represented
in canonical form and the operations $u \bullet v$ in the residue class ring are
polynomials operations $u \bullet v$ modulo the Gröbner basis: $E'(u \; v)$. The

completion procedure proceeds by enumerating all least upper bounds with respect to $\underset{E}{\rightarrow}$ of the leading terms of all pairs of polynomials in E. The results of the two ambiguous reductions are subtracted, reduced $\underset{E}{\overset{*}{\rightarrow}}$ and checked for 0. If the test fails, the non-zero polynomial augments E. Buchberger has shown that $\underset{E}{\rightarrow}$ can always be extended to a noetherian confluent reduction system in a finite number of steps. In his proof it is crucial that the ideal generated by E and E' stays always the same. He has closely investigated the posibilities of saving reduction and extension steps. The special case of two polynomials is the polynomial greatest common divisor algorithm and the special case of linear polynomials is the Gaussian elimination algorithm for linear systems. So, these two algorithms are also Knuth-Bendix type extension algorithms. It is easy to see that the word problem for commutative semigroups reduces to the set membership problem for polynomial ideals [19]; here Buchberger's algorithm is a feasable alternative to G. Hermann's decision method [20]. Applications, implementations in algebraic systems and variations of Buchberger's algorithm are described in [21, 22, 23, 24, 25, 26].

Still more general is Bergman's constructive proof for the diamond lemma in ring theory. Let k be a commutative associative ring with 1 and <X> the already introduced free monoid with the same 1, and k<X> be the free associative k-algebra on X. Reduction rules are pairs $s = (l_s, r_s)$ where $l_s \in X^*$ and $r_s \in k<X>$. Let I be the ideal of k<X> generated by the elements $r_s - l_s$. To enforce finite termination Bergman assumes a semigroup partial ordering $\leq$ on <X> compatible with the reduction rules which means that any monomial in r_s precedes the monomial l_s. Finally the descending chain condition is required. Bergman then shows that all ambiguities are resolvable iff all elements of k<X> have canonical forms iff the irreducible elements forming the k-submodule $k<X>_{irr}$ are an ample set of k<X>/I. Bergman gives many applications and studies several algebraic complete reduction systems in detail, in particular he gives an argument which leads also to a simple proof of termination of Buchberger's algorithm [27], which may replace the original proof which resembles the proof of Kruskal's tree embedding theorem [28].

Finally, we want to study in this section the question whether Bergman's and Buchberger's algorithms can be obtained as special instances of the Knuth-Bendix extension process. We have to take in addition to the ground term reduction rules (l_s, r_s) the axioms of the ring k, of the monoid X* and of the monoid algebra k<X>. Given the element $l_s - r_s$ as a sum of terms, say $t_1 + t_2$, how do we form from the equation $t_1 + t_2 = 0$ in the ideal I a reduction rule, more precisely should we form $t_1 + t_2 \to 0$ or $t_1 \to - t_2$, given $t_2 < t_1$ in the partial order? Since the terms form an abelian group under addition, we need the axioms of an abelian group, written additively:

(r1) $x+y = y+x$

(r2) $(x+y)+z = x+(y+z)$,

(r3) $x+0 = x$,

(r4) $x+(-x) = 0$,

(r5) $-0 = 0$,

(r6) $-(-x) = x$,

(r7) $-(x+y) = (-x)+(-y)$.

This complete reduction system is taken from [29] where the first two axioms are not used as computation rules but taken care of during the reduction and unification process. Then the Knuth-Bendix extension procedure added to (r3) and (r4) the rules (r5) - (r7).

Suppose we add $t_1 \to - t_2$. Then the polynomial $t_1 + t_2$ becomes $(-t_2) + t_2$ which reduces by (r2) and (r4) to 0.

Suppose we add $t_1 + t_2 \to 0$ as reduction rule (r8) instead of $t_1 \to - t_2$. The superposition algorithm finds a unification (in fact a match) between the subterm $(x+y)$ in (r2) and $t_1 + t_2$ in (r8): $\{x \leftarrow t_1,\ y \leftarrow t_2\}$. The least upper bound reads therefore

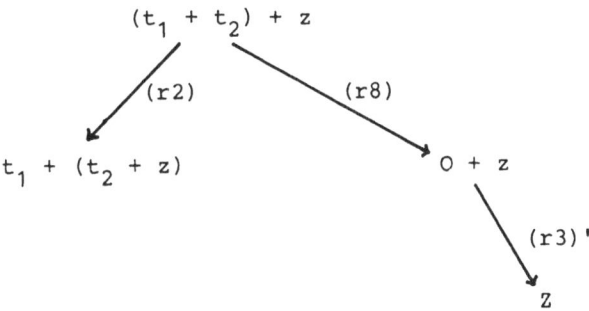

Hence we add

(r9) $t_1 + (t_2 + z) \to z$.

Unification people call such a rule an extended rule, in this case to

(r8), and if (r2) is not used for reduction it is automatically added
by the associative-commutative (ac) unification algorithm. Next there
is a further unification possible between rule (r4) and the subterm
$(t_2 + z)$ in the new rule (r9): $\{x \leftarrow t_2, z \leftarrow (-t_2)\}$. Therefore the
ambiguously reducible term becomes

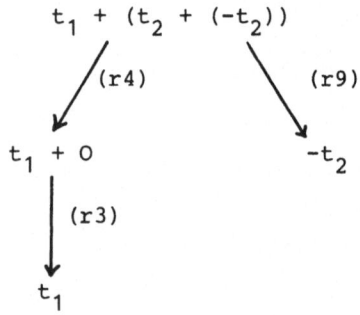

and the Knuth-Bendix extension procedure adds the rule

$$(r10) \qquad t_1 \rightarrow -t_2$$

by which by the previous rule (r8) is eliminated. Therefore, no matter
how we start, $t_1 \rightarrow -t_2$ is added. More generally, we have the

<u>Lemma</u> Let $t = t_1 + t_2 + \ldots + t_r$ be an element of k<X> such that
$t_1 > t_2 > \ldots > t_r$. If the equation $t = 0$ is added to the abelian group
axioms, the Knuth-Bendix extension procedure will add the equation as
reduction $t_1 \rightarrow - t_2 - \ldots - t_r$.

Let t_i now be of the form aA with $a \in k$, $a \neq 0$, and $A \in X^+$. By the
preceding Lemma the equation $aA = t_1 \in$ k<X> will be added as $A \rightarrow a^{-1}t_1$,
if $aA > t_1$, since the multiplication between elements of k and X* obeys
the abelian group axioms, multiplicatively written this time. Hence the
form of Bergman's reduction rules from $X^+ \times$ k<X> is automatically found
by the Knuth-Bendix process.

Next we want to know, whether the ambiguously reducible terms will be
found by the superposition algorithm. We work now in the free semigroup X^+ since only lefthand sides of the rules are involved. We have
the only axiom

(A) $\qquad (xy)z \rightarrow x(yz)$

Given a rule

(R) $\qquad$ $X(XY) \rightarrow r_s$

we get (as above) the match $\{x \leftarrow X, y \leftarrow XY\}$ and the ambiguous term

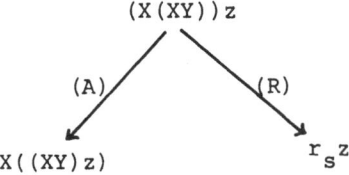

$$(X(XY))z$$
$$(A) \swarrow \qquad \searrow (R)$$
$$X((XY)z) \qquad r_s z$$

resulting by (A) in

(R_c) $\qquad$ $X(X(Yz)) \rightarrow r_s z$

If we consider the second rule

R_2 $\qquad$ $X(YY) \rightarrow r_s,$

we find a unification possible between the subterm $X(Yz)$ of (R_c) and
the left hand side of R_2: $\{z \leftarrow Y\}$ such that

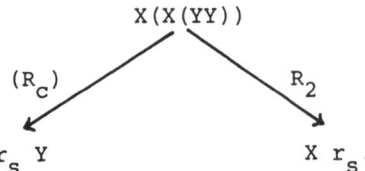

$$X(X(YY))$$
$$(R_c) \swarrow \qquad \searrow R_2$$
$$r_s Y \qquad X r_s.$$

The example shows that the Knuth-Bendix algorithm enumerates Bergman's
overlap ambiguities and even with empty unifiers also the inclusion
ambiguities are found automatically. We state without a formal proof
the

Lemma Given a set E of equations in k<X> and a partial order $\leq$ with
descending chain condition. The Knuth-Bendix decision algorithm tests
whether all ambiguities are resolvable and therefore whether E defines
a complete reduction system compatible with $\leq$.

In order to implement this test one needs ac-unification for which some
algorithms are known, unfortunately without proofs of correctness for general terms. If
not all most general unifiers are found some critical pairs may be
missed what invalidates the decision or stops the completion process
too early. Commutativity destroys finite termination and even commutative

unification with associativity as reduction rule leads to cyclic permutations of variables in the reduction process. The problem is solved for left linear systems (where the variables in a term of a left hand side are all distinct) by Huet. However, groups and rings have no left linear reduction systems.

Still another application of complete reductions can be made to language recognition by complete grammars. Let G be a context free grammar. We interpret the non-terminals as constant operators (may be with attributes as parameters). Then one single binary concatenation operator is used to construct strings of the monoid $(N \cup T)^*$. The productions are symmetrized to a Thue-system and the axioms of a monoid are added. Submitted to the Knuth-Bendix completion procedure we obtained complete grammars, usually the right side of productions became left sides of reduction rules and additional non-context-free rules from superpositions, mainly with the associativity law, resulted. A string of terminals, written with the same concatenation operator is then reduced by the complete grammar corresponding to a bottom up parse, non-deterministic with respect to the next rule applied and to the next subterm rewritten. If the canonical form of the string is the start symbol of the grammar it is accepted otherwise rejected.

Acknowledgement

I thank Dr. Siekmann for introducing me to the important work of Huet and Mr. Küchlin for many discussions.

References

[1] E. Lauer, Algorithmen für symmetrische Polynome, Diplomarbeit, 1976, Fachbereich Informatik, Universität Kaiserslautern

[2] D.E. Knuth, P.B. Bendix, Simple Word Problems in Universal Algebras, "Computational Problems in Abstract Algebra", Ed. J. Leech, Oxford and New York 1969

[3] G. Huet, Confluent Reductions: Abstract Properties and Applications to Term Rewriting Systems. Journ. ACM, Vol. 27, No. 4, October 1980, pp. 797-821

[4]   G. Huet, D. Oppen, Equations and Rewrite Rules: a Survey, "Formal
      Languages: Perspectives and Open Problems", Ed. R. Book, Academic
      Press, 1980

[5]   G.M. Bergman, The Diamond Lemma for Ring Theory, Advances in Math.
      29 (1978), 178-218

[6]   N. Dershowitz, Orderings for Term-rewriting Systems, Proc. 20th
      Symposium on Foundations of Computer Science (1979), 123-131

[7]   N. Dershowitz, Z. Manna, Proving Termination with Multiset
      Orderings. Comm. ACM, 22 (1979), 465-476

[8]   Z. Manna, S. Ness, J. Vuillemin, Inductive Methods for Proving
      Properties of Programs, Comm. ACM, 16 (1973), 491-504

[9]   M. Newman, On Theories with a Combinatorial Definition of
      "Equivalence". Annals of Math. 43, 2 (1942), 223-243

[10] A. Church, J.B. Rosser, Some Properties of Conversia, Transactions
      of AMS 39 (1936), 472-482

[11] D.E. Knuth, Top-Down Syntax Analysis, Acta Informatica 1 (1979),
      79-110

[12] J.A. Robinson, A Machine-Oriented Logic Based on the Resolution
      Principle, Journ. ACM 12 (1965), 32-41

[13] M.S. Paterson, M.N. Wegman, Linear Unification, J. of Computer
      and System Sciences 16 (1978), 158-167

[14] G. Huet, D.S. Lankford, On the Uniform Halting Problem for Term
      Rewriting Systems, Rapport Laboria 283, IRIA, Mars. 1978

[15] G. Birkhoff, On the Structure of Abstract Algebras, Proc.
      Cambridge Phil. Soc. 31 (1935), 433-454

[16] I.D. Macdonald, A Computer Application to Finite p-Groups,
      J. Austral. Math. Soc. 17 (1974), 102-112

[17] V. Felsch, A Machine Independent Implementation of a Collection
      Algorithm for the Multiplication of Group Elements, Proceedings
      of the 1976 ACM Symposium on Symbolic and Algebraic Computation,
      159-166

[18] D.R. Musser, Algorithms for Polynomial Factorization, Ph.D Thesis,
      Techn. Rep. No. 134 Comptr. Sci. Dept. U of Wisconsin - Madison,
      Madison, Wis., Sept. 1971

[19] E. Cardoza, R. Lipton, A. Meyer, Exponential Space Complete Problems
      for Petri Nets and Commutative Semigroups, Proc. of the Eight ACM
      Symposium on Theory of Computing, May 1976, 50-54

[20] Grete Hermann, Die Frage der vielen Schritte in der Theorie der
      Polynomideale, Math. Ann. 95 (1926), 736-788

[21] B. Buchberger, Ein Algorithmus zum Auffinden der Basiselemente
      der Restklassenringe nach einem nulldimensionalen Polynomideal,
      Dissertation, Universität Innsbruck, 1965

[22] B. Buchberger, A Theoretical Basis for the Reduction of Polynomials
      to Canonical Forms, SIGSAM-Bulletin of the ACM, 39 (Aug. 1976),
      19-29.

[23] B. Buchberger, A Criterion for Detecting Unnecessary Reductions
      in the Construction of Gröbner-Bases, Proceedings EUROSAM 1979,
      Marseille, Springer Lecture Notes in Computer Science, Vol. 72,
      (1979) 3-21

[24] R. Shtokhamer, A Canonical Form of Polynomials in the Presence
      of Side Relations, Physics Dept., Technion, Haifa, Israel,
      Technion PH-76-25, 1976

[25] M. Lauer, Kanonische Repräsentation für die Restklassen nach
      einem Polynomideal, Diplomarbeit, Fachbereich Informatik, Univer-
      sität Kaiserslautern, Oktober 1976,
      Extended Abstraction, Proceedings of the 1976 ACM Symposium on
      Symbolic and Algebraic Computation, 339-345

[26] S.T. Schaller, Algorithmic Aspects of Polynomial Residue Class
      Rings, Ph.D. Thesis, Comp. Sci., Techn. Report 370, October 1979,
      Comp. Sciences Dept. U. Wisconsin, Madison

[27] B. Buchberger, Private communication

[28] J.B. Kruskal, Well-quasi-ordering, the Tree Theorem and Vazsonyi's
      Conjecture, Trans. Amer. Math. Soc. 95 (1960) 210-225

[29] J.M. Hullot, A Catalogue of Canonical Term Rewriting Systems,
      Techn. Report CSL-113, April 1980, SRI International, Comp. Sci.
      Laboratory

A NOETHERIAN REWRITE SYSTEM FOR IDEMPOTENT SEMIGROUPS

J. Siekmann   P. Szabó

Universität Karlsruhe
Institut für Informatik I
Postfach 6380
D-7500 Karlsruhe

ABSTRACT: Let B be a semigroup with the additional relation

$$\forall\, w \in B.\ ww = w$$

B is called a band or an idempotent semigroup [CP61]. It is shown in this paper that the replacement rules (rewrites) resulting from the axiom of idempotence:

(i) $xx \rightarrow x$

(ii) $x \rightarrow xx$

can be replaced by the *Noetherian, confluent, conditional* rewrites (i.e. a terminating replacement system having the Church-Rosser-Property):

(iii) $xx \rightarrow x$

(iv) $xyz \rightarrow xz$ if $x \overset{CI}{=} z$ and $xy \overset{CI}{=} z$.

These rewrites are used to obtain a unique normal form for words in B and hence are the basis for a decision procedure for wordequality in B.

The proof techniques are based upon *term rewriting systems* rather than the usual algebraic approach, and alternative and simpler proofs of a result reported earlier by Green and Rees (1951) and Gerhard (1970) are obtained.

For space limitations all proofs are omitted, but may be found in [SS81a].

1. MOTIVATION

1.1 Confluent Noetherian rewrite systems [HO80] are of considerable practical importance in computer science (e.g. compiler construction, abstract data types [GHM78]), in automated theorem proving [LO78], in computer algebra [KB70] and in unification theory [RSSU79].

In this paper attention is confined to the equational theory consisting
of the two axioms of *associativity* and *idempotence*, because any axiom
set which includes the axiom of idempotence could not so far be used
for a term rewriting system due to the non-Noetherian (i.e. non-
terminating) nature of the replacement rule:

$$x \Rightarrow xx.$$

Once the result for associativity and idempotence is established, it
is possible to obtain confluent rewrite systems for larger sets of
axioms, for example using the technique of coding the remaining
equations into a single one [GER70, theorem 4.33].

Also it is easy to obtain a confluent rewrite system in the absence of
associativity (see section 4.4).

1.2 A confluent Noetherian rewrite system for an equational theory T
can be used to obtain a *unique normal form* for terms and is therefore
often an important prerequisite for a *unification algorithm* in T. The
T-unification algorithm, where T consists of the axioms of associativity
and idempotence [SS81] is based on the rewrites proposed in this paper.

1.3 Let F_A be the free semigroup generated by the alphabet A and let
B_A, the free band generated by A, be F_A/I, where I is the smallest
congruence on F_A containing the relation $\{(ww,w)|w \in F_A\}$. It is not
obvious whether or not two different words w_1 and w_2 in F_A determine
the same element in B_A. An algorithm, based on the work of Green and
Rees [GR62] and Gerhard [GER70], which decides whether or not $w_1/I = w_2/I$
is presented in [HOW76]. This algorithm is based on the following
observation: For a word $w \in F_A$ let C(w) be the *content of w*, i.e. the set
of letters of A appearing in w.

RULE C : If $C(y) \subseteq C(z)$ and $C(x) = C(z)$ then x y z = x z.

RULE C is used as the basis for our second rewrite.

1.4 It should be noted that the structure resulting from associativity
and the single rule

$$(i) \quad xx \Rightarrow x$$

(i.e. without rule (ii) $x \Rightarrow xx$) has been investigated under the name of
'nonrepetitive words' ([HA78], chapter 1.8), but is very different from
the structure investigated here: for example, there exist infinitely
many nonrepetitive words [HA78 p. 36], whereas idempotent semigroups
are finite [GR52]. Also *there is no confluent rewrite system for (i)*
alone (see counterexample 2).

To provide some insight into the problems involved, we present a few examples.

Given two words w_1, $w_2 \in F_A$ let us write $w_1 \overset{I}{=} w_2$ iff they constitute the same element in B_A.

A word uvvw $\in F_A$ may be replaced by uvw, which still represents the same element in B_A. We write uvvw $\underset{c}{\rightarrow}$ uvw for such an *elementary c-transition* and $u \underset{c}{\overset{*}{\rightarrow}} w$ for a chain of elementary c-transitions. Similarily: uvw $\underset{e}{\rightarrow}$ uvvw, and $u \overset{*}{\rightarrow} w$ is a chain of elementary c- or e-transitions. Then:

(1.4.1) $\qquad w_1 \overset{I}{=} w_2$ iff $\exists v.w_1 \overset{*}{\rightarrow} v$ and $w_2 \overset{*}{\rightarrow} v$.

But this is a very unsatisfactory situation: because of the e-transitions there is no unique element v and in general it is not at all easy to see whether or not there exists such a word v.

Hence our intention to replace $\underset{e}{\rightarrow}$.

A word $w \in F_A$ is *terminal* if $\not\exists v.$ $w \underset{c}{\rightarrow} v$ and let TER(w) be the set of all terminal words obtainable from w:

$$\text{TER}(w) = \{\hat{w} \mid w \overset{*}{\rightarrow} \hat{w} \text{ and } \hat{w} \text{ is terminal}\} .$$

Using this definition (1.4.1) could be replaced by:

(1.4.2) $\qquad w_1 \overset{I}{=} w_2$ iff $\text{TER}(w_1) \cap \text{TER}(w_2) \neq \emptyset$.

Since TER is always finite this would solve the problem.

Counterexample 1:

Let $w_1 = abc$ and $w_2 = abc\ b\ abc$.
Then $\text{TER}(w_1) = \{abc\}$; $\text{TER}(w_2) = \{abc\ b\ abc\}$
and hence $\text{TER}(w_1) \cap \text{TER}(w_2) = \emptyset$, thus $w_1 \overset{I}{\neq} w_2$.
However:
$w_1 = \underline{abc} \underset{e}{\rightarrow} ab\ \underline{abc} \underset{e}{\rightarrow} \underline{ab}\ \underline{abc}\ babc \underset{c}{\rightarrow} abc\ b\ abc = w_2$
and hence $w_1 \overset{I}{=} w_2$, which falsifies (1.4.2). □

This counterexample can be generalized to the following observation, which will be utilized later:

1. *Proposition 1:* $\qquad \forall u,\ w \in F_A$

$\qquad\qquad\qquad\qquad w\ u\ w \overset{*}{\rightarrow} w$ if u is a subword of w.

If we define $w\ u\ w \underset{cc}{\rightarrow} w$ as a single cc-transition, (1.4.1) could be replaced by:

(1.4.3) $w_1 \overset{I}{=} w_2$ iff $\exists v. w_1 \overset{*}{\rightarrow} v$ and $w_2 \overset{*}{\rightarrow} v$
where $\rightarrow$ are only c- and cc-
transitions.

Since both transitions terminate, this would be a basis for a Noetherian
and confluent rewrite system, but:

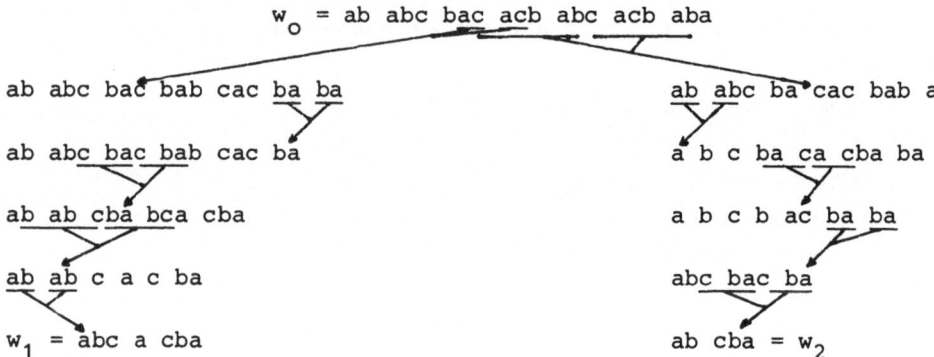

Hence we have two words w_1, $w_2 \in F_A$ with $w_o \overset{*}{\rightarrow} w_1$ and $w_o \overset{*}{\rightarrow} w_2$, i.e.
$w_1 \overset{I}{=} w_2$; but w_1 and w_2 cannot be further reduced by $\overset{}{\underset{c}{\rightarrow}}$ nor by $\overset{}{\underset{cc}{\rightarrow}}$ and
$w_1 \neq w_2$.

This example leads to our final generalization:
1. *Proposition 2:* $\quad \forall\ u,\ v,\ w \in F_A$
$\quad uvw \overset{*}{\rightarrow} uw$ if $C(v) \subseteq C(u) = C(w)$.

2. THE PROBLEM

Let A be a non-empty set (the alphabet) and let A* denote the set of
all finite words (including the empty word) in the alphabet A. Under
the binary operation of concatenation of words the free semigroup F_A
on A* is obtained. Let B_A be the semigroup with the additional defining
relation

$$\{ (ww,\ w) : w \in F_A \}.$$

Interest is in the problem of deciding whether or not two words w_1,
$w_2 \in A*$ determine the same element in B_A.

An algorithm for the solution of this problem is known [HO76, IV.4].
However motivated by the considerations above, we are interested in
confluent and *Noetherian rewrite systems* and *normal forms*, such that

$$\{\forall x. x^2 = x\} \vdash w_1 = w_2 \quad \text{iff} \quad \|w_1\| = \|w_2\| \quad \text{for } w_1, w_2 \in A^*$$

where $\|w\|$ is the normal form of a word $w \in A^*$ obtained by the rewrite system to be established below and $\vdash$ denotes provability.

3. NOTATION AND DEFINITIONS

Let $T \vdash u = v$ denote that equation $u = v$ is provable from the set of closed equations T in a suitable logical calculus (that $u = v$ is true in T). This is abbreviated to $u \overset{T}{=} v$, we say is *T-equal* to v.

We are interested in theories T consisting of combinations of the following three axioms:

$$\begin{aligned}
&\text{(ASS)} && \forall\, u,\, v,\, w \in A^*. && ((uv)w) = (u(vw)) \\
&\text{(ID)} && \forall \qquad\; w \in A^*. && ww = w \\
&\text{(COM)} && \forall \qquad\; v,\, w \in A^*. && vw = wv
\end{aligned}$$

For example, $\{\text{ID,COM}\} \vdash u = v$ is then abbreviated to $u \overset{IC}{=} v$ and $\{\text{ID}\} \vdash u = v$ is abbreviated to $u \overset{I}{=} v$.

Let $|w|$ be the *length* (number of symbols) of word $w \in A^*$; as usual $\cup$ denotes *set union* and $\subseteq$ denotes *set inclusion*. Let V be a denumerable set, $A \cap V = \emptyset$, (the set of variables) and let $AV := \{A \cup V\}$. A *substitution* σ is an endomorphism on AV^* defined as follows:

(i) For $v \in V$ $\sigma(v) = v$ almost everywhere (i.e. except for finitely many points) and

(ii) $\sigma(a_1 \ldots a_n) = \sigma(a_1)\, \sigma(a_2) \ldots \sigma(a_n)$, $a_i \in AV$ and $\sigma(a) = a$, $a \in A$.

A substitution σ is represented as the finite set of pairs $\sigma = \{(v_1|w_1) \ldots (v_m|w_m)\}$ for $v_i \in V$ and $w_i \in AV^*$. The set of substitutions is SUB.

Sign $\in$ is used for set membership and $\blacktriangleleft$ for the occurrence relation: u occurs in w, $u \blacktriangleleft w$, iff $w = w_1\, u\, w_2$ for u, w, w_1, $w_2 \in AV^*$. For $w \in AV^*$, $\text{Var}(w) = \{v | v \in V \text{ and } v \blacktriangleleft w\}$ is the set of variables occurring in word w.

Using this notation we define our second important notion:
The set of pairs

$$Rc = \{(1_1 \to r_1 \text{ if } \Psi_1 \overset{T}{=} \Sigma_1) \ldots (1_n \to r_n \text{ if } \Psi_n \overset{T}{=} \Sigma_n)\}$$

is called a *conditional rewrite system* if $\text{Var}(r_i) \subseteq \text{Var}(1_i)$ for $1 \le i \le n$ and $\Psi_i \overset{T}{=} \Sigma_i$ is a set of T-equations over AV^*. The relation $\overset{Rc}{\to} \subseteq A^* \times A^*$

is defined as:

$u \xrightarrow{Rc} v$ iff $u = u_1 \, w \, u_2$ and there exists $\sigma \in$ SUB and $(1 \to r$ if $\Psi \stackrel{T}{=} \Sigma) \in$ Rc such that $w = \sigma(1)$ and $v = u_1 \, \sigma(r) u_2$ and $\sigma(\Psi) \stackrel{T}{=} \sigma(\Sigma)$ is true, where $u, u_1, u_2, v, \sigma(r), w \in$ AV*.

Example 2: Let $I_c = \{(xyx \to x$ if $xy \stackrel{CI}{=} x)\}$.

Then dabc b abcd $\xrightarrow{I_c}$ dabcd, with $\sigma = \{(x|abc)(y|b)\}$, $u_1 = u_2 = d$, $w = abc \, b \, abc$ and

$$\sigma(xy) = abcb \stackrel{CI}{=} abc = \sigma(x) \quad .$$

This rewrite system allows us to replace the word wvw by w if $C(v) \subseteq C(w)$, where $C(w)$ is the content of word w as define before. This is a generalization of 1. Proposition 1.

$$R = \{(1_1 \to r_1), (1_2 \to r_2), \ldots, (1_n \to r_n)\}$$

is called a *rewrite system* if $Var(r_i) \subseteq Var(1_i)$, $1 \le i \le n$. Different definitions for conditional rewrite systems have been proposed in [BDJ79]. The relation $\xrightarrow{R} \subseteq A^* \times A^*$ is defined as:

$u \xrightarrow{R} v$ iff $u = u_1 \, w \, u_2$ and there exists $\sigma \in$ SUB and $(1 \to r) \in R$ such that $w = \sigma(1)$ and $v = u_1 \, \sigma(r) \, u_2$ for $u, u_1, u_2, v, \sigma(r), w \in A^*$.

$\xrightarrow[*]{R}$ is the reflexive, transitive closure of $\xrightarrow{R}$. We shall omit the super-script R if the set of rewrites in question is determined from the context and write $\xrightarrow{*}$.

Example 1: Let $I = \{(xx \to x)\}$ be a rewrite system. Then aabc $\xrightarrow{I}$ abc, with $\sigma = \{(x|a)\} = \varepsilon$, $w = aa$, $u_2 = bc$.

The relationship between T-equality and rewriting systems becomes apparent, when we can set

$$R_T = \{(u_1 \to v_1), \ldots, (u_n \to v_n), (v_1 \to u_1), \ldots, (v_n \to u_n)\}$$

for the equational theory $T = \{u_1 = v_1, u_2 = v_2, \ldots, u_n = v_n\}$ with u_i, $v_i \in$ AV*. Such rewriting systems are the basis for a mechanical treatment of T-equality on a computer [HO80].

3. *Definition 1:* (the obvious rewrite system for idempotence)

$$I_0 = \{(xx \xrightarrow{e} x), (x \xrightarrow{c} xx)\}$$
where $\xrightarrow{e}$ is a step by *extension*
and $\xrightarrow{c}$ is a step by *collaps*.

Using the above definition of a rewrite
system we obtain the relations $\underset{c}{\Rightarrow}$ and $\underset{e}{\Rightarrow}$
and $\overset{I_o}{\longrightarrow} = \underset{c}{\Rightarrow} \cup \underset{e}{\Rightarrow}$.

With 3. Def. 1 we arrive at an important equivalence, which we shall not
prove here:

3. Lemma 1: $\forall u, v \in A^*$.

$u \overset{I}{=} v$ iff $\exists w \in A^*$ such that

$u \overset{I_o}{\underset{*}{\longrightarrow}} w$ and $v \overset{I_o}{\underset{*}{\longrightarrow}} w$.

We say a relation $\rightarrow$ is *Noetherian* iff there is no infinite sequence:
$u_1 \rightarrow u_2 \rightarrow u_3 \rightarrow \ldots$.

3. *Definition* 2: A relation $\rightarrow$ is *confluent* iff

$\forall u, v, w \in A^*$: if $u \overset{*}{\rightarrow} v$ and $u \overset{*}{\rightarrow} w$ then

$\exists z \in A^*$ with $v \overset{*}{\rightarrow} z$ and $w \overset{*}{\rightarrow} z$.

3. *Definition* 3: A relation $\rightarrow$ is *locally confluent* iff

$\forall u, v, w \in A^*$: if $u \rightarrow v$ and $u \rightarrow w$ then

$\exists z \in A^*$ with $v \overset{*}{\rightarrow} z$ and $w \overset{*}{\rightarrow} z$.

4. RESULTS

We now replace the obvious rewrite system I_o of 3. Definition 1. by
the following conditional rewrite:

4. *Definition* 1:

Let $I := \{ (xx \underset{c}{\Rightarrow} x),$

$(xyz \underset{cc}{\Rightarrow} xz$ if $x \overset{CI}{=} z$

$xy \overset{CI}{=} z) \}$

Let $\rightarrow := \underset{c}{\Rightarrow} \cup \underset{cc}{\longrightarrow}$, where the relations $\underset{c}{\Rightarrow}$ and $\underset{cc}{\longrightarrow}$ on A^*
are obtained according to the definition of a
conditional rewrite system.

This definition is based on the decidability of CI-equality, i.e. the
decidability of word equality in commutative bands, which is obvious,
then for two words u, w in a commutative band u = w (i.e. $u \overset{CI}{=} w$) iff
$C(u) = C(w)$. In a sense 4. Def. 1 reduces the problem of equality in

bands to the problem of equality in commutative bands.

4.1 *Soundness of →.*

We have to show that I is a *correct (sound)* system in the sense that if $w_1 \overset{*}{\to} w_2$ then $w_1 \overset{I}{=} w_2$. This is easily seen for $w_1 \underset{c}{\to} w_2$, but less obvious for $w_1 \underset{cc}{\to} w_2$.

4. *Lemma* 1: $\forall v, w \in A^* :$

$\qquad$ if $w \overset{CI}{=} wv$ then $wvw \overset{I}{=} w$.

4. *Lemma* 2: $\forall u, v, w \in A^*$

$\qquad$ If $u \overset{CI}{=} w$ and $uv \overset{CI}{=} w$ then $uvw \overset{I}{=} uw$.

This lemma states Rule C in our notation, which was observed in [BR64], [MC54] and [GER70] also.

4. Lemma 1 and 4. Lemma 2 prove the following soundness theorem:

---
4. *Theorem* 1: (Soundness) $\forall u, v \in A^*$

$\qquad\qquad$ If $u \overset{*}{\to} v$ then $u \overset{I}{=} v$.

4.2 *Confluence of →.*

As usual, we first demonstrate the local confluence by considering the three possible combinations of $\underset{c}{\to}$ and $\underset{cc}{\to}$.

4. *Lemma* 3: $\forall u, v, w \in A^*.$

$\qquad$ If $u \underset{c}{\to} v$ and $u \underset{c}{\to} w$ then $\exists z \in A^*$
$\qquad$ such that $v \overset{*}{\to} z$ and $w \overset{*}{\to} z$.

4. *Lemma* 4: $\forall u, v, w \in A^*.$

$\qquad$ If $u \underset{c}{\to} v$ and $u \underset{cc}{\to} w$ then $\exists z \in A^*$
$\qquad$ such that $v \overset{*}{\to} z$ and $w \overset{*}{\to} z.$

4. *Lemma* 5: $\forall u, v, w \in A^*.$

$\qquad$ If $u \underset{cc}{\to} v$ and $u \underset{cc}{\to} w$ then $\exists z \in A^*$
$\qquad$ such that $v \overset{*}{\to} z$ and $w \overset{*}{\to} z.$

This demonstrates the local confluence of → and proves the following theorem.

---
4. *Theorem* 2: → is a Noetherian, confluent relation.

Some reader may be more familiar with the notion that → "is terminating and has the Church-Rosser-Property"; we say $\rightarrow$ is canonical.

4.3 *A Decision Procedure Based on* $\rightarrow$.

A word $w \in A^*$ was called terminal if there does not exist a word v with $w \rightarrow v$. Since $\rightarrow$ is Noetherian, for every word $w \in A^*$ there exists a word $\bar{v}$ with $w \overset{*}{\rightarrow} \bar{v}$ and $\bar{v}$ is terminal, and since $\rightarrow$ is confluent, $\bar{v}$ is unique.

We denote the terminal word of $w \in A^*$ as $\|w\|$, which is called the *normal form* of w.

---

4. *Theorem* 3: $\qquad\qquad \forall u, v \in A^*.$

$$u \overset{I}{=} v \quad \text{iff} \quad \|u\| = \|v\| \quad .$$

In applications the problem of $w \overset{I}{=} v$ is usually not presented in A^* but in TERM, where TERM is the least set such that

$$\text{(i)} \quad A \subset \text{TERM}$$
$$\text{(ii)} \quad \text{if } t_1, t_2 \in \text{TERM} \quad \text{then } f(t_1, t_2) \in \text{TERM}$$

where f is a binary function symbol with

(ASS) $\quad \forall a, b, c \in A.$ $\qquad f(f(a,b)c) = f(a, f(b,c))$

(ID) $\qquad \forall a \in A.$ $\qquad\qquad f(a,a) \quad = \quad a$

Define a homomorphism φ between $\tilde{w} \in \text{TERM}$ and $w \in A^*$ as

$$\varphi(\tilde{w}) = \begin{cases} \tilde{w} & \text{iff } \tilde{w} \in A \\[2ex] \varphi(u)\varphi(v) & \text{iff } \tilde{w} = f(u,v) \end{cases}$$

i.e. $\quad \varphi(\tilde{w}) \rightarrow w$.

Then: $\quad \{\text{ASS}, \text{ID}\} \vdash \tilde{w}_1 = \tilde{w}_2 \quad \text{iff} \quad \{\text{ID}\} \vdash \varphi(\tilde{w}_1) = \varphi(\tilde{w}_2)$.

Hence we have as an obvious consequence:

4. *Corollary:* $\qquad \forall \tilde{w}_1, \tilde{w}_2 \in \text{TERM}.$

$$\{\text{ASS}, \text{ID}\} \vdash \tilde{w}_1 = \tilde{w}_2 \quad \text{iff} \quad \|\varphi(\tilde{w}_1)\| = \|\varphi(\tilde{w}_2)\| \quad .$$

4.4 *Idempotence without Associativity*

Let $I_1 = \{(f(x,x) \rightarrow x)\}$ and let $\underset{c}{\rightarrow}$ be the associated relation on words in TERM.

I_1 is locally confluent on TERM:

4. *Proposition* 1: $\quad \forall u, v, w \in \text{TERM}$ with $u \underset{c}{\rightarrow} v$ and $u \underset{c}{\rightarrow} w$ there exists $z \in \text{TERM}$ such that

$$v \xrightarrow[c]{*} z \quad \text{and} \quad w \xrightarrow[c]{*} z \; .$$

Since $\xrightarrow[c]{}$ is locally confluent and Noetherian:

4. *Proposition* 2: $\xrightarrow[c]{}$ is confluent on TERM.

Using the confluence of $\xrightarrow[c]{}$ we have the following theorem, which is proved analoguously to 4. Theorem 3:

---

4. <u>*Theorem* 4</u>: $\forall u, v \in$ TERM:

$\{ID\} \vdash u = v \quad \text{iff} \quad \| u \| = \| v \|$

where the normal form $\| \cdots \|$ is obtained by $\xrightarrow[c]{}$.

Acknowledgement: In an earlier version of this paper we only proposed a particular instance of RULE C as a basis for the second rewrite. We are most greatful to H. Jürgensen, Technische Hochschule Darmstadt, who gave us the decisive hint to the relevant literature of semigroup theory, which greatly improved the paper.

REFERENCES

[BDJ79]   D. Brand, J. Darringer, J. Joyner "Completeness of Conditional
          Reductions"; Proc. of the Workshop on Automated Deduction,1979

[BR64]   T.C. Brown "On the Finiteness of Semigroups in which $x^r = x$";
          Proc. Cambridge Phil. Soc. 60, 1964

[CP61]   A.H. Clifford, G.B. Preston "The Algebraic Theory of Semi-
          groups"; American Math. Society, 1961

[GR52]   J.H. Green, D. Rees "On Semigroups in which $x^r = x$"; Proc.
          Cambridge Phil. Soc. 48, 1952

[GHM78]   J.V. Guttag, E. Horowitz, D.R. Musser "Abstract Data Types
          and Software Validation"; Com. of the ACM, vol 21,no 12, 1978

[GER70]   J.A. Gerhardt "The Lattice of Equational Classes of Idempotent
          Semigroups"; J. of Algebra, 15, 1970

[HO80]   G. Huet, D. Oppen "Equations and Rewrite Rules: A Survey";
          Techn. Report CSL-111, SRI International, California

[HOW76]   J.M. Howie "An Introduction to Semigroup Theory", Academic
          Press, 1976

[HA78]   M.A. Harrison "Introduction to Formal Language Theory",
          Addison Wesley, 1978

[HUE77]   G. Huet "Confluent Reductions: Abstract Properties and
          Applications to Term Rewriting Systems"; 18th IEEE Symp. on
          Foundations of Comp. Sci., 1977

[KB70]   D. Knuth, P. Bendix "Simple Word Problems in Universal
          Algebras", in: Computational Problems in Abstract Algebra,
          (ed) J. Leech, Pergamon Press, 1970

[LO78]   D. Loveland "Automated Theorem Proving", North Holland Publ.
          Comp., 1978

[MC54]   D. McLean "Idempotent Semigroups"; Americ. Math.Mon.61, 1954

[RSSU79] P. Raulefs, J. Siekmann, P. Szabó, E. Unvericht "A Short
          Survey on the State of the Art in Matching and Unification
          Problems", Bulletin of EATC, Oct. 1978

[SS81a]   J. Siekmann, P. Szabó "A Noetherian Rewrite System for
          Idempotent Semigroups", Universität Karlsruhe, 1981 (to
          appear in "Semigroup Forum", Springer 1981)

[SS81b]   J. Siekmann, P. Szabó "Unification in Idempotent Semigroups";
          Univ. Karlsruhe, Institut für Informatik I (in preparation).

ON THE COMPLETENESS OF CONNECTION GRAPH RESOLUTION

W. Bibel

Technische Universität München

Connection graph resolution is a refinement of resolution introduced by Kowalski in the early seventies /2/. However, it is still an open problem whether this proof rule (like resolution) is complete in the strong sense that for any unsatisfiable formula any sequence of selections of connections to be resolved upon leads to a refutation provided each connection has a finite chance to be selected.

Recently, the present author has represented this problem within his matrix formalism and has provided in it a simple proof for the completeness of this rule in the weak sense that there exists some refutation /1/. It is easy to see that this proof also applies for a more restricted definition of this proof rule which in certain cases generates less connections than the original rule. Therefore this restriction, which can be easily added in implementations, potentially leads to a smaller search space with little effort and costs. It applies in cases where the parent clauses are connected with more than one connections; such parallel connections have not to be inherited into the resolvent. It also applies in certain cases where a literal is contained in both parent clauses.

On the basis of this definition the author has what he believes is the main part of a proof for the completeness of this restricted rule in the strong sense. It specifies for any connection graph a so-called kernel which is a set ot sets of paths satisfying certain properties, and for each such kernel a degree which is a natural number less than 2^n where n is the number of connections in the graph. In each step a kernel produces a new kernel with smaller degree. The kernel properties imply that the empty clause is contained in the matrix when the degree becomes zero. Obviously, with these properties the remaining proof is a simple induction on the degree.

By an example handed over to the author by N. Eisinger and C. Walther it turned out, however, that there is still a gap in the present proof. It could be closed by showing that the restriction with respect to parallel connections mentioned above may be generalized to any pair of connections which is inherited in the course of the derivation from an originally parallel pair of connections. We conjecture that this is in fact true. But it seems that this open part of the proof still requires considerable efforts in addition to those already invested into the existing decidedly non-trivial part.

/1/ W. Bibel, On matrices with connections, Journal of ACM (to appear).

/2/ R. Kowalski, A proof procedure using connection graphs, Journal of ACM <u>22</u> (1975) 572 - 595.

Generating Small Models of First Order Axioms

K.M.Hörnig

TU München, Postfach 20 24 20, 8000 München 2, West Germany

Abstract:

A method for obtaining models of a set of first order sentences obeying certain restrictions is derived from the logical concept of satisfiability. It is explained how systematic proof procedures for propositional logic, developed earlier, can be used to implement this method.

We describe here a method to obtain models of sentences (i.e. closed formulas) of first order predicate calculus. In order to obtain an efficient algorithm we have to put restrictions on these sentences. These restrictions, however, still allow many applications of this algorithm. Our main application arises in the design of a partially automatic system for program sythesis, called LOPS, which is currently being implemented in the project "Beweisverfahren" at the TU München [3].[1] There we are often faced with a large search space consisting of sentences which we have to search for valid statements. This search would be very extensive, in fact infeasible in most cases, if we had no tools to guide it. One of these tools is provided by a look over the shoulders of a human programmer. In order to guide his search for valid statements this programmer might draw a small, lucid picture of the situation he's dealing with. In this case two conditions are usually fulfilled:

1. the situation can be described by means of a small set of rather simple axioms
2. these axioms have a small model, the picture.

As an example take the problem of finding the biggest element of a strict linear ordering. A correponding picture might be:

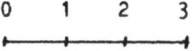

---

1) This project is headed by W. Bibel and supported by the DFG.

It will be exactly these two conditions under which the algorithm we shall
describe now works satisfactorily. It should be noted that there are a lot
more potential applications of such a model construction.

Before we can describe this construction, we have to make precise what we
mean by model and axiom. For simplicity we restrict ourselves to a language
without function and constant symbols. Once the method is clear, there should
be no doubt that this restriction is not harmful.

defn. 1:

The language L consists of

numerals: $0,1,2,\ldots$

variables: $x,x1,x2,\ldots$, $y,y1,y2,\ldots$

predicate symbols: $P,P1,P2,\ldots$ $R,R1,R2,\ldots$

logical symbols: $\neg,\&,\vee,\to,\leftrightarrow,\forall,\exists$

auxiliary symbols: $(,),,$

Atomic formulae, formulae, bound and free variables are defined as usual.

A formula with no free variables is called closed or a sentence.

We let $F,F1,F2,\ldots$ denote formulas, $S,S1,S2,\ldots$ sentences.

Examples:

a) $\exists$ x1 P(x1,x2,x3)

b) $\forall$ y$\exists$x1(P(y) $\to$ $\forall$x2R(x1,x2,y))

Both a) and b) are formulae, but only b) is a sentence.

A sentence S of the language L, where $(R1,\ldots Rk)$ is an exhaustive list
of the predicate symbols in S, and i_j $(j = 1,\ldots,k)$ indicates the number
of arguments of Rj, will sometimes be denoted by $S(R1^{i_1},\ldots,Rk^{i_k})$.
A model M over A of S is a structure $(A,\underline{R1},\ldots,\underline{Rk})$ where A is a set of the
form $\{0,1,\ldots,N\}$ with $N > 0$, $\underline{Ri}$ is a subset of A^{i_j} (i.e. the set of i_j-tuples
of elements of A) $(j = 1,\ldots,k)$, and M satisfies S $(M \models S)$ in the sense
described inductively below:

(let n_r range over A)

(a) $M \models Rj(n_1,\ldots,n_{i_j}) <=> (n_1,\ldots,n_{i_j}) \in \underline{Ri}$

(b) $M \models \neg S1 <=>$ not $M \models S1$

(c) $M \models S1 \& S2 <=> M \models S1$ and $M \models S2$

   $M \models S1 \vee S2 <=> M \models S1$ or $M \models S2$

   $M \models S1 \to S2 <=> M \models \neg S1$ or $M \models S2$

   $M \models S1 \leftrightarrow S2 <=> M \models S1$ iff $M \models S2$

(d) $M \models \forall xF1(x) <=>$ for all $n \in A$: $M \models F1(n/x)$

   $M \models \exists xF1(x) <=>$ there is some $n \in A$: $M \models F1(n/x)$,

   where F1(n/x) is the result of substituting all occurrences of x in F1
   by n.

Example:

A strict linear ordering R can be described by the following sentences (read "x less than y" for $R(x,y)$):

(A.1) $\forall x \neg R(x,x)$

(A.2) $\forall x \forall y (x \neq y \longrightarrow R(x,y) \vee R(y,x))$

(A.3) $\forall x \forall y \forall z ((R(x,y) \ \& \ R(y,z)) \longrightarrow R(x,z))$

A model M of the conjunction of these sentences is given by $(A,\underline{R})$ where A= {0,1,2,3} and

$\underline{R} = \{(0,1),(0,2),(0,3),(1,2),(1,3),(2,3)\}$.

The reader should notice how the model $(A,\underline{R})$ captures the essential information of the picture above.

Our choice of the elements of A is arbitrary. We could have used other natural numbers, characters, LISP - atoms etc.. Our interpretation of satisfaction is well-known in mathematical logic (see [9]) and is due to Tarski. The advantages of this definition of model will be explained in the following paragraphs.

The first useful observation is that, once we have fixed A, we can find for each axiom S a sentence S' which does not contain $\longrightarrow$, $\longleftrightarrow$, $\forall$, $\exists$ and is satisfied by exactly the same models over A as S. For $\longrightarrow$ and $\longleftrightarrow$ this is done using their usual logical definitions, namely $S1 \longrightarrow S2 <=> \neg S1 \vee S2$ and $S1 \longleftrightarrow S2 <=> (S1 \ \& \ S2) \vee (\neg S1 \ \& \ \neg S2)$. Here we make no use of A, whereas for the elimination of $\forall$ and $\exists$ A is essential. It can be easily seen that for $A = \{0,1,\ldots,N\}$:

$M \models \forall x F1(x) <=> M \models F1(0) \ \& \ \ldots \ \& \ F1(N)$ and

$M \models \exists x F1(x) <=> M \models F1(0) \vee \ldots \vee F1(N)$.

Another fact of mathematical logic is, that one can construct a sentence S'' which is satisfied by exactly the same models over A as S', and in which any $\neg$ - sign occurs only immediately before some predicate symbol. Unnegated and negated atomic subformulae of S'' are called <u>literals</u>. Let $L,L1,L2,\ldots$ denote literals. The negation of a literal L will be denoted by ^1L. Clearly $^1(^1L) <=> L$. We say that S'' is in <u>A-normal form</u>.

In view of the above observations we can assume that all axioms are in A-normal form.

For formulas in A-normal form there is a very simple and useful representation by matrices. The usefulness of matrices for purposes of theorem-proving has been well established in [1] and [2]. The efficient algorithms of [2] combined with some facts about the relationship between validity of theorems and satisfiability of formulas are the basis of our approach to model construction. Let us first recall some definitions from [1].

<u>defn. 2:</u>

<u>Matrices</u> over a set of literals V are defined inductively as follows:

(a) any member of V is a matrix

(b) if $Q1,\ldots,Qn$ are matrices then the set $\{Q1,\ldots,Qn\}$ is a matrix $(n \geq 0)$.

$\emptyset$ will denote the empty matrix.

Given a matrix Q of the form $\{C1,\ldots,Cn\}$, the C_i will be called <u>clauses</u> of Q, $(i = 1,\ldots,n)$.

We say that $\underline{Q\text{ represents }S}$, if Q is interpreted as the conjunction of all its clauses, each clause as a disjunction of its elements and so on in this alternating way.

Example: $Q = \{\{\{L1, {}^{1}L1\}, L2\}, L1, \{{}^{1}L1, {}^{1}L2\}\}$

represents $((L1 \ \& \ {}^{1}L1) \lor L2) \ \& \ L1 \ \& \ ({}^{1}L1 \lor {}^{1}L2)$.

A $\underline{\text{path}}$ through a matrix Q is a set of literals defined inductively:

(a) there is exactly one path through a literal L: $\{L\}$

(b) let $Q = \{C1, \ldots, Cn\}$; if n=0 or if $Ci = \emptyset$ for some i then there is no path through Q. Otherwise for any n matrices Qi, s.t. $Qi \in Ci$ and for any n paths Pi through Qi (i = 1,...,n) the set $P1 \cup P2 \cup \ldots \cup Pn$ is a path through Q.

L is called $\underline{\text{complementary}}$ to ${}^{1}L$ and vice versa.

A path is called $\underline{\text{complementary}}$ if it contains a complementary pair of literals.

A matrix is called $\underline{\text{complementary}}$ if each path through it is complementary.

Example:

The matrix Q above contains the paths

$\{L1, {}^{1}L1\}$ $\{L1, {}^{1}L1, {}^{1}L2\}$ $\{L2, L1, {}^{1}L1\}$ $\{L2, L1, {}^{1}L2\}$

as can be seen from a more illustrative presentation:

```
  L1  1L1           1L1
              L1
    L2            1L2
```

Hence Q is complementary.

The algorithms (1.3) and (6.1) of [2][2] have the following important property: if a matrix Q is not complementary then the algorithm after (non-successful) termination has obtained a non-complementary path through Q.

Now we state the important

theorem 1: (folklore)

Let S be the conjunction of a finite set of axioms in A-normal form. Let Q be a matrix representing S. If there exists a non-complementary path P through Q, then P determines a model of S. Moreover every model of S over A is an extension of some model determined by some non-complementary path.

---

2) We claim that we have obtained a combination of these two algorithms (as conjectured in [2]), which enjoys the virtues of both of them.

We sketch a proof of theorem 1 and indicate what we mean by "determines" and "extension".

Let $S = S(R1^{i_1},...,Rk^{i_k})$.

For $j = 1,...,k$ define $\underline{Rj} := \{(n_1,...,n_{i_j}) \in A^{i_j} \mid Rj(n_1,...,n_{i_j}) \in P\}$

We claim that $(A,\underline{R1},...,\underline{Rk})$ is a model of S, call it the <u>canonical model</u> <u>determined by P</u>. This can be proved using induction on the structure of Q. Conversely if we are given a model $M = (A,\underline{R1},...,\underline{Rk})$ of S, the process of checking that M satisfies S will yield a non-complementary path through Q.

This path consists of all literals which have to be satisfied by M. If we construct the canonical model for this path, we obtain some M'. It may happen that M' ≠ M, but all relations of M' will be subsets of the corresponding relations of M and thus M is called an extension of M'. Furthermore we can obtain all such extensions M' by extending the relations of this model subject to the restriction that the negated sentences in the path remain satisfied.

What we have explained so far amounts to:

<u>theorem 2:</u>

There is an algorithm which, when applied to a finite set of axioms in the language L which possess a model of size $N > 0$, yields such a model. All such models can be obtained by small variations of this algorithm.

The rest of this paper is devoted to some modifications of the path-checking algorithms as described in [2], which can be made in this context and yield considerable speed-up of the algorithm.

In order to do this it is necessary to be more explicit about the algorithms in [2]. For our purposes it suffices to know the basic idea of them. For simplicity let all elements of the matrix Q be literals. We choose a clause C of Q and then an element L of C. We look for another clause C' which contains ^1L. If we find such a clause, we proceed by choosing an element of this clause different from ^1L and repeat what we did before. This can be pictured as follows:

$$\begin{array}{cccccccc} & ^1L1 & & ^1L2 & & ^1L3 & \cdot & \cdot & \cdot & \cdot \\ L1 & & L2 & & L3 & & \cdot & \cdot & \cdot & \cdot & \cdot \\ \cdot & & \cdot & & \cdot \\ \cdot & & \cdot & & \cdot \\ \cdot & & \cdot & & \cdot \end{array}$$

All paths containing the selected links are complementary. We may , however, run into the sitation where no such link can be established:

$$^1L1 \quad ^1L2 \quad ^1L3 \quad ^1L1 \quad ^1L5 \quad \cdot \quad \cdot \quad \cdot$$

```
  1L1    1L2    1L3    1L1    1L5   · · ·
L1    L2    L3    L4    L5    ·
 ·     ·     ·     ·     ·     ·
 ·     ·     ·     ·     ·     ·
 ·     ·     ·     ·     ·
```

The partial path {L1,L2,L3,L4} has been called <u>active</u> in [2], since it is
a candidate for extension to a non-complementary path. In the special situation
of this example, we can find a link which makes it possible to continue,
namely $l = \{L1, {}^1L1\}$:

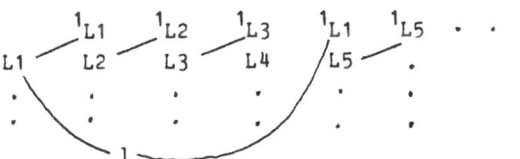

However, if a continuation like that is not possible, then Q is complementary
iff the remaining clauses of Q which have not been involved so far form a
complementary matrix. For those readers who are familiar with [2] we remark
that algorithms (1.3) and (6.1) at this point forget about the active path
constructed so far. In the model-construction-algorithm this deletion must
be omitted.
Proceeding this way we either end up with an active path going through Q
(i.e. Q is not complementary) or we go on to consider the paths of Q which
are pictured by dots. Briefly one can say that the algorithm establishes
the complementarity of paths through Q in a <u>systematic</u> way until it either
finds a non-complementary path or has exhausted all possibilities.

We are now going to describe how this systematic behaviour can be modified
to benefit the construction of models.

1. Since the set of axioms is in A-normal form, the matrix Q in question
has a rather special structure. The axioms give rise to a partition of the
clauses of Q (we collect all clauses which come from the first axiom into
the first group, etc.). We note that if an axiom begins with $\forall$, then the
clauses belonging to it look very much alike (they are instances of a common
generalization). $\exists$ has a similar effect inside the clauses. This allows
that we don't need to generate all of Q in order to find a non-complementary
path. We explain this using as an example the following three axioms to be
interpreted in $A = \{0,1\}$:
S1: $\forall x \, \neg R(x,x)$
S2: $\forall x \, \exists y \, R(x,y)$
S3: $\exists x \, Q(x)$

We pick an axiom (say S1) and if it is of the form $\forall$ x1,...,xn S, we pick
any substitution for (x1,...,xn) (say x ==> 0 in the example). This yields
a clause which in the present example consists only of the literal ¬R(0,0),
for which we have to find a complement in one of the remaining clauses.
Among these we may distinguish two disjoint subsets. First, we check
the remaining substitutions for (x1,...,xn). Here, this is only x ==> 1
which doesn't yield the desired complement. Then we look for further axioms
which contain the same relations. Clearly, axioms like S3 can be neglected.
In our case the substitution x ==> 0, y ==> 0 in S2 succeeds. But the
corresponding clause in A-normal form is {R(0,0),R(0,1)}. Therefore,
if we continue this process, we will obtain for example:

¬R(0,0) —— R(0,0)   ¬ R(1,1) —— R(1,1)   Q(0)

R(0,1)   R(1,0)

This ex mple is poorly chosen with respect to demonstrating the efficiency
of this approach. But as soon as the axioms get more complex and the size
of the intended model bigger, one can realize the economy. With a suitably
chosen representation of the axioms it is possible to work with the
axioms rather than with a large array of literals which obviously saves a
lot of memory.

2. It is not hard to see that the order in which the axioms are chosen has
some influence on the speed of the algorithm. We have no mathematical theory
to select an optimal order, but propose instead to try some strategies at
this point. The choice of such strategies may change the efficiency
but not the systematic feature of the algorithm. One such strategy could
be to start with small clauses, since having big clauses on the right increases
the chances of finishing an active path.

An implementation of this algorithm along these lines has not yet been carried
out, but is one of the next tasks in the current project. A preliminary version
of it, based more on heuristic than on systematic features, is running and
has obtained several interesting models. More on this version can be found
in [3].

Conclusion:
We have presented a method to obtain models of theories with finite models.
This method is systematic and based on the connection between satisfiability
and provability. For the latter notion powerful algorithms are known which
can be modified to work efficiently as model constructors. We do not know
whether this approach is entirely new, but we have found no mentioning of
it in some relevant papers using models, like [5] - [8]. The only work we
know of which takes a similar point of view is [4]. Bledsoe's and Ballantine's
technique is more ambitious than ours since it is not subject to the two

restrictions at the beginning of this paper. On the other hand the lack of these restrictions entails the use of higher order theorem proving or similar methods and thus has to be less systematic. We feel that our method is preferable in cases like LOPS, where above restrictions pose no problems.

Acknowledgement. We wish to thank Dr. W. Bibel for his encouragement and many valuable suggestions which he contributed to this research.

Bibliography:

[1] W. Bibel

On Matrices With Connections
JACM (to appear)

[2] W. Bibel

A Comparison Of Several Proof Procedures
AI-Journal (to appear)
shortened version in:
Proc. AISB-80 Conference on Artificial Intelligence
Amsterdam (1980)

[3] W. Bibel, K.M. Hörnig

LOPS - A System Based On A Strategical Approach To
Program Synthesis
Proc. International Workshop On Program Construction
Chateau de Bonas
INRIA Le Chesnay (1980)

[4] W.W. Bledsoe, A.M. Ballantine

On Automatic Generation Of Counterexamples
ATP-44A, Univ. of Texas at Austin (1979)

[5] H. Gelernter

Realization Of A Geometry Theorem Proving Machine
Proc. Int. Conf. Information Processing
Paris, UNESCO House (1959) 273-282

[6] L.J. Henschen

Semantic Resolution Of Horn Sets
Adv. Papers Int. Joint Conf. Artificial Intell.
Tbilisi U.S.S.R. (1975)

[7] R. Reiter

A Semantically Guided Deductive System For Automatic
Theorem Proving
IEEE Trans. On Elec. Computing C-25(1976) 328-334

[8] J.R. Slagle

Automatic Theorem Proving With Renamable And
Semantic Resolution
JACM 14 (1967) 687-697

[9] R.M. Smullyan

First Order Logic
Springer, Ergebnisse der Mathematik und ihrer
Grenzgebiete Bd. 43 (1968)

Program Verification at Stanford:
Past, Present, Future

Wolfgang Polak
Computer Systems Laboratory
Stanford University

1. History of the Stanford Verifier

1.1. Early Beginning

In late 1971 Shigeru Igarashi, Ralph London, David Luckham, and Robin Milner were working at the Stanford Artificial Intelligence Laboratory. At the same time Niklaus Wirth was visiting the Computer Science Department at Stanford. Robin Milner was implementing LCF [25, 26], a formal system to reason about programs based on Dana Scott's logic of computable functions.

David Luckham's attempts to verify programs with the early version of LCF proved tedious and frustrating; reliance on a simpleminded proof-checker forced the user to feed very detailed proof steps to the system. It was Luckham's feeling that a practical verification system ought to be based on more powerful theorem proving capabilities. At the same time Ralph London was very tediously writing out manual correctness proofs for simple compilers for pure Lisp [18]. Those experiences prompted the idea for a new, easier to use program verifier.

So, Igarashi, London, and Luckham set out to develop a *practical* verifier. Pascal was chosen as the programming language accepted by this new verifier simply because Wirth, the authority on the language, was at Stanford. Their initial approach was to use explicit path traces based on Floyd's theory [6], as had been done previously by Jim King [16] and was pursued later by Peter Deutsch [5]. But during the initial design phase the novel idea was born to use Tony Hoare's axiomatic proof rules [11] as a reduction system, that is, a system which *reduces* statements about programs in Hoare's logic to statements in first order logic.

The key idea was to give a set of proof rules that was unambiguous, i.e. in any situation at most one rule is applicable. Such a set of rules can be used in a straightforward way to generate verification conditions. The group developed suitable rules for a subset of Pascal including assignment, while loops, conditionals, recursive functions and procedures (declaration and call), and one-dimensional arrays.

Formal assertions were included in programs by augmenting Pascal with certain kinds of documentation statements. Entry and exit conditions had to be provided for each function and procedure; an assert statement was required for each loop and label. The assertion language was first order logic, including full quantification. Auxiliary (free) functions and predicates could be used to introduce new concepts in the assertion language.

Work progressed in parallel. Igarashi and Luckham developed a set of proof rules and proved their soundness and completeness while Ralph London implemented the reduction

---
This research was supported by the Advanced Research Projects Agency of the Department of Defense under Contract MDA 903-80-C-0159.

system. This program became known as "verification condition generator" (VCgen). In summer of 1972 the first version of the "Stanford Verifier" was operable. In addition to the verification condition generator the system contained a simple parser for the input language. The system was coded in Lisp 1.6 and running on the Stanford PDP10 system.

It was planned to use the Allen/Luckham resolution prover [2] to prove verification conditions but only few proofs have actually been mechanized in this way. In fact, an interface between the output of VCgen and the resolution prover was never completed.

Examples handled with the very first system include factorial, exchangesort (including mechanical proof of VCs), binary search, and the McCarthy/Painter compiler [24]. A complete description of the facilities of the first verifier and the underlying theory can be found in [13]. It is interesting to note, that Igarashi, London and Luckham allready proposed to include modal operators in the assertion language (see [13] p.1), an idea that has found much recent attention.

In summer 1972 both Igarashi and London left Stanford.

1.2. Nori Suzuki

Early experiments showed that the resolution prover was not very well suited for program verification; it was too general and consequently too slow. Norihisa Suzuki joined the verification group as a graduate student of Luckham in October 1972; design of a better theorem prover was his first task. Another member of the group at this time was Friedrich vonHenke.

Verification conditions arising from practical problems require two kinds of reasoning. For one, most programs depend on very deep mathematical properties. For example, a program that permutes elements of an array according to a given permutation (see [34] for one such program) may depend on theorems like "each permutation consists of disjoint cycles" or "each permutation can be written as a sequence of exchange operations". Proofs of these theorems require sophisticated reasoning in number theory and cannot be expected to be automated in the near future. On the other hand, given suitable theorems about the problem domain the remaining reasoning to prove verification conditions is very shallow.

The key idea of the new prover design was to separate difficult and easy proofs, leaving the former to the user while automating the latter. Difficult to prove facts could be given to the prover as theorems and lemmas, called the logical basis.

The logical basis was given as a set of *rules*. In addition to purely logical content, rules contained heuristic information indicating how the theorem prover should use them.

There were two kinds of rules, inference rules and rewrite rules. The syntax

$$\text{goal } P \text{ sub } Q \wedge R$$

expressed the formula $Q \wedge R \supset P$. It indicates that P is to be proven from Q and R by subgoaling. Rewrite rules, suggested by Luckham, were inspired by W. Bledsoe's work in theorem proving in topology. Suzuki's implementation proved their usefulness [39]. Rewrite rules had the syntax

$$\text{axiom } f \leftrightarrow g.$$

This rule specifies that each occurence of f is to be replaced by g. Logically, it expresses the equality $f = g$. Rules were applied by the system by pattern matching; pattern variables in formulas had to be explicitly marked as such.

Since integer arithmetic occurs very frequently in verification, Suzuki included a special module dealing with arithmetic. It's design was ad hoc and tailored to the particular problems that arose from verification experiments.

There was no provision to deal with quantifiers, so the assertion language was restricted to quantifier free first order logic. Although slightly inconvenient, this was not a severe restriction. For any quantified formula $\forall x.P(x,y)$ one can define a new predicate $R(y) \equiv \forall x.P(x,y)$; necessary properties of $R(y)$ can be supplied by rules.

But Suzuki did not stop here; another major contribution is the extension of VCgen to handle complex data structures. The term $\langle x, [i], e \rangle$ was introduced to denote the array x after e had been assigned to position i. This new notation presents a significant advantage over the rather clumsy conditional notation if $i = j$ then e else $x[i]$ (going back to McCarthy) used in the early version of the verifier.

Analogously with array terms $\langle a, [i], e \rangle$ Suzuki introduced the notation $\langle r, .c, e \rangle$ denoting the record r after assigning e to the record field $r.c$.

A major breakthrough to handle pointers was the introduction of the "reference class." A reference class is a part of the computation state that cannot be manipulated by a Pascal program; it can only be used in the assertion language. For each pointer type $\uparrow T$ the reference class $\#T$ is defined to be the set of objects of type T pointed to by pointers of type $\uparrow T$. In this framework dereferencing of a pointer p can be described as "indexing the corresponding reference class by p"; Suzuki used the notation $\#T \subset p \supset$ Assigning to a pointer means changing a particular element of the reference class; it can be described in analogy to the array and record assignment by the term $\langle \#T, \subset p \supset, e \rangle$. For the compiler writers the analogy between a reference class and the heap will be obvious.

Even today no better technique has been devised to reason about pointers. The concept of reference classes appeared so important to the designers of Euclid that they made it part of their language [17]; Euclid "collections" are nothing but reference classes (see conclusion section of [23]).

Other innovations introduced by Suzuki were changes in the proof rules. For example, the new "while" rule was

$$\frac{I \wedge B\{S\}I, \; P \supset I \wedge \forall s.(I \wedge \neg B \supset Q)}{P\{\text{while } B \text{ do } S\}Q}$$

where I is the invariant and s is the list of variables changed in the body S. This rule does not require the programmer to state obviously invariant properties in the loop invariant.

Similarly, the restriction that each label had to be followed by an assertion was removed; it was merely required that any loop constructed with goto's was cut by at least one assertion. However, this may not be an improvement at all; the complications in VCgen may outweigh the flexibility gained in writing assertions.

David Luckham and Friedrich vonHenke were active users of the new verifier. Their verification experiments provided valuable feedback for the development of the system. Much of the effort at this time was directed towards establishing what kinds of programs could be analyzed with the verifier. Their examples included sorting and unification programs and progressed to more and more complex problems, e.g. pointer manipulations. Examples in this area include reachability in lists, the root and sentinal problem, and the Schorr–Waite marking algorithm. The need to develop methods of integrating the use of verifiers into the programming process was realized soon. Early published research from 1973 – 1974 includes [39, 40, 10].

A complete description of the new verifier with examples demonstrating the capabilities of the system is given in Suzuki's thesis [41]. Suzuki worked with the verification group until late 1975.

1.3. The theorem prover

Although Suzuki's prover was a vast improvement over a resolution systems theorem proving still was the bottleneck of verification. At about the time when Suzuki left Derek Oppen joined as a full time research associate with primary responsibility for theorem proving. The overall concept of user supplied rules and fast special purpose modules (e.g. for arithmetic and data structures) was generally accepted as useful and should be retained.

Initially, Oppen redesigned and recoded parts of Suzuki's prover. Many problems in the code were eliminated and the rule language was changed. Replacement rules now used the more mnemonic syntax

replace x by y.

In addition to backward subgoaling the concept of active "forward" deduction was introduced. A rule of the form

from a infer b

would cause the prover to infer b whenever a was known. To be consistent, the syntax of subgoaling rules was changed to

infer b from a.

Explicit mentioning of pattern variables was eliminated; rather any free variable was taken to be a pattern variable. A constant declaration is allowed to override this default.

In fall 76 Greg Nelson, then a graduate student, contributed a very significant new idea. He proved the following important theorem (stated here informally):

> Let T_i be theories satisfying certain constraints (see $\begin{bmatrix} 29, 30, 31 \end{bmatrix}$ for details) and let D_i be complete decision procedures for T_i. The decision procedures D_i can be combined to a complete decision procedure D for the union $T = \bigcup \{T_i\}$ of the individual theories by merely communicating equalities among the D_i.

This theorem prompted a complete redesign of the prover; it provided the basis for a systematic combination of special purpose decision procedures and a general rule facility. Design and implementation was undertaken by Oppen, Nelson, and Scherlis.

In the new prover a potentially unlimited number of independent decision procedures communicate via a common data base of equalities, called E–graph. Equalities between terms of certain types are passed to the appropriate decision procedures which in turn will *propagate* new equalities to be entered in the graph. At any time the E–graph was closed under equalities; e.g. if $f(x)$ and $f(y)$ were terms in the E–graph and the equality $x = y$ was propagated then the equality $f(x) = f(y)$ was deduced.

The new prover is characterized by the following features: (i) systematic design that guarantees some limited form of completeness; (ii) refutation based (as opposed to subgoaling in Suzuki's prover); (iii) functions as a simplifier. The latter point is particularly important for verification: while a theorem prover may give the possible answers "valid", "unsatisfiable", or "I don't know", a simplifier will return the simplest formula equivalent to its input. Thus, if a formula is valid, the result of simplification will be *true*. (To some extend Suzuki's prover behaved like a simplifier.)

Let us briefly outline the principal operation of the simplifier. An input formula is normalized into *cond*-normal form, i.e. using only the ternary boolean connective **if a then b else c**. Let ρ be a context, i.e. the conjunction of all equalities in the E–graph.

A formula of the form **if** p **then** a **else** b in context ρ is simplified recursively as follows:

$$\rho' \leftarrow \rho \wedge p;$$
if $inconsistent(\rho')$ then $return(simplify(b, \rho));$
$a \leftarrow simplify(a, \rho');$
$$\rho' \leftarrow \rho \wedge \neg p;$$
if $inconsistent(\rho')$ then $return(a);$
$p \leftarrow simplify(p, \rho);$
$return(\text{"if } p \text{ then } a \text{ else } b\text{"});$

To add an atomic formula p to a context simply means to add the equality $p = true$. A context is inconsistent if $true = false$.

Initially, decision procedures were provided for rationals under addition and inequalities, lists under *car*, *cdr*, and *cons*, and data structure terms for array, record and pointer operations. Thus, the prover was complete for the union of these theories and the theory of uninterpreted function symbols.

The decision procedure for rationals was implemented by Nelson. It uses the simplex algorithm to determine if a set of inequalities has a non-empty solution space. If no solution is possible the given set of inequalities is inconsistent. The simplifier has no decision procedure for integers; all integers are treated as rationals. For example, the equation $x + x = 1$ does not lead to an inconsistency.

One important feature contributing to the overall performance of the system is the pattern matcher which is implemented as integral part of the E-graph. Matching is done on equivalence classes rather than syntactic terms. For example, given the equality $f(2) = 3$, the pattern $f(x)$ will match the term 3 with the binding $x \leftrightarrow 2$.

A special module "rule handler" dealt with rules provided by the user. It interfaces (at least conceptually) with the rest of the prover like just another decision procedure. But the rule handler cannot be complete, of course, since it depends on rules written by the user.

The rule handler for this new system was designed and implemented by Bill Scherlis. Although it uses a syntax similar to the previous prover, rules have substantially different semantics. For example, a replace rule **replace** a **by** b will cause the equality $a = b$ to be added to the E-graph as soon as a suitable match for a has been found; no replacement is done. Forward and backward inference rules have a different semantics since no subgoaling is done. A detailed description of the rule handler can be found in $\begin{bmatrix}38\end{bmatrix}$ (also unpublished manuscript by Scherlis).

Unfortunately some problems in the interfacing of rule handler and E-graph still exist today. One problem area is the matching of arithmetic expressions. Since matching is semantic rather syntactic a pattern of the form $a + b$ is not meaningful since it will match any term x with infinitely many bindings $a \leftrightarrow x - b$ for arbitrary binding of b.

A manual mode is not yet inplemented in the simplifier. Some limited tracing facilities are available. However, the facts that the simplifier tries to derive a contradiction and operates with *cond*-normal form make trace information difficult to interpret.

1.4. User inferface

In parallel with the development of a better theorem prover, work continued to improve the user interface of the system. A notable deficiency of Suzuki's system was its parser. Error messages were not very informative and only a minimum of semantic checks were performed. For example, it was the programmer's responsibility to guarantee absence of aliasing.

Richard A. Karp made the system much friendlier to its users by implementing a new parser for programs and rules. A semantic phase checked all restrictions on the applicability of proof rules as well as the usual type and declaration constraints mandated by Pascal. The input language was extended to cover almost full Pascal. Notable omissions are reals, the with–statement, and variant records.

Steve German, a Harvard student on leave at Stanford, recoded VCgen. Some inconsistencies in VCgen were eliminated and additional language constructs not previously handled were included. Rules for procedure and function call were generalized. A description of the proof rules now used in the system is contained in [38].

Friedrich vonHenke coded a top level command interpreter for the system. The user no longer has to write Lisp syntax like (*parse* (*file ver*)), rather the system accepts a more natural command language, e.g. *parse file.ver;*. The available commands include requests for status information, writing of transcripts, changing of parameter settings, and commands for tracing.

Steve German developed a special version of the verifier called runcheck. Runcheck proves the absence of many common runtime errors. Steve had earlier worked with Ben Wegbreit on the synthesis of loop invariants. He used this experience and employed invariant synthesis techniques so that absence of runtime errors can be checked for a large class of programs without requiring annotations from the user [7, 8].

German's program uses two techniques to derive invariants. First, obviously invariant properties are detected by inspection of the loop body. Second, the partially annotated program will be supplied to the verifier and the simplified verification conditions are analyzed to infer additional invariants. This latter technique appears very promising and should be useful in a more general setting to provide feedback about possible errors in the program and insufficient invariants.

2. The present system

2.1. Overview

In figure 1 the structure of the present system is shown. The input language for programs and rules, and top level commands is as described in the previous section. The semantic module passes abstract syntax trees as well as symbol table information to VCgen. Rules and verification conditions are stored internally and can be reused for different proof attempts.

Specification and consistency analysis of a substantial number of programs (hundreds) has been undertaken with the aid of our verifier over the past few years. The collection of verified programs includes numerous small examples (one page of Pascal code), but also some large programs. For example a complete compiler for a Pascal-like language (about 150 pages of code) has been checked for consistency using the verifier; this is believed to be the largest verification task ever undertaken with the assistence of a mechanized verifier [35].

Theory of specification of some classes of programs (notably sorting) has reached an acceptable degree of standardization. Verification of pointer manipulation programs has progressed and a number of standard pointer algorithms have been specified and verified. However, this area seems to require development of high level specification concepts beyond the theory of reference classes (or collections) and their axiomatization.

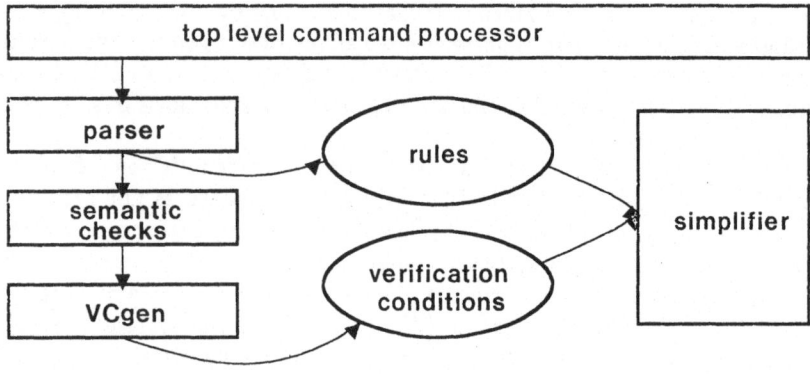

Fig. 1

The Stanford verifier is frequently used in class work. Various industrial and governmental groups have begun to experiment with the verifier. Several versions have been distributed over the ARPAnet and are running on PDP-10 installations under TOPS-10 and TOPS-20 operating systems.

2.2. Methodology

The initial verification paradigm was to take a complete Pascal program, find suitable annotations, and submit it together with a suitable logical basis to the verifier. Although this mode of operation is imperative to verify certain well established algorithms it is not desirable for program development. The main problems involved here are to find suitable invariants and to determine a suitable logical basis. Both problems require a complete understanding of the program's operation and the programmer's intentions. This information is very difficult to reconstruct after the design of a program is completed; even good informal documentation is only of limited help.

The above problems are avoided if program development and verification go hand in hand. In fact, significant future progress in the practical application of program verification will most likely come from methodological advances. Even if we can improve current theorem provers by orders of magnitude, suitable methodology will be imperative for success. If a program is developed using stepwise refinement the verification on each level will be related to that of the previous level; the only new proof steps are those corresponding to the latest refinement step. Any error in the design is detected at the earliest possible time.

The concept of a logical basis fits smoothly into this paradigm. With successive design decisions new formal concepts are introduced and added to the logical basis. At any given time the logical basis represents all assumptions (design decisions) on which the implementation is based. For example when the designer decides to implement the type stack with an array and an index pointing to the top element a suitable definition specifying how this representation is to be mapped into stacks is provided. In this way details of the underlying theory are developed in a top down fashion in parallel with the program development.

However, the concepts of logical basis appears to be controversial and has drawn heavy criticism from both opponents and proponents of verification. A frequent criticism is that a proof is only valid if it is based on first principles of number or set theory. The philosophy of the Stanford verifier is to give relative consistency proofs between the program text and the logical basis. It is our firm belief, that even if significant progress is made in automatic theorem proving the concept of a logical basis will be necessary to tackle programs of any significance. Theorems and lemmas in a logical basis are of purely mathematical nature and can often be taken from mathematical text books.

2.3. Examples

We will explain the use of the Stanford verifier with two examples. The following program is the Pascal version of a function defined by Ikuo Takeuchi.

```pascal
pascal
function tak(x, y, z : integer) : integer;
exit (x ≤ y ∧ tak = y) ∨ (x > y ∧ ((y ≤ z ∧ tak = z) ∨ (y > z ∧ tak = x)));
begin
  if x ≤ y then
      tak ← y else
      tak ← tak(tak(x − 1, y, z), tak(y − 1, z, x), tak(z − 1, x, y));
end;
```

The reason this program is presented here is that its verification conditions are formulas in the theory of rationals under addition and inequalities. Since the simplifier is complete for this theory it is guaranteed to prove or disprove these verification conditions without any rules or user interaction. The two conditions generated by the verifier are:

$$
\begin{aligned}
&(\neg(x \le y) \land (x - 1 \le y \land tak(x - 1, y, z) = y \lor \\
&\qquad\qquad y < x - 1 \land (y \le z \land tak(x - 1, y, z) = z \lor \\
&\qquad\qquad\qquad\qquad z < y \land tak(x - 1, y, z) = x - 1)) \land \\
&(y - 1 \le z \land tak(y - 1, z, x) = z \lor \\
&\; z < y - 1 \land (z \le x \land tak(y - 1, z, x) = x \lor \\
&\qquad\qquad x < z \land tak(y - 1, z, x) = y - 1)) \land \\
&(z - 1 \le x \land tak(z - 1, x, y) = x \lor \\
&\; x < z - 1 \land (x \le y \land tak(z - 1, x, y) = y \lor \\
&\qquad\qquad y < x \land tak(z - 1, x, y) = z - 1)) \land \\
&(tak(x - 1, y, z) \le tak(y - 1, z, x) \land \\
&tak(tak(x - 1, y, z), tak(y - 1, z, x), tak(z - 1, x, y)) = tak(y - 1, z, x) \lor \\
&tak(y - 1, z, x) < tak(x - 1, y, z) \land \\
&(tak(y - 1, z, x) \le tak(z - 1, x, y) \land \\
&tak(tak(x - 1, y, z), tak(y - 1, z, x), tak(z - 1, x, y)) = tak(z - 1, x, y) \lor \\
&tak(z - 1, x, y) < tak(y - 1, z, x) \land \\
&tak(tak(x - 1, y, z), tak(y - 1, z, x), tak(z - 1, x, y)) = tak(x - 1, y, z))) \\
&\to \\
&\quad x \le y \land tak(tak(x - 1, y, z), tak(y - 1, z, x), tak(z - 1, x, y)) = y \lor \\
&\quad y < x \land (y \le z \land tak(tak(x - 1, y, z), tak(y - 1, z, x), tak(z - 1, x, y)) = z \lor \\
&\qquad\qquad z < y \land tak(tak(x - 1, y, z), tak(y - 1, z, x), tak(z - 1, x, y)) = x))
\end{aligned}
$$

and

$$(x \leq y$$
$$\rightarrow$$
$$x \leq y \wedge y = y \vee$$
$$y < x \wedge (y \leq z \wedge y = z \vee z < y \wedge y = x))$$

The simplifier takes 2.35 seconds to simplify both conditions to *true*.

Next, let us consider a more realistic example in some detail. We will design a parser for context free grammars and demonstrate the technique of simultaneous program development and verification.

As a first step of the program development we define the underlying concepts. Sequences are elements of the free monoid (A^*) over some alphabet A. We use $\circ$ as the concatenation operator, Λ as the empty sequence, *first*, *rest* have their obvious meaning, and $\langle a \rangle$ denotes the sequences of just one element a. We have the following axioms for sequences:

$$u \circ \Lambda = \Lambda \circ u = u, \quad (u \circ v) \circ w = u \circ (v \circ w)$$
$$first(\langle a \rangle \circ u) = a, \quad rest(\langle a \rangle \circ u) = u$$

A context free grammar is a tuple $\langle N, T, P, s \rangle$ where

$$s \in N, \quad P \subseteq N \times (N \bigcup T)^*$$

We define a binary relation $\Rightarrow \subseteq (N \bigcup T)^* \times (N \bigcup T)^*$ as follows:

$$u \circ \langle x \rangle \circ v \Rightarrow u \circ w \circ v \quad iff \quad (x, w) \in P$$

Let $\Rightarrow^*$ be the reflexive, transitive closure of $\Rightarrow$, i.e.

$$u \Rightarrow^* v \quad iff \quad u = v \vee u \Rightarrow v \vee \exists w (u \Rightarrow^* w \wedge w \Rightarrow^* v)$$

We use functions *embed*, *projt*, and *projn* to convert between sequences in N^*, T^*, and $(N \bigcup T)^*$. The predicates *ist* and *isn* test whether an element of $N \bigcup T$ is in N or T.

To parse a string $w \in T^*$ means to determine whether $\langle s \rangle \Rightarrow^* embed(w)$; the problem of outputting a parse tree is ignored in our example.

To express the above definitions in the rule and assertion language we use the abbreviations:

$$
\begin{array}{rcl}
\Lambda & - & null \\
\langle a \rangle & - & list(a) \\
u \circ v & - & concat(u, v) \\
u \Rightarrow^* v & - & isderiv(u, v) \\
(x, w) \in P & - & isprod(x, w)
\end{array}
$$

The theory of context free languages can then be expressed by the rules

ref : infer $isderiv(x, x)$;
trans : infer $isderiv(x, concat(u, concat(w, v)))$ from
$\qquad isderiv(x, concat(u, concat(list(n), v))) \wedge isprod(projn(n), w)$;

Additional rules defining the theory of sequences are necessary for the proof, these can be found in appendix D.

We will only prove that the parser is correct if no parsing error occurs. In any error situation we assume that the program does not terminate. This technique is very convinient since it allows us to ignore abnormal situations during verification. In practice, the parser will be embedded in a larger program. In this case "non-termination" can be achieved by jumping to an error handler outside the parser or by raising a suitable exception. With this error convention the correctness of the parser can be stated by the simple exit assertion

$$isderiv(list(s), embed(w)).$$

We will implement the basic algorithm of a nondeterministic push down automaton accepting a context free language in a top-down fashion. This algorithm can be described in terms of a pushdown stack p and three sequences, the initial input $w0$, the current input w, and the input already read wr. At any time we will maintain $w0 = wr \circ w$ and $s \Rightarrow^* embed(wr) \circ p$. This relationship will become the obvious invariant of our implementation.

The algorithm starts in the situation $w = w0, wr = \Lambda, p = \langle s \rangle$. The input is successfully parsed if we can achieve the final situation $w = \Lambda, wr = w0, p = \Lambda$ which entails $\langle s \rangle \Rightarrow^* embed(w0)$. The program repeatedly performs the following steps:

— If $first(p) \in T$ and $first(p) = first(w)$ then set $wr = wr \circ first(w)$, $p = rest(p)$ and $w = rest(w)$.

— If $first(p) \in N$ then set $p = v \circ rest(p)$ such that $\langle first(p), u \rangle \in P$.

Based on the above remarks we write an "abstract" program (appendix B). We call this program abstract because it will contain operations, structures, and concepts from the underlying formal theory. For the purpose of the verification of this program these mathematical (abstract) objects are assumed to have their usual mathematical meaning.

In each refinement step certain of the mathematical objects will be replaced by a suitable implementation. A definition relating the concrete implementation to the implemented objects is added to the logical basis.

In this first program we assume the existence of a procedure *selprod* that selects a suitable production for a given nonterminal symbol. We omit the implementation of *selprod*; in the refined version of the program we will pass a "look ahead" parameter to *selprod*. Thus, an implementation of *selprod* for LL(1) grammars is then obvious.

Further, we assume a procedure *error* which is used to report syntax errors. Its specification requires that it must not terminate normally (exit *false*). Upper case letters are used to denote abstract objects while lower case letters describe objects in the programming language. All declarations are omitted.

For the parser the verifier generates 7 verification condition all of which can be proved by the simplifier in 10 cpu seconds. A typical example is:

$$(\text{P} \neq \text{NULL} \wedge$$
$$\text{ISDERIV}(\text{LIST}(\text{S}), \text{CONCAT}(\text{EMBED}(\text{WR}), \text{P})) \wedge$$
$$\text{W0} = \text{CONCAT}(\text{WR}, \text{W}) \wedge$$
$$\neg \text{IST}(\text{FIRST}(\text{P})) \wedge$$
$$\text{U\_0} = \text{SELPROD\_RHS}(\text{PROJN}(\text{FIRST}(\text{P})), \text{U}) \wedge$$
$$\text{ISPROD}(\text{PROJN}(\text{FIRST}(\text{P})), \text{U\_0})$$
$$\rightarrow$$
$$\quad \text{ISDERIV}(\text{LIST}(\text{S}), \text{CONCAT}(\text{EMBED}(\text{WR}), \text{CONCAT}(\text{U\_0}, \text{REST}(\text{P})))) \wedge$$
$$\quad \text{W0} = \text{CONCAT}(\text{WR}, \text{W}))$$

Here names containing the symbol "_" are new variables and function symbols introduced by VCgen.

Next we will refine the program. This means that we consider any of the abstract objects in our program and decide upon a concrete implementation. In practice we proceed in several steps; for space reasons we merely show one such step.

The sequence w is given by the input file ($infile$). Since we refer to the first element of this sequence very frequently we separate it from the file and store it in a variable l. Also we introduce a boolean flag, say e which is true if the input sequence is empty. Thus w is represented by a triple ($infile, l, e$). An abstraction function $seq1abs$ maps the implementation into abstract sequences. It is defined as

$$seq1abs(infile, l, e) = \text{if } e \text{ then } null \text{ else } concat(list(l), infile)$$

wr is an abstract entity only used in assertions and virtual code; no implementation is necessary.

p is used as a stack with the difference that we push whole sequences at a time. We represent p by an array together with an index pointing to the top element. The same representation is used for the intermediate variable u. We define

$$seq2abs(a, 0) = null$$
$$seq2abs(a, i + 1) = concat(seq2abs(a, i), list(a[i + 1])).$$

We introduce procedures *push, pop, top* etc. operating on p and u with the obvious meaning. Their implementation and proof are immediate and left to the reader.

Finally, the sets N, T, and $N \bigcup T$ have to be implemented. For simplicity we assumed that N and T are both represented as integers. Then union $N \bigcup T$ is implemented as a record type

record *kind* : (*terminal, nonterminal*); *value* : *integer* end

(the verifier does not allow variant records) with the abstraction function *ntabs*:

$$x.kind = terminal \quad iff \quad ist(ntabs(x))$$
$$x.kind = nonterminal \quad iff \quad isn(ntabs(x))$$
$$x.value = \text{if } ist(ntabs(x)) \text{ then } projt(ntabs(x)) \text{ else } projn(ntabs(x))$$

The refined program is shown in appendix C; appendix D contains the complete set of rules necessary to verify this program.

3. Plans for the future

The current staff of the program verification group is engaged in a variety of research projects aimed at the development of general programming tools integrating verification, compilation, debugging, and program maintenance (see section 3.3).

One recently completed project was the development of a compiler for ADA. Central goal of this project was to study compilation techniques for ADA tasking constructs. This compiler is to be used in the design and implementation of a verified operating system for a multiprocessor minicomputer system.

Also, research is going on in several more theoretic areas. One example is an attempt to describe concurrency by means of infinite operation sequences. Other areas include application of Scott/Strachey semantics in program verification (e.g. [36]) and new directions of theorem prover design.

In this section we will look at the research efforts directed towards improvement of the Stanford verifier in more detail.

3.1. Improvements of the current system

Like any program of significant size the verifier requires constant maintenance. Some of the known "bugs" are obvious coding errors that can be eliminated easily. Others, however, are design problems that require more basic research. One example is the treatment of arithmetic terms by the pattern matcher; a satisfactory solution requires the development of general techniques to deal with commutative and associative operators.

Due to the verifier's organization in parser, verification condition generator, and prover it adapts easily to new languages. We are planning to construct a verifier for ADA in the near future. The semantic concepts of ADA are very similar to those of Pascal. Some additional research is required to handle certain aspects of ADA for which no proof rules are known as yet. Some problem areas are Ada packages, exception handling [20], and multi-tasking.

Steve German will continue to work on runcheck. His main emphasis is on improvements of techniques to synthesize invariants as well as check for new runtime errors. Here Ada introduced a wealth of new errors that can be checked for.

Introduction of new users to verification methodology is still rather primitive. Class examples and experiments done by users on other net sites indicate that more documentation and a better user interface are called for. Development of a better user interface will be a main are of improvement. The problems here are not so much technical but rather human engineering problems. Here are two obvious examples.

The system has to provide more feedback for the user as to why a particular verification condition cannot be simplified to *true*. This situation can be due to an incomplete logical basis, errors in the program, or insufficient invariants.

The relation between a verification condition and the corresponding path of the program should be made more transparent to the user. Or better even, a failing proof should be related to a particular point in the program, the possible source of an error.

We mentioned earlier that verification should be integral part of program development. The current verifier supports this paradigm only to a limited extent. For example, it accepts "complete" Pascal programs. Instead we want the verifier to accept program fragments of the kind arising during top down program design.

To facilitate reasoning about complex data structures we are looking for high level assertion language concepts. Some examples in the right direction have been proposed by Reynolds in [37]. More research in this area is necessary, however. In particular reasoning about pointers is still very tedious and asks for more abstract concepts.

The current division of the verifier into verification condition generator and prover imposes a useful structure on the system and provides great flexibility for experiments with new languages as well as new provers. However, this structure of the verifier may not be the ideal one. It may be more appropriate to have a prover that reasons directly about programs rather than about verification conditions. In this case the relation of a failing proof to the offending part of the program will be much more obvious. Also, there may be significant computational advantages.

3.2. The next theorem prover

The two main areas of improvement of the simplifier are a better user control and extension to the assertion and rule languages.

The obvious way to implement user control is to add interactive features to the system. Interactive proof mode is important to debug proofs, i.e. to find out why a particular set of rules does not lead to a proof or why exactly a verification condition is not provable. However, interactive mode should be the exception rather than the rule; verifying large programs by stepping a prover through each verification condition individually is not feasible.

The alternative to interactive mode are heuristics. These are present in a crude form as rules. In a future prover the present rule language will be replaced by two languages, a purely logical language to specify lemmas and axioms, and a "hunch" language to specify heuristics. The new hunch language will be more powerfull than the present rule language; for example, it will allow to program proofs. A good example in this direction is the new LCF implementation at Edinburgh [9]. The interactive mode will be useful to find suitable heuristics for a problem domain.

Several extensions to the rule and assertion languages are desirable. One such extension that will be added to the next system is the introduction of types. Type checking in rules and assertions will detect many errors which are otherwise only found after tedious "debugging of proofs".

The next step after types is the introduction of theories in the sense of [3, 27]. Each theory may come equipped with special heuristics or decision procedures. However, further research has to provide more insight in the problem of combining and extending theories.

In some situations the absence of quantifiers from the assertion language causes inconveniences. Although quantifiers can systematically be avoided by introducing new predicate symbols and a suitable axiomatization, proceeding in this way may lead to clumsy and complicated formulation of concepts. However, here is a tradeoff between convenience and efficiency of the prover. Introducing unrestricted quantification will slow down proofs and may render the whole system useless.

3.3. New verification and program development tools

Following the idea that verification and program development are inseparable, tools for both activities should be integrated into one programming system, or programming environment.

Obvious components of such a system are

- a language oriented display editor (for example [42, 1]),
- an interpreter,
- symbolic debugging facilities,
- a general verifier,
- specialized verifiers such as runcheck, and
- a data base with canned program modules.

Clearly, this list is open-ended. But note, that most of the tools mentioned above are fairly well undestood; the problem seems to be to integrate them all into a coherent system. Initial plans are considered for such a system.

The above ideas can be carried a step further. Instead of taking a program fragment and refining it, it would be much easier for both the verifier and the programmer to explain refinement steps to an intelligent verification system. Such a system would change the program as well as check which parts of existing proofs are affected by the refinement and have to be redone. Some of the refinement steps may be suitable for abstraction and codification in the form of "canned" program transformations; however, it is likely that any set of predefined transformations will prove to be insufficient and that a language in which steps of program refinements and associated proofs can be described may eventually be more useful.

Program verification is related to program transformation and program synthesis techniques; it may be most useful when it becomes an integral part of such advanced programming tools.

Acknowledgements

I thank David Luckham for providing valuable information about the early days of the Stanford verifier. His careful reading has improved the initial draft of this paper. Also, I thank Annie Discepolo for her comments and suggestions.

Bibliography

An attempt was made to give a complete bibliography of papers pertaining to the Stanford Verifier; not all references are cited in the text.

[1] Alberga, C. N., et. al.: *A program development tool*, Research report RC 7859, IBM 1979.

[2] Allen J. R. : *Stanford Resolution Theorem Prover: A user manual*, Stanford Artificial Intelligence Lab. Operating Note, 1971..

[3] Burstall, R. M., Goguen, J. A.: *Putting theories together to make specifications*, Int. Joint Conf. on Artifical Intelligence, Boston 1977.

[4] Cartright, R., Oppen, D.: *The Logic of Aliasing*, STAN-CS-79-740.

[5] Deutsch, L. P.: *An interactive program verifier*, Report CSL-73-1, XEROX PARC, 1973.

[6] Floyd, R. W.: *Assigning Meanings to Programs*, Proceedings of Symp. in Applied Mathematics 19 (1967).

[7] German, S.M.: *Automating proofs of the absence of common runtime errors*, Proc. 5th. ACM Symp. on Principles of Programming Languages, Tucson, 1978, pp 105-118.

[8] German, S.M.: *An extended semantic definition of Pascal for proving the absence of common runtime errors*, STAN-CS-80-811.

[9] Gordon, M., Milner, R., Wadsworth, C.: *Edinburgh LCF*, Report CSR-11-77, University of Edinburgh.

[10] von Henke F. W., Luckham D. C.: *Automatic Program Verification III: A Methodology for Verifying Programs*, AIM-256, 1974.

[11] Hoare, C. A. R.: *An Axiomatic Basis of Computer Programming*, CACM 12, Oct, pp 576-580 (1969).

[12] Hoare, C. A. R., Wirth, N.: *An Axiomatic Definition of the Programming language Pascal*, Acta Informatica, 2 (1973), pp.335-355.

[13] Igarashi, S., London, R. L., Luckham, D. C.: *Automatic Program Verification 1: Logical Basis and Its Implementation*, Acta Informatica, Vol 4, pp 145-182 (1975).

[14] Jensen, K., Wirth, N.: *PASCAL, User Manual and Report*, Springer, New York, Heidelberg, Berlin, 1976.

[15] Karp, R. A.: *Proving Concurrent Programs Correct*, STAN-CS-79-783.

[16] King, J. C.: *A program verifier*, Ph. D. Thesis, CMU, 1969.

[17] Lamport, B.W., et. al.: *Report on the programming language Euclid*, Sigplan Notices, Vol. 12, No. 2, 1977.

[18] London, R. L.: *Correctness of two compilers for a LISP subset*, AIM - 151, Stanford University, 1971.

[19] London, R.L. et al: *Proof rules for the programming language Euclid*, Acta Informatica, Vol 10, No 1 (1978).

[20] Luckham, D. C., Polak, W.: *ADA Exceptions: Specification and Proof Techniques*, STAN–CS–80–789.

[21] Luckham, D. C., Suzuki, N.: *Automatic Program Verification IV: Proof of Termination Within a Weak Logic of Programs*, AIM-269, October 1975.

[22] Luckham, D. C., Suzuki, N.: *Automatic Program Verification V: Verification-Oriented Proof Rules for Arrays, Records and Pointers*, AIM-278, March 1976.

[23] Luckham, D. C., Suzuki, N.: *Verification of Array, Record, and Pointer Operations in Pascal*, ACM TOPLAS 1/2, 1979.

[24] McCarthy, J., Painter, J.: *Correctness of a Compiler for Arithmetic Expressions*, AIM-40, Stanford University 1966.

[25] Milner R.: *Implementation and applications of Scott's Logic for Computable Functions.*, in: Proceedings of the ACM Conference on Proving Assertions about Programs, Las Cruces, 1972.

[26] Milner, R.: *Logic for Computable Functions: Description of a Machine Implementation*, AIM-169, May 1972.

[27] Nakajima. R., Honda, M., Nakahara, H.: *Hierarchical program specification and verification - a many-sorted logical approach.*, Acta Informatica, Vol 14, Fasc. 2, 1980.

[28] Nelson, C. G., Oppen, D. C.: *Simplification by Cooperating Decision Procedures*, AIM-311, April 1978.

[29] Nelson, C. G., Oppen, D. C.: *Simplification by Cooperating Decision Procedures*, TOPLAS 2/1,1979.

[30] Nelson, C. G., Oppen, D. C.: *Fast decision procedures based on congruence closure*, JACM 27/2, 1980.

[31] Nelson, C. G., Oppen, D. C.: *Fast decision procedures based on UNION and FIND*, Proc 18th Annual Symp. on Foundations of Comp. Science, Providence, RI, 1977.

[32] Oppen, D. C.: *Complexity, convexity, and combinations of theories*, TCS 12/3, 1980.

[33] Oppen, D. C.: *Reasoning about recursively defined data structures*, JACM 27/2, 1980.

[34] Polak, W.: *An exercise in automatic program verification*, IEEE Transactions on Software Engineering, SE-5/5 (1979).

[35] Polak, W.: *Theory of compiler specification and verification*, STAN–CS–80–802.

[36] Polak, W.: *Program verification based on denotational semantics*, Proc. 8th. ACM Symp. on Principles of Programming languages, Williamsburg, 1981.

[37] Reynolds J.C.: *Reasoning about arrays*, Communications of the ACM 22.5, 1979, 290-299.

[38] Stanford Verification Group: *Stanford Pascal Verifier User Manual*, Stanford Verification Group Report No. 11, 1979.

[39] Suzuki, N.: *Automatic Program Verification II: verifying programs by algebraic and logical reduction*, STAN-CS-74-473.

[40] Suzuki, N.: *Verifying Programs by Algebraic and Logical Reduction*, Proceedings of Int'l Conf on Reliable Software, IEEE, pp 473-481 (1975).

[41] Suzuki, N.: *Automatic Verification of Programs with Complex Data Structures*, AIM-279, February 1976.

[42] Teitelbaum, R. T.: *The Cornell Program Synthesizer: A microcomputer Implementation of PL/CS*, Cornell TR 79-370, 1979.

Appendix A

The following is the transcript of a verifier session; input from the user is indicated by italics.

r verify

Hi Wolf, welcome to the Pascal Verifier.
Version June 11 1980
Type 'HELP;' for help

>*read tak.pas;*

Reading file: TAK.PAS[VER,WP]
SYNTAX SCAN COMPLETE.
PROGRAM PARSED.
CPU SECONDS:0.374

>*status;*
Verification Conditions:
MAIN 1 VCs
TAK 2 VCs
No rulefiles
No rules

>*printvc;*

Unsimplified Verification Condition: MAIN 1

TRUE

Unsimplified Verification Condition: TAK 1

$(\neg(X \le Y) \wedge$
$\ldots$

$$TAK(TAK(X-1,Y,Z),TAK(Y-1,Z,X),TAK(Z-1,X,Y))=X))$$

Unsimplified Verification Condition: TAK 2

$(X \le Y$

...

...

$\quad Y = X))$

$>simplify\ tak;$

Simplified Verification Condition: TAK 1

TRUE

Simplified Verification Condition: TAK 2

TRUE

Appendix B

The following is a first draft of the parser developed in secion 2.3.

```
procedure selprod(nterm : N; var rhs : SEQUENCE);
exit ISPROD(nterm, rhs);
external;

procedure error;
exit false;
external;

entry w = w0;
exit ISDERIV(LIST(S), EMBED(W0));

begin
  WR ← NULL;
  P ← LIST(S);
  invariant ISDERIV(LIST(S), CONCAT(EMBED(WR), P))
        ∧W0 = CONCAT(WR, W)
  while P ≠ NULL do
  begin
    if IST(FIRST(P)) then
    begin
      if W = NULL then error;
      if PROJT(FIRST(P)) = FIRST(W) then
      begin
        P ← REST(P);
        WR ← CONCAT(WR, LIST(FIRST(W)));
        W ← REST(W)
```

```
        end else error
    end else begin
      selprod(PROJN(FIRST(P)), u);
      P ← CONCAT(u, REST(P))
    end;
  end;
  if W ≠ NULL then error;
end.
```

Appendix C

Refinement of the program in appendix B leades to the following program.

```
type nttype = record kind : (terminal, nonterminal); value : integer end;
    SEQUENCE = (NULL); %virtual type %
    NT = (STARTSYMBOL); %virtual, we do not specify concrete
            representation of STARTSYMBOL %
    ntarray = array[1 : 500]of nttype;
    termfile = flle of integer;

var e : boolean;
    l, ut, pt : integer;
    t : nttype;
    uv, pv : ntarray;
    w0, infile : termfile;
    WR : SEQUENCE; %virtual variable %

%virtual procedure %
procedure WRITE(var f : SEQUENCE; x : integer);
initial f = f0;
exit f = CONCAT(f0, LIST(x));
external;

function eof(f : termfile) : boolean; exit true; external;

procedure read(var f : termfile; var e : integer);
initial f = f0;
exit f0 = CONCAT(LIST(e), f);
external;

procedure error; exit false; external;

procedure selprod(nterm : integer; var uv : ntarray; ut, lookahead : integer);
exit ut ≥ 0 ∧ ISPROD(nterm, SEQ2ABS(uv, ut));
external;

procedure push1(x : nt);
global(var pv, pt);
initial pv = pv0, pt = pt0;
```

```
exit SEQ2ABS(pv, pt) = CONCAT(LIST(x), SEQ2ABS(pv0, pt0));
external;


procedure push(uv : ntarray; ut : integer);
global(var pv, pt);
initial pv = pv0, pt = pt0;
entry ut ≥ 0;
exit SEQ2ABS(pv, pt) = CONCAT(SEQ2ABS(uv, ut), SEQ2ABS(pv0, pt0));
external;


function empty(pt : integer) : boolean;
global(pv);
exit empty = (SEQ2ABS(pv, pt) = NULL);
external;


procedure pop;
global(var pt; pv);
initial pt = pt0;
entry SEQ2ABS(pv, pt) ≠ NULL;
exit SEQ2ABS(pv, pt) = REST(SEQ2ABS(pv, pt0));
external;


function top(pv : ntarray; pt : integer) : nttype;
entry SEQ2ABS(pv, pt) ≠ NULL;
exit NTABS(top) = FIRST(SEQ2ABS(pv, pt));
external;

%main program %
entry w0 = infile ∧ ¬empty(infile);
exit ISDERIV(LIST(STARTSYMBOL), EMBED(W0));
begin
  WR ← NULL;
  pt ← 0;
  push1(STARTSYMBOL);
  read(infile, l);
  e ← false;
  invariant ISDERIV(LIST(STARTSYMBOL), CONCAT(EMBED(WR), SEQ2ABS(pv, pt))) ∧
      W0 = CONCAT(WR, SEQ1ABS(infile, l, e))
  while not EMPTY(pt) do
  begin
    t ← top(pv, pt);
    pop;
    if t.kind = terminal then
    begin
      if e then error;
      if t.value = l then
      begin
        WRITE(WR, l); %virtual call %
        if eof(infile) then e ← true else read(infile, l)
      end else error
```

```
    end else begin
      selprod(t.value, uv, ut, l);
      push(uv, ut)
    end;
  end;
  if not e then error;
end.
```

Appendix D

The following set of rules is required for the verification of the refine version of the parser.

rulefile(*sequences*)

constant *null*;
ass :   whenever $concat(u, concat(v, w))$ from *true* infer
           $concat(u, concat(v, w)) = concat(concat(u, v), w)$;
$first$:   whenever $first(x)$ from *true* infer $x = concat(list(first(x)), rest(x))$;
$rest$:   whenever $rest(x)$ from *true* infer $x = concat(list(first(x)), rest(x))$;

$emb1$:   replace $embed(null)$ by $null$;
$emb2$:   replace $embed(concat(x, y))$ by $concat(embed(x), embed(y))$;
$emb3$:   replace $embed(list(projt(x)))$ by $list(x)$;

$null1$:   replace $concat(null, x)$ by x;
$null2$:   replace $concat(x, null)$ by x;

rulefile(*grammar*)

ref :   infer $isderiv(x, x)$;
$trans$:   infer $isderiv(x, concat(u, concat(w, v)))$ from
           $isderiv(x, concat(u, concat(list(n), v))) \wedge isprod(projn(n), w)$;
$nterm$:   infer $isn(x)$ from $\neg ist(x)$;

rulefile(*refine*)

constant *null, terminal, nonterminal, value, kind*;
from *true* infer $terminal \neq nonterminal \wedge value \neq kind$;
from $x \neq terminal$ infer $x = nonterminal$;

$seq1$:   whenever $seqlabs(f, l, e)$
           from $e = true$
           infer $seqlabs(f, l, e) = null$;
$seq2$:   whenever $seqlabs(f, l, e)$
           from $e = false$
           infer $concat(list(l), f) = seqlabs(f, l, e)$;

$eo1$:   from $eof(x)$ infer $x = null$;

io2 :   replace *eof(x)* by *empty(x)*;

arr1 :   replace *seq2abs(a, 0)* by *null*;
arr2 :   replace *rest(seq2abs(a, t))* by *seq2abs(a, t − 1)*;
arr3 :   replace *first(seq2abs(a, t))* by *a[t]*;
arr4 :   replace *seq2abs(⟨a, [at + 1], x⟩, at + 1)* by
           concat(list(ntabs(x)), seq2abs(a, at));
arr5 :   replace *concat(list(ntabs(a[at + 1])), seq2abs(a, at))* by
           seq2abs(a, at + 1);

nt1 :   from *x.kind = terminal* infer *ist(ntabs(x))*;
nt2 :   from *x.kind = nonterminal* infer *isn(ntabs(x))*;
nt3 :   replace *x.value* where *ist(ntabs(x))* by *projt(ntabs(x))*;
nt4 :   replace *x.value* where *isn(ntabs(x))* by *projn(ntabs(x))*;

A SYSTEM FOR UNDERSTANDING CONTINUOUS GERMAN SPEECH

H.-W. Hein
Universität Erlangen-Nürnberg
Lehrstuhl für Informatik 5 - Mustererkennung
Martensstrasse 3, D-8520 Erlangen

Abstract

In 1979 we started the development of an experimental German speech understanding system [1,2]. It should be speaker independent and accept connected speech of good signal quality. All components and their underlying models should be independent of each other as far as possible. This will enable an easy exchange of components and various experiments in constructing different systems out of existing modules.

Understanding strategy will be tailored to parallel computing purposes. In the first project phase parallelism is simulated on software level, in a second phase the system will be implemented on a parallel computer.

1. Understanding system structure

1.1. The concept of understanding

The general concept of understanding, our system is based on, is shown in Fig.1. The incoming speech signal's data is stored in a central database. Three types of knowledge will be consulted to understand the utterance:

* method knowledge (algorithms which are not necessarily specific for the speech understanding task),

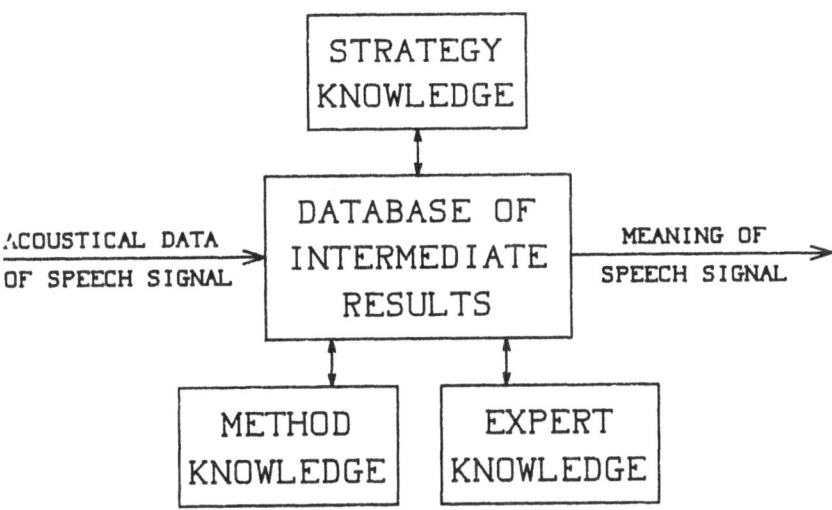

Fig. 1: The concept of understanding

* expert knowledge (linguistic and statistic information about the German language together with algorithms to handle it),
* strategy knowledge (analysis control, intermediate results estimating, and performance optimization concepts applied to the actual system configuration).

From the activities of the knowledge modules will accrue lots of intermediate and often contradictory results, all to be stored and administrated in the common database to be available in further analysis steps.

Analysis proceeds as long as the results about the meaning of the speech signal are vague. If one of the emerging alternatives in meaning becomes clearly estimated best, it finally is put out as "what was understood".

1.2. The speech understanding system

The structural principles of the speech understanding system are drawn from experiences with the HEARSAY-II system [3] and pay regard to both, the general understanding concept and parallel processing conditions. An example of a speech understanding system is shown in Fig.2. Knowledge is divided into several knowledge modules depending on linguistic categories.

Theoretically all these knowledge modules, each running on an own processor of a parallel computer, will have simultaneous access to the intermediate analysis results ("hypotheses") stored in a database.

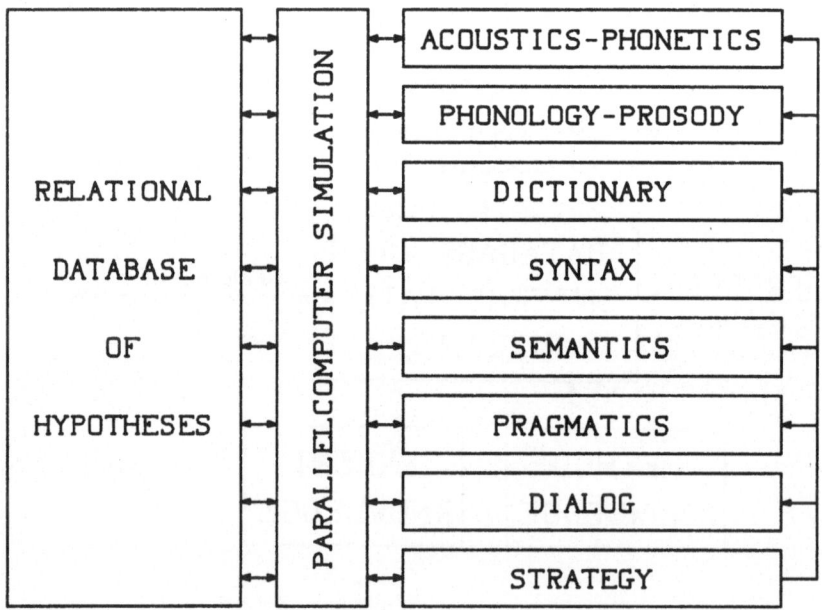

Fig. 2: The speech understanding system

Strategy knowledge remains an extra module. In connection with its analysis and optimization and control functions the strategy module is able to do some scheduling tasks by tuning behaviour parameters of other modules. The necessity for this becomes obvious considering a possibility of understanding system structures with more active modules than processors available.

The principles of our approach enable moreover the construction of understanding systems with multiple occurrence of e.g. very time consuming modules, working in parallel at different sectors of the database.

1.3. The database of hypotheses

To enable parallel access to the analysis information it contains, the database is modularized. This is done in a natural manner by comprising hypotheses of equal type to certain "abstraction levels". Main levels are those of phone hypotheses ("phone level"), word hypotheses ("word level"), sentence structure hypotheses ("syntax level"), and sentence meaning hypotheses ("semantic level").

Some more non-intuitive levels may be introduced depending on future experiences. The input signal data is thought of as the hypotheses at the lowest abstraction level.

Because most of the modules produce and require analysis results only at some of those abstraction levels, the number of database access conflicts will be fewer from the very start. Generally it may be appropriate, at the lower abstraction levels of the database of hypotheses, to modularize in addition into time sectors accessable by several occurrences of one module in parallel.

We are developing a relational database system which will enable easy construction of suitable modularized databases of hypotheses for any experimental need.

1.4. The knowledge modules

Each knowledge module can perform two tasks using its special knowledge or methods:

* create a hypothesis and
* estimate a hypothesis.

This is done by consideration of already existing hypotheses and their estimates. Knowledge modules are strictly independent of each other, because they communicate through hypotheses, which are uniformly structured. Modules thus may be developed independently by different human "module specialists" without knowing the whole system.

Moreover this concept easily enables running of analysis processes with humans acting through an online terminal as modules within an automatic understanding system. Experiences drawn out of such experiments may lead to the definition of new or alternative knowledge modules.

1.5. Parallel computing and the understanding strategy module

A basic principle of analysis is that it will be mainly, but not strictly bottom-up. That corresponds with the system's aim to understand a sentence, but not to recognize it by all means. The advantage of parallel computing would be better utilized, if hypotheses on higher abstraction levels can be made without waiting for a complete analysis of the underlying levels.

Naturally it is expected that during the course of analysis the lower level knowledge first is involved much more extensive than higher level knowledge, and later vice versa. But the earlier an examination feedback by higher knowledge occurs the smaller the quantity of superfluously analysed alternatives at lower levels will be held.

The understanding strategy mainly has to balance between two critical states of system performance:

* an excessive consideration of analysis alternatives at each level would require an unrealistic amount of processing time and memory space,
* an immoderate restriction in following alternative analysis paths increases the average error rate too much.

To solve this problem the strategy module (Fig.3) is provided with knowledge about

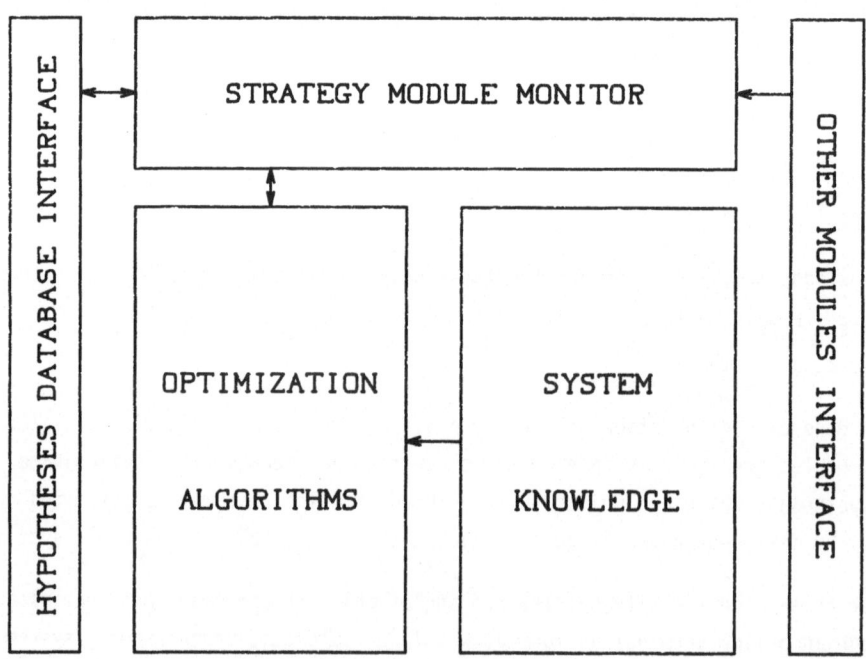

Fig. 3: The strategy module

all available software and hardware (or pseudo-hardware) modules:

* into what abstraction levels the database of hypotheses
  is modularized,
* what knowledge modules exist, what abstraction levels they access, and how
  (heuristic data) their time behaviour and analysis behaviour is,
* how much common memory is available, how many processors exist, and what
  maximum answer delay is tolerable.

The strategy module optimizes understanding processes by influencing them three-
fold:

* by changing the distribution of the entire processor time among
  the knowledge modules,
* by changing the distribution of a module's processor time share
  between creating new and estimating old hypotheses,
* by alteration of hypotheses estimates and by deletion of low
  estimated hypotheses.

Purposeful algorithms for the optimization task can be drawn from Operations
Research or Artificial Intelligence.

2. Usage of linguistic knowledge

2.1. The zero-dictionary

Zero-dictionary we name a collection of word-related linguistic data, currently under construction and thought to be expanded continuously. It is organized by means of
the relational database system and contains for each wordform entry its textual and
phonetical representation, further morphemic, syntactic and semantic categories.

The zero-dictionary is not used directly by knowledge modules during speech analysis.
When constructing a certain speech understanding system only that amount of linguistic
knowledge is extracted from the zero-dictionary as will be directed by the intended
experiment.

Extraction is done using a "preprocessor" for each concerned module. The preprocessor, besides, transforms the extracted linguistic knowledge to a data structure which
is well adapted to the respective module's algorithms.

2.2. The ATN-grammar

For the speech understanding system an augmented transition network (ATN) grammar
for the German language is developed [4]. The ATN concept is thought to be very useful
to model the syntax of a natural language.

As the zero-dictionary, the ATN-grammar will be fully or partially introduced to a speech understanding system with the help of a preprocessor. The internal data structure of the grammar knowledge is then subject to the parser, used in the syntax module.

2.3. The dictionary module

Fig.4 shows the organization of this module, which is prototypical of the other knowledge module's structure.

Active part of the dictionary module is a monitor, able to communicate through an interface with the database of hypotheses. The database interface already belongs to the database system, so it is standardized.

The monitor passes relevant hypotheses to the module's algorithmic part and relevant hypotheses of that part back to the database. What is assumed to be "relevant" at a certain time depends on several of the module's behaviour parameters. This "module strategy" data can be altered by the strategy knowledge module at any time of an analysis process. The strategy module interface is standardized, too.

Two types of knowledge are contained in the dictionary module. First a dictionary, extracted from the zero-dictionary and therefore subject to change. Further the module is provided with statistic data about relative grades of identity between those phones used for phonetic representation of words in the dictionary and those phones equivalently recognized from the acoustics-phonetics module.

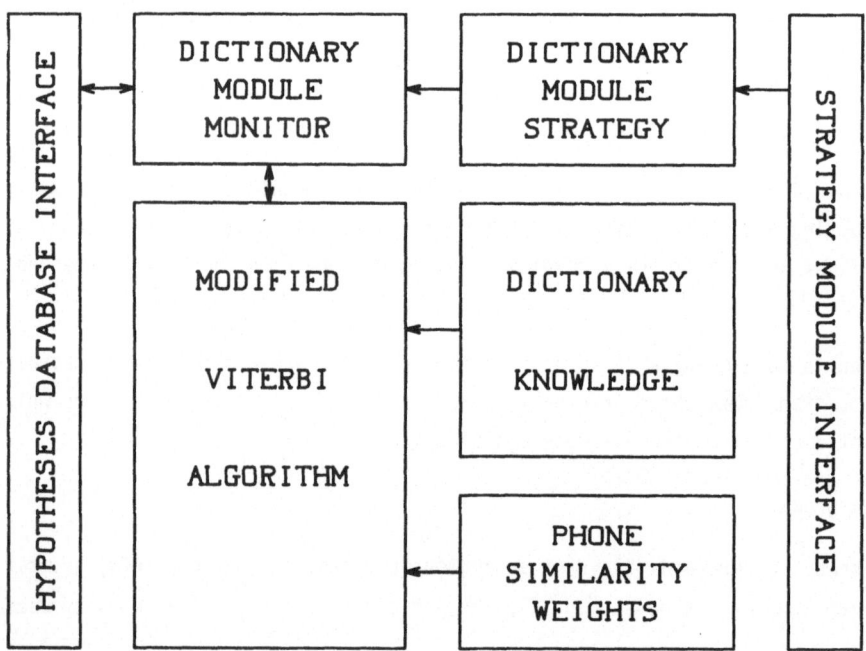

Fig. 4:   The dictionary module

The main part of the dictionary module is its modified Viterbi algorithm [5]. For two given strings of (phone) symbols it computes a measure of similarity.

The Viterbi algorithm essentially searches for the shortest sequence of elementary operations required to transform one of the strings into the other. Elementary operations are: delete a symbol, insert a symbol, and replace a symbol.

The strings may be of different length. The modified algorithm not only counts the needed operations but summarizes them weighted with the available phone similarity knowledge. Moreover it can be provided to consider knowledge about symbol context, e.g. occurrence frequency of phone pairs, triples etc.

The dictionary module uses the modified Viterbi algorithm for:

* estimating word hypotheses of other modules,
* optimizing estimates of word hypotheses by slight boarder corrections,
* finding the best fitting dictionary word for a given portion of the phone hypotheses level,
* finding the best fitting portion of the phone level for a given dictionary word.

2.4. The syntax module

One part of the syntax module is an "island-parser" which is adapted to the special situation found in speech understanding at the sentence structure level. The island-parser is able to work direction independent and to cope with recognition gaps at the word hypotheses level.

It is used to analyse for a given word sequence ("island") the possibility to be part of a correct sentence. During an understanding process it keeps the parsing information of the islands, to save computing expense when expanding an existing island with a new word hypothesis to the left or to the right ("island-extension"), or when joining two islands into one ("island-collision").

Another part of the syntax module is an appropriate preprocessed extract of the already mentioned German ATN-grammar.

3. Usage of task specific and of mandatory knowledge

3.1. The pragmatics module

Often ambiguities in the meaning of a sentence can be solved if the sentence context is known. Semantic variance of many key words then will be restricted. Conversely pragmatic knowledge can be useful to produce word and semantic hypotheses within an understanding process.

The first pragmatics module developed for the understanding system concerns the German Intercity-Train-System. It contains concepts about spatial and temporal laws of nature, geographic knowledge, timetables and fares.

From this module the input speech signals are expected to be retrieval demands about its knowledge.

3.2. The semantics module

Corresponding to the linguistic idea of semantics, this module should be provided with general concepts for meanings of words and sentences. Semantic knowledge can be used like pragmatic knowledge to reduce ambiguities during an analysis but also to verify sentence hypotheses if being significant at all.

3.3. The dialog module

One spoken sentence has to be seen practically always as being part of a dialog between man and machine. Knowledge of certain discourse patterns, introduced into the speech understanding system by adding a dialog module, therefore may be very helpful.

If the course of the actual dialog is available, the intention of the following sentence may be foreseeable up to a certain extent.

Further, sentences in spoken language often are fragmentary or refer to previous ones. To supplement incomplete sentences with those redundant parts, which had been dropped by a speaker, will be another task of the dialog module.

3.4. The phonology-prosody module

It is emphasized by linguists that utterances contain syntactic and semantic information coded prosodically [6]. Analysis of stress patterns, voice melody, speech acceleration and retardation, together with phonological knowledge of coarticulation effects may be important, when searching not only for word boundaries at phone level but also for syntactic and semantic key words at word level.

In contrary to automatic understanding of typed sentences in the field of Artificial Intelligence, where it plays an important role, morphemic analysis will be of less benefit in Speech Understanding. Boundaries between the morphemic items of words, even boundaries between words themselves are in most cases unrecognizable bottom-up, because not spoken and so far not contained in the acoustical data of an utterance. Moreover, word prefixes or word endings normally are weakly articulated respectively swallowed by an average speaker.

It follows that a phonology-prosody module should be introduced to a speech analysis process to compensate this general absence of morphemic precision in spoken language.

4. Understanding system performance

4.1. Parallelcomputer simulation

During the first phase of understanding system development, parallel computing is simulated. The principle parallelcomputer structure which is introduced in this phase, keeps the evolving modules from being interfered with special solutions for problems, evoked only by a certain parallel computer system.

The simulated computer model therefore is more abstract and consists of several independent processors, each possessing private memory. A common memory, which is divided into parallel accessible segments, can be used by all processors. If two or more processors try to access the same memory segment simultaneously, their demands are randomly sequenced. The number of processors, memory sizes and the common memory segmentation are adaptable to all experimental requirements. Parallel processing of a chosen pseudo-hardware configuration is realized with the SIMULA programming language coroutine concept [7].

4.2. The acoustics-phonetics module

Because it is independently realized using a computer with signal processing devices, the acoustics-phonetics module is simulated within the speech understanding system, too. The "acoustics-phonetics module" in this context simply contains the acoustic and phonetic data, offline produced by the system which is described in [8].

4.3. Hypotheses, estimates, and module interaction

The uniform data structure of the modules intermediate results, stored and administrated in the common database is the "hypothesis". It mainly consists of a statement about a portion of the speech signal and some estimates giving a possible rank for that statement. In addition, a hypothesis has some pointers to other hypotheses, being its logical or temporal predecessors, competitors, or successors.

Further a hypothesis belongs to a certain level of abstraction depending on the knowledge of the module it was created by. Naturally, this module will give the hypothesis a first estimate. Later on, as long as the hypothesis remains in the database, it can be estimated complementarily by other modules. All estimates become independent parts of the hypotheses and are matter of change at any time.

The hypotheses estimates coming from the strategy module, which has access to all abstraction levels, are calculated out of the other module's singular estimates. This is done with consideration of the trustworthiness of the involved modules, being part of the strategy knowledge.

A speech analysis starts with the acoustics-phonetics module writing a spoken sentence into the database, phone by phone. The strategy module simultaneously activates some other modules depending to its plans and knowledge. These modules then try, within the limits of their behaviour parameters initialized by the strategy module, to do something purposeful accessing the database. From time to time the strategy module inspects the database and changes hypotheses estimates, module behaviour and scheduling, if necessary. The analysis of an utterance stops, when a well enough estimated hypothesis at sentence meaning level is found, or when the appointed analysis time is exceeded. In the second case the longest partial interpretation will be result of the analysis.

5. Conclusion

A stepwise approach is necessary to develop for a certain speech understanding task a solution which complies with practical requirements, e.g. high reliability and realtime performance.

First the system's understanding rate has to be optimized through many simulation experiments, then it may be implemented on a parallel computer to speed up the analysis process. Further improvement in processing time will come from special hardware realizations of some algorithms (e.g. classifier, pattern-matcher, parser) which will be used frequently.

Acknowledgement

The author wishes to thank A. Brietzmann, A. Cieslik, G. Görz, Prof. G. Nees, Prof. H. Niemann, P. Regel, and all student contributors for their former and their further commitment to the Erlangen Speech Understanding Project.

References

[1] Niemann, H., Hein, H.-W.: A Program System of Parallel Processes for Understanding Continuous Speech. Computing, Suppl.3, 141-148 (1981)

[2] Hein, H.-W., Niemann, H.: Expert Knowledge for Automatic Understanding of Continuous Speech. Signal Processing: Theories and Applications (Kunt, M., de Coulon, F., eds.), 647-651. Amsterdam: North-Holland (1980)

[3] Lea, W. A. (ed.): Trends in Speech Recognition. Englewood Cliffs (N.J.): Prentice-Hall (1980)

[4] Brietzmann, A.: Eine ATN-Grammatik des Deutschen für die Automatische Sprachverarbeitung. Diplomarbeit, Lehrstuhl für Informatik 5 (Mustererkennung), Universtiät Erlangen (1980)

[5] Forney, G. D.: The Viterbi Algorithm. Proc. IEEE, Vol.61, No.3, 268-278 (1973)

[6] Artemov, V. A.: Intonation und Prosodie. Phonetica, Vol.35, 301-339 (1978)

[7] Dijkstra, E. W.: Co-operating Sequential Processes. Programming Languages (Genuys, F., ed.), 43-112. London: Academic Press (1968)

[8] Regel, P.: Automatische Extraktion phonetischer Symbole aus kontinuierlich gesprochener deutscher Sprache. DFG-Kolloquium "Digitale Sprachverarbeitung", 37-40. Göttingen (1980)

VERARBEITUNG VON EXTERNER UND INTERNER SITUATION IN ÜBERZEUGUNGSSYSTEMEN

Katharina Morik
Universität Hamburg, Germanisches Seminar

Some notions are introduced to describe requirements for modelling natural language as an action determining and determined by an external situation, referring an internal situation.

1. BEGRIFFSKLÄRUNG

Die im Titel genannten Begriffe bedürfen einer Erläuterung. Zunächst zur Eingrenzung der KI-Systeme, von denen hier die Rede sein soll. Aus der Linguistik kommend, interessieren mich KI-Systeme, die natürliche Sprache verarbeiten, insofern, als sie bei der Explizierung, Überprüfung und Entwicklung von Erklärungen sprachlichen Verhaltens helfen können. Wird Sprache als zielgerichtetes Handeln in Situationen aufgefaßt, so rückt Subjektivität in den Bereich linguistischen Interesses. Systeme, die Subjektivität in der Wissensbasis, in den Inferenzprozessen wenigstens zu einem Teil modellieren, sollen hier ÜBERZEUGUNGSSYSTEME (belief systems) heißen.

Nun zu den beiden anderen Begriffen im Titel, die an Fillmore[1] angelehnt sind:

Die EXTERNE KONTEXTUALISIERUNG bestimmt die Situation, in der der Text angemessen benutzt werden kann.

Die EXTERNE SITUATION ist also die Situation, in der der Text stattfindet (Kommunikationssituation).

Die INTERNE KONTEXTUALISIERUNG bestimmt die Situation, von der der Text handelt.

Die INTERNE SITUATION ist also die Situation, auf die der Text verweist.

Ein Beispiel zur Illustration:

Franz und Otto sitzen zusammen. Otto hustet. Franz sagt:

"Mein Onkel hatte wochen-, ach, monatelang so einen leichten Husten. Es wurde dann immer schlimmer. Schließlich hatte er starke Schmerzen und erst dann ist er endlich zum Arzt gegangen. Der sagte dann, daß er eine Lungenentzündung hätte, schlimme Sache. Also, ich an deiner Stelle würde gleich zum Arzt gehen."

Der Text realisiert die Handlung RATGEBEN und verweist dabei auf eine interne Situation, die darin besteht, daß Franz' Onkel Husten und schließlich Schmerzen hatte, weshalb er zum Arzt ging. Der Arztbesuch ist nun wiederum die externe Situation für die Handlung INFORMIEREN des Arztes.

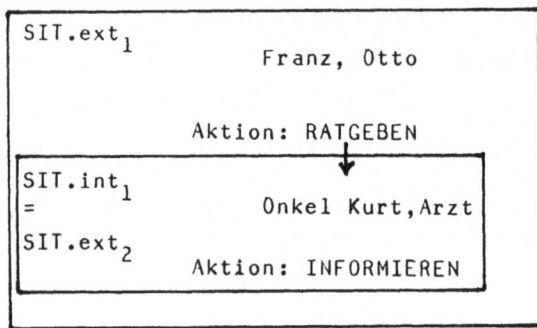

2. BESTANDSAUFNAHME

Die interne Kontextualisierung und die Repräsentation des zum Verstehen
der internen Situation notwendigen Weltwissens wurde in der KI im Bereich
des Geschichten-Verstehens bearbeitet. Die Subjektivität des Verstehens-
prozesses hat Carbonell [2] aufbauend auf Arbeiten von Abelson [3] modelliert. Ich werde auf sein System POLITICS als einem Beispiel subjektiver Verarbeitung der internen Situation später eingehen.
Die externe Kontextualisierung wurde bisher nicht explizit formalisiert.
Dennoch wird situationsinadäquate Rede wohl aus jedem natürlichsprachigen
Anwendungssystem ausgeschlossen. Dies geschieht aber durch den Systemrahmen, der für eine bestimmte Situation, in der zu einem bestimmten Thema
zu einem bestimmten Zweck Dialoge geführt werden, maßgeschneidert ist.
Die Bearbeiter konzipieren das System so, daß die Texte, die in der An-
wendungssituation adäquat sind, auch verstanden und nur solche erzeugt
werden können. Ähnlich gehen Systeme für aufgabenorientierte Dialoge vor.

Die externe Situation selbst wird bei Auskunftsystemen und Systemen auf-
gabenorientierter Dialoge zum Teil expliziert. Ein Handlungsplan, der entweder (Grosz [4]) parallel zum Dialog ausgeführt wird, oder für dessen
Ausführung Informationsfragen vom Benutzer gestellt werden (GUS [5])
stellt den Bezug für die Fragen und kooperativen Antworten dar.
Der Benutzer, als ein Akteur in der externen Situation, hat durch den
Systemrahmen vorgegebene Oberziele, die während des Dialoges spezifiziert
werden. Insofern ist ein, wenn auch eingeschränktes, Partnerbild immer-
hin gegeben. Und, indem der Benutzer und das System tatsächlich zu einem
bestimmten Zweck, sei es für die Reiseplanung oder den Zusammenbau einer
Pumpe, kommunizieren, stellen die produzierten Texte auch im eigentlichen
Sinne Texte dar: nämlich [6] Text-in-Funktion-in-Situation.
Das Sytem aber, der zweite Akteur in der externen Situation, pflegt so
kooperativ zu sein, daß es über keine eigenen Ziele verfügt, sondern für
den Benutzer plant. Damit erkennt es das sprachliche Verhalten des Benutzers als zielgerichtetes und berücksichtigt somit einen Teil dessen Subjektivität. Das System selbst beinhaltet aber keine Simulation zielge-

richteten sprachlichen Handelns.

Die erst kürzlich in HAM RPM implementierte Hotel-Szene [7] versucht, Sprecherstrategien zu modellieren. Das System spielt die Rolle des Hotel-Managers, der am Telefon Fragen über Hotelzimmer beantwortet. Da er das Ziel hat, seine Zimmer zu vermieten, richtet er seine Antworten nach dem, was er als Ziele des Kunden aus dessen Fragen entnimmt. Damit ist ein Schritt in Richtung subjektiver Verarbeitung der externen Situation getan. Bekannt ist auch das Beispiel PARRY [8] , das in diesem Zusammenhang genannt werden sollte.

Mit dieser kurzen Bestandsaufnahme sollte gezeigt werden:
daß es sowohl bei der Verarbeitung der internen, wie auch bei der der externen Situation Modellierungen subjektiver, zielbezogener Prozesse gibt - oder Ansätze dazu;
daß aber bei der Verarbeitung der internen Situation die externe sozusagen aus dem Systemrahmen herausgeschoben wird, während bei der Verarbeitung der externen Situation keine interne vorkommt.

Es scheint aber plausibel zu sein, daß die Verfahren subjektiver, zielgesteuerter Verarbeitung der externen und der internen Situation nicht grundverschieden sind. Außerdem ist es der Normalfall sprachlicher Handlungen, daß sie
- zur Voraussetzung eine externe Situaion haben,
- die sie gleichzeitig (mit-)konstituieren und
- verändern,
- während sie auf eine (mehrere) interne Situation verweisen.
Die Frage nach der Beschaffenheit eines Rahmens, in dem externe und interne Situation verarbeitet werden können, scheint mir daher berechtigt. Gelingt es, ihn zu finden, so bestünde die Möglichkeit:
- Zusammenhänge zwischen beiden Prozessen zu explorieren,
- den kommunikativen Aspekt auch bei interner Kontextualisierung zu berücksichtigen,
- eingeschachtelte Situationen adäquat zu behandeln ((in-)direkte Rede).
Es geht mir hier nicht um die Vorstellung eines implementierten Systems, sondern zunächst einmal darum, Vorbedingungen für die Integration subjektiver Prozesse, die auf die interne und solcher,die auf die externe Situation bezogen sind, abzuklären.

3.POLITICS

Mehrere Voraussetzungen, die für die Modellierung der beiden Prozesse erfüllt sein müssen, hat m.E. Carbonell [2] bereitgestellt. Deshalb gehe ich auf sein System POLITICS hier kurz ein.
Er modelliert subjektives Verstehen von Ereignissen aus dem Themenbereich

der US-Außenpolitik.

Das Überzeugungssystem besteht in seinem wesentlichsten Teil aus Zielbäumen, die eine Sichtweise der US-Außenpolitik beschreiben sollen, und zwar 30 Zielbäume der USA, 15 der UdSSR und 10 anderer Länder, sowie aus Strategien und Plänen. Carbonell implementierte zwei strukturgleiche Versionen: ein liberales und ein konservatives Überzeugungssystem.

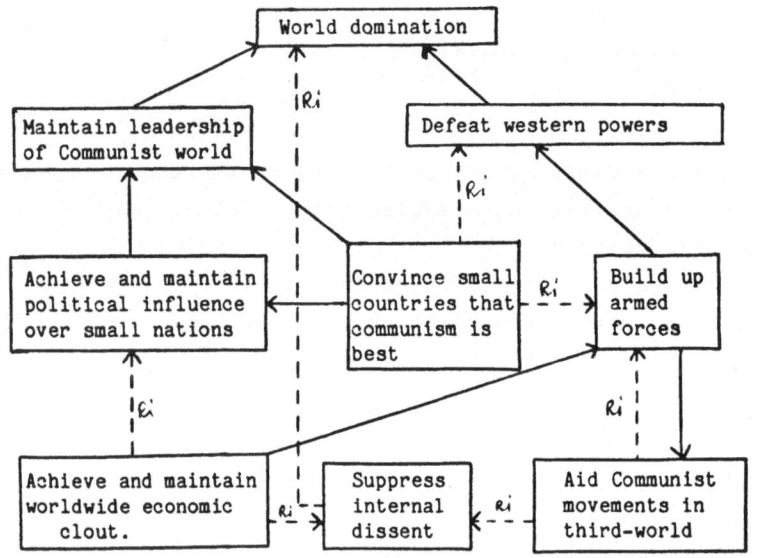

sowjetischer Zielbaum in US-konservativer Ideologie

Ein Zielbaum hat zwei verschiedene Kantenarten zwischen Zielen: relative Wichtigkeit (RI) und Unterziel.

Strategien werden als Meta-Pläne zur Angabe eines prinzipiellen Lösungsverfahrens eines Ziel- oder Plankonfliktes angegeben. Dem liegt eine Klassifikation der Konflikte zugrunde.

Das System analysiert einen Text über ein außenpolitisches Ereignis in Richtung eines bekannten Zieles. Handlungen werden als direkte oder strategische Durchsetzung von Zielen aufgefaßt. Das Ergebnis des subjektiven Verstehens ist die Zuschreibung von Zielen zu Akteuren - damit eine Begründung des geschilderten Verhaltens - und ein Plan, was die USA als nächstes tun sollten - damit eine Erwartungshaltung.

Die Ziele steuern den Inferenzprozeß insofern, als nur das betrachtet wird, was ein Ziel oder einen Plan konservativer bzw. liberaler Außenpolitik berührt.

Carbonell gibt ferner eine Beschreibungsmöglichkeit für Persönlichkeitsmerkmale an: Abweichungen von einem Normzielbaum für persönliche Ziele, den er für Nordamerikaner aufstellt, charakterisieren ebenso die Persön-

lichkeit, wie Vorlieben oder Abneigungen für/gegen bestimmte Strategien.
In den modellierten Fällen liberaler und konservativer Überzeugungen
findet eine direkte Identifizierung mit den USA statt. Deshalb ist der
von Carbonell angegebene IDENTIFIZIERUNGSALGORITHMUS trivialerweise
schnell am Ziel. Dieser Algorithmus ist aber als Ansatz zur Verbindung
der internen Situation mit den Zielen des Hörers notwendig und wichtig.

Die interne Kontextualisierung geschieht in POLITICS einmal über den
Systemrahmen (Thema: US-Außenpolitik), zum anderen über Scripts. Einen
Zusammenhang zwischen Überzeugungen und Zielen zu einem Thema und den
persönlichen Zielen (Konsistenzforderungen?) stellt Carbonell nicht dar.

Carbonell hat einige Prozesse und Informationen formalisiert, die für die
subjektive Verarbeitung von internen Situationen aus einem Themenbereich
nötig sind.

4. ERFORDERNISSE UND MÖGLICHKEITEN

Sollen nun zielgerichtete Prozesse für die Verarbeitung externer und interner Situation genutzt werden, so muß das Modell erweitert werden.
Auf der folgenden Seite ist skizziert, welche Prozesse und Wissensbasen
vorhanden sein müssen.
Zunächst genügt es nicht, nur einen Themenbereich anzunehmen, da exter-
ne und interne Situation meistens nicht aus dem selben Thema stammen.
Ein Thema enthält mehrere Situationen. Situationen, die bereits einmal
instantiiert wurden, werden in dieser spezifizierten Form zu Episoden.
Stereotype Situationen können als Scripts [9] dargestellt werden, auch
sie können, spezifiziert, im EPISODENGEDÄCHTNIS abgelegt werden.
Nichtstereotype Situationen werden durch
- Partnerbilder, die, um Bewertungen formalisieren zu können, je einen
  Zielbaum enthalten,
- einen Zielbaum des Simulates selbst,
- eine Repräsentation der Handlungen und
- eine Szenen-Repräsentation   beschrieben.

Einzelne Handlungen werden durch Akteure, Aktion, Voraussetzungen, be-
absichtigte Ergebnisse und Seiteneffekte repräsentiert.
Parallel oder als Teil von nichtsprachlichen Handlungen oder als einzige
Handlung müssen nun auch Sprechhandlungen dargestellt werden. Wir können uns die Einträge in das Handlungsschema bei Sprechakten etwa so den-
ken:
AKTEURE sind der Sprecher, der oder die Hörer und der Kreis von Menschen,
für den die Äußerungen im Weiteren bestimmt sind.
AKTION ist der Name eines Sprechaktes. Dabei kann auf andere Sprechakte
verwiesen werden oder ein (mehrere) neues Ziel für die Planung kreiert

PERSON/GRUPPE A:

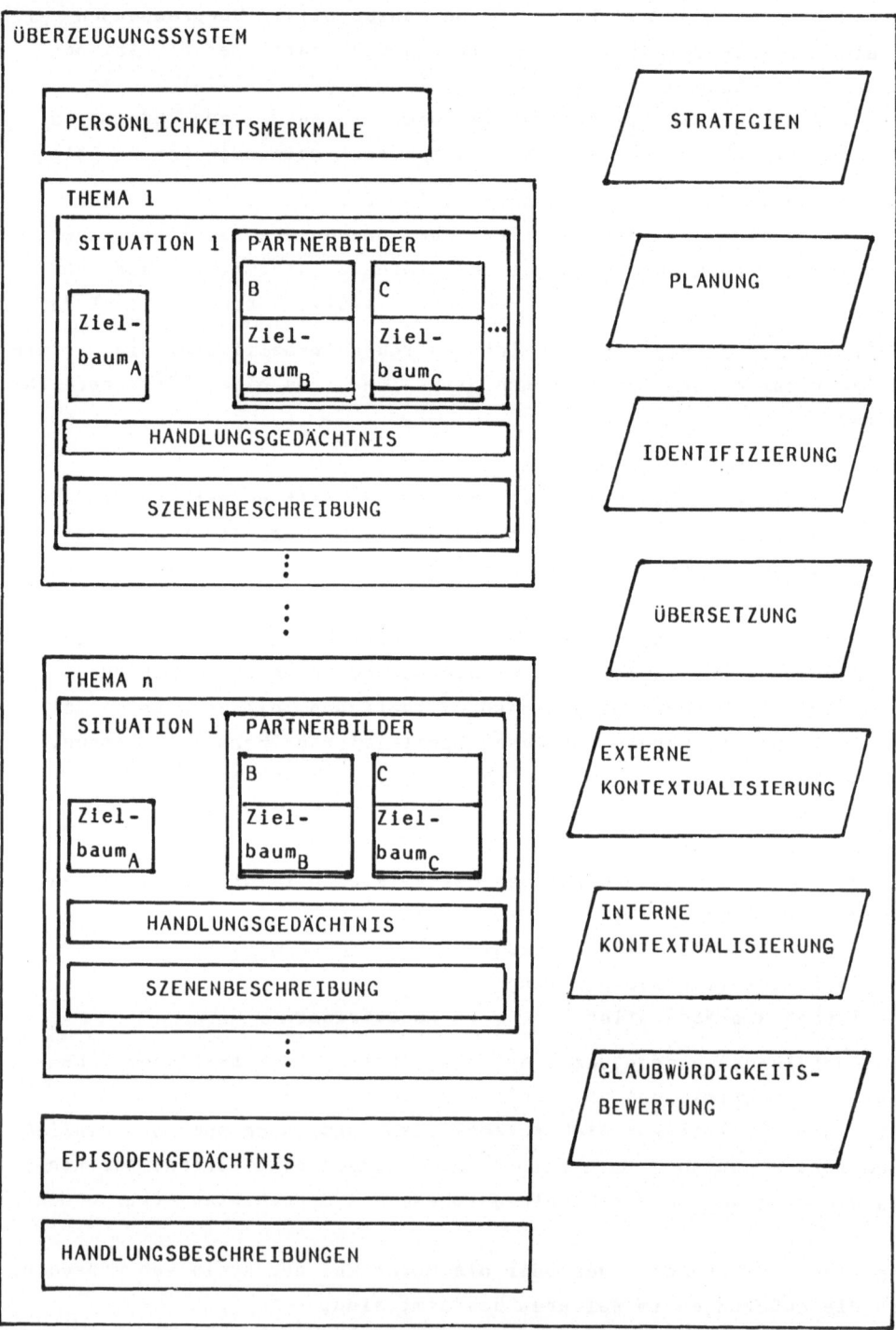

generelles Überzeugungssystem

werden.

VORAUSSETZUNGEN lassen sich durch die Sprechaktbedingungen, die frei-
lich einer genaueren Kategorisierung unterworfen werden müßten, angeben.
Das INTENDIERTE ERGEBNIS ist im Wesentlichen der perlokutive Akt.

Auf dieser handlungsbezogenen Abstraktionsstufe können Sprechhandlungen
in die Planung mit einbezogen werden.

Beispiel:

AKTEURE   A an B

AKTION   RATGEBEN $*H_B$

               $Ziel_{neu\ 1_A}$: B glaubt, daß $\neg H_B$ wichtigeres $Ziel_B$ bedroht

und/oder $Ziel_{neu\ 2_A}$: B glaubt, daß H_B wichtigeres $Ziel_B$ fördert

und/oder AKTEURE   A an B

           AKTION   INFORMIEREN $\mathcal{E}H_A$

VORAUSSETZUNGEN

1. Kommunikationskanal (A,B)

2. Gleichsprachig (A,B)

3. A glaubt, H_B ist besser als H_B

4. A glaubt, B tut nicht H ohne $RATGEBEN_A$

5. Gleichberechtigt (A,B)

BEABSICHTIGTES ERGEBNIS

B glaubt, daß H_B besser ist, als $\neg H_B$

($*$, $\mathcal{E}$ geben Modalität an; H_X ist eine Handlung, die von X ausgeführt wird)

Die IDENTIFIZIERUNGSREGELN, die Carbonell angegeben hat, erhöhen das In-
teresse, wenn der Hörer eine Übereinstimmung seiner Ziele mit denen eines Akteurs in der Geschichte feststellen kann, wenn die Ziele eines
Akteurs der internen Situation mit den eigenen in Konflikt stehen, oder
wenn Ziele eines Menschen, mit dem sich der Hörer identifiziert, von
Handlungen in der internen Situation berührt werden. Verallgemeinern wir
dieses Konzept, so können wir Regeln formulieren, deren Bedingungsteil
- Zielübereinstimmung,
- Zielkonflikt   oder
- Konflikt bzw. Übereinstimmung der Konsequenzen (Ergebnisse und Seiteneffekte) mit Zielen oder Plänen des Hörers beschreibt,
und deren Aktionsteil genauere Angaben als nur die Steigerung des Interesses enthält.

Beispiel: Wenn $Z_{i_J} = Z_{j_U}$ und $P_{i_J}(Z_{i_J})$ und $Konsequenz_{i_J}$,

            dann überprüfe $Konsequenz_{i_U}$ für $Ziele_U$ und $Pläne_U$

(U,J: Akteure; $P_{i_J}(Z_{i_J})$: $Plan_i$ von J für J's $Ziel_i$)

Nun sollen Identifizierungsregeln auch "umgekehrt" verwendet werden
können, so daß, wenn jemand das Ziel hat, U möge Konsequenz$_i$ für
sich überprüfen, er den Bedingungsteil wahr macht oder über ^{U}eine Episode, die den Bedingungsteil beschreibt, informiert.
Tatsächlich kann mit diesem Mittel modelliert werden, wie Franz im oben
angeführten Beispiel dazu kam, die Geschichte seines Onkels zu erzählen.
Das im Handlungsmuster RATGEBEN kreierte Ziel für Franz: 'Otto glaubt,
daß nicht zum Arzt zu gehen,wichtigeres Ziel von Otto bedroht' kann
dadurch erreicht werden, daß Otto überprüft, ob die Konsequenz des un-
terlassenen Arztbesuches auch Ottos Ziel(e) betreffen würde. Franz nimmt
aufgrund seiner Partnerbilder von Otto und von Kurt dies an. Anzumerken
ist hier die Schwierigkeit, Unterlassungen und ihre Konsequenzen zu modellieren, was gerade bei P-goals [9] wesentlich ist.

Die ÜBERSETZUNGSKOMPONENTE muß u.a. eine Verbindung zwischen der Sprech-
aktebene und realen Äußerungen herstellen. Zu dieser viel diskutierten
Verbindung sind aus der KI von Cohen und Perrault [10] und Allen [11]
Lösungsvorschläge gekommen. Ihr Verfahren beruht sehr stark darauf, daß
der Hörer Ziele und Pläne des Sprechers leicht erschließen kann, so daß
dann mit Hilfe der angenommenen Hindernisse im Plan des Hörers die Äußerung als Sprechakt erkannt werden kann.
Das von linguistischer Seite vorgeschlagene Verfahren der Konversations-
postulate [12] will C.Sidner versuchen, für ihr Projekt bei BBN zu nutzen. Es liegt aber noch kein Bericht vor. Ferner sei auf B.Bruce hingewiesen [13] .
Bei der Textgenerierung wirken Regeln der EXTERNEN KONTEXTUALISIERUNG
stark ein, die Informationen aus der externen Situation benutzen (z.B.
um zu entscheiden, wie Onkel Kurt referenziert wird, wieviel über das
Script ARZTBESUCH als bekannt vorausgesetzt werden kann etc.)

Die INTERNE KONTEXTUALISIERUNG markiert je eine Situation als aktuelle
interne und als externe Situation. Daß für ein künstliches System die
externe Situation markiert werden muß, liegt darin begründet, daß es sie
nicht (wie der natürliche Sprecher/Hörer) unmittelbar wahrnehmen kann.
Bisher wurde die interne Situation entweder über Schlüsselwörter/-muster
(SAM) [14] aufgefunden oder mit Hilfe von Plänen neu konstruiert (PAM)
[15] . Experimente, wieweit die Markierung der internen von der der externen Situation abhängen kann (damit das Erzählen einer Episode einen
Ratschlag darstellen kann, muß es sich um die und die interne Situation
handeln) oder umgekehrt (nach dem zu urteilen, was er ihr sagt, scheint
es sich um die externe Situation 'Romance' zu handeln), liegen, soweit
ich weiß, noch nicht vor.
Die als aktuell markierten Situationen können verändert (spezifiziert)

werden. Da hier nur an eine natürlichsprachige Ein-/Ausgabe gedacht ist,
können Situationsveränderungen nur mitgeteilt oder durch Texte ausgeführt
werden. Episoden können also nur dann "erlebt" werden, wenn sie ausschließlich sprachliche Handlungen beinhalten. Andere Episoden können
nur dem Episodengedächtnis zugeführt werden, wenn sie als glaubwürdig
bewertet werden. Die Bewertung nach GLAUBWÜRDIGKEIT [3] ist dabei in
hohem Maße abhängig von den eigenen Zielen und den angenommenen der
anderen Akteure in externer und interner Situation.

Ich hoffe, schon die Auflistung der Wissensbasen und Prozesse, die für
die Modellierung interner und externer Situationen und ihrer Rolle bei
der Sprachverarbeitung benötigt werden, macht die Komplexität deutlich,
die in natürlichsprachiger Kommunikation begründet ist.
Um den als Beispiel angeführten Text von Franz an Otto als Ratschlag zu
verstehen oder zu erzeugen, ist ein zur Zeit noch unrealistisch hoher
Aufwand erforderlich. Dabei handelt es sich um einen gewöhnlichen Text,
wie er in alltäglicher Sprachverwendung ständig vorkommt.
Die Skizze eines generellen Überzeugungssystems zeigt also einerseits,
was noch nicht erarbeitet wurde und deckt den Anteil der impliziten
Berücksichtigung der externen Situation am Gelingen einer guten System-
Performanz auf (Anwendungssysteme, aufgabenorientierte Dialoge).

Andererseits ermöglicht sie, vorhandene Ansätze in einen Zusammenhang
zu stellen und zu vergleichen. Es läßt sich zeigen, wie in der Bestandsaufnahme angedeutet, daß Teilkomponenten bereits realisiert sind, und
plausibel machen, daß einige Verfahren für die Verarbeitung beider Situationen verwendet werden können.

LITERATURHINWEISE

[1] FILLMORE,C. "PRAGMATICS AND THE DESCRIPTION OF DISCOURSE"
in: Schmidt,S.J.(ed) "Pragmatik II" S.83 München 1975

[2] CARBONELL,J.G. "SUBJECTIVE UNDERSTANDING: COMPUTER MODELS OF BELIEF
SYSTEMS" Yale University 1979

[3] ABELSON,R.P. "COMPUTER SIMULATION OF 'HOT' COGNITION"
in: Tomkins,S.(ed) "Computer Simulation of Personality" 1963 S.277

ABELSON,R.P. "THE STRUCTURE OF BELIEF SYSTEMS"
in: Schank,R.C./Colby,K.M. "Computer Models of Thought and Language"
1973 S.287

[4] GROSZ,B. "FOCUSING AND DESCRIPTION IN NATURAL LANGUAGE DIALOGUES"
Stanford 1979

[5] BOBROW,B./KAPLAN,R.M./KAY,M./NORMAN,D.A./THOMPSON,H./WINOGRAD,T.
"GUS. A FRAME-DRIVEN DIALOG SYSTEM"
in: AI VIII S.155 1977

[6] SCHMIDT,S.J. "TEXTTHEORIE"
München 1973

[7] JAMESON,A. "THE NATURAL LANGUAGE SYSTEM HAM RPM AS A HOTEL MANAGER: SOME REPRESENTATIONAL PREREQUISITES" Hamburg 1980

[8] COLBY,K.M. " ARTIFICIAL PARANOIA: A COMPUTER SIMULATION OF PARANOID PROCESSES" 1975

[9] SCHANK.R.C./ABELSON.R.P. "SCRIPTS.PLANS.GOALS AND UNDERSTANDING" Hillsdale 1977

[10] COHEN.P.R./PERRAULT.C.R. "ELEMENTS OF A PLAN-BASED THEORY OF SPEECH ACTS" Toronto 1979

[11] ALLEN.J.F."A PLAN-BASED APPROACH TO SPEECH ACT RECOGNITION" Toronto 1979

[12] GRICE.P."LOGIC AND CONVERSATION"
in: Cole,P./Morgan,J.L.(eds) "Syntax and Semantics III"   S.41
N.Y.,S.Francisco,London 1975

GORDON.D./LAKOFF.G."CONVERSATIONAL POSTULATES"
Papers from the 7th Regional Meeting, Chicago Linguistic Society
1971   S. 63

[13] BRUCE.B."BELIEF SYSTEMS AND LANGUAGE UNDERSTANDING" BBN 1975

[14] CULLINGFORD.R.E."SCRIPT APPLICATION: COMPUTER UNDERSTANDING OF NEWS-PAPER STORIES" Yale University 1978

[15] WILENSKY.R."UNDERSTANDING GOAL-BASED STORIES" Yale University 1978

STRUCTURES FOR KNOWLEDGE-BASED CHESS PROGRAMS

K.v.Luck , B.Owsnicki

Univ. Hamburg , Institut für Informatik

This paper describes some ideas for structuring chess knowledge about the strategic middle-game. These structures may serve as basic ideas for the design of a knowledge-based chess program.

1. INTRODUCTION

At least since 1973/74, when H.Berliner published his articles, it became apparent to almost every chess programmer that conventional Shannon-type chess programs suffer from structural shortcomings. Research on removal or reduction of these weaknesses proceeds into three general directions.

First, special hardware and skillful techniques taken from the field of software engineering are used to press back the effects of insufficient structures.

Further on, chess programmers try to insert knowledge about the problem of chess into tree search and evaluation procedures by quantifying certain properties of the position.

The third possibility is to base a chessplaying system upon knowledge, which has been collected during centuries in the field of chess. This is the possibility which we are following, too.

This approach enables us to develop a structure for chess knowledge with regard to the contents and not under technical demands. Especially, this knowledge can be made explicit.

We, personally, don't know any approach in this direction, which can claim to have seized the knowledge as a whole or even to have worked up with it structurally. So we, too, have worked only on a part of this area, namely strategic middle-game. We will come back to what we mean by this expression later.

First of all, we would like to state two pretensions which we are not going to follow. We don't believe, that a system based upon our approach will play better or even more flawless than today's strong conventional programs. We only want it to have different flaws.

Further on, we are not convinced, that the structures we are going to present in this paper have any equivalence with structures that allow human cognitive performance in chess. What we tried to do is to merely make knowledge useful, knowledge that deals with the problem and with problem solving procedures and has been made explicit by competent chess players.

2. THE STRUCTURE OF THE PROBLEM AND THE APPROACH

Besides the fascination of chess as a hobby or as a profession, for us it has an additional bearing. Chess can serve as an example for a non-trivial problem, whose complexity doesn't result from the representation of states and the handling of state transformations in this domain, but from the large number of states and paths to a desired state as well as from a non-cooperative environment. Among others, the fact, that the actors in this domain are not provided with the possibility to agree on 'peaceful co-existence', is a part of this non-cooperative environment.

As indicated above, there exists a store of knowledge, collected during the last centuries and partially documented, which enables a person to develop useful solutions for the problems of this domain in a finite amount of time.

Attempting to utilise this knowledge we have to reduce the complexity mentioned above. Therefore we have tried to develop formal structures, which enable us to perform a classification of board situations. The main property of a class is the existence of knowledge about adequate general proceeding. From now on, we will refer to this kind of proceeding as a *theme*.

Every theme requires additional knowledge about the development of a concrete way of proceeding in a concrete situation of the class associated with the theme. We will refer to this concrete proceeding as *strategy*. Finally, this strategy has to be subject to a limited analysis of its feasibility.

The development of strategy, in our case, is nothing else than the application of existing knowledge. Thus, a system based upon our approach will be helpless if put into a situation which is unknown to it, that is a situation belonging to no class at all.

We do not deal with the problem of 'learning', which in our case means the ability to introduce new classes of situations and to develop associated themes including their concretising procedures.

As a main topic of our approach, we don't try to determine situation-dependent strategic goals, for which a proceeding has to be developed to reach this goal. We only attach to every theme a value (measured in 'pawn units') corresponding to the expectation of a positional and/or material advantage resulting from the succesful execution of the strategy.

So-called *final situation classes* are associated with every theme, because there has to be a possibility to declare a strategy as being successful even without complete execution.

Several classes of situations and the associated themes have been developed, among others, by H.Kmoch in a work known as standard chess literature.

Our hope that this kind of chess knowledge can be used for problem
solving has been supported by the research done by DeGroot, Chase, Simon
and others.

3. STRUCTURING CHESS KNOWLEDGE
3.1 CLASSIFICATION

Our approach uses a two-level classification of chess positions. The
first (obligatory) step is to remove all the pieces from the board exept
pawns of either color. This step is called *reduction* of the actual position and is performed in order to enable an analysis of the bare 'pawn
skeleton' or pawn structure. The *installation* of a definite theme depends
in the first place on certain parts of an actual pawn structure, which
therefore has to be represented and recognised.

The representation of pawn structures is based on research done by
S.T.Tan, who uses *pawn relations* and *pawn-relations graphs* to build up a
system for pawn endgames. Tan himself refers to Kmoch, who defined certain relations between two pawns and by using these relations developed
a very useful system for the description of pawn structures. So, for example, he defined the relation between two pawns of opposite color, which
stand 'face to face' unable to move one step foreward (white pawn on d4,
black pawn on d5), as a 'ram', the relation between two pawns, who could
capture each other in the next move as a 'lever', and so on.

Tan uses 11 relations, as shown in Tab.1, which give an almost complete
description of the actual pawn-structure on the board.

	name	graphical notation	code
hostile relations:	counterpawn	< - >	1
	ram	< + >	2
	sentry	< .. >	3
	lever	< . + . >	4
friendly relations:	duo	=	5
	twin	= ×	6 (inverse: 7)
	potential protector	= >	8 (inverse: 9)
	protector	= / = >	10 (inverse: 11)

Tab.1

Pawn relations for a complete position may be represented as a collection of single relations of the form '(pawn x,pawn y)∈ rell' or as a colored, directed graph, the pawn-relations graph or PR-graph, as in Fig.1.

Pawn relations can be derived easiliy from the actual position using a
rather simple procedure, which is the only component of the whole system
that has been implemented.

Normally, the installation of a theme does not depend on the actual
pawn structure as a whole, but on certain parts or even on a single pawn,
like the isolated queen pawn (IQP). So, for example, let's have a look
at Pos.1, which represents a well-known pawn structure (well-known to
chess players, that is!).

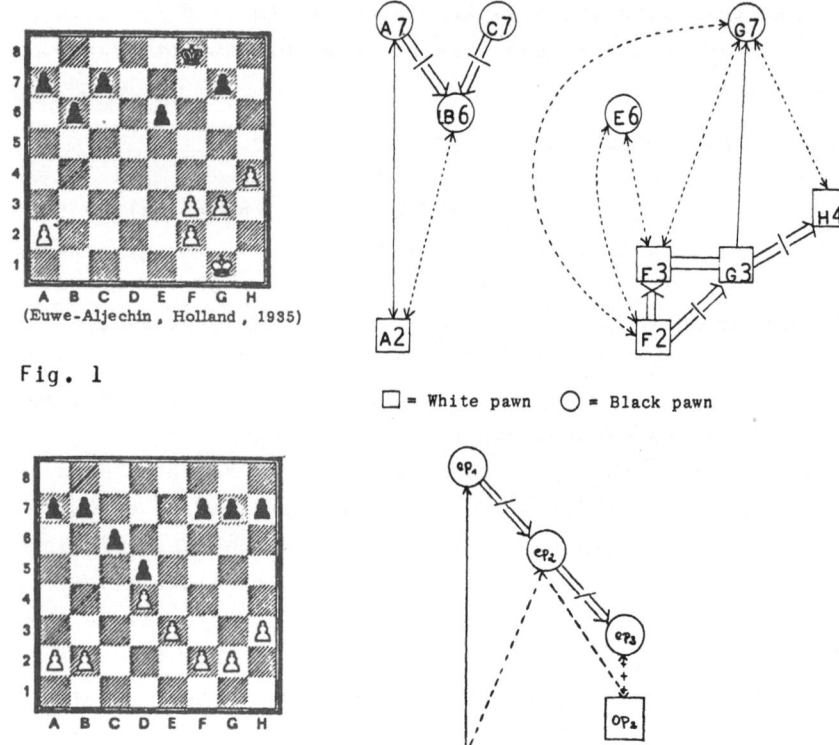

(Euwe-Aljechin, Holland, 1935)

Fig. 1

□ = White pawn   ○ = Black pawn

Pos. 1

Fig. 2

This structure normally arises out of the Queen's Gambit and, from white's side, may lead into a theme called minority attack, because two white queen-side pawns will attack three black pawns. That means that it will be sufficient to consider only the queen-side pawn structure (a,b, c,d-files) to enable the installation of the minority attack. Fig.2 shows the pawn relations for the queen-side pawn structure, which serves as a *cliché* that can be matched with an actual position and, if recognised, can suggest the installation of the theme 'minority attack'.

Unfortunately, there is a great variety of themes that depend not on the bare pawn structures like the minority attack. Consider, for example, Pos.2, which shows a thematic situation of a white knight against a bad black bishop.

The black bishop is bad, because it is hemmed by his own center pawns on the c-, d- and e-file, and there is no realistic hope that these pawns will be able to leave their position during the next moves. In this situation an analysis of the pawn structure, a so-called pawn chain, may lead to the supposition that there may exist a bad bishop on one side. Therefore, after recognising the pawn chain cliché, it is a minor problem to check for this bad bishop situation using a fairly complicated procedure.

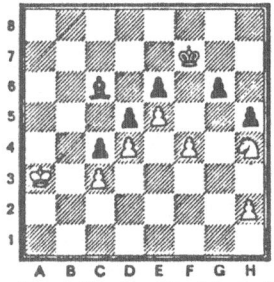

Pos. 2

(Burn-Aljechin, Karlsbad, 1911)

3.2 THE STRUCTURE OF THEMES

For the next considerations - the structure of an abstract theme - we will first have a look at chess theory which will tell us something about the way to lead the minority attack, which will serve us as an example of a theme whenever we need one. So, M.Euwe, former Chess World Champion, explains the procedure for Pos.3 :

" ... advance the queen-wing (a4 and b4), move the heavy pieces to the b and c file (queen rook at b1, if possible, king rook at c1 and queen at c2). Further on, it is often valuable to occupy the front square on a semi-open file (c5) with a knight."

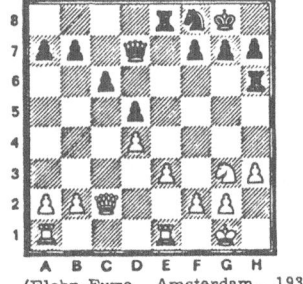

(Flohr-Euwe, Amsterdam, 1932))

Pos. 3

For our approach it is very important to notice the characteristics of explanations like these :

- a theme is a sequence of pre-defined actions, not the statement of a fixed thematic goal to be reached by manoeuvres that have to be newly developed;
- themes may (and normally will) have resulting positions which describe the successful completion of this sequence. E.g., the minority attack may lead to positions in which the black queen pawn is isolated or in which the black QBP is backward on the semi-open c-file.

Therefore, we can divide a theme into several more or less distinct manoeuvres which we called *stratagems*, an expression taken from A.Nimzović, a famous Latavian Grandmaster of the Twenties.

Roughly spoken, a stratagem is a triple

(piece-type , starting square , ending square)

with the meaning that the piece indicated has to be moved from its actual starting square to the designated ending square, e.g. the knight has to be moved from g3 to c5.

During the execution of a theme some major restrictions have an influence on all the stratagems. So, for instance, the 'knight to c5'-stratagem can work only if there is a knight on g3, which means that a preceding stratagem must not exchange this knight against any of the opponent's light pieces. This trivial restriction leads us to the concept of *material resources*, which are essential to the feasibility of any stratagem.

On the other hand, there are not only material restrictions connecting the stratagems, but also some positional characteristics of the situation have to be present, if a stratagem has to be executed successfully. Chess theory, for instance, tells us that it is important to keep the black pawn on its square c6, if we wish to execute a minority attack. If this pawn can advance to c5 without being sacrificed the minority attack has failed (maybe another theme arises out of this position, but it will have nothing to do with the minority attack at all). Therefore, a black pawn on c6 is a *positional resource* of most of the stratagems (among others, of course).

Positional resources resemble installing pawn clichés in several ways, so that it looks reasonable to use pawn relations to represent positional resources during the execution of a theme.

We even use pawn relations to define the characteristics of the resulting positions, that can occur after the successful completion of a certain theme. So, we are able to describe the black IQP or the backward QBP in terms of relations, which enables the system to recognise the success of its operations and may even lead to an instant installation of an adequate subsequent theme, e.g. a theme entitled 'play against the opponent's IQP'.

So far, a theme is not more than a bunch of stratagems loosely connected by their mutual resource demands. But there is more knowledge to be brought into a certain theme. In our example, it is meaningful to move the heavy pieces (at least one of them) to the c-file first, in order to prevent the black QBP from advancing, and to advance the own QNP afterwards, which suggests a temporal ordering of the stratagems in any theme.

Further, not all the stratagems are of the same importance for the success of the theme, e.g. the knight's march from g3 to c5 is sometimes useful, but it is not an obligatory stratagem in the minority attack.

This means that the overall structure of an abstract theme consists of a rather small number of stratagems, which are connected by resources, a *temporal ordering relation* and a *relative importance relation*. The

first relation states that one stratagem has to be finished before the
other one starts, the second one defines that one stratagem's execution
is more important than the execution of the other one. Both relations are
irreflexive, asymmetric and transitive, they may be represented as a directed, colored graph, the *thematic ordering graph* or *TO-graph*. The complete TO-graph for our minority attack including the definitions of the
stratagems is shown in Fig.3.

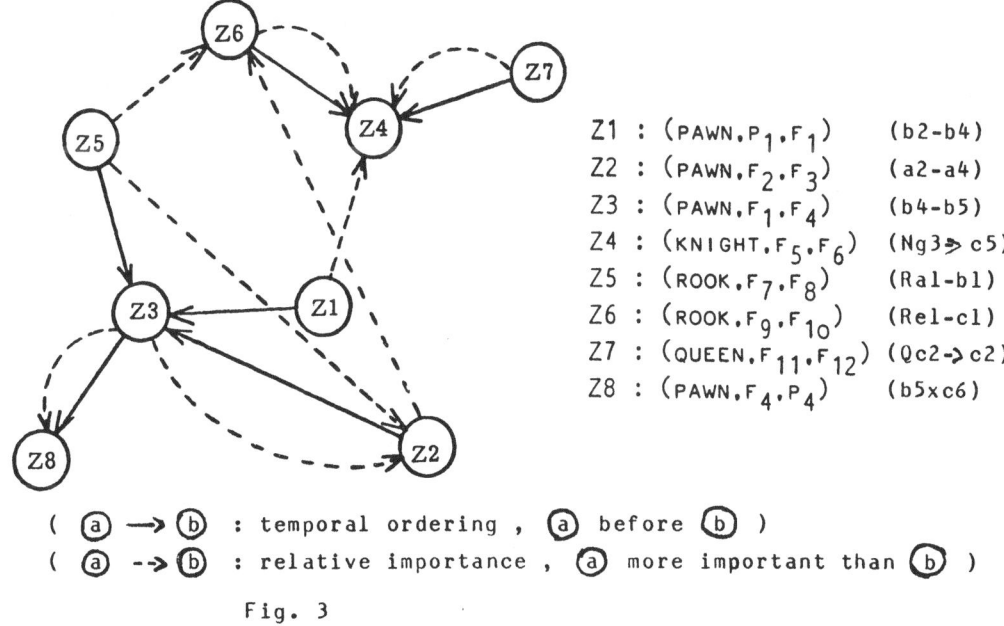

$Z1$: (PAWN, P_1, F_1) (b2-b4)
$Z2$: (PAWN, F_2, F_3) (a2-a4)
$Z3$: (PAWN, F_1, F_4) (b4-b5)
$Z4$: $(\text{KNIGHT}, F_5, F_6)$ (Ng3➤c5)
$Z5$: (ROOK, F_7, F_8) (Ra1-b1)
$Z6$: $(\text{ROOK}, F_9, F_{10})$ (Re1-c1)
$Z7$: $(\text{QUEEN}, F_{11}, F_{12})$ (Qc2➤c2)
$Z8$: (PAWN, F_4, P_4) (b5xc6)

((a) ⟶ (b) : temporal ordering , (a) before (b))
((a) -⇢ (b) : relative importance , (a) more important than (b))

Fig. 3

3.3 CONCRETISING A THEME

The next problem in the application of chess knowledge is the concretising of an abstract theme represented by its TO-graph in an actual
game situation. Imagine, for example, Pos.3 shifted one file to the right
which makes only minor changes in the thematic situation, if at all. Now
the queen has to be placed on d2 instead of c2, the knight aimes at d5
instead of c5 and so on. We cannot fix all those squares in the abstract
theme to predefined squares on the board without losing all flexibility
needed for reasonable play. A lot of chess knowledge has to be given to
the system to recognise that the square c2 is in fact an arbitrary square
on the semi-open file but not on the first rank, because this one is re-
served for the king rook. It is actually not a great problem to assign
pieces and squares to every parameter in Pos.2, but removing the white
rook from a1 and placing it on d3 changes the whole situation and should
result in moving the rook from e1 to b1 and moving the rook from d3 to c3!

Even this small example shows one of the major shortcomings of the system structure: it seems to be nearly impossible to attach one specific

concretising procedure to every stratagem because for proper handling
of this problem stratagems need knowledge about the overall structure of
the theme and about the internal structure of other stratagems. The concept of splitting knowledge into independent pieces in this first approach
reaches its limits when applied to the development of a concrete theme.
Therefore, we will look for mechanisms to represent knowledge about these
dependencies between stratagems to return to the concept of procedural
attachment (by the way, we are even looking for the knowledge itself!).

Anyway, not all the stratagems are causing trouble like this. Normally,
all stratagems involving pawn movements are easy to handle because the
pawns are fixed in the process of recognising the clichés. So, pawn op_1
in the installing cliché is the one that later on advances until it forms
a lever with ep_2. Also, the final square for the knight is defined as the
square lying directly in front of ep_2.

The process of concretising results in a modified TO-graph in which
stratagems are either deleted, because they require pieces that are not
on the board anymore, or added, e.g. removing a bishop from the back rank
that hinders rook movement, or taken from TO-graph, all provided with actual parameters, which are obtained by an analysis of the position. This
new graph is called *concrete thematic ordering graph* or *CTO-graph*.

So far, the system is provided with knowledge about how to play a theme
if there is no opponent player who follows quite opposite intentions. The
opponent will normally counter-act in one of the following two manners:
 - defend directly against our theme (direct counterplay)
 - play his own theme, with minimal effort spent on direct defence
   (indirect counterplay).

Knowledge about direct counterplay is thematic knowledge as well as the
TO-graph. It can be represented as a collection of stratagems, so-called
direct anti-stratagems, which are a part of the theme. Thus, they also
underly the process of concretising, but in this context we are confronted with even greater problems than before, because we cannot make
any assumptions about the dependencies between the anti-stratagems as we
could with our stratagems.

Indirect counterplay, in principle, can be handled like the original
theme following the same procedures, as described above. This results in
a collection of *indirect anti-stratagems*, who are treated just like the
direct anti-stratagems. Unfortunately, we can only handle opposite themes, if we have knowledge about them. If the opponent plays an unknown
theme, it leaves the system helpless, since there is no 'plan recognition feature'.

3.4 Move generation

Considering the complete theme with its CTO-graph and anti-stratagems we are now confronted with the last problem to obtain an adequate stratigical move from the system. Moves can be generated only if there is a stratagem which contains this move as its only or first move.

Some problems arise out of the fact that some stratagems require more than one move until they are completed, e.g. the 'knight to c5'-stratagem. These stratagems will be split into a 'first move' and a remainder stratagem using Botvinnik's method of trajectories, which may be checked for tactical safety.

At a fixed state of theme execution there are only few candidate stratagems for the generation of the next move. This, in the first place, is due to the temporal ordering in the CTO-graph, which prevents some stratagems from execution because their ancestor stratagems are not yet completed. All candidates together with all anti-stratagems are collected in a so-called *pool*, which connects them to the move generation module.

After determining the first or only moves of the pool-stratagems, all these moves together with the first or only moves of the anti-stratagems are used to construct the *thematic tree*. The thematic tree search procedure mainly checks the positions in the tree, whether any resource demands are violated (material and/or positional) or whether there occurs a final position which, as stated above, indicates the success of the whole theme. Violation of any resource demands leads to a refutation of the corresponding move in this actual situation. If there remains more than one thematically legal move, we choose the one that belongs to the most important stratagem. Importance of stratagems is determined by considering the relative importance edges that lead to this stratagem in the CTO-graph.

If the move chosen terminates a stratagem, this stratagem is removed from the CTO-graph and its temporal successors will now become candidates for the next move. If the move doesn't terminate a stratagem, this stratagem is replaced by its remainder.

If there is no thematically legal move, some operations can be performed, such as looking for standard auxiliary stratagems, inserting more thematic stratagems into the pool (higher-order anti-stratagems), or, in the worst case, cancelling the whole theme because its execution has irrevocably failed.

If there is an extra-thematic advantage (normally material), that can be realised only with an extra-thematic move, one can imagine a conventional Shannon-type program, provided with some kind of interrupt facility that can realise this gain if it exceeds the pre-defined thematic value.

4. CONCLUSION

In our attempt to present structures that enable a strategic approach
to the problem of chess, it probably became apparent that there are, a-
bove the basic structures which at first glance appear to be very simple,
one or more levels of considerably more complex structures.

Our first approach still contains a relatively large number of solutions
for the problem of understanding even a part of these structures, which
can only be justified pragmatically. For us, however it seems to be important to go on in this direction.

Not by chance, we used several methods and formalisms of AI. This kind
of problem, as roughly sketched above, is one of the topics in AI in the
area of representation of knowledge and inference techniques. Especially,
we are influenced by the dicussion about Frames, Scripts, Belief Systems
etc. The special domain we worked with doesn't allow to use these methods
directly. But we made use of the ideas of these methods, which are not
fully discussed now, because they seem to be pragmatically feasible.

Yet we are, at the moment, far away from even considering an implementation of a system based upon our approach, not to mention to issue any
statements about the likely playing strength of this system.

REFERENCES

Berliner, H.J.   Chess as Problem Solver
                         Carnegie-Mellon Univ. Comp. Science Dept. 1974

Botvinnik, M.M.   Computers, Chess and Long-range Planning
                         Heidelberg Science Library 1970

Chase, W.G.   The Mind's Eye in Chess
   Simon, H.A.   in: Chase (ed.):Visual Information Processing
                            Academic Press 1973

DeGroot, A.D.   Thought and Choice in Chess
                         The Hague:Mouton 1965

Euwe, M.   Urteil und Plan im Schach
                         de Gruyter 1967

Kmoch, H.   Die Kunst der Bauernführung
                         Siegfried Engelhardt Verlag 1967

v.Luck, K.   Strukturen des strategischen Schachspiels
   Owsnicki, B.   Univ. Hamburg (unpublished) 1980

Nimzovič, A.   Mein System
                         Das Schach-Archiv 1965

Pitrat, J.   A Chess Combination Program which uses Plans
                         Art. Intell. 8 1977

Schank, R.C.   Scripts, Plans, Goals and Understanding
   Abelson, R.P.   Lawrence Erlbaum

Tan, S.T.   Describing Pawn Structures
                         in: Clarke (ed.):Advances in Computer Chess 1
                            Edinburgh Univ. Press 1977

INFORMATIONSGEWINNUNG DURCH AUTOMATISCHES ERZEUGEN ZIELBEZOGENER FRAGEN

Sven Müller

Abteilung für Informatik I der Universität Bonn

Inhaltsübersicht   Es wird eine Strategie untersucht, die es einem Computerprogramm erlauben soll, in einer ihm unbekannten "Umwelt" "Fragen" zu erzeugen, um sich - mit Hilfe der erhaltenen Antworten - Klarheit über die Struktur der Umgebung zu verschaffen. Die Strategie geht davon aus, daß die mit einer Antwort übertragene Information quantifizierbar ist. Fragen werden so gestellt, daß sie mit den zu erhaltenen Antworten mindestens zu erwartende Informationsmenge maximal wird. Die Strategie wurde in einem Computerprogramm konkretisiert und am Beispiel der Frage-Antwort-Situation beim Spiel "Mastermind" überprüft.

Abstract   The aim of this - experimental - paper is to examine a strategy which enables a computer program to generate automatically questions in an unknown environment. The program assumes that it is possible to measure the amount of information received by the answer. It tries to generate questions in order to maximize the minimum amount of expected answer-information. This strategy was implemented and verified by the example of the question-and-answer problems with an extended version of the game of 'mastermind'.

EINFÜHRUNG

Tom   "Denk' Dir eine Zahl zwischen 0 und 99 aus und antworte mir auf jede Frage nur mit "Ja" oder "Nein". Wieviele Fragen werde ich Dir wohl stellen müssen, bis ich die gedachte Zahl erraten habe?"

Jerry "Keine Ahnung! Vielleicht 25?"

Tom   Wetten, daß ich es in weniger als 8 schaffe?"

Bekanntlich benötigt man hier $\left|\log_2 (100)\right|$ = 7 Fragen maximal, wenn man so fragt, daß die beiden Antworten "Ja" und "Nein" gleichwahrscheinlich sind. Daher rührt auch die Basis 2 des Logarithmus.

Jerry (versucht Tom reinzulegen)
"Wieviele Fragen aber brauchst Du, wenn Du mir nur noch eine Zahl als Frage vorlegen darfst und ich Dir sage, wieviele Ziffern an der richtigen und an einer falschen Stelle vorkommen? Mehr oder weniger?"

Tom   "Natürlich erheblich mehr! Sagen wir etwa 13."

Jerry "Weit gefehlt! Sogar weniger, nämlich nur 5!"

Tom   "Das Spiel gefällt mir nicht."

Diesmal errechnet sich die Anzahl: $\left|\log_2 (100)\right|$ = 5; es gibt hier zwar 5 verschiedene Antworten (Anzahl positionsrichtig, Anzahl positionsfalsch): {(0,1), (1,0), (0,0), (0,2), (2,0)}, wovon aber nur 3 ungefähr gleichwahrscheinlich sind, die beiden letzten aber bereits die Lösung darstellen und in die Basis des Logarithmus nicht "eingehen".

Jerry "Spielst Du gerne Master-Mind?"

Tom   "Au ja! Soll'n wir gleich mal?"

Jerry "Hab'n wir doch gerade!!"

Tom   "????"

Im Vorgriff auf die weitere Darstellung kann hier schon gesagt werden, daß eine Strategie gefunden wurde, mit deren Hilfe es möglich ist, automatisch Fragen zu erzeugen, daß die mit den Antworten erhaltene Informationsmenge maximiert wird. Der verfolgte Denkansatz geht davon aus, daß die Information, die mit einer Antwort übertragen wird, von der Bedeutung der Antwort unabhängig gemessen werden kann. Eine Auswahl aus vom Programm intern erzeugten Fragekandidaten erfolgt derart, daß die ausgewählte Frage die Wahrscheinlichkeiten des Auftretens einzelner Antworten einander annähert. Bekanntlich ist die mittlere mit einer Antwort übertragene Information dann am größten. Diese einfache Strategie hat sich im Spezialfall des hier untersuchten Spieles außerordentlich gut bewährt. Wie später noch zu sehen sein wird, ist die Komplexität von Mastermind (bei entsprechender Wahl bestimmter Spielparameter) außerordentlich groß - wesentlich größer als z.B. beim Schach. Trotzdem gelingt es dem fragenerzeugenden Programm, mit Hilfe dieser ja ziemlich unspezifischen Strategie, besser oder mindestens genauso gut zu spielen wie ein geübter menschlicher Spieler. Beim Schach z.B. kann das - obwohl sehr problemspezifische Bewertungs- und Auswahlkriterien verwendet werden - (noch) nicht behauptet werden. Die Selektionskraft der vorgeschlagenen Methode, die hier außerordentlich hoch ist, muß natürlich noch eingehender untersucht werden. Da die zugrundeliegende Theorie, die Informationstheorie von SHANNON u.a., sehr allgemein und gut abgesichert ist, bin ich, was den Erfolg der Methode auf anderen Gebieten angeht, sehr zuversichtlich.

Der Leser, der mit den Spielregeln von "Mastermind" vertratut ist, kann den nachfolgenden Abschnitt übergehen.

Spielregeln Ziel des Spieles ist es, ein Wort fester Länge über einem endlichen
Alphabet zu erraten: Ein Mitspieler, der sich dieses Wort ausgedacht hat, beantwortet jeden Rateversuch mit der Bekanntgabe der Anzahlen der darin positionsrichtigen
und positionsfalschen Zeichen. Diese "Antwort" kann jetzt dazu verwendet werden,
eine neue "Frage" zu erzeugen u.s.w., bis das vom Mitspieler ausgedachte Wort erraten ist. Könnte dieses Wort mit weniger als einer vorher vereinbarten Zahl von Rate-
versuchen gefunden werden, dann gilt das Spiel als gewonnen.

DEFINITION DES PROBLEMS

Zwei verschiedene und sich vielleicht ausschließende Ziele kann man während des
Spiels verfolgen:

  a) in möglichst kurzer Zeit unter Verwendung eventuell aller zur Verfügung
     stehender Fragemöglichkeiten das Lösungswort zu finden, oder

  b) mit möglichst wenigen Fragen unter Verwendung von möglichst viel Antwort-
     Information das Lösungspattern zu finden.[1]

Es soll das zweite Ziel weiterverfolgt werden. Das bedeutet jedoch nicht, daß die
zum Finden der Lösung nötige Zeit überhaupt keine Rolle spielen soll. Auch zu anderen Problemen lassen sich ja Verfahren angeben, die mit möglichst wenigen "Zügen"
eine Lösung finden, falls eine Lösung existiert. Sie sind aber wegen der dazu be-
nötigten Zeit völlig undurchführbar. Das vollständige Durchsuchen des Spielbaumes
beim Schach kann als Beispiel dafür gelten.

ÜBERBLICK ÜBER DIE KOMPLEXITÄT DES SPIELES

BERECHNUNG DER ZUGMÖGLICHKEITEN

Für den Entwurf eines Programmes, das in der Lage sein soll, Fragen[1] aus den gegebe-
nen Antworten selbst zu erzeugen, ist es sinnvoll, sich zunächst einen Überblick
über die Anzahlen verschiedener Pattern und Antwort-Tupel zu verschaffen.

Wird die Anzahl der zur Auswahl stehenden Zeichen mit Z, mit L die der zur Verfügung
stehenden Positionen bezeichnet, dann gibt es bekanntlich Z^L verschiedene Worte.[1]
Die Berechnung der Anzahl der auf eine Frage möglichen Antwort-Tupel (s,w) ist
nicht ganz so einfach. Die Anzahlen s der positionsrichtigen und w der positionsfalschen Zeichen in der Frage genügen immer den folgenden Bedingungen:

$$s \text{ kann nicht negativ sein} \qquad (1)$$

$$w \text{ kann nicht negativ sein} \qquad (2)$$

$$\text{die Summe } s+w \text{ kann nicht größer als L sein} \qquad (3)$$

---

[1] "Pattern", "Worte", "Fragen" werden synonym verwendet.

(1) bis (3) bedeuten, daß die Zahl der bewerteten Zeichen in der Frage nicht größer sein kann, als das Fragepattern Positionen hat. Es ist zum Beispiel unmöglich, daß in einer Frage aus vier Zeichen fünf positionsrichtig sind, oder daß in derselben Frage drei Zeichen an der falschen und vier Zeichen an der richtigen Stelle stehen. (3).

Da beide Variablen s und w je L+1 verschiedene Werte annehmen können (von 0 bis L), ergibt sich zunächst eine Anzahl von

$$k = \frac{(L+1) \cdot ((L+1)+1)}{2} \qquad (4)$$

mögliche Antworten. Unter diesen Antworten ist allerdings eine, die noch nicht durch die Bedingungen (1) bis (3) ausgeschlossen wird: Da es unmöglich ist, daß in einem Pattern L-1 Zeichen positionsrichtig und genau ein Zeichen positionsfalsch steht, kann es auf eine vorgelegte Frage nie mehr als

$$k = \frac{(L+1) \cdot (L+2)}{2} - 1 \qquad (5)$$

Antworten geben.

Beispiel: Bei einem Spiel mit neun Farben auf fünf Positionen ist Z=9 und L=5. Es gibt dann 9^5=59049 verschiedene Pattern und 6·7/2 -1 = 20 verschiedene Antworten pro Frage. Die Anzahl der möglichen Antworten auf eine einzelne Frage läßt sich noch besser abschätzen, wenn man bedenkt, daß nur höchstens soviele Zeichen positionsfalsch sein können, wie es verschiedene Zeichen pro Frage gibt.

DER BAUM DER MÖGLICHKEITEN FÜR EIN 2-POSITIONEN/3-ZEICHEN - SPIEL

Auch wenn es im 2-Positionen/3-Zeichen - Spiel nur neun verschiedene Pattern {AA AB AC BA BB BC CA CB CC} und nur fünf verschiedene Antworten { (0,0) (1,0) (0,1) (2,0) (0,2)} gibt, ist eine Darstellung aller möglichen Spielsequenzen z.B. als Baumstruktur zu umfangreich (unendlich). Läßt man in einer solchen Darstellung jedoch alle Antworten fort, die aufgrund der Vorgeschichte nicht mehr gegeben werden können, verzichtet man weiterhin auf die Notation aller derjenigen Pattern, die aufgrund der Vorgeschichte nicht mehr Lösung sein können, und verzichtet man außerdem noch auf eine Darstellung derjenigen Pattern, die durch eine konsistente Umbenennung auf schon Dargestellte abgebildet werden können, dann lassen sich diese Spielverläufe einigermaßen übersichtlich in Form der Abb. 1 darstellen.

ZIELKONSISTENTE FRAGEN

Es ist sicherlich wenig sinnvoll, eine Frage, die schon einmal gestellt wurde, noch einmal zur Beantwortung vorzulegen: man erhielte genau dieselbe Antwort, die schon beim ersten Stellen dieser Frage gegeben wurde. Bei der Erzeugung plausibler Fragepattern wird man also darauf verzichten, diese Pattern noch einmal zu generieren. Wie später formal noch gezeigt wird, ist ein 9-Farben/5-Positionen - Spiel mit vier bis fünf Fragen beendbar. Da die Anzahl aller Z^L möglichen Pattern immer wesentlich

311

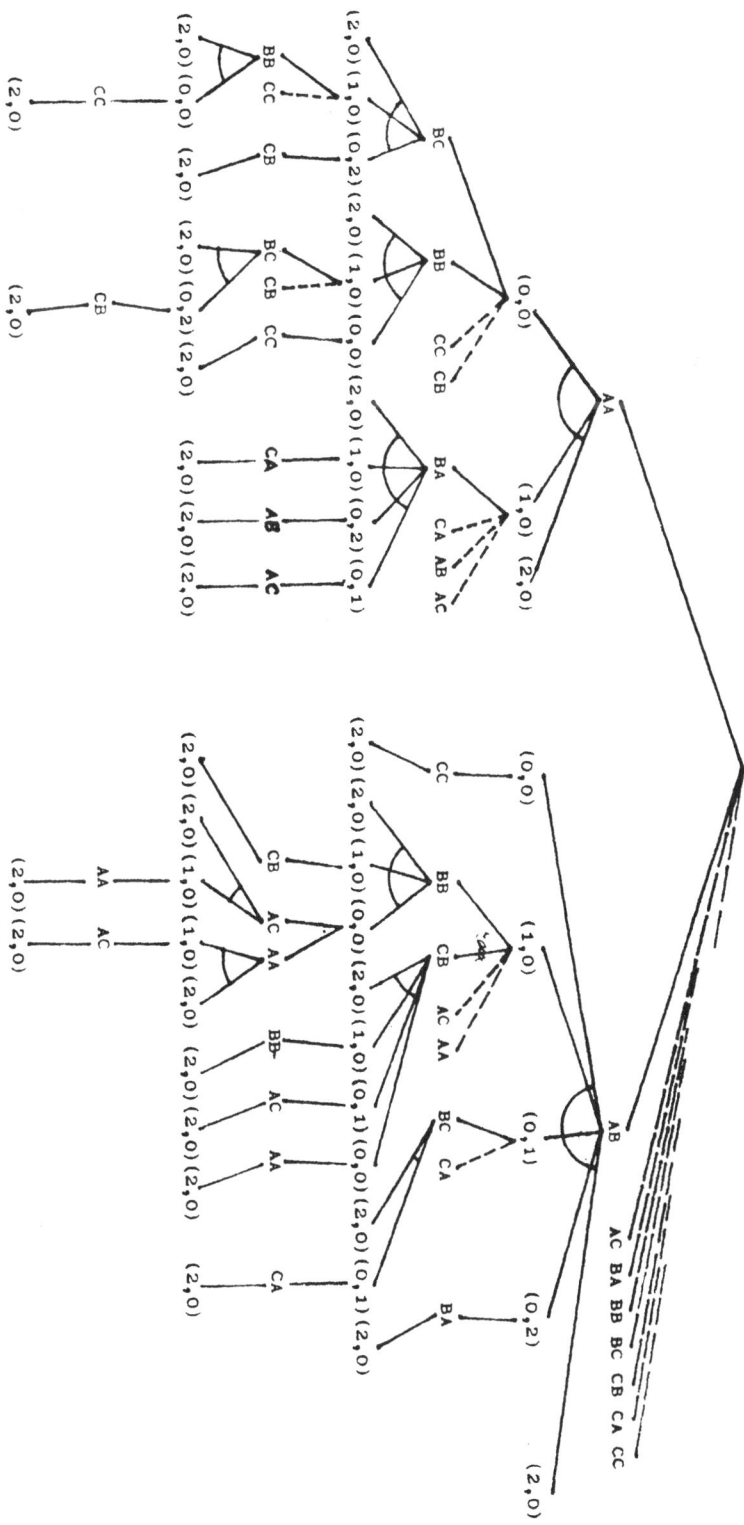

Abbildung 1

größer ist, als die Anzahl derjenigen Fragen, die in einer Spielsequenz gestellt werden müssen, ist das nicht-mehr-Generieren schon gestellter Fragen zwar sinnvoll, kann aber zu keiner bedeutsamen Verringerung des Suchbereichs beitragen.

Eine zweite, wesentlich restriktivere Begrenzung der Menge der plausiblen Pattern erhält man dann, wenn man fordert, daß auf eine potentielle Frage aufgrund der Vorgeschichte die Antwort (L,0) noch möglich sein soll, die Frage also Lösung sein kann. Durch diese Forderung wird unter anderem vermieden, daß schon gestellte Fragen neu generiert werden. Bekommt man auf die Frage AB die Antwort (0,0), dann weiß man, daß die Lösung weder A oder B enthalten kann. Kein Pattern, das A oder B enthält, kann mehr Lösung sein.

Auf der anderen Seite kann jedes Fragepattern, auf das die Antwort (L,0) noch gegeben werden kann, mit dem Lösungspattern identisch sein. Diese Beobachtung führt zu der folgenden

DEFINITION: Ein Fragepattern, auf das die Antwort (L,0) erfolgen kann, soll
zielkonsistent heißen.

Stellt man ausschließlich zielkonsistente Fragen, dann ist es immer möglich, daß das Spiel mit der nächsten Frage beendet ist.

Bemerkung: Die erste Frage ist immer zielkonsistent.

PROBLEME BEI DER ERZEUGUNG PLAUSIBLER PATTERN

Die Beobachtung, daß die Menge aller zielkonsistenten Fragen immer das Lösungspattern enthält, legt nahe, zur Erzeugung plausibler Pattern gerade die zielkonsistenten Fragepattern zu verwenden. Zwei Probleme müssen dann untersucht werden:

1) Bringt das ausschließliche Verwenden zielkonsistenter Pattern tatsächlich die erhoffte Beschränkung der Menge der zu untersuchenden Pattern?

2) Werden durch die ausschließliche Verwendung zielkonsistenter Pattern "wertvolle", d.h. spielverkürzende Pattern übersehen?

Zu 1): Bedenkt man, daß die erste Frage immer zielkonsistent ist (man kann ja mit der ersten Frage zufällig die Lösung erraten), dann hat man hier wieder das Problem, alle Z^L verschiedenen Pattern untersuchen zu müssen.

Auf der anderen Seite sind alle Teilbäume isomorph, deren Wurzel-Pattern sich nur in den Bezeichnungen noch nicht verwendeter Zeichen unterscheiden: Daß die Wurzel des linken Teilbaumes in Abb. 1, z.B. AA statt BB heißt, ist insofern uninteressant, als dieser Baum die gleiche Struktur und damit die gleiche Maximaltiefe hat wie der in Abb. 1 eingetragene. Das erklärt, warum die in Abb. 1 gestrichelt eingetragenen Äste nicht weiterverfolgt werden müssen. Im allgemeinen sind zu Beginn eines Spiels nicht alle Z^L verschiedenen Pattern, sondern nur alle Min(L,Z) verschiedenen Wurzeln nicht isomorpher Teilbäume zu untersuchen. Auf den anderen Ebenen des Baumes gilt das gleiche Argument rekursiv für bis dahin noch nicht verwendete Zeichen.

<u>Zu 2)</u>: Unter bestimmten Bedingungen existieren tatsächlich nicht-zielkonsistente Pattern, deren Beantwortung dem Fragenden wesentlich mehr Information liefert, als jede zielkonsistente Frage; deren Verwendung also weniger Fragen erfordert, um das Lösungspattern eindeutig festzulegen. Ein kleines Beispiel soll diese Situation veranschaulichen:

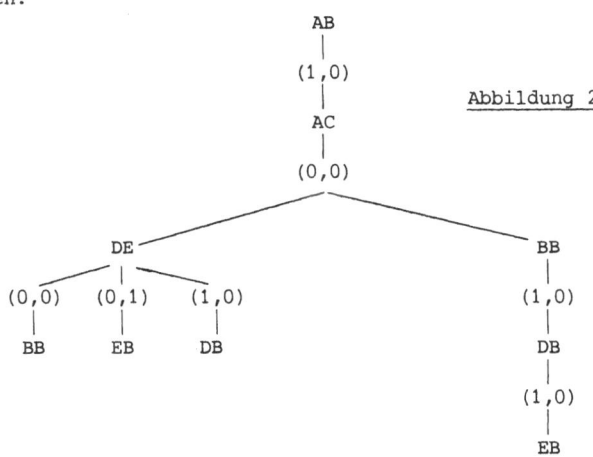

Abbildung 2

In einem 2-Positionen/5-Farben - Spiel wurde AB gefragt und mit (1,0) beantwortet. Zielkonsistente Fragen sind jetzt noch: AA AC AD AE BB CB DB und EB. Angenommen, der Fragende entschließt sich, AC zu setzen, und er erhält als Antwort (0,0). Er weiß jetzt zwar, daß das Lösungspattern die Zeichen A und C nicht enthalten kann und daß außerdem B an der zweiten Position stehen muß; stellt er jetzt jedoch weiter ziel-konsistente Fragen BB DB EB, dann hat er viermal fragen müssen (o.B.d.A. ist EB die Lösung), bevor er die Lösung sicher kennt. Hätte er stattdessen nicht-zielkonsistent DE gefragt, dann wäre jetzt schon mit der Antwort die Lösung eindeutig festgelegt (linker Zweig in Abb. 2).

Daß in diesem Fall ein nicht-zielkonsistentes Pattern der spielverkürzende Fragekan-didat vor allen zielkonsistenten Pattern ist, liegt daran, daß einige Zeichen - bei zielkonsistentem Fragen - erst sehr spät verwendet werden. Das nicht-zielkonsi-stente Pattern DE enthält genau die noch nicht verwendeten Zeichen!

DIE ERZEUGUNG ZIELBEZOGENER PATTERN

Das Lösungspattern kann nach Definition nur durch Stellen einer zielkonsistenten Frage gefunden werden. Die zielkonsistenten Fragepattern wird man also bei der Er-zeugung plausibler Pattern berücksichtigen müssen. Einige zielkonsistente Pattern sind zu anderen zielkonsistenten äquivalent, was die Topologie der Teilbäume angeht, in denen sie Wurzel sind. Deshalb muß man nicht alle zielkonsistenten Pattern gene-rieren. Es bleibt das Problem der nicht-zielkonsistenten Pattern, die in bestimmten Fällen die Suche nach der Lösung besser als eine zielkonsistente Frage voranbringen können. Sind diese Pattern wieder unter allen Z^L möglichen Worten zu suchen, dann wäre, was die Beschränkung des Suchbereiches angeht, nicht viel gewonnen. Im Gegensatz zu den zielkonsistenten Fragen konnte hier kein Merkmal gefunden werden, durch das sich diese Pattern sicher identifizieren ließen. Eine Vielzahl von automatisch erzeugten Spielsequenzen zeigte aber bisher ohne Ausnahme, daß immer dann, wenn einige Zeichen erst sehr spät in einer Frage verwendet wurden, das Stellen nicht-zielkonsistenter Fragen schneller zur Lösung geführt hätte. Das läßt vermuten, daß es günstig ist, möglichst am Anfang einer Fragesequenz alle Zeichen in Fragen auftreten zu lassen.

Die plausiblen Pattern, die einer weiteren automatischen Bewertung unterzogen werden, sind also auf der einen Seite alle nichtäquivalenten zielkonsistenten Pattern, auf der anderen Seite Pattern, die nur Zeichen enthalten, die in bisher gestellten Fragen noch nicht vorgekommen sind, auch wenn diese Fragen nicht zielkonsistent sind. Diese Worte werden im Folgenden "zielbezogen" genannt. Durch die Einbeziehung dieser zweiten Gruppe nicht notwendig zielkonsistenter Fragepattern, die nur aus noch nicht verwendeten Zeichen bestehen, soll vermieden werden, daß immer wieder unter allen möglichen Pattern zielbezogene Fragen gesucht werden müssen.

BEWERTUNG DER ZIELBEZOGENEN PATTERN

Ein einzelnes Pattern läßt sich nicht sinnvoll bewerten. Ein Blick auf Abb. 1 zeigt, daß das gleiche Pattern an ganz verschiedenen Positionen im Spielbaum auftreten kann. Der Wert eines Pattern läßt sich vielmehr dann sinnvoll bestimmen, wenn man weiß, wie lang der Faden von der Wurzel bis zum Ende des Spiels ist, auf dem das zu bewertende Pattern liegt. Je kürzer dieser Faden ist, umso besser ist das Pattern zu bewerten.

Kann man den Spielbaum bis zum Ende des Spiels expandieren, dann läßt sich eine optimale statische Bewertungsfunktion angeben: Da alle Blätter Antwort-Knoten vom Typ (L,0) sind, weiß man hier genau, wieviele Fragen nötig waren, bis die Lösung gefunden worden ist. Bewertet man diese Blätter mit -(Tiefe), führt Rückbewertungen durch (Maxima für den Fragenden, Minima für den Antwortenden), dann erhält man die korrekte Bewertung derjenigen Fragepattern, die auf der ersten Ebene des Baumes zur Auswahl stehen. In Abb. 1 erkennt man, daß die Frage AB mit -6 bewerter wird, also einen höheren Wert erhält, als die mit -8 bewertete Frage AA. Stellt man AA als erste Frage, dann kann es immer passieren, daß man vier Fragen stellen muß, bis man die Antwort (L,0) erhält; im AB-Zweig des gleichen Spielbaumes kommt man dagegen immer mit höchstens drei Fragen zum Ziel. (Man darf natürlich nicht auf eine eventuelle Antwort (1,0) hin BB oder AA fragen.)

Die statische Bewertung -(Tiefe) der Blätter des Spielbaumes führt in Verbindung mit Rückbewertungen nach dem Minimax-Verfahren immer zur richtigen Auswahl einer zielbezogenen Frage.

SCHWIERIGKEITEN MIT DEM VORGESCHLAGENEN VERFAHREN

Das Problem schein gelöst: eine Methode zur Erzeugung zielbezogener nächster Fragen ist gefunden, eine absolut richtige statische Bewertungsfunktion ist vorhanden, und mit Hilfe des Minimax-Verfahrens lassen sich die Fragenkandidaten für den nächsten Zug rückbewerten. Mit der angegebenen Methode läßt sich immer diejenige Sequenz von Fragen bestimmen, die auf dem kürzesten Weg zum Ziel führt.

Bedenkt man aber, daß dem Fragenden an jedem Knoten $O(Z^L)$ Alternativen, dem Antwortenden $O(L^2)$ Alternativen zur Verfügung stehen, dann genügt es, L oder Z genügend groß zu machen, um zu Rechenzeiten zu gelangen, die jede vorgegebene Schranke überschreiten. Schon für die übliche Dimensionierung des Spiels: 5 Positionen / 9 Zeichen kommt man in den Bereich zu langer Ausführungszeiten. Diese Problematik taucht hier ja nicht zum erstenmal auf. Für das Schachspiel läßt sich ja leicht eine absolut richtige statische Bewertung der Endsituation des Spiels angeben, die - rückbewertet - in jeder Situation Auskunft darüber geben kann, was als nächstes zu tun ist.

Generiert man aber nur einen Teil der Spielbäume, dann muß man auch Knoten bewerten können, die nicht Endknoten des Spiels sind. Eine solche statische Bewertung soll im nächsten Abschnitt vorgestellt werden.

DAS KONZEPT DER ANTWORT-INFORMATION

Der Begriff der Information, die der Fragende mit den Antworten erhält, soll nun präzisiert werden. Aus diesen Überlegungen kann dann unmittelbar eine neue statische Bewertungsfunktion gewonnen werden.

Faßt man den Antworter als Nachrichtenquelle im Sinne der Informationstheorie /1/ auf und sei zunächst probeweise angenommen, daß alle Antworten mit etwa der gleichen a-priori Wahrscheinlichkeit gegeben werden, dann wird mit jeder Antwort die Informationsmenge

$$I = \sum_{i=1}^{k} -p_i \cdot ld(p_i) \qquad (6)$$

übertragen. p_i ist die Wahrscheinlichkeit, mit der die i-te Antwort gegeben wird. k berechnet sich nach Gleichung (5). ld(x) sei der Logarithmus zur Basis 2. Bei k möglichen Antworten gilt:

$$p_i = p = \frac{1}{k} \qquad (7)$$

Es gilt also für gleichwahrscheinliche Antworten

$$I_G = ld(k) \qquad (8)$$

Ein Zahlenbeispiel: im 5-Positionen/9-Farben - Spiel berechnet sich die im Mittel pro Antwort übertragene Information zu I = ld((5+1)(5+2)/2 - 1) = 4.322 Bit/Antwort.

Zu bemerken ist noch, daß die im Mittel pro Antwort übertragene Information n u r

von der Anzahl der Positionen und nicht von der Anzahl der zur Verfügung stehenden
Farben abhängt.

EINE ABSCHÄTZUNG DER ZAHL ZU STELLENDER FRAGEN

Mit Hilfe der eben eingeführten Modellvorstellung vom Antworter als Nachrichtenquelle
im Sinne der Informationstheorie läßt sich die Zahl der Fragen abschätzen, die im
Mittel zu stellen sind, bis dem Fragenden das Lösungspattern bekannt ist:

$$\text{Anzahl der Fragen } F = \frac{ld(Z^L)}{I_G} \tag{9}$$

Ein Zahlenbeispiel: Z = 9 Zeichen, L = 5 Positionen, F = $ld(9^5)/ld(6 \cdot 7/2 -1)$ = 3.667
Fragen. Zwischen drei und vier Fragen wird man nach diesem Modell stellen müssen,
bevor die Lösung eindeutig festliegt, vorausgesetzt, die verschiedenen Antworten
kommen ungefär gleich häufig. Für Z = 3 Zeichen, L = 2 Positionen ist F = 1.365. Man
wird also zwischen zwei und drei Fragen stellen müssen, bis man die Antwort (2,0) erhält.

Die mit diesem Modell berechneten Anzahlen zu stellender Fragen stimmen gut mit dem
überein, was ein geübter menschlicher Spieler an Fragen benötigt. Diese erste heuri-
stische Überprüfung des Modells läßt die Vermutung zu, daß es sich auch bei der Verwendung zur Konstruktion einer neuen statischen Bewertungsfunktion bewährt.

EINE ZWEITE STATISCHE BEWERTUNGSFUNKTION

Die mittlere mit einer Antwort übertragene Information wird bei gleichwahrscheinli-
chem Auftreten der Antworten maximal: Der Spieler wird seine Fragen in irgendeiner
geeigneten Weise so zu stellen versuchen, daß am Ende alle Antworten mit ungefähr
derselben Häufigkeit aufgetreten sind.

Es stellt sich also das Problem, ob es möglich ist, so zu fragen, daß die erhaltenen
Antworten alle möglichst die gleiche relative Häufigkeit besitzen. Da der Fragende
die auf seine Frage möglichen Antworten kennt und die Menge dieser Antworten durchaus nicht immer alle möglichen Antworten enthält, kann er versuchen, seine nächste
Frage so aus den zielbezogenen Fragen auszuwählen, daß die zu dieser Frage gehörende
Menge von Antworten möglichst wenige der schon erhaltenen Antworten enthält. Unter
diesem Gesichtspunkt ist eine Frage dann besonders schlecht zu bewerten, wenn ihre
zugeordnete Menge möglicher Antworten nur Antworten enthält, die schon früher gegeben wurden. Das Stellen immer der gleichen Frage ist das krasseste Beispiel hierzu:
Die zugehörige Antwortmenge umfaßt genau die Antwort, die beim ersten Stellen dieser
Frage gegeben wurde.

Im allgemeinen läuft die Bewertung zielbezogener Fragen jetzt so ab: Ein Baum zielbezogener Fragen mit den zugehörigen Antworten wird soweit expandiert,wie es die
vorhandenen Resourcen (Zeit, Speicherplatz) sinnvoll erscheinen lassen. Ein Blatt
ist dann statisch umso besser bewertet, je gleichverteilter die Antworten auf dem

<u>Kantenzug von der Wurzel bis zu diesem Blatt sind</u>. Nach unserem Modell wäre die auf diesem Weg dem Fragenden zur Verfügung stehende Information dann am größten. Diese statischen Bewertungen werden jetzt nach dem Minimax-Prinzip bis zu den Fragekandidaten auf der ersten Ebene des Baumes rückbewertet. Diejenige Frage, die so den größten Wert erhält, wird jetzt tatsächlich gestellt. Selbstverständlich kann die Entscheidung, wie weit ein Teilbaum weiter zu expandieren ist, dynamisch von den Bewertungen, die in vorher untersuchten Ästen vorgenommen worden sind, abhängig gemacht werden (Alpha-Beta-Pruning) /2/. Diese und andere Details der Programmierung werden in /3/ ausführlich besprochen.

Der wesentliche Vorteil des Verfahrens liegt darin, daß nun nicht mehr der Spielbaum bis zum Ende expandiert werden muß, damit man sinnvoll statisch bewerten kann, sondern man kann innerhalb des Baumes jede Antwort bewerten. Das eröffnet die Möglichkeit, Mastermind-Probleme in Angriff zu nehmen, bei denen es eine astronomisch hohe Zahl von Spielverläufen gibt (z.B. mehr als 10^{130} bei 10 Positionen und 20 Zeichen bei höchstens 10 Fragen).

Schon beim oft angeführten 5-Positionen/9-Farben - Spiel ist der mittlere Verzweigungsfaktor wesentlich höher als z.B. beim Schach: i m m e r   59049 Möglichkeiten für den Fragenden, ca. 20 Möglichkeiten für den Antwortenden. Beim Schach rechnet man mit ca. 30 Möglichkeiten für jeden Spieler. Die Schwierigkeiten, die sich schon bei dieser vergleichsweise geringen Zahl von Alternativen ergeben, sind hinlänglich bekannt. Mit dem hier vorgeschlagenen Verfahren sind schon automatisch Mastermind-Probleme der Größe 10-Positionen/20-Farben in vertretbaren Zeiten gelöst worden.

Das Programm ist auf einer Mikrocomputeranlage "Tandy TRS-80" entwickelt worden. Es ist zum allergrößten Teil in BASIC geschrieben und benötigt 11,5 kBytes Hauptspeicherplatz. Ein kleinerer Teil - der Mastermind-Vergleich - ist wegen der Häufigkeit seiner Verwendung in "inneren Schleifen" in Maschinensprache geschrieben worden.

LITERATUR

/1/ Bauer, F.L., Goos, G., Informatik, Eine einführende Übersicht, Erster Teil, Berlin, Heidelberg, New York, Springer-Verlag, 1971

/2/ Nilsson, N.J., Problem-Solving Methods in Artificial Intelligence, New York, McGraw-Hill Book Company, 1971

/3/ Müller, S., Informationsgewinnung durch Automatisches Erzeugen zielbezogener Fragen, Informatik Berichte Nr. 31, Universität Bonn (erscheint 1981)

Lecture Notes in Computer Science